Data Structures via C++
Objects by Evolution

Data Structures via C++

Objects by Evolution

A. Michael Berman
Rowan College of New Jersey

New York   Oxford

OXFORD UNIVERSITY PRESS

1997

Oxford University Press

Oxford   New York
Athens   Auckland   Bangkok   Bogota   Bombay
Buenos Aires   Calcutta   Cape Town   Dar es Salaam
Delhi   Florence   Hong Kong   Istanbul   Karachi
Kuala Lumpur   Madras   Madrid   Melbourne
Mexico City   Nairobi   Paris   Singapore
Taipei   Tokyo   Toronto

and associated companies in

Berlin   Ibadan

Published by Oxford University Press, Inc.,
198 Madison Avenue, New York, New York, 10016
http://www.oup-usa.org

Library of Congress Cataloging-in-Publication Data
Berman, A. Michael.
Data structures via C++ : objects by evolution / A. Michael
Berman.
p.   cm.
Includes bibliographical references and index.
ISBN 0-19-510843-4
1. C++ (Computer program language)   2. Data structures (Computer
science)   3. Object-oriented programming (Computer science)
I. Title.
QA76.73.C153R69 1996
005.7'3—dc20   96-42323
                                                                      CIP

Printing (last digit): 9 8 7 6 5 4 3

Printed in the United States of America
on acid-free paper

For Ann, Adam, and Alice

Contents

Preface   xiii

Chapter 1   **Software Engineering and Computer Programming**   *1*

1.1   Software Engineering and Computer Science   2
    1.1.1   Data Structures and Abstract Data Types   4

1.2   The Software "Life Cycle"   9
    1.2.1   The Waterfall   9
    1.2.2   Critiques of the Waterfall   12
    1.2.3   Documentation   13

1.3   Why C++?   14

Chapter 2   **Designing Software: Two Approaches**   *19*

2.1   Why Design?   20

2.2   Top-Down Design   21

2.3   The Object Alternative   25

2.4   Which Method Is Better, TDD or OOD?   31

Chapter 3   **Software Reliability**   *37*

3.1   Risks of Faulty Software   38

3.2   Testing   40
    3.2.1   A Taxonomy of Errors   40
    3.2.2   Approaches to Testing   44
    3.2.3   Two Techniques for Unit Testing   47

3.3   Applying Program Correctness Techniques   50
       3.3.1   Assertions   50
       3.3.2   Preconditions and Postconditions   52
       3.3.3   Loop Invariants and Proving Termination   53
       3.3.4   Insertion Sort   57

Chapter 4   Abstract Data Types, Classes, and Objects   67
4.1   Problem: Computing with Time   68
4.2   Describing Data Types   69
       4.2.1   What's an ADT and Why Use It?   69
       4.2.2   A Time ADT   71
4.3   ADT Implementation and Code Reuse   74
       4.3.1   Code Reuse: Don't Reinvent the Wheel   74
       4.3.2   Implementing a Time ADT   75
4.4   Information Hiding, Encapsulation, and Views   77
4.5   Creating Encapsulated ADTs Using the C++ Class   78
       4.5.1   Declaring the Time Class   79
       4.5.2   Creating ADTs for C++ Classes   81
       4.5.3   Creating Clients for C++ Classes   83
       4.5.4   Implementation for C++ Classes   84
4.6   Using Standard C++ Class Libraries   85
       4.6.1   Using C++ Libraries for Input and Output   86
       4.6.2   Using the C++ String Library   89
4.7   ADTs, Objects, and Object-Oriented Programming   92

Chapter 5   Efficiency   99
5.1   Selecting Good Algorithms   100
5.2   The Many Faces of Program Efficiency   101
5.3   Algorithms for Searching   103
       5.3.1   Linear Search   104
       5.3.2   Binary Search   108
5.4   Analysis of Some Simple Sorting Algorithms   114
       5.4.1   Selection Sort   114
       5.4.2   Bubble Sort   119

Chapter 6   Recursion   127
6.1   Solving Problems with Recursion   128
       6.1.1   A Very Simple Example   128
       6.1.2   The Nature of Recursion   130
6.2   Recursive Definitions   130
6.3   Applying Recursion to Sorting and Searching Problems   135
       6.3.1   Recursive Search Algorithms   135
       6.3.2   Quicksort: A Recursive Sorting Algorithm   139

6.4   How Is Recursion Implemented?   151
    6.4.1   What Happens When a Function Is Called?   151
    6.4.2   What Happens When a Recursive Function Is Called?   152
    6.4.3   Is Recursion Inefficient?   153

Chapter 7   **Lists**   *161*
7.1   Problem: A Membership Management Program   162
7.2   The List ADT   162
7.3   Implementing Lists   164
    7.3.1   A Header File for the List ADT   164
    7.3.2   Implementation via Arrays   166
    7.3.3   Implementation via Linked Lists   170
    7.3.4   Dynamic Memory Allocation   179
7.4   The Inorder List ADT   183
7.5   Variations on a Linked List   190
    7.5.1   Dummy Head Nodes   190
    7.5.2   Circular Linked Lists   196
    7.5.3   Doubly Linked Lists   197
7.6   A Dynamic Linear List   200
7.7   The Membership Management Program Revisited   202

Chapter 8   **Stacks**   *211*
8.1   Problem: Robot Navigation   212
8.2   The Stack ADT   215
8.3   Implementing the Stack 1: Array   216
8.4   Creating Generic Classes with Templates   221
8.5   Implementing the Stack 2: Dynamic List   225
8.6   Applications of the Stack ADT   227
    8.6.1   Building a Calculator with a Stack   227
    8.6.2   How Is Recursion Implemented? Part 2   232
8.7   The Robot Navigation Problem Solved   237

Chapter 9   **Queues**   *251*
9.1   Problem: Computer Network Performance   250
9.2   The Queue ADT   254
9.3   Implementing a Queue 1: Array   256
9.4   Implementing a Queue 2: Dynamic List   262
9.5   Simulation: Modelling a Computer Network   265

Chapter 10   **Tables**   *279*
10.1   A Data Structure to Support Retrieval by Key   280
    10.1.1   The Routing Problem   280
    10.1.2   Defining the Table ADT   281
10.2   Implementing a Table   282
    10.2.1   A Simple Implementation That Doesn't Quite Work   282

10.3 Hash Tables for Fast Retrieval   285
    10.3.1 Hash Functions   285
    10.3.2 Picking a Good Hash Function   287
    10.3.3 Methods of Handling Collisions   288
    10.3.4 A Complete Implementation   292
    10.3.5 Chained Hashing   297
10.4 Using Tables   302

Chapter 11   **Trees**   *307*
11.1 Introducing Trees   308
    11.1.1 Talking About Trees   308
    11.1.2 Binary Trees   309
    11.1.3 An Application: Expression Trees   311
11.2 Building the Binary Tree   314
    11.2.1 The Binary Tree ADT   314
    11.2.2 Implementing a Binary Tree   315
    11.2.3 A Sample Client for the Binary Tree   318
    11.2.4 Using the Binary Tree: Expression Trees Revisited   321
11.3 Tree Traversal   325
    11.3.1 Three Tree Traversal Algorithms   325
    11.3.2 Using Tree Traversals   329
    11.3.3 Implementing Tree Traversals   330
11.4 Binary Search Trees   336
    11.4.1 An Ordered Tree ADT   336
    11.4.2 Implementing the Binary Search Tree   340
11.5 Reuse Through Inheritance: A Hierarchy of Trees   345
11.6 Performance of Binary Trees   353
    11.6.1 The Shapes of Binary Trees   353

Chapter 12   **Graphs**   *361*
12.1 Example: Keeping Track of Course Prerequisites   362
12.2 Basic Graph Concepts and Terminology   363
12.3 Creating Graph ADTs   365
    12.3.1 Data Structures to Model Graphs   365
    12.3.2 Defining Graph ADTs   368
    12.3.3 A Hierarchy of Graphs   374
12.4 Implementing and Using Adjacency List Graphs   376
    12.4.1 Implementing Lists with Iterators   376
    12.4.2 The Adjacency List Abstract Base Class   380
    12.4.3 The Undirected and Directed Adjacency List Graphs   381
    12.4.4 Topological Sort   384
12.5 Implementing and Using Adjacency Matrix Graphs   390
    12.5.1 Implementation of the Adjacency Matrix Classes   390
    12.5.2 Finding the Transitive Closure   393

Appendix A   A Brief Review of C++   *401*
Appendix B   C++ for the Pascal Programmer   *447*
Appendix C   C++ for the C Programmer   *455*
                Bibliography   *463*
                Index   *465*

Preface

I have written *Data Structures via C++: Objects by Evolution* for a typical second semester course in computer science and programming, similar to what the Association for Computer Machinery (ACM) Curriculum dubbed CS2. I would expect that most students using this book will have some background in C++, but that this background will not include some of the more advanced topics covered in the text. I have also successfully used this book with students who have learned to program in another language, such as Pascal, by including the material that can be found in the appendices. A prior or concurrent course in discrete mathematics is useful, but not required to use this book. To fully understand the more analytical portions, precalculus is recommended.

The material in a CS2 course provides the student with the fundamentals needed for future study in the field of computer science, as well as the basics of software engineering. I find that the course has a wonderful balance between theory and practice that makes it challenging and rewarding. My students tell me that once they've completed the course upon which I've based this book, they really feel like they've started to understand what computer science, and software engineering, are all about. Furthermore, years later they tell me that they've used what they learned over and over again. This makes the CS2 course one of the most satisfying to teach and to take, as well as one of the toughest for the student and the instructor.

In addition to covering the "traditional" CS2 topics, such as recursion, linked lists, stacks and trees, this book provides a gentle introduction to the concepts of object-oriented programming, particularly encapsulation and inheritance. Certain advanced topics in C++, such as abstract base classes, friend classes, and operator overloading are presented so that the student can apply these object-oriented concepts in the C++ language. My goal is that by the end of the course the student will understand the fundamental goals of software engineering, the basic tools of algorithm analysis, the use of abstract data types and classes, and techniques for building simple data structures and will be able to apply these concepts in an object-oriented way using C++. By mastering these concepts and techniques the student will be well-prepared for future study in computer science and ready to begin to apply what he or she knows to software engineering projects, in an academic program or in the workplace.

To the Student

Nearly every time I teach this course, a student who's having trouble will come to my office after a difficult exam and report, "Well, I read the book, I don't understand why I'm having trouble." What he or she doesn't understand is that you can't read a computer science book like you would read a novel. Many of the ideas are difficult, some are subtle, and you have to read *actively* if you want to get the full value. First of all, do as many of the exercises as you can. Many of the exercises go beyond the material in the text, so to get the full value of the book you have to try these exercises. Second, don't just read the code—attempt to trace how it works, either by hand or by loading it into your system and using a debugger or other tracing technique. Finally, when it's time to do the lab projects, make sure you understand the question before you spend a lot of time developing the solution.

Answers to many of the exercises can be found on the World Wide Web site for this book, `<http://www.rowan.edu/evolve/>`. Please take a look at the web site for other materials that I hope you will find useful to you. Sample solutions for many of the lab projects will be provided to your instructor—for obvious reasons, you won't find them at the web site.

Depending on your C++ background, you may occasionally find a construct that you've never seen or perhaps have forgotten about. You may find Appendix A useful as a reference in such cases.

When I first studied the material in this course, I found it tremendously exciting. For the first time, I felt like I really was starting to understand how to program a computer and think about problem solving in a sophisticated way. My greatest hope is that you will find some of the same excitement that I felt, and that you'll feel that this book provides you good value for your hard-earned money. If you have comments or questions, or want to give me suggestions that I can incorporate into future editions, feel free to send me e-mail at `berman@rowan.edu`.

To the Instructor

It seems that computer science changes constantly. When I began teaching the subject, just about a decade ago, the World Wide Web and Java and Windows NT hadn't been invented yet; few people knew about the Internet or C++; and nobody that I knew was teaching anything about object-oriented programming. Now, it's hard for me to imagine teaching a computer science course without using the Web, and C++ and object-oriented programming are widely used and often taught to first-year students.

Much of the writing on object-oriented programming and other object-oriented technologies emphasizes its revolutionary nature—the world becomes objects, and nothing's the same again. Unfortunately, viewing object orientation as a radical new way of thinking about software induces paralysis in many computer science instructors and departments. They have become convinced by the loud voices that insist that everything we did before is wrong, and that unless we start over from scratch and take a revolutionary approach, our students will remain in the Dark Ages.

I *do* believe that there's a revolutionary aspect to object-oriented programming, but that doesn't mean that everything that came before doesn't matter anymore. Nor does it mean that in a course like Introductory Data Structures (CS2 in the ACM curriculum) we should throw out all the material that we've developed over the last 20 or 30 years. Instead, I believe that there's an evolutionary path, one that keeps the best ideas and techniques that we know and uses the powerful concepts of object-oriented programming to structure them in a new way. I have based this book on such a philosophy.

Thus you will find here classes, inheritance, and certain advanced C++ language constructs. But you will also find recursion, efficiency analysis, linked lists, and trees. Perhaps the day will come when the wide availability of powerful object-oriented libraries will mean that few of our graduates will ever encounter a linked list directly. But that day certainly hasn't come yet, and even when it does, I believe that an intelligent user of a list will benefit from an understanding of the techniques for programming linked lists, even if he or she never needs to write one from scratch.

One of the important and beneficial impacts of the growth of object-oriented programming has been an increased emphasis on the importance of software engineering concepts. My book reflects this emphasis, particularly including material on design, reliability, and testing. A CS2 course that emphasizes software engineering concepts doesn't substitute for more advanced study in the area, but it does prepare the student for what is to come. Furthermore, many of my students "escape" to industry after just a year or two of instruction, so it's important that I help them to understand and appreciate the issues early on, even if it's only at an introductory level.

Despite the rapid pace of change in computer technology, I find that much (but not all) of what I teach now has remained the same over the past ten years. That's reassuring. After all, if I'm teaching completely different things now, what about those poor students from ten years ago? Our challenge is to figure out what really matters in the field of computer science, to determine the material that is fundamental and will continue to serve our students in years to come. This isn't easy, but I hope that this book will serve as one reasonable model.

Using this Book

My approach is somewhat unusual in that there's quite a bit of material in the first six chapters before you get to some of the "traditional" CS2 topics such as linked lists and stacks. Some class testers have found that they spent too much time on these chapters and thus found it hard to finish the data structures material later on in the course. Here are a few thoughts about using each chapter that I hope will help you pace the course appropriately for your audience. I've indicated a typical number of lectures for each chapter, based on a 75-minute lecture period. You'll need to make adjustments based on the length of your lectures, the background of your students, the length of the semester or quarter, and whether or not you have a closed laboratory associated with the course.

	Chapter	Notes	Number of Lectures	Number of Labs
1	Software Engineering and Computer Programming	This chapter can be assigned reading or covered as introduction.	1	
2	Designing Software: Two Approaches	You can cover this material quickly for general exposure or emphasize if desired.	1–3	0–1
3	Software Reliability	Should certainly cover testing; program correctness can be omitted if you desire.	1–3	1
4	Abstract Data Types, Classes, and Objects	Depending on student's background, much of this may be review. Be sure to cover C++ classes if new.	1–4	0–2
5	Efficiency	Light coverage OK if your course doesn't emphasize algorithm analysis.	1–3	1
6	Recursion	May be review, but don't rush through if not.	1–3	1
7	Lists	Most students find this material difficult. If list variations are skipped, you may wish to cover later.	3–4	1–2

	Chapter	Notes	Number of Lectures	Number of Labs
8	Stacks	Include coverage of templates.	2	1
9	Queues	Simulation can be omitted.	1–2	0–1
10	Tables	This chapter can be skipped.	0–2	0–1
11	Trees	There's a lot of material here. You can skip evaluation trees and performance section.	2–4	1–2
12	Graphs	This chapter can be skipped.	1–3	0–1

Based on the table, here's a sample calendar for a one-semester course consisting of 30 lectures and 15 closed labs in 15 weeks.

Week	Lectures	Closed Lab
1	Introduction; Design	
2	Design	Design
3	Testing; begin Invariants	Testing
4	Finish Invariants, begin ADTs	Invariants
5	ADTs and C++ Classes	ADTs/Classes
6	Efficiency	Efficiency
7	Recursion	Recursion
8	Exam; begin Lists	Lists
9	Lists	Lists
10	Stacks	Stacks
11	Queues; begin Tables	Queues
12	Tables; begin Trees	Tables
13	Trees	Trees
14	Finish Trees; begin Graphs	Trees
15	Graphs	Graphs

The above schedule assumes that your students are reasonably competent with basic C++ and are ready to tackle some difficult topics quickly. It also assumes that you have a closed lab. The next schedule represents a more pessimistic approach—little or no C++ background, no closed labs, and a less sophisticated audience. You can certainly make it work, you just can't cover as much material. Here's one possible schedule that covers the early chapters in less detail, allowing more time for C++, recursion, and linked lists.

Week	Lectures
1	Introduction; C++ fundamentals
2	Testing; more C++
3	ADTs; more C++
4	Finish ADTs; more C++
5	Efficiency; finish C++ fundamentals
6	Recursion
7	Recursion; Exam
8	Lists
9	Lists
10	Stacks
11	Finish Stacks; start Queues
12	Tables
13	Trees
14	Trees
15	Graphs

Using Exercises and Laboratory Projects

Throughout each chapter you'll find exercises. Some require pencil and paper and some are simple coding problems—typically requiring a small modification of an example in the book. My primary purpose for the exercises is to encourage the student to be an active learner and to reinforce (and in some cases, go beyond) the material in the book. Generally, exercises should take the average student from a few minutes to no more than an hour. Many of the simple coding exercises could serve as lab projects for a closed lab. Answers to selected exercises can be found at the World Wide Web page <http://www.rowan.edu/evolve/>.

Programming Laboratory Problems are designed to serve as longer projects for a closed or open lab. Depending upon the project and upon the student, these problems may take from a few hours to 20 or 30 hours or more. Some of the shorter labs would be suitable for closed lab sessions, although few could be completed entirely within a two-hour lab period. The author will provide sample solutions to some of the lab projects—write me at `berman@rowan.edu` or contact an Oxford University Press representative at `college@oup-usa.org`, for more information.

Internet Resources

Extensive support for the users of this book is provided via the World Wide Web. The main entry point for these resources is at `<http://www.rowan.edu/evolve/>`. In addition to the complete source code for the book, you will find materials, software, and web links that will be useful for the course, including answers to many of the exercises. I would be glad to correspond with any students or instructors using this book via e-mail to `berman@rowan.edu`. Certain additional materials, such as sample exam questions, will be made available directly to instructors; contact me or your Oxford University Press representative at `college@oup-usa.org`, for more information.

Instructors at institutions that have difficulty accessing these resources via the Internet should contact an Oxford University Press representative, who can arrange for you to receive the materials in an alternative form.

Acknowledgments

I would not have had the opportunity to write this book without my teachers and mentors at Rutgers University. My sincere thanks for an excellent education go to Matthew Morganstern (who first introduced me to data structures), Ann Yasuhara, Bill Steiger, Barbara Ryder, Don Smith, Martin Dowd, Yehoshua Perl, Endre Szemeredi, Michael Saks, and Diane Souvaine. I was also fortunate to have Tom Marlowe of Seton Hall University and Lori Pollock of the University of Delaware on my dissertation committee. Arnold Rosenberg at Duke University was a great influence on my teaching during a short interlude there. I owe a particular debt to Ken Kaplan of Rutgers, who encouraged and mentored me and taught me a lot about what it means to be a teacher. My dissertation advisor Marv Paull has been as an important role model, as well as a friend, and taught me that writing a book can be a kind of research. Thanks, Marv.

I began teaching at Glassboro State College in 1988. Since then, Glassboro State has become Rowan College, and by the time you read this may be Rowan University. Throughout this time, I have found it to be a remarkably supportive place that has made it possible for me not only to learn and grow as a teacher, but also to have the time and support I've needed to complete this book. I'd like to thank my deans, Minna Doskow and Pearl Bartelt, who have been generous and supportive throughout my time at Rowan. The Office of Academic Computing, under the direction of Jack Cimprich, has always done everything possible to make sure that I had the hardware and software that I needed for this project. I would like to thank everyone from Academic Computing: Bruce Klein, Karlton Hughes, and Kyle Cassidy (all former students of mine) as well as Stuart Cleveland, Ken Denton, Clare Lafferty, and John Logan. Dan Greenspan and Mark Sedlock have done such a great job of managing our Unix network that I've been able to ignore it for weeks while I worked on this book.

I have been lucky to be part of an excellent computer science department at Rowan College. I want to particularly thank Don Stone, Seth Bergmann, and Nancy Tinkham for teaching from early drafts of the book and giving me many corrections and improvements. Don was particularly diligent at rooting out errors. Thanks also for their support to Khaled Amer, Ganesh Baliga, and Jianning Xu. Leigh Weiss helped me maintain my sanity (if not my deadlines) by dragging me out of my office and off to sail on the Chesapeake Bay. I could thank many colleagues from other departments at Rowan, but I have to note in particular Karen Magee-Sauer, Bob Newland, Ron Czochor, and Dick Scott, who constantly remind me why I like being at a teaching-oriented college. I appreciate all that Evelyn Amato does to help make the day-to-day demands of the computer science department rest as lightly on me as possible so that I can teach and write. Michael Lukasavage at our Duplicating Center did a great job getting copies of this book put together.

Many students have contributed to this book, not least by suffering through early, partial, error-laden drafts; I thank them all for their generosity and their patience. I received particularly useful feedback from Marc Balzamo, Joyce Barton, Chuck Deal, Beth Morris, Todd Seidenberg, Tony Sikora, Ted White, and Brian Wischet. Joe Pellegrino has had the unenviable task of testing my software while I have been changing it almost as fast as he can test it. Joe deserves the credit for finding many errors, and I have to take the blame for any that remain. I received anonymous written comments from dozens of students who class-tested the manuscript; I read every one of them carefully and was able to make some useful improvements based upon them. Mark Sedlock has developed algorithm animation software that I am using to create animations that serve as an adjunct to this book; for more information, see `<http://www.rowan.edu/evolve/>`.

I have had the benefit of the generous spirit of many other computer scientists as I have developed these books. In addition to the anonymous referees, who made many corrections and suggestions, I have learned from discussions and correspondence with Owen Astrachan, Barbara Boucher-Owens, Barry Burd, Doug Cooper, Rick Decker, Robert Duvall, Michael Feldman, Mac Grigni, Stuart Hirschfeld, Daniel Hyde, David Levine, Chris Nevison, Dung "Zung" Nguyen, Rich Pattis, Eugene Wallingford, Richard Zaccone, and Lynn Ziegler. While I have been influenced by the individuals listed, it would be incorrect to assume that all of them endorse this book—I know that some of them do things quite differently from the way I do. Thanks also to Mary Laude of Sun Microsystems for bringing a "real-world" perspective to the material on testing. Judy Mullins, Lewis Barnett, Daniel Hyde, and Rick Mercer class-tested the manuscript and provided useful feedback. Rick Mercer and I have spent many a happy hour discussing the ins and outs of teaching object-oriented programming, C++, and computer science. Rick's been a friend, a teacher, a critic, and a support, and this book wouldn't be what it is without his contribution. Thanks, Rick!

I have been privileged to meet and work with many fine people in the college text book world. My primary editor, Bill Zobrist, helped me even before he inherited this project. His contagious enthusiasm and his generous spirit have always made dealing with Oxford University Press pleasant and easy. Oxford editor Krysia Bebick has shepherded me through the completion of the book with great competence and good humor. I'd like to thank as well many others who encouraged and helped me in various ways throughout this process, including my original acquisitions editor Emily Barrosse at Saunders College Publishing, Richard Bonnacci, Lynne Doran-Cote, Carter Shanklin, Halee Dinsey, and Jim Leisy.

Thanks to artist Nina Deckert of Berkeley, California for her wonderful cover art.

Finally, thanks to my wife, Ann G. Walker, my son, Adam, and my daughter, Alice, for making it all worthwhile.

Data Structures via C++

Objects by Evolution

Chapter 1 Software Engineering and Computer Programming

Overview

A preview and a context for the subjects covered in this book.

Chapter Objectives

1. To outline the relationship between computer science, software engineering, and the topics covered in this book.

2. To define the terms data structures and abstract data types.

3. To provide an overview of the process of software development

4. To describe the rationale for using the programming language C++.

1.1   Software Engineering and Computer Science

The subject matter of this book lies at the intersection of two closely related fields: *software engineering* and *computer science*. The computer scientist studies *algorithms* and methods for implementing algorithms on the computer. An algorithm describes a method for solving a problem. Computer science became a discipline about 50 years ago, although its roots in mathematics go back much farther. The software engineer develops methods for efficiently building reliable software systems. The formal study of software engineering only goes back to the late 1960s.

While these two fields certainly overlap, they have different goals. The computer scientist tries to discover the fundamental principles that underlie computer software and hardware. The software engineer applies these principles to construct better software systems. The titles "computer scientist" and "software engineer" serve as convenient labels, but many computing professionals straddle both disciplines. Because of its historical roots, most students who study computers earn degrees in computer science, even though their career goals lie in the field of software engineering. Furthermore, every software engineer requires a firm grounding in the theories and techniques of computer science.

In 1991, a task force established by the preeminent professional organizations in our field—the Association for Computing Machinery (ACM) and the Computer Society of the Institute for Electrical and Electronic Engineering (IEEE-CS)—studied the undergraduate computing curriculum. They concluded that three processes encompass the work of the computing professional: theory, abstraction, and design.

Theory   *Theory* includes definitions and axioms, theorems, proofs, and the interpretation of results. In other words, it's a lot like what mathematicians do. In this book, you will learn about some of the theories that computer scientists have derived to help them understand and compare different algorithms. Most computer science focuses primarily on theory. A "pure" computer scientist, if there is such a thing, is concerned about using theory to understand fundamental principles of computing. The software engineer, on the other hand, uses theory in a pragmatic way; for example, a theory may suggest which of two algorithms is likely to be more efficient for solving a particular problem.

Abstraction   *Abstraction* comes from the experimental sciences. It includes developing models of the world, using these models to generate hypotheses, designing experiments to test these hypotheses, and analyzing the results. We will be using abstraction to build *models* to simplify our understanding of complicated systems. A model is created by abstracting essential features from the "real world" by stripping out features so that we can focus on the core of a problem. For example, suppose you need to "flip a coin" as part of a program that studies probability. For this purpose, the cash value of the coin, its color, its size, and the picture on it are irrelevant to the task of flipping a coin and getting heads and tails. We can model a coin for this purpose as a function that randomly generates "heads" or "tails" since that's what we really care about.

Abstraction also comes into play when we use experiments. In many cases, the theory of computer science can't tell us all we need to know about a particular algorithm and technique. We can create experiments to test alternate approaches, another use of abstraction.

Design   The process of ***design*** comes from the world of the engineer. The design process includes requirements, specifications, program design and implementation, and testing and analysis. These are the steps in constructing practical software systems, and are at the core of the field of software engineering.

To study the material in this book, you will adopt the perspectives of both computer scientist and software engineer as you use the three processes—theory, abstraction, and design. Figure 1.1 illustrates in an impressionistic way the author's view of the relationship among these areas. I hope this diagram will help you place the roles of the computer scientist and the software engineer in perspective. Please remember that any fixed dividing line between these roles is arbitrary and artificial.

Figure 1-1   *The concerns of the computer scientist and the software engineer*

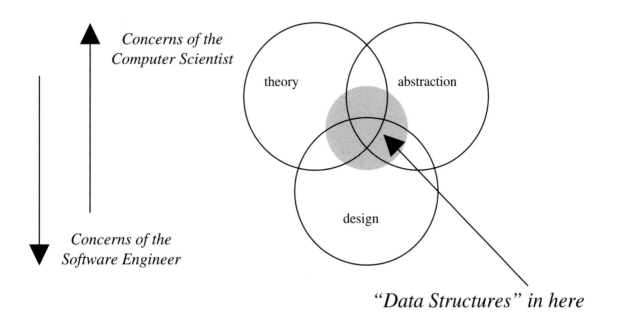

In your first computer science course or courses, you probably spent a lot of time engaged in the activity generally known as "computer programming." You may be wondering at this point, "Where does programming fit into the picture?" Computer scientists use programs to model processes and test algorithm performance (abstraction); software engineers use programs to build software systems (design). Programming is an important part of computer science and software engineering, but only a part of each field.

1.1.1   Data Structures and Abstract Data Types

I've been tossing around the term *data structures* without a definition. I've written this book for a course often called Data Structures, although it's also known by the name Intermediate Programming. Computer science faculty often refer to this course by the generic title Computer Science 2 or CS 2, which came from an influential ACM curriculum study in the 1970s. Regardless of what you call it, the course has changed over the years, and the study of data structures now forms only one part of the subject matter, although it's still certainly at the heart of this material.

Data Structures   What is a data structure? We'll use the following working definition:

Definition 1-1   A **data structure** consists of a base storage method (e.g., an array) and one or more algorithms that are used to access or modify that data.

Consider, for example, a data structure to represent a pair of dice used in a game. The base storage could be a pair of integer variables, each storing an integer in the range from 1 to 6. Relevant algorithms operating upon the dice would be "roll"— pick random numbers between 1 and 6 and store them in the integer variables—and "add"—add the two integers together to get the total. In Code Example 1-1, we demonstrate the use of a dice data structure.

Code Example 1-1   *A program demonstrating a dice data structure*

```
// cx1-1.cpp
// Code Example 1-1: a dice program that does not use an adt
//
// Illustrates the solution to a "dice simulation", without using
// abstract data types. Compare this approach to cx1-2.cpp.

#include "dslib.h" // contains standard header files for this book
#include <stdlib.h>
int main()
{
   int die1, die2, total;
   randomize(); // initialize the pseudorandom number generator
```

```
die1 = random(6) + 1; // random(6) returns random number between 0 and 5
die2 = random(6) + 1;
total = die1 + die2;
cout << "first die: " << die1 << ", second die: " << die2 << endl;
cout << "total for roll is: " << total << endl;
return 0;
}
```

While representing the dice as a pair of integers works pretty well for something so simple, keeping track of the "high level" concepts in your program (e.g., dice) using a "low level" model (e.g., integers) starts to break down as you attempt to develop more complicated systems (e.g., a deck of cards). And it becomes incredibly complex when it's used to develop a large software system. Suppose you were developing a system to support air traffic control, and needed to store and update the location of airplanes, and information about speed, distance, flight rules, fuel, runways, wind, weather, and so forth. The simple variables and arrays you've probably learned to use in your previous programming experience just aren't so simple when you have hundreds of them to keep track of. Aggregating the parts into data structures doesn't provide an adequate way to control the complexity of a complicated system. Clearly we need something more powerful.

Abstract Data Types This need to control complexity drives us to organize systems via levels of abstraction. Software engineers and computer scientists have observed that we can separate the specification for a data structure—what it does—from the implementation of a data structure—how it does it. This powerful idea leads us to the abstract data type.

Definition 1-2 An ***abstract data type (ADT)*** is a well-specified collection of data and a group of operations that can be performed upon the data. The ADT's specification describes what data can be stored (the ***characteristics*** of the ADT), and how it can be used (the ***operations***), but not how it is implemented or represented in the program.

An ADT specification may be quite formal, written in a ***specification language***, or may be an informal description in English. Likewise, an implementation could be a program in a particular programming language such as C++ or Pascal or could be a pseudo-code description. Here's a sample ADT definition for our pair of dice. We'll explain the format for specifying an ADT in Chapter 4, but your intuitive understanding should be clear for now.

ADT 1-1 Dice

Characteristics:

- Represents a pair of 6-sided dice that can be rolled to get a random sum between 2 and 12.

Operations:

int roll()

> *Precondition:* None.
>
> *Postcondition:* A random value between 1 and 6 is stored for each of the dice.
>
> *Returns:* The sum of the two dice values, lying between 2 and 12.

int die1()

> *Precondition:* The dice have been rolled at least once.
>
> *Postcondition:* None.
>
> *Returns:* The value of the first die.

int die2()

> *Precondition:* The dice have been rolled at least once.
>
> *Postcondition:* None.
>
> *Returns:* The value of the second die.

Because the ADT doesn't specify the *how*, there will generally be more than one data structure that can be used to implement it. By using the ADT approach, we have **decoupled** the specification of data from the details of implementation. Two big advantages follow from this decoupling:

1. The software development process can become less complex, because implementation details can be "pushed down" to a lower level of abstraction.

2. The software developed becomes more flexible, because we can change the implementation (e.g., to take advantage of a particular piece of computer hardware or a particular operating system) without changing the specification.

We will develop these ideas extensively in Chapter 4. Code Example 1-2 illustrates the ADT approach in C++ code. Note that the definition of the ADT serves as an excellent form of documentation within the code.

Code Example 1-2   *A program using a Dice ADT*

```
// cx1-2.cpp
// Code Example 1-2: a dice program that uses an adt
//
// Illustrates the solution to a "dice simulation", using
// abstract data types. Compare this approach to cx1-1.cpp.
//
// Dice ADT
//
// Characteristics:
```

```
//      Represents a pair of 6-sided dice, that can be rolled to get a
//      random sum between 2 and 12.
//
// Operations:
// int roll()
//      Preconditions: none
//      Postcondition: A random value between 1 and 6 is stored for each of
//         the dice.
//      Returns: The sum of the two dice values, lying between 2 and 12
// int die1()
//      Precondition: The dice have been rolled at least once.
//      Postcondition: None
//      Returns: The value of the first die.
// int die2()
//      Precondition: The dice have been rolled at least once.
//      Postcondition: None
//      Returns: The value of the second die.
// Note on encapsulation: The representation of the dice is contained within
// global variables -- we'll see shortly a better way to do this.
#include <iostream.h>
#include <stdlib.h>
#include "dslib.h"
int dice_1, dice_2;
int roll()
{
   // note -- you don't really want to call randomize every time you roll the
   // dice, but for this simplified design you don't have much choice.
   randomize();
   dice_1 = random(6) + 1;
   dice_2 = random(6) + 1;
   return dice_1 + dice_2;
}

int die1()
{
   return dice_1;
}

int die2()
{
   return dice_2;
}

// end of Dice ADT

int main() // test program to demonstrate Dice ADT
{
   cout << "The value rolled is: " << roll() << endl;
   cout << "The first die was: " << die1() << endl;
   cout << "The second die was: " << die2() << endl;
   return 0;
}
```

Before we go any further, it's useful to see where the issues you'll be dealing with in this class fit in the overall process of software development. So we'll put on our "software engineer" hat for the rest of this chapter. In subsequent chapters, we'll move more to the theoretical side of the map and examine some of the theory that underlies the course we call Data Structures.

Exercise 1-1   In the software distribution for this book you can find the programs cx1-1 and cx1-2, representing the data structure and ADT described above.[1] Read, compile, and compare these two programs.

Figure 1-2   *One version of the waterfall model of software development*

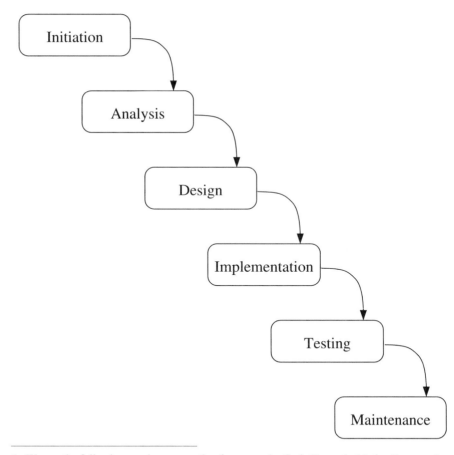

---

1. We use the following naming convention for our code: Code Example *i-j*, the *j*th example in Chapter *i*, will get the name cx*i-j*. For more information, see the software distribution.

Exercise 1-2   Design a different implementation of Dice, and modify cx1-1 to reflect your new implementation. How is the "main" function in cx1-1 affected by your change?

Exercise 1-3   Design a different implementation of Dice, and modify cx1-2 to reflect your new implementation. How is the "main" function in cx1-2 affected by your change?

Exercise 1-4   Some games for young children use colored squares on a board and a spinner that, in effect, picks one of the colors at random. Suppose that the game has five colors—red, green, blue, yellow, and orange. Design a Spinner ADT.

Exercise 1-5   Implement your Spinner from Exercise 1-4.

1.2   The Software "Life Cycle"

The goal of the software engineer is to develop quality software systems and to deliver them on time at a reasonable cost. In the past computer scientists had a difficult time achieving this goal for systems of even moderate complexity. The perception of a "software crisis"—too many software systems were of poor quality, delivered late, and too costly—motivated the creation of software engineering as a discipline. Today, we have techniques that can help us achieve our goal, if we learn these techniques and apply them to our development projects. I hope that the following description of the software life cycle will give you some insight into the software development process, but don't be deceived; this quick review will just give you a gloss on the subject, and you'll need to do quite a bit more study if you wish to become a competent software engineer.

1.2.1   The Waterfall

One of the first contributions of software engineering was the creation of formal models of the software development process. The most widely used model is called "*the waterfall*." There are many variations on this model; our composite version appears in Figure 1-2.

The waterfall model consists of a sequence of steps that lead in an orderly manner (one hopes) from the initial idea to the completed software system. Each step, as shown in Table 1-1, produces one or more *deliverables*, which are passed to the next step below. These deliverables are usually documents or the software itself. The names given to these deliverables vary from one organization to another.

Table 1-1   *The waterfall model: A summary of the players and the deliverables*

Phase	Who Performs	Deliverable
Initiation	Managers	Request for development
Analysis	Systems analyst	Functional specification
Design	Systems architect	Design specification
Implementation	Programmer	Documented code
Testing	Systems tester	Test plan and report
Maintenance	Maintenance programmer	

Initiation   In the *initiation* step, an individual or a group perceives the need for a software system. In the case of a business system, it might be a corporate executive who believes that the operation of the organization could be improved if a new system were developed. Engineers might initiate a software project because of the need for software to control a processor embedded in a product such as a jet engine or an oven. A scientist could initiate the development of new software to analyze experimental data. An entrepreneur might become aware of a need in the marketplace and could initiate the development of software to fulfill the need. The deliverable from the initiation step might be called something like "Request for Software Development." The initiation step could also include substeps such as the following:

- *Feasibility study.* Could anyone build such a system?

- *Examination of alternatives.* Is there an alternative to building the system that might be better?

- *Cost-benefit analysis.* Do the potential benefits of building such a system exceed the likely costs?

- *Make-or-buy study.* Should we develop a new system or try to buy it from someone else?

The tasks of the initiation step are often undertaken by individuals who are not primarily computing professionals: businesspersons, scientists, engineers, economists. In some cases, a software engineer may serve as a consultant to the process.

Analysis   In the *analysis* step the exact requirements of the system are determined. Typically, a professional known as a *systems analyst* performs the analysis. The systems analyst serves as an interface between the people who understand the goals and purpose of the software system—the *domain experts*—and the software engineers who will build the system. Systems analysts often interview the prospective users of the system. Ultimately, the analyst creates a document known as a *functional specification* which relates, in some detail, the exact functions that the system needs to provide as well as any special requirements—such as minimum performance limits—that the system must satisfy. Often the organization that needs the software contracts with an outside firm to develop the system; in this case, the functional specification may form part of the legal agreement between the contractor and the customer.

Design

In the *design* phase of software development, the designer uses the functional specification to construct an abstract model—a blueprint—of the system to be built. The work of the software designer has some similarity to the work of an architect; in fact, systems designers are sometimes known as **system architects**. Just as an architect's plan for a building does not specify the exact location of every nail, the system designer attempts to develop an overall plan for the software system, without paying attention to low-level details. The deliverable from the design phase is sometimes called a **technical specification**, a **coding specification**, or simply a *design*.

We consider software design to be the most critical and difficult step in the development of a software system. A good design leads to a system that can be implemented successfully and maintained relatively easily. A bad design may be impossible to implement, and if implemented, a nightmare to maintain. Of course, most designs lie somewhere in between these extremes. Unfortunately, software developers have a tendency to rush through the difficult work of design (when, after all, no "real" work is getting done) and get into the implementation without a completed design. Skimping on the design phase often leads to a poorly designed system and usually means that developers never document the design decisions that they make. Because of the importance of the design phase, we'll devote further study to it in Chapter 2.

Implementation

You are already familiar with implementing software; the primary task of the **implementation** phase is writing code in a programming language such as C++. In addition, implementation typically includes developing system and user documentation; we'll have more to say about that later. Implementation goes relatively smoothly when the programmers have a good, well-documented, design to work from.

Testing

In recent years, software developers have recognized the need to allow sufficient time for careful **testing** of software. Testing consists of developing a **test plan** that specifies the expected behavior of the system for a set of sample inputs and then running the software and comparing the actual results with the test plan. While good design and development techniques can greatly reduce the number of errors in software, we have no substitute for well-planned, thorough testing. On large projects, the people responsible for the testing may consist of a specialized staff that works only on testing and not on implementation. For systems of more modest size, the programmers and the testers may be the same people. Because testing provides the final line of defense against unreliable software, it's a critical step in the software development process, and we'll look at it in some detail in Chapter 3.

Maintenance

Maintenance describes everything that happens to the system after the users begin to use the system. *Maintenance* is a strange term—after all, software doesn't wear out like a pair of tires or require oiling like a sewing machine. Instead, the need for software maintenance arises from three sources:

1. *Latent errors.* Bugs become apparent after testing and need to be repaired.

2. *Adaptive maintenance.* We design a software system to fit into a particular environment. This environment includes the hardware and system software and also the real-world environment of the users. As this environment changes—hardware advances, operating systems are upgraded, management objectives change, laws are modified—aspects of the system become obsolete and must be repaired.

3. *Enhancement.* Users will inevitably see ways that the system can be improved and functionality added. If such changes are cost effective, the system may be modified to incorporate them.

Software developers regard maintenance as dirty work. Since maintaining an existing system lacks the glamour of developing a new one, in many cases the least experienced programmers end up responsible for maintenance. This provides a good training experience for apprentice programmers, but doesn't always enhance user satisfaction. Because all the other phases of development take place in a relatively condensed time period, those responsible for each phase can usually receive answers to their questions from those who worked on previous phases. Conversely, the maintenance programmer may be working on a system five or ten years old; the original developers have moved on, so he or she is completely dependent on the available documentation when trying to understand design and implementation choices. Without a detailed understanding of the design of the system, changes to the system may introduce new problems and make future maintenance even more difficult.

1.2.2   Critiques of the Waterfall

The waterfall model of software development has a great deal of influence, but it is not without its critics. They argue that the waterfall describes a way of working that is expensive, slow, and unrealistic. Some question whether design and implementation can really be separated and point out that research on real software development projects shows that much of the design actually gets done concurrently with the implementation. In many cases, it just seems to be too difficult to know how to do the design until certain implementation issues are resolved. Other critics suggest that writing functional specifications without exposing users to pieces of a working system results in a specification for the wrong system.

Prototypes   The construction of *prototypes* has become one of the most common variations on the standard waterfall model. A prototype is a preliminary version of the system that can be used to illustrate the specifications, test design concepts, and help the developers better understand the problem to be solved. Developers build a prototype with less care than the final product, because they intend to throw it away and start over. In some cases, different software tools may be used to build the prototype. For example, you can build a working model using a ***fourth-generation language*** (4GL) associated with a database system such as Oracle, Foxpro, or Paradox, or a ***graphical user interface (GUI)*** tool such as Visual Basic. This model may lack the polish and performance required for the final product but will serve the purposes of experimentation and insight that we want a prototype to provide.

Reusability   Software engineers have observed that a huge amount of work goes into "*reinventing the wheel*"—that is, designing and implementing software quite similar to (and sometimes exactly the same as) software that has been developed before. Building a large software system "from scratch" involves too much unnecessary work. By building and using ***reusable software*** we can begin to view the development process as proceeding by assembling reusable components rather than creating everything from the ground up. Mathematical programmers have been the most successful at reusing software; libraries of mathematical subroutines have been popular for many years. But outside the well-defined world of mathematical functions, reusability has been more elusive.

In recent years, ***object-oriented programming*** techniques have made reusability more effective; we'll discuss reusable objects in Chapter 4. The notion of reusable objects doesn't really fit naturally in the waterfall model; this lack has driven the development of new models of software development. Reusing objects has mostly to do with reusing implementations, but software engineers have also been interested in reusing designs. One of the most active and promising movements in this direction has been the development of **design patterns**. A design pattern "systematically names, explains, and evaluates an important and recurring design" (Gamma et al., p. 2). Design patterns thus help the designer by providing a library of other designer's work to draw upon when creating a new design.

Despite the shortcomings of the waterfall model of system development, it continues to have tremendous influence in software development. Even projects that adopt other techniques, such as prototyping, often use some variant of the waterfall model.

1.2.3   Documentation

To the system developer, documentation is a difficult and time-consuming task that seems to get in the way of the more interesting work of design and implementation. On the other hand, from the point of view of the maintenance programmer, there's never enough documentation, or it's inaccurate or impossible to use. The professional software engineer accepts the responsibility to provide adequate, accurate documentation.

Developers produce three broad classes of documentation as part of a software system. First, users require documentation to instruct them in the use of the system. Many organizations employ one or more professional ***technical writers*** to produce user documentation. Ideally, the technical writer works in close conjunction with the software engineer to assure the accuracy and usefulness of user documentation. Next, documentation intended for the designers, implementors, and maintainers of the system is needed. Software engineers usually produce *system documentation* as part of their professional responsibilities. System documentation will include the design, notes on implementation, test plans and results, and so forth. One form of system documentation that you've probably seen before consists of the comments embedded in the code. Finally, the clients of the developers may demand certain documentation; this documentation certifies the progress of the development process and the techniques used. Government projects typically require such documentation. This work may be done by the software engineers alone, or in conjunction with a technical writer.

In upcoming chapters, we'll look at certain aspects of software engineering in more detail. But first, we discuss our choice of C++ as the implementation language for this book.

Exercise 1-6   What are the pluses and minuses of using comments in source code for systems documentation?

1.3   Why C++?

Bjarne Stroustrup originally began developing C++ at Bell Laboratories in the early 1980s. C++ was built upon the C language as a base, but was intended to improve upon it in the following ways:

1. It allows the programmer to create new types that can be added to the language; that is, it supports *data abstraction.*

2. It supports object-oriented programming.

3. It improves on certain aspects of C; it's a "better C."

Since then it has gone through various versions and had substantial extensions and improvements made to the original specification, while maintaining the design principles of the original language. Today, C++ is close to approval by an international standards committee (ISO SC22-WG21). This book corresponds as closely as possible to this upcoming standard.

In the past, most data structures texts used Pascal as the implementation language. Why is C++ a better choice? The way in which programmers think about data structures has undergone an evolution over the last 30 years. The first insight was that the specification and implementation of a data structure could be separated and that this separation could be used to improve the design process. This is the notion of an abstract data type (ADT), discussed in Section 1.1.1, that was popularized by influential books such as Wirth's *Algorithms + Data Structures = Programs*. This concept is implemented by building **modules** and was part of the motivation for the design of languages such as Modula-2 and Ada. By the time Pascal became popular in the classroom, Wirth (the designer of Pascal) was already on to Modula-2. Students continue to struggle to build modules in Standard Pascal, which really doesn't provide language-level support for the module, or they use the extensions provided in Borland's Turbo Pascal, which does support modules but is limited to the DOS platform. Modula-2 has never made substantial inroads into the classroom.

In the meantime, computer scientists began to look beyond the ADT to the **object.** An object can be viewed as an ADT that supports the concepts of **inheritance**—new objects can be created that share features of previously created objects—and **polymorphism**—you can request an object to do something without knowing exactly what kind of object it is, and the object will "figure out" how to process the request appropriately. In my view, object-oriented programming (OOP) is a natural extension of modular programming, that is, programming with ADTs. The first OO language to achieve wide use was Smalltalk. Smalltalk has had a tremendous influence on the development of OOP and continues to enjoy substantial popularity, but it puts substantial demands on the hardware and on the programmer.

At the same time, the growth of small computers and availability of good C compilers has made C an international standard. The popularity of C++ has been driven by the combination of a large base of C programmers and a move toward object-oriented programming. Because C forms a subset of C++, the transition to OOP is eased by a familiar syntax and similar tools.

Our approach is to begin with modular programming, which we see as a subset of OOP, and progress towards OOP. We see this as a natural progression that is more easily motivated than an objects-only approach. C++ supports this well, since it can be used to do almost any style of programming from something that looks almost like assembly language programming to something quite like Smalltalk and everything in between. It's our philosophy that the student is best served by learning a range of approaches and tools. The hybrid nature of C++ lets us explore these various approaches, within a single language. We hope that the result is students that not only have gained a facility with a language rapidly gaining in popularity, but who also understand a range of design principles and philosophies and can then work within or choose among multiple models of program design.

In the next chapter, we look at two of the most influential design approaches: top-down design, and object-oriented design.

Exercise 1-7 Determine the name and version number of the C++ compiler you will be using for your course. What standards, if any, does your compiler correspond with?

Exercise 1-8   Determine which of the following relatively recent features of C++ your compiler supports: templates, exceptions, namespaces, Standard Template Library.

Chapter Summary

- The subject matter of this book includes topics from computer science—the study of the principles that underlie computer software and hardware—and software engineering—the application of those principles to the development of software systems.
- Three processes encompass the work of the computing professional: theory, abstraction, and design.
- Data structures implement abstract data types.
- The waterfall model represents the process of software development.
- Software engineers often supplement the waterfall model with development of prototypes.
- The trend toward reusable software has driven the development of new models of software development.
- C++ supports data abstraction and object-oriented programming.

Programming Laboratory Problems

Lab 1-1   Using the Dice ADT from Section 1.1.1, write a program to measure the results of rolling 1000 pair of dice. Keep track of how many times the pair sums to each possible value between 2 and 12, and print out a histogram of the results.

Lab 1-2   Using the Dice ADT from Section 1.1.1, write a program that plays the game craps. In craps, the player makes a bet, then rolls a pair of dice. If the first roll is 7, the player wins the bet; if the first roll is 2, 11, or 12, the player loses. Otherwise, the total is called the "point," and the player rolls pairs of dice until the dice add up to the point again (a winner) or until 7 is rolled (called "craps," a loser).

Lab 1-3   Design and implement an ADT to represent a coin flip. Your ADT should have an operation, "flip," which randomly returns a value, "heads" or "tails," each time it is called. Test your ADT in a program that flips 10,000 coins and reports the number of heads and tails.

Lab 1-4   Design and implement an ADT for money. Note that money cannot be represented accurately by a floating point number, because of rounding. Test your ADT by writing a program that simulates a cash register—the user enters amounts, which are added together, and a total is reported. You can enhance your program by adding a tax computation and a way to back out a transaction after it has been entered.

Lab 1-5   Find a program that you wrote last semester. Write a functional specification for the program. Develop, in consultation with your instructor, a significant improvement to the program, and write a revised functional specification for the new program. Modify your program to correspond with the new specification. What things about the way you wrote your original program made it easier to modify? What things made it harder?

Lab 1-6   Find a program that you wrote in a language other than C++, and convert it to C++. In what ways is the program different in C++ than it was in the original language?

Lab 1-7   The C++ standard includes a definition of a string ADT. C++ also supports the traditional "C"-style string (char *). Write a program, using a string ADT, that creates a string of length 1000, puts random characters into the string, and then counts the number of times the letter *A* is found. Rewrite the program using "C"-style strings. Using the "stopwatch" class provided in this book, compare the performance of the two programs. If you see no difference, try making the problem bigger. Report the performance difference, if any, between the two string implementations.

Lab 1-8   (For those already familiar with C++ classes) Rewrite the Dice ADT as a C++ class. Test your class by instantiating several dice objects. What are the advantages of using a C++ class? Are there any disadvantages?

Lab 1-9   Design an ADT and a data structure for storing an e-mail header. You can assume that the following fields are required, From, To, Reply To, Date, and Subject, and that each line can be stored in a single string. Implement your ADT and a program that tests it by first prompting the user to enter the data for the header and then printing it out. (*Hint:* I recommend you use C++ strings, *not* C (char *) strings.)

Lab 1-10   Using the facilities provided by your implementation of C++, write a program that uses a graphical user interface (GUI) to open a window, read a word, and convert it to uppercase. What abstraction mechanisms does the GUI software use?

Chapter Vocabulary

abstract data type (ADT)	implementation
abstraction	inheritance
adaptive maintenance	initiation
ADT characteristics	latent error
ADT operations	maintenance
algorithm	make-or-buy study
analysis	model
coding specification	module
computer science	object
cost-benefit analysis	object-oriented programming
data abstraction	polymorphism
data structure	prototype
decoupling	reusable software
deliverable	software engineering
design	specification language
design pattern	systems analyst
domain expert	systems architect
enhancement	system documentation
examination of alternatives	technical specification
feasibility study	technical writer
fourth-generation language	testing
functional specification	test plan
graphical user interface (GUI) tool	theory
	the waterfall model

Chapter 2 Designing Software: Two Approaches

Overview

An introduction to the significance and principles of software design.

Chapter Objectives

1. To understand the role and importance of design in the software lifecycle.
2. To learn about top-down design methods.
3. To learn about object-oriented design methods.
4. To consider the relative advantages of each method.

2.1   **Why Design?**

What does design have to do with programming? Can't the programmer just depend on someone else to do the design and then simply write the code? Isn't design an issue for builders of big software systems but more or less irrelevant for the typical computer science student?

The fact is, *every time you write a program, no matter how small, you are a designer.* For example, you decide whether to include some code within a function or to break it out into a separate function. If you're using "traditional" coding techniques, you select the variables you will use and determine how they will be passed around in the program. If you've been introduced to object-oriented programming, you think instead of your objects and how they interact. You design a user interface when you write user prompts. So you are *designing* a program, not just writing the code—the question is, will you do so consciously or unconsciously? More importantly, will you design your software well or poorly?

We often evaluate designs subjectively, but we can apply certain principles. Your goal is to create a software system that is

- *Usable.* People can use the software to solve the problems it is intended to solve.
- *Reliable.* The system runs without crashing and provides correct results.
- *Maintainable.* Problems with the software can be corrected with relative ease, and the software can be updated to meet future needs.
- *Reusable.* The software we develop should be based as much as possible on reusable components, to reduce costs and improve reliability, and should generate new reusable code that can be used for future projects.

A good design helps you achieve these goals. A bad design makes the program difficult to code in a reliable, maintainable way. Of course, just like designs for houses or cars or microcomputer motherboards, most designs have good and bad features.

In this chapter, we'll look at two *design methodologies,* or methods for creating designs. The first, *top-down design (TDD),* has been the most popular approach for the last two decades. A top-down design *decomposes* large problems into smaller ones, each of which can be solved separately. The second method, *object-oriented design (OOD),* has been growing in influence and popularity for the last ten years or so. In OOD, we focus on the data that the system manipulates and break up the overall system into **objects.** The remainder of the chapter describes the two methods and provides examples.[1]

2.2 Top-Down Design

Suppose you want to plan a large party, like a wedding reception. If you're an organized sort of person, you would sit down and make a list of the major tasks you need to undertake. Depending on your preferences, and your budget, the list might look something like this:

1. Find and book a hall.

2. Arrange for catering.

3. Hire a deejay.

4. Create the guest list and send invitations.

For each of these tasks, there are a number of subtasks. Finding and booking a hall involves identifying candidate locations, determining availability on the desired date, negotiating price and terms, and so forth. Similarly, the other tasks on the list have subparts. But your list of four items gives a good outline of the entire task; it decomposes the overall problem—plan a party—into four subtasks. Each of these subtasks could be further decomposed, and so on.

This problem-solving strategy is the basis of top-down design.[2] While there are many variations, this approach generally starts with the initial problem, breaks it into several smaller problems, and then applies the same method to each smaller problem, until each problem is of a "reasonable" size.

Video Rental System   Let's look at an example. Suppose you're given the following specification:

> *Video Rental System: Build a software system to support the operation of a video rental store. The system should automate the process of renting tapes and receiving returned tapes, including calculating and printing patron bills, which may or may not be done at the same time the tape is returned. The system must also give the clerk access to information about the tapes, such as the number of copies on the shelf of any given video owned by the store. The*

---

1. We're using the term *methodology* a bit loosely here; often it's used to mean one very specific set of rules for creating a design, such as "The Booch Methodology." More correctly, top-down design and object-oriented design can be viewed as families of methodologies.

2. Many other names have been used to describe more-or-less the same approach, including *top-down decomposition, algorithmic decomposition,* and *functional decomposition.* While each of these terms has a different shade of meaning, they are all based on the same concepts.

system must be able to add new customers and tapes to and remove them from the database. Each patron and each copy of each tape are to be associated with a unique bar-coded label.

For a real system, we would normally develop a more detailed requirements specification, but this limited specification will serve our purposes now.

To apply TDD, begin by observing that we can classify the operation of the system into three general categories: transactions (checking tapes in and out); queries (information about patrons and tapes); and modifications (adding and deleting tapes and patrons). We use this as the initial decomposition, illustrated in Figure 2-1, in the form of a *structure chart*.

Figure 2-1   *Structure chart for initial decomposition of video rental system*

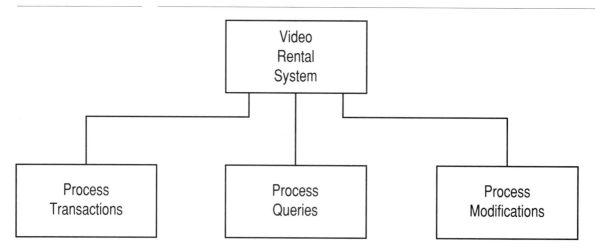

There's certainly not enough detail yet—it would not be a good idea to start writing code from a description as vague as "process transactions." We need to repeat the process, further decomposing the subparts until they represent simple problems that can be solved directly. We call the process of breaking the problem into finer and finer pieces *refinement.*

Refinement   Let's refine "process transactions." As noted in the requirements, there are two transactions: renting a tape and returning a tape. To rent a tape, we first need to look up information on the tape—if a patron tries to rent a tape that's already out, there's a problem. We also need to verify that the patron has a valid rental card and doesn't owe a lot of money to the store. The exact parameters for blocking a rental when a patron is delinquent would be specified in the requirements; it's certainly outside the software engineer's scope of responsibility to determine the policies of the store. Assuming the rental is approved, the patron database and the tapes database need to be updated to reflect the rental. Thus the "rent tape" procedure can be summarized:

1. Verify tape information.

2. Validate patron.

3. Update tape information.

4. Update patron information.

When the tape is returned, the process is reversed, and a bill is computed. If the patron pays the bill at the time of the return, then this transaction can be combined with the return. But the patron might return a tape without paying, so the system must allow customers to simply pay bills. At this point, we see we need to add "pay bill" as one of our transactions. A structure chart illustrating the "process transactions" subsystem is shown in Figure 2-2.

Figure 2-2   *Structure chart for "process transactions"*

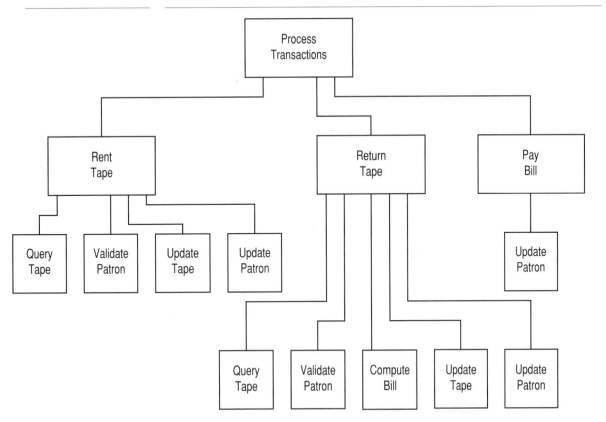

Note that many of the subparts are repeated here. This alerts us to opportunities to reduce the amount of work required by the implementation, since some parts of the system can serve more than one master. Of course, we might have been more specific in naming these parts; for example, there might be a subtask under "rent tape" labelled "verify tape available" and one under "return tape" named "verify tape is out." In this case, we would have to observe that these two processes can be merged into a single module ("query tape") that checks on the status of a tape, since in the two cases the steps taken are likely to be quite similar. By noting these similarities, we can reduce the size of the system and avoid redundant code.

A structure chart for the full system is shown in Figure 2-3. Note that this is just one possible top-down decomposition of this system; I encourage you to generate a different one. For any reasonably complicated problem, there is no one right or best TDD. Whether you find the lack of a single "correct" answer liberating or frustrating depends on your attitude and problem-solving abilities.

Coupling and Cohesion

While the process of developing a good design takes experience and insight, you can apply principles to judge the quality of a design. The most prominent criteria in common use are *coupling* and *cohesion*. Cohesion refers to the degree to which the parts of the design "hang together" well. When examining a particular subpart, you can ask whether the work that it performs naturally fits together as a single piece. Take, for example, the subpart "process modifications." The various processes subordinate to "process modifications" certainly have a consistent relationship—all have to do with data modification within the system. Thus the pieces of the "process modifications" portion of the system have a logical relationship that "holds them together." The "rent tape" and "return tape" subprocesses have even stronger cohesion—they consist of a sequence of operations that must be performed together in order to complete the task of renting a tape. In a good design, subparts exhibit good cohesion. Good cohesion leads to subparts that logically fit together and work together and thus can be programmed and tested more easily.

Coupling refers to connections between separate parts of the design. For example, if different subparts have to communicate with each other, we say that the design has a high degree of coupling. We want to avoid coupling. After all, we want our top-down decomposition to lead to subparts that can be understood and programmed separately. But if the subparts really have significant connections with one another, we can't really understand each piece independently.

Exercise 2-1 Starting from the original specification on page 21, use top-down decomposition to develop your own design for the video rental system. Compare your design with the one in Figure 2-3. What do you like better about the book's design? What do you like better about yours? Which design has better cohesion? Which has less coupling?

Figure 2-3   *Final decomposition of video rental system*

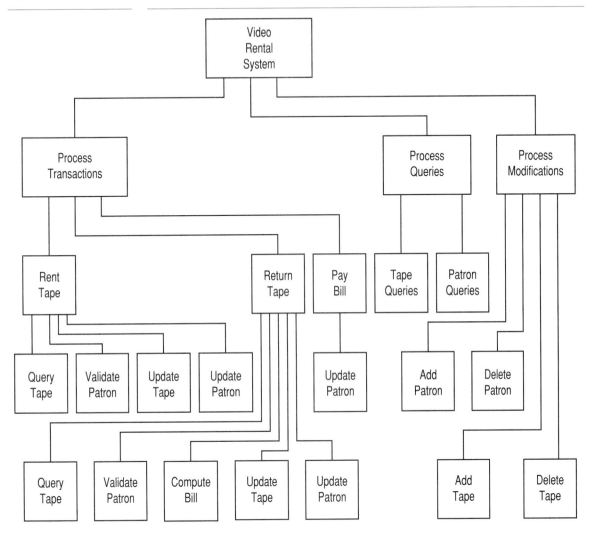

2.3   The Object Alternative

The leading alternative approach to TDD is object-oriented design (OOD). The growth in the popularity of OOD has generally paralleled the growth in popularity of object-oriented programming, but it's important to note that these are related but distinct disciplines. That is, one can design a system using OOD and implement it using a "traditional" language such as Pascal or C; OOD methods have even been employed for systems built with COBOL and Assembler Language. It's also possible to design with TDD and implement using OOP.

Many methodologies have been proposed for OOD. A methodology consists of techniques for creating the design and a language for describing it. Most OOD methodologies are based on the following basic idea: use the requirements specification to "find the objects" in the system, and then describe these objects in a more-or-less formal way. I've based the methodology we'll use in this book on a simplification of the "responsibility-driven approach" of Wirfs-Brock, Wilkerson, and Wiener. Rather than getting bogged down in the details of the method, let's go directly to an example.

How can we describe the video rental system using objects? We can start by looking at the real-world objects that the system manipulates—most obviously, the tapes and the customers. Some of these real-world objects will correspond to objects in our design. This direct correspondence between the world and our software model is the most appealing motivation for OOD. However, you are warned not to take this correspondence too far—as we will see, not all of the "objects" in the system correspond in an obvious way to concrete, real-world objects; furthermore, we don't restrict our software objects to behave like their real-world counterparts. Instead, we generally talk about *all* the objects in the system as if they are capable of "doing things." This **anthropomorphism**—attribution of human capabilities to things—helps us tremendously in the design.

Classes   Each "type" of object that we identify will form a ***class.*** For example, all the tapes in the system will form the Tape class.[3] Likewise, the Patron class will represent the customers. What we informally refer to as "finding the objects" is more properly "finding the classes." A class serves as a kind of blueprint or form that describes the attributes and behavior of an object; as such, it's similar (but not identical) to the notion of a ***type,*** for example, the `int` type in C++. A single object is referred to as an ***instance*** of the class; thus, a particular tape will be an instance of the Tape class, and a particular customer will be an instance of the Patron class.

How can we find the other classes we need for the video rental system? One popular technique is to develop ***scenarios.*** For example, imagine the process of checking out a tape. When a customer walks up to the counter to rent a tape, he or she hands the tape to the clerk, who scans the bar codes for the tape and for the patron. By "walk-

---

3. Actually, in a more sophisticated design, we might break the tapes into two or more classes; for example, new releases, general tapes, and children's tapes might each form a class, and the individual tapes would each be instances of one class. The same idea applies to the Patron class.

ing through" the scenario and considering the steps required, we may realize the need for additional classes.

The bar code scanner is attached to a console that displays information to the clerk and allows him or her to enter additional information. The physical setup is illustrated in Figure 2-4. We can use the hardware to help us understand the classes that we need. For example, we can create a Console class to model the part of the system responsible for communicating with the clerk. Likewise, a Scanner class will be responsible for reading the bar codes, and a Printer class can print the customer's bill.

Figure 2-4   *The video rental console*

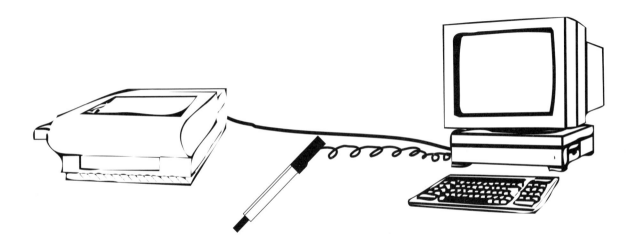

Responsibilities   Before we go any further, note that we have begun to describe each class in terms of its **responsibilities.** This is the fundamental idea behind **responsibility-driven design.** The responsibilities of a class consist of the information an object maintains and the actions an object can perform (Wirfs-Brock et al., p. 61). Also note that the classes have to work together to do the job; for example, the Console class will need to communicate with the Scanner class in order to determine which tape is being processed.[4] Classes that work together are referred to as **collaborators.**

Given these concepts, we can outline our design process as follows:

---

4. A more precise way to make this statement would be "An instance of the Console class will communicate with an instance of the Scanner class," but this language is cumbersome. The risk of the more concise form is confusion between objects and classes.

1. Find the classes.

2. Determine the responsibilities of each class.

3. Determine who collaborates with each class.

We don't mean to imply that OOD is "as easy as 1-2-3." The designer does not simply perform each step and then forget about it. For example, when determining the responsibilities of each class, the need for additional classes often becomes apparent. Conversely, you might find you have a class with no responsibilities—in which case you discard it. The designer (or designers) work back and forth among these steps to create the design, which may change with each iteration.

Let's list the classes in the current design for the video rental system:

- Tape
- Patron
- Console
- Scanner
- Printer

What are the responsibilities of an instance of the Tape class? Certainly it must contain fixed information about the tape such as its name and perhaps the running time and rating (e.g., G, PG, R). Furthermore, we give each tape instance the responsibility for keeping track of whether or not it's currently rented, and if rented, the date it's due back in the store. It will return this information in response to a query about its location. In order for the tape to maintain this information, we will assign it the responsibility of checking itself in and out. We summarize these aspects of the Tape class in Table 2-1.

Table 2-1   *Tape class*

Class	Responsibilities
Tape	Keep track of tape identification data
	Check self out
	Check self in
	Answer queries about the location of self

Instances of the Patron class will also have identifying information (name, address, phone number, bar code, etc.) and will need to keep track of two kinds of information—tapes rented and billing data. Patron data (unlike Tape data) is likely to change. Our Patron class is shown in Table 2-2.

Table 2-2   *Patron class*

Class	Responsibilities
Patron	Keep track of patron identification data Update patron identification data Update list of rented tapes Update billing information

Now let's look at the Console class.[5] The operator of the system will use Console to interface with the rental system. Even though there might only be one physical console, we'll refer to an instance of class Console, to make it clear that Console is a class just like the others. A console will need to provide a way to check tapes in and out, to respond to queries about tapes and patrons, and to add and remove tapes and patrons, and so forth, as you can see in Table 2-3.

Table 2-3   *Console class*

Class	Responsibilities
Console	Check tapes in and out Find the location of tapes Find out about patrons Add and remove tapes Add, update, and remove patrons Update patron billing information

Finally, we examine the Scanner and the Printer classes. Note that the physical elements of the system may inspire us to create classes, but there is no necessity to restrict the behavior of the classes we design to the exact capabilities of the physical objects. After all, we already have tapes that check themselves in and out! So we've decided to put the responsibility for looking up the identity of a tape or a patron into the Scanner class, rather than having it simply read a bar code (see Table 2-4).

Table 2-4   *Scanner class*

Class	Responsibilities
Scanner	Read a bar code and return either a tape or a patron

---

5. For the moment, we're assuming that there's a single console in the store; see Exercise 2-4.

The Printer class is quite simple—upon receiving the appropriate request, it prints patron's bills and receipts, as shown in Table 2-5.

Table 2-5   *Printer class*

Class	Responsibilities
Printer	Print bills Print receipts

Collaborators   Now that we've listed the classes and their responsibilities, we need to determine, for each class, the other classes that it needs in order to do its job. For example, the Console will need to collaborate with every other class in order to fulfill its responsibilities. On the other hand, the Scanner needs to collaborate with the Tape and Patron classes (in order to identify the bar code it reads), but it has no particular need to rely upon the Printer, or, less obviously, the Console. With this in mind, we present Table 2-6, which completes the first phase of the design; it contains a list of classes, responsibilities, and collaborators.

Table 2-6   *Video rental system: Classes, responsibilities, and collaborators*

Class	Responsibilities	Collaborators
Tape	Keep track of tape identification data Check self out Check self in Answer queries about the location of self	
Patron	Keep track of patron identification data Update patron identification data Update list of rented tapes Update billing information	Tape
Console	Check tapes in and out Find the location of tapes Find out about patrons Add and remove tapes Add, update, and remove patrons Update patron billing information	Patron Tape Scanner Printer
Scanner	Read a bar code and return either a tape or a patron. (This suggests that a database that links bar codes to tapes and patrons is maintained by the Scanner class.)	Tape Patron

Table 2-6   *Video rental system: Classes, responsibilities, and collaborators*

Class	Responsibilities	Collaborators
Printer	Print bills Print receipts	Tape Patron

The next step in the design is to examine carefully the classes and responsibilities, comparing them with the requirements to assure that the system can meet them. Another factor to consider is the number of responsibilities each class has. For example, the Console class seems to do a lot—is there a reasonable way to break it up into two or more classes, each of which would be simpler? Careful examination of the design may lead to adding new classes, combining two or more classes into one, and noting where responsibilities were omitted. In the perfect world, this process of "debugging" the design would be complete before implementation began; however, it's more likely that once implementation commences, errors and omissions in the design will have to be corrected.

There are many details we've omitted at this point. In particular, we will want to examine the classes to determine whether any of them contain features that can be shared between classes. This will make more sense after we've discussed inheritance, so we put off this discussion until later in the text.

Exercise 2-2   Describe some of the scenarios that might be useful in finding objects for the video rental system.

Exercise 2-3   Explain the relationship between the notion of collaborators, discussed in this section, and coupling, discussed in the top-down design section.

Exercise 2-4   We developed the design assuming that the store has a single console. More realistically, we'd expect a typical store to have several, all communicating with a central database. How does this require us to change the design, if at all?

2.4   Which Method Is Better, TDD or OOD?

If there were a definite answer to the question posed by the section heading, there would be no need to look at two different approaches to design. Instead, our equivocal answer is, "It depends." TDD has been used extensively from the 1970s up to the present day (and was probably used before then, except that people didn't know that what they were doing had a name!). OOD began to be discussed in the early 1980s, and since then has grown steadily in popularity. While OOD methods dominate new development, TDD still has a tremendous impact within industry.

As we all know, it's hard to make predictions about the future. Although OOD will continue to grow in popularity and continue to dominate, many systems will still be developed using top-down methods. So I believe it's most useful for the student to have some familiarity with both methods. After all, even if *you* are certain that OOD is the way to go, you may not be the one making the decision. Furthermore, for many years there will be a lot of software originally designed using TDD that will need to be maintained.

That being said, OOD has substantial advantages over TDD. A designer builds a model that abstracts features of the world. It seems that the object model, by combining data and behavior into classes, does a better job of modeling most problems. If you have never really thought about design before, I suggest that you concentrate your energies on the object-oriented approach. If you have experience with TDD, you may have a harder time getting used to OOD, but I encourage you to learn to think in this new way. There's a saying, "If all you have is a hammer, everything looks like a nail," but we need more than a hammer to build a house. OOD is a flexible and effective tool that all software engineers ought to have in their toolboxes.

Chapter Summary

- A good design helps lead to software that is usable, reliable, maintainable, and reusable.
- In top-down design, you decompose a large problem into smaller and smaller subproblems until the size of each subproblem is manageable.
- You can use a structure chart to document a top-down design.
- Consideration of coupling and cohesion can help you evaluate the quality of a design.
- An object-oriented design begins by identifying objects in the specification and creating classes that can represent these objects.
- Scenarios can help identify the classes needed in an OOD.
- The responsibilities and collaborators of each class should be determined.
- Top-down design and object-oriented design each have their place, but object-oriented design has become the preferred method for most new development.

Programming Laboratory Problems

For each of the following specifications, you can develop a top-down design, an object-oriented design, or both.

Lab 2-1   *Library circulation system.* The library circulation system will keep track of every book, video, and audio recording in the library, as well as library cardholders. Each time a book is checked out or returned the system must keep track of it. Books can be added to the library's collection and also removed. Due dates for books should be tracked, as well as notices sent out for materials that are more than a week overdue. Fines for overdue materials should be calculated, and a record kept of the amount owed by each cardholder. Library patrons should be able to determine the availability of a book and also get a list of the books they have checked out.

Lab 2-2   *Radio program database.* Jean Shave, a deejay at WCPP radio, wants to keep track of all the music she plays each week. For each number, the system should keep track of the name of the song, the artist, and the album on which it appeared. The system should be able to list all the songs played on a particular date and also to display all the times a particular song was played.

Lab 2-3   *Racquetball court scheduling system.* The Happy Hacker's Health Club has three racquetball courts. Each court can be reserved for a one-hour period.

The desired software system will allow the club attendant on duty at the front desk to keep track of court reservations. Facilities should be provided for making a reservation, cancelling a reservation, checking to see whether a court is free, and printing out the daily schedule for the three courts.

Lab 2-4   *Content analysis system.* This system reads a text from standard input, breaks it up into words, and keeps track of every word and the context in which it appeared. Once the text has been processed, the user can make queries about particular words. In addition to keeping track of the number of times each word appears, the system should also compute the average word length and the average number of words per sentence. In addition, the context for each word should be recorded by keeping track of the word before and the word after each word in the text. For example, if you were to check the context of the word *context* in this paragraph, your output would look like this:

```
context appears 4 times:
--
the * in
the * for
the * of
word * in
```

The "*" stands for each occurrence of the query word.

Lab 2-5   *Emerald Green Lawn Care.* The Emerald Green Lawn Care Company uses a special portable lawn analysis system to determine the mix of chemicals that will make a lawn as green as possible. The system takes a sample of grass and soil, as well as the date and the air temperature; automatically analyzes (under computer control) the samples; mixes a chemical potion to be applied to the lawn; and fills a tank with the appropriate mix. The system keeps track of the time and date on which this chemical application is made to the lawn.

Lab 2-6   *Editorial system.* An editor for a monthly newsletter wants to keep track of articles for each issue. Various authors submit articles, which have to be edited, typeset, and placed within the magazine. The system should keep track of the status of each article, the set of articles prepared for each issue, and the placement of articles within the issue.

Lab 2-7   *Sailboat autopilot.* An autopilot system for a sailboat automatically steers the boat toward a specified compass heading (i.e., the direction the boat is sailing). It consists of the following: a magnetic flux compass that determines the current heading; a control unit that lets the sailor specify the desired compass heading; a motorized belt that adjusts the sailboat's rudder to attempt to maintain the desired heading; and a microprocessor that controls the operation of the system. The microprocessor will receive input from the compass and from the control unit and will move the motor as appropriate to set the heading of the boat.

Lab 2-8   *Image viewer.* Image viewer software reads a file in a standard graphics format (such as JPEG, GIF, or TIFF) and displays it on the screen. Design an image viewer that can read files in many different formats, display them, and perform simple transformations such as rotation and zooming in and out. Your viewer should also allow the user to convert the software to a new format with a "Save as" command. As you create your design, think about reusability across computer platforms, such as Unix, MS Windows, and Macintosh. What parts of the design can be platform independent, what parts must be platform dependent, and can you partition the design to make large chunks of it platform independent?

Lab 2-9   *Wireless telephone cell.* A single cell in a cellular phone system communicates with the cellular phones in its area and connects them to the telephone network. The cell must be able to initiate and break contact for calls as well as pass them to adjacent cells when the phone moves from one area to another. When a call is initiated, the cell must verify that the phone has a valid identifier and that the user is registered to use the system (by communicating with a user database via the telephone network). Once the phone has been validated, the cell requests the telephone network to set up a circuit and then monitors the call as long as it remains within the local cell, passing it off to an adjacent cell if the phone moves or terminating the call if appropriate.

Lab 2-10   *Box office system.* The box office system for the Glass Apple Performing Arts Center keeps track of all tickets available for a series of performances at the center. Each ticket specifies a particular seat at a particular performance. The system should support individual ticket purchases, as well as subscription purchases for a number of performances. Ticket buyers should be able to express a preference for the area in the theater in which they would like to sit and also be able to reserve blocks of tickets for groups. The system should calculate invoices for purchases and keep track of money owed. Note that you need to include a way to add new performances as they are scheduled.

Chapter Vocabulary

anthropomorphism

class

cohesion

collaborators

coupling

decomposition

design methodology

instance

maintainable

object

object-oriented design (OOD)

refinement

reliable

responsibility (of class)

responsibility-driven design

reusable

scenario

structure chart

top-down design (TDD)

type

usable

Chapter 3 Software Reliability

Overview

A discussion of the risks of faulty software and techniques for making software more reliable.

Chapter Objectives

1. To understand the professional responsibility of the computer scientist and software engineer to avoid risks.

2. To be able to use testing to identify and correct faulty software.

3. To use program correctness techniques to reduce software errors.

3.1   Risks of Faulty Software

A few years ago, the operator of a pool maintenance company in New Jersey got the idea to use his computer to monitor his customer's pool heaters. Using a microcomputer and a modem, he developed a program that would connect by phone with the heaters, check for correct operation, and adjust the temperature. After a few weeks of operation, he got a frantic call from one of his clients—the water in the pool was 100° and rising! He drove to the pool and adjusted the temperature by hand. Later he was able to find a bug in his program. Fortunately, nobody was injured by the scalding water.

A patient at the East Texas Cancer Center in March 1986 was not so lucky. He was receiving radiation therapy for cancer from a machine called the Therac-25. Here's a description of what happened:

> *The patient . . . was taken into the treatment room and placed face down on the treatment table. The operator then left the treatment room, closed the door, and sat at the control terminal. . . . The operator was isolated from the patient, since the machine apparatus was inside a shielded room of its own. The only way the operator could be alerted to patient difficulty was through audio and video monitors. On this day, the video display was unplugged and the audio monitor was broken.*

> *After the first attempt to treat him, the patient said that he felt like he had received an electric shock or that someone had poured hot coffee on his back. He felt a thump and heat and heard a buzzing sound from the equipment. Since this was his ninth treatment, he knew that this was not normal. He began to get up from the treatment table to go for help. It was at this moment that the operator hit the "P" key to proceed with the treatment. The patient said that he felt like his arm was being shocked by electricity and that his hand was leaving his body. He went to the treatment room door and pounded on it. The operator was shocked and immediately opened the door for him. He appeared shaken and upset. . . .*

> *In actuality, but unknown to anyone at that time, the patient had received a massive overdose, concentrated in the center of the treatment area. After-the-fact simulations of the accident revealed possible doses of 16,500 to 25,000 rads in less than 1 second over an area of about 1 cm.*

> *During the weeks following the accident, the patient continued to have pain in his neck and shoulder. He lost the function of his left arm and had periodic bouts of nausea and vomiting. He was eventually hospitalized for radiation-induced myelitis of the cervical cord causing paralysis of his left arm and*

both legs, left vocal cord paralysis (which left him unable to speak), neuro-genic bowel and bladder, and paralysis of the left diaphragm. He also had a lesion on his left lung and recurrent herpes simplex skin infections. He died from complications of the overdose five months after the accident. (Leveson and Turner, pp. 27-28)

At least six people were seriously injured by the Therac-25, and two died as a direct result of their injuries. After extensive examination, it was determined that a bug in the software was a direct cause of the accidents. In addition, there were other, related problems:

- Inadequate testing: while the system as a whole was operated under test conditions, there was no systematic attempt to test whether or not the software operated as specified.

- Too much faith in software control: hardware interlocks on older systems were removed on the Therac-25.

- Poor documentation: the system displayed the message "Malfunction 54," but the operator's manual did not include a description for this message.

- Poor user interface: it was easy for operators to enter inconsistent commands that could be harmful to patients.

The tragic effects of the Therac-25 resulted from a combination of the factors. Better software and hardware design and proper testing procedures might well have saved lives.

Costs of Software Errors

Medical devices, airplanes and transit systems, weapons and power plants—in any of these environments, errors in software can be fatal. But even when lives are not at stake, the risks of unreliable software are substantial. A programming error in an AT&T telecommunications switch effectively shut down AT&T's long-distance service for nine hours, blocking approximately 5 million calls (Neumann, p. 15). Errors in accounting and financial software can cost millions of dollars, as well as damaging the reputation and stability of the companies involved. For example, a software error at the Bank of New York cost an estimated $5 million in 1985 (Wiener, p. 10). When software errors strike a small company, the dollar values involved may be less impressive, but the impact can be even more devastating for those involved.

As a future (or practicing) computer science professional, you have a moral and ethical obligation to apply the best we know about software development to the products you help to produce. In this chapter, we examine two areas related to the design and implementation of reliable software. First, we look at techniques for testing software. Next, we examine some approaches that help to reduce the number of errors during the design and implementation phases. It's beyond the scope of this book to make you an expert in either of these areas, but I hope to provide a base level of knowledge that you can expand upon as you continue in your computer science education. Designing and implementing computer software can be a lot of fun, but it's a serious business too, because many individuals will be depending on the software you write in order to do their jobs, solve problems, go from place to place, and maybe even to save lives. With the power of the computer comes responsibility; it's up to you to take it.

Exercise 3-1   In the United States, engineers in traditional fields such as civil or mechanical engineering are usually licensed by state boards, which set minimum standards for education and competence. Currently, no state has a similar system for software engineers. What would be the advantages, and disadvantages, of adopting licensing for software engineers?

Exercise 3-2   Access the Usenet newsgroup "comp.risks," and start reading the messages found there. You'll find it's a gold mine of interesting and important information about problems caused by the use and misuse of computers and related technologies.

Exercise 3-3   Suppose all the computers in the world suddenly stopped working tomorrow. What would the effect be on you and your family?

Exercise 3-4   Give an example of a problem you've encountered due to faulty software and how it affected you.

3.2   Testing

3.2.1   A Taxonomy of Errors

Testing is the search for software errors. The goal is to find as many errors as possible, so they can be removed, making the software as reliable as possible. Before we discuss approaches to testing, it will be useful to classify the types of errors encountered in software.

Syntax Errors   Students learning to program generally spend more time with ***syntax errors*** than with any other kind. The *syntax* of a programming language is the formal rules that specify the structure of a legal program; that is, a program that the compiler for the language can compile successfully. That doesn't mean that the program does anything useful, or even that it will run, but only that it will compile. Syntax errors are, by definition, the errors that the compiler can detect. Normally, the presence of even a single syntax error prevents the successful completion of the compilation process.

Here's an example. The syntax of C++ requires that every identifier be defined before it is referenced. If you submit the following code to a C++ compiler, it will generate an error message along the lines of "x is not defined."

```
int main()
{
  int i, j;
  x = 0; ...
}
```

While the student finds syntax errors frustrating, they are really the easiest kind of error to deal with. The compiler does the testing for you—there's no chance of finding a syntax error in a program after it's in use, because you can't successfully compile a program with a syntax error, and hence you can't use it! The programmer uses the compiler to detect the syntax errors and then fixes them. A programmer experienced with a language will have few syntax errors and will be able to fix them quickly.

Validity Errors   If a program runs but gives the "wrong answer" or in some other way fails to meet its specification, we say that it has a *validity error.* These errors are also known as *logic errors,* because they often (but not always) stem from errors in the logic of the program. You've probably run into validity errors in software you've used. Unfortunately, most of the software that is in use today contains many validity errors. The errors that resulted in the serious consequences described in the previous section were primarily of this type.

Validity errors may result from a mistake made when going from one phase to the next in the software development process. In the simplified waterfall model presented in Section 1.2, this would be either when going from analysis, or requirements, to design or from design to implementation. If the designer misinterprets the requirements and creates a faulty design, the final product will contain the error, even though the programmer may have implemented the (faulty) design correctly. Likewise, a correct design implemented incorrectly will result in one or more errors in the software. We can say that errors of this type result from a failure to "build the system right."

Verification Errors   On the other hand, it's quite possible for errors to occur even if the designers and implementors make no mistakes at all. This can occur if there is an error in the requirements; that is, the requirements analysis fails to describe the system that is really needed. We call this a *verification error.* A common source of verification errors results from overlooking important factors when developing the requirements. A famous example of this occurred in 1960 when a military system in Thule, Greenland, reported a massive missile attack; it turned out that the system had detected the moon rising over the horizon! (Neumann, p. 38) The system was implemented correctly, but the requirements failed to take the moon into account. When an error of this type occurs, we say that we have "built the wrong system."

Run-Time Errors

A *run-time error* is really a special case of a validity error, but because it appears in a rather different way it is often considered separately. A run-time error occurs when a program suddenly terminates execution—when it "crashes." A typical cause of a program crash is a misuse of memory, for example, a misuse caused by an array reference out of bounds. Another cause is division by zero, which on most systems causes the program to terminate. Depending on the environment, a run-time error can be quite hazardous—for example, if the software for an air-traffic control system crashes, the consoles for the controllers will go blank. In other environments, a program crash is more annoying than dangerous. Programs that enter infinite loops are not quite the same as programs that crash, but the effect is roughly equivalent, since in most cases the operator is forced to terminate execution of the program.

A run-time error occurs because of a failure to correctly implement the design. While run-time errors can be dramatic, in many cases they are not as insidious as other kinds of validity errors. That's because you know right away when you have a run-time error: the program crashed, so you know there's a problem that needs to be fixed. An error that results in incorrect output may be much more subtle and, hence, harder to find and to fix.

Many of the bugs that are the most difficult to detect and diagnose arise when software operates in a *real-time environment.* In a real-time environment, the operation of the software depends upon various tasks operating with strict timing constraints. For example, the operating system has to deal directly with devices such as disk drives, input devices, network interfaces, and so forth. Other systems collect data from instrumentation or control hardware devices, such as the microprocessor in an automobile. A particularly tricky environment in which to work is a *multiprocessor system*—a computer with more than one processor. While multiprocessor systems were once considered exotic, they've become commonplace in larger servers and workstations; such systems bring new challenges to the design and implementation of error-free software.

In some situations, it may be difficult to guarantee that a program will never terminate unexpectedly. For example, as we will see in Chapter 7, some programs request new memory during program execution. If this is the case, there's always a chance that when the program wants more memory, there is no more available to it. In this case, the requirements should state the course of action for the program to follow: either terminate or continue to try to operate without the extra memory. Of course, if the program does terminate, it should do so "gracefully," by providing full information to the user about the reason for termination and saving any data that it can.

Maintenance Errors

Maintenance errors are not a distinct type of error; these are errors of whatever type that are introduced during the maintenance phase of the software life cycle. Introducing new errors during software maintenance is one of the most common causes of errors in software. Typically, the original authors of the software do not end up maintaining it. The maintenance programmer has to understand the code well in order to avoid making errors. Often, a lack of documentation makes the problem tougher. If the software was designed carefully at the start, it helps; for example, excessive coupling makes it hard to understand small chunks of the code without understanding the whole thing. When software engineers design and implement code with the assumption that it will be modified in the future, maintenance errors will be relatively less common. As we will see, special care must be used in testing the changes made during program maintenance.

Costs to Repair Errors

All software errors have a potential cost, especially when the software is released containing the error. The cost of repairing an error is closely related to the type of error, where in the lifecycle it occurs, and when it is detected. Basically, the greater the distance between where the error is made and where it is detected, the greater the cost to repair it.[1] Let's consider two extremes.

A syntax error is typically made and repaired by the same person. No testing is required to find it, other than attempting to compile the code. While the programmer may have to use a reference manual or get help from another programmer in order to understand and correct the error, most syntax errors are fixed quickly and at low cost.

At the other extreme, an error in program requirements that is not detected early on has the potential to be extremely expensive. If the error or omission is faithfully reproduced in the design and the code, the wrong system will be built. Once this error is detected, there are two choices: settle for a system that doesn't really do what is needed, or go back through all the phases of the life cycle—analysis, design, implementation, and testing—to correct the error. While good design techniques may help to isolate the problem, this process may still take a substantial amount of time and require a lot of money. Thus an early investment in reviewing the requirements and design will pay off in that it helps to assure that the correct system is built in the end.

Exercise 3-5   Give two or three examples of syntax errors you frequently encounter in C++.

Exercise 3-6   Write a simple function in C++ that will result in a run-time termination. Run the program and observe the results. How could the function be modified to avoid termination or to terminate "gracefully"?

---

1. According to Mary Laude, a member of the technical staff at Sun Microsystems and a testing engineer, fixing an error in the field costs about three times as much as fixing the same error before release.

Exercise 3-7   The following function contains a validity error of a sort that's quite common.

```
int sum(int a[], int n)
{
// precondition: a is an array subscripted from 0 to n-1
  int i, total(0);
  for (i = 0; i <= n; i++)
    total += a[i];
  return total;
}
```

Find the bug and fix it.

3.2.2   Approaches to Testing

Black-Box vs.
Glass-Box   There are two fundamental approaches to testing.

1. ***Black-box testing.*** In black-box testing, only the inputs to and outputs from the program are considered. That is, no attention is paid to the source code. The testers create input/output sets by using the requirements and the design to predict the output for a particular input. The program runs with the specified input, and the results are compared to the predicted output.[2]

2. ***Glass-box testing.***[3] When using glass-box testing, the tester consults the source code to design the tests. Glass-box testing uses the notion of *code coverage* in an attempt to test as many possible paths through the code as feasible. (Usually, it's impossible to test every possible path, because there are too many.)

Most software developers use black-box testing alone, but glass-box testing has become more popular because of automated tools that assist the tester in devising and cataloging the test procedures. We will assume from now on that when we refer to testing, we are talking about black-box testing.

Unit vs. System
Testing   *Unit testing* refers to the testing of individual pieces of a larger software system. The units might be individual functions, or they might consist of groups of functions or modules. In a system designed using OOD, the units might be the classes of the system. There should be a close link between the design of the system and unit testing—a good design contains enough detail about the individual parts of the program

---

2. The terminology of testing doesn't apply very well to modern interactive programs, where the output might consist of a sequence of commands, mouse-button presses, and so forth. The principle is the same, but the input/output sets might look more like scripts: the user does this, and gets this response, etc.

3. Also called *white-box testing* and *clear-box testing*.

so that meaningful tests can be created. Unit testing is extremely important, because it is often easier to identify subtle bugs by the careful testing of individual units then by testing the entire system.

After unit testing is complete, a **system integration** or *system build* is performed, and system testing can begin. A system tester depends more upon the specifications than the design, since he or she will be looking for errors in the overall operation of the system. When errors are identified during the system test, they will have to be referred back to the point in the process at which the error was made, which may not always be easy to determine. The errors are corrected, and then the process moves forward—design, implementation, unit testing—until system testing can be repeated.

When the exact specification of a system has been incorporated into a contract between a customer and a software development contractor, acceptance testing may be required. In acceptance testing, the customer supervises the testing or contracts with a third party to perform the tests. Often, the tests are designed by associating them with specific requirements in the functional specification. This is referred to as *functional testing.* Only when all required tests have been passed will the acceptance test be completed; typically, the contractor will not receive part or all of the payment for the software until the system passes acceptance testing.

In recent years it has become common for **system testing** to include a phase called **beta testing.** In beta testing the software is released to a subset of the potential users who begin using the software and find latent bugs. Beta testing has value to a commercial software company beyond the identification of bugs. By providing early versions of the software to selected individuals, the company helps those individuals prepare for the transition to the new software. This encourages the beta testers to be loyal to the software they are testing.

Who Does Testing? You have probably been testing your own software in school, and this is a practice not uncommon in small-scale, informal development. But a sophisticated software engineering operation will usually have a team specially trained and dedicated to testing. There are definite advantages to this approach, at least for organizations that can afford it. Testing is a speciality, and those who work regularly at it can develop expertise beyond that commonly found among programmers. Furthermore, the programmers may have little or no incentive to find their bugs — in many cases, once they're done with this project, they can go on to another and let a separate staff of maintenance programmers clean up behind them. The testing staff, on the other hand, justifies their reason for being by finding bugs and assuring reliable software.

Test Plans The method used to test software bears a strong resemblance to the scientific method, which can be summarized as follows: one uses observations about the world to create theories about its behavior; these theories are tested by experiment and are modified accordingly. Testing software is quite similar. Based on the specification and design, one can create experiments that test the behavior of the system. If a test fails—assuming that the test was correctly derived from the specification—it tells us that the software is not behaving in the manner predicted. Of course in the scientific world, when an experiment fails to conform to our theory, we change the theory. In software testing, a failed experiment requires instead that we change our "world" (the software) to conform to our theories (our specifications and design).

The tester begins by creating **test plans**. These plans must be derived directly from the specification and the design. Here's an example of a very simple specification that we can use to write a test plan:

> *Write a program,* Max, *that reads in a sequence of integers and outputs the value of the greatest integer.*

The tester uses this specification to write a sequence of input/output pairs, for example:

```
Input:    2 8 1919 28 7 -3 1

Output:   1919
```

How does the tester decide which inputs to test? Obviously, except for very simple programs, to list every possible input would require a prohibitive amount of time. Take, for example, the video rental system described in Chapter 2. Listing every possible video tape, patron, and transaction would clearly be impossible. While there are no hard and fast rules, some guidelines are helpful:

1. *Test typical cases.* Ideally, inputs are collected from the environment where the program will be used. Another, less-useful possibility is to use a random number generator to pick a range of cases.

2. *Test extreme cases.* For this problem, some of the extreme cases might be very few (1 or 2) inputs, all negative numbers, all numbers the same, or a very large list of numbers (if there is some maximum limit, this should be tested). In this problem, you would want to make sure you test an input in which the largest is in the first position and an input in which it is in the last position.

3. *Test invalid inputs.* While we can't expect good answers from bad data, we can expect the program to do something reasonable like complaining about the input and explaining what it expected. A complete specification should state what actions should be taken, although it's usually not possible to predict the complete range of potential inputs the system might see. As much as possible, the software ought to behave well, even when unexpected events occur.

A (partial) test plan for Max is given in Table 3-1. The Type column refers to the three types of tests listed above.

Table 3-1   *Test plan for Max program*

Test	Input	Output	Type
1	2 38 2 938 20 47 2 -109 0 38	938	1
2	100 29 28 10 4 -3 84 17 -9	100	2
3	938 2847 17273 2867 238 19288	19288	2
4	-1 -2 -3 -4 -5 -6 -9	-1	2
5	1 1 1 1 1 1 1 1 1 1 1	1	2
6	2.5 .09 1 2 3	error	3
7		error	3

Exercise 3-8   Write a test plan for a function `void sort(int a[], int n)` that sorts the array `a`.

Exercise 3-9   Write a test plan for a function `float mpg(float milesDriven, float gallons)` that computes miles per gallon for a specified number of miles driven and gallons purchased.

Exercise 3-10   Write the `mpg` function from Exercise 3-9, a main program to test it, and use your test plan to test the function.

3.2.3 Two Techniques for Unit Testing

You may have wondered how it is possible to test pieces of a system without testing the whole thing. In many software development projects, the programmers have to be able to test parts of their software independently because different programmers are implementing different parts concurrently. Even when all pieces of a system are available, unit testing is desirable. How can this be accomplished?

Drivers   There are two basic techniques for unit testing. The first is the construction of *drivers*. Suppose you are working on a project and have been assigned to write a function `max` with the following specification:

```
int max(int a[], int n)
Inputs: a is an array of n integers
Returns: the value of the largest integer in array a
```

Presumably, somewhere in the larger system your function will be called, but you really don't know when or how. Furthermore, as specified, the function has no input or output, so how will you get the data into the array, and how will you check the value returned? The answer is a driver: a program whose sole purpose in life is to test `max`. Code Example 3-1 is a sample test driver for `max`.

Code Example 3-1   *Test driver for* max *function*

```
// cx3-1.cpp
// Code Example 3-1: Test Driver for Max Function

#include <iostream.h>

int max(int a[], int n);   // defined in cx3-3.cpp; link with the driver

int main()
{
    int a[100], i;
    cout << "Max driver\n";
    cout << "Enter each input to max terminated by -9999\n";
    cout << "Length of input must be <= 100\n";
    for (i = 0; i < 100; i++) {
        int val;
        cin >> val;
        if (val == -9999) // termination sentinel
            break;
        else
            a[i] = val;
    }
    cout << "\nMax is " << max(a, i) << '\n';
    cout << "\n\n";
    return 0;
}
```

Stubs   In some cases, the developer faces the inverse situation: the code under construction includes calls to one or more functions that are not yet available. Perhaps another programmer is responsible for these functions. In other cases the same programmer is writing both but wants to start testing the logic of the calling function before writing the called functions. To test a function that contains calls to unavailable functions, the programmer needs a placeholder for the function that hasn't yet been written—a **stub.** A stub stands in for a function until the real one is available.

Typically, a stub is designed to do two things:

1. Print an "I'm here" message.

2. Return a plausible value (if required).

The first step isn't absolutely required, but it's usually handy for debugging. An "I'm here" message generally includes the name of the function, plus the values of the actual parameters in the call. For example:

```
function max called with values: 2 38 2 938 20 47 -2 109 0 38
```

Unless the function return type is void, the function has to return a value. In order for the calling program to operate correctly, this returned value has to be something reasonable. Depending on the logic, you might be able to return a constant—maybe returning 1000 from the Max function will work for a particular application. Another possibility is to get an input value from the tester before continuing. Code Example 3-2 contains a stub for a function median based on this second strategy.[4]

Code Example 3-2   Sample stub for function median

```
// cx3-2.cpp
// Code Example 3-2: Stub for Median Function

#include <iostream.h>

int median(int a[], int n)
{
    // This is a stub for the function median; the real function supplied later
    cout << "function median called with n = " << n << ", a[] = ";
    int i;
    for (i = 0; i < n; i++)
        cout << a[i] << '\t';
    cout << "\nType in value you want median to return:";
    int return_value;
    cin >> return_value;
    return return_value;
}
```

Exercise 3-11   Write a stub for a function void sort(int a[], int n) that sorts the array a.

Exercise 3-12   Write a driver for a function void sort(int a[], int n) that sorts the array a.

Exercise 3-13   The function double min2(double a, double b) takes two floating-point numbers a and b and returns the smaller of the two. Write a stub for min2 that prints out a and b and prompts the user to enter the smaller number.

Exercise 3-14   Write the function min2 described in Exercise 3-13. Write a test plan for min2. Write a driver for min2 and use it with your test plan to test min2.

---

4. The median of a list of numbers is the value "in the middle" such that half the numbers are smaller than or equal to the median and half are larger or equal to the median.

3.3 **Applying Program Correctness Techniques**

An important research area in computer science in the last 20 years has been the development of techniques for ***proving program correctness.*** The idea is simple: if we can express the specification for a program using the language of mathematical logic and if we have sufficient understanding of the exact meaning of the statements in our programming language, then we can construct a formal, mathematical proof that the operation of the program corresponds to the specification. If you have such a proof, then in theory there's no need for debugging at all. Since the program has been proven correct, why test it? Note that the best testing can do is find errors; because it's not possible to test all possible combinations of inputs for a program of any complexity, testing can't *prove* the program correct.

Even if we agree on the goal of proving program correctness, program correctness techniques still can't guarantee reliability. First of all, program-proving techniques prove that a program corresponds to a specification, but that doesn't prove the specification is correct! Testing will still be required to demonstrate that we've "built the right system." Furthermore, how can we guarantee that the argument for a particular proof is correct? Just as it's possible for a program to contain errors, the argument accompanying the program can have bugs as well. Proofs produced using formal techniques can be quite long and difficult to read. Most proofs in the literature have been created for programs that are relatively small, compared to the ever-growing systems produced by software engineers, although there are significant exceptions.

Despite some skepticism on the part of many software engineers that program proving can ever be widely practiced in a formal way, there is general agreement that techniques that come out of this research can have a profound effect in improving the reliability of software. In this section, we introduce some of these techniques and show how they can be applied in an informal manner to improve our software and to help us avoid bugs. I strongly recommend that all computer science students learn more about proving program correctness, but the formal study of that subject is outside the scope of this book.

3.3.1 **Assertions**

An ***assertion*** is a precise statement about the behavior of a program at a particular spot in its execution. The intention is that if the assertion can be shown to be true, the program is operating correctly at that point. For an example, we return to function max, which is shown in Code Example 3-3.

Code Example 3-3   Function max

```
// cx3-3.cpp
// Code Example 3-3: max function

int max (int a[], int n)
{
    // assertion 1: a is an array with subscripts ranging from 0 to n-1
    int max_val(a[0]), i;

    for (i = 1; i < n; i++)
        // assertion 2:  (max_val >= a[k] for 0 <= k < i) and
        //               (max_val = a[j] for some j, 0 <= j < i)
        if (max_val < a[i])
            max_val = a[i];

    // assertion 3: (max_val >= a[k] for 0 <= k < n) and
    //              (max_val == a[j] for some j, 0 <= j < n)
    //              i.e., max_val is equal the value of largest int in array a
    return max_val;
}
```

Preconditions Each assertion in max makes a claim about the state of the function at a particular point. The first assertion simply states that the array a is indexed from 0 up to n-1. Nothing in max makes this true; rather, we're assuming that it holds when max begins to execute. A claim about the state of a function, or a section of code, that we expect to be true before execution is called a ***precondition.***

Loop Invariants The second assertion claims that certain conditions hold on each iteration of the for loop in max. Such an assertion, called a ***loop invariant,*** attempts to capture something important about the operation of a loop. Because programmers often make mistakes when specifying loops, loop invariants provide an important tool for creating reliable loops. The details of this particular loop invariant are a bit complicated, so we defer them until Section 3.3.3.

Postconditions Assertions positioned at the end of a function, or in some cases at the end of a block of code such as a loop, are referred to as ***postconditions***. The postcondition for max promises that the value returned by the function will indeed be equal to the largest value in the array.

To make a formal proof of correctness, we must show that if the precondition is true, then the postcondition must be true, by using the loop invariant. As promised, we won't present a formal proof of correctness; however, we'll show that constructing informal arguments of this nature will help us to construct more reliable software.

3.3.2   Preconditions and Postconditions

Preconditions and postconditions are special assertions that describe the operation of a function. If A_1 is a precondition for a function f, and A_2 is the corresponding postcondition, then we claim that the function operates as follows:

> *If, when function* f *is called,* A_1 *is true, then, when the function returns,* A_2 *is true.*

Perhaps this is easier to understand in terms of a concrete example. Here is the description of the pre- and postconditions for function max:

> *If, when function* max *is called, it is true that* a *is an array ranging from 0 to* $n - 1$*, then, when function* max *returns, the value returned is equal to the largest value in* a*.*

The precondition and postcondition constitute a *contract* between the caller of the function (called the **client**) and the function itself. The client has an obligation to meet any preconditions; if these preconditions are met, then the function guarantees to make the postcondition true when control is returned to the client. Note that if the client fails to make the precondition true, then the results are unpredictable—the function makes no particular claim about what it will do, or even if it will do anything in this case. Looking again at function max, we see that if the client passes an invalid value for n, there is no way that the function can guarantee that it will return the correct value. In fact, if n is *larger* than the array, calling max might even cause the program to crash, since function max will be accessing memory that doesn't belong to the array.

Why not simply check the preconditions upon entry to the function? In some cases this can be done, but in many instances it cannot. For example, there's no way in C++ to check the length of an array. Even when it is possible to check the preconditions, there may be a performance penalty to checking a condition that the client may already have checked. The client is in the best position to know whether or not the precondition is true.

The value returned by a function, if any, can be viewed as a kind of postcondition. For documentation purposes, this book specifies the value returned by the function separately from the postconditions. Other authors choose to fold together the return value with other postconditions. The two approaches are logically equivalent, and it's just a matter of style and convention as to which one you use.

The interface between functions is a likely location for program bugs. If the client function misinterprets the requirements of the function it is calling, the results may be a program error. Careful attention to preconditions and postconditions makes such errors much less likely. From now on, we'll state the preconditions and post-conditions as part of the specification for each function. You should include pre- and postconditions as comments when writing functions; they serve as a particularly useful form of documentation.

Sometimes it's convenient when specifying a pre- or postcondition to be able to refer to, for example, "the value of array a before the function is called" or "the value of a after the function executes." We'll use the convention that $variable_{pre}$ refers to the state of `variable` when the function is called, and $variable_{post}$ refers to the state after returning from the function.

Exercise 3-15 Write appropriate preconditions and postconditions for a `min` function; that is, a function that takes an array and its length as arguments and returns the value of the smallest item in the array.

Exercise 3-16 Write appropriate preconditions and postconditions for a `maxpos` function. `Maxpos` is similar to `max`, but instead of returning the value of the largest item it returns its index in the array.

Exercise 3-17 Write appropriate preconditions and postconditions for the function `addone(int a[], int n)`, which takes as input an array a of `int`s of length n and adds one to each element in the array. Use the notation a_{pre} and a_{post} to refer to the state of a before and after calling `addone`.

3.3.3 Loop Invariants and Proving Termination

You've probably already seen in your programming experience that loops are a major source of program errors. A loop invariant is a special kind of assertion that is used to reason about the operation of loops. When used with care and experience, loop invariants can improve the reliability of software by leading to correct loops.

The formal definition of a loop invariant is easy to understand: a loop invariant is an assertion that is true at the beginning of each iteration of a loop. The trick is to find *useful* loop invariants, that is, loop invariants that tell us something about how the loop works.

Max *Function with Invariant*

Let's look once more at the `max` function loop; we reproduce it here:

```
int max_val(a[0]), i;
for (i = 1; i < n; i++)
    // loop invariant:  (max_val >= a[k] for 0 <= k < i) and
    //                  (max_val == a[j] for some j, 0 <= j < i)
    if (max_val < a[i])
        max_val = a[i];
```

Before we consider whether the assertion is really satisfied, let's consider some other loop invariants we might have used. First of all, anything that is always true is a loop invariant, for example, i == i is certainly true at every iteration of the loop, but it doesn't tell us anything about the operation of the loop. Second, the loop control condition is also an invariant, by definition: at each iteration of the loop, i < n is true. Again, this doesn't really tell us anything we didn't know before.

Now let's consider our proposed invariant, and ask what it tells us. Suppose the invariant is correct, that is, at each iteration of the loop the invariant is true. The loop termination condition, i < n, means that we keep looking as long as i is less than n, so when the loop ends i >= n; if the invariant is still true, then, substituting for i,

```
(max_val >= a[k] for 0 <= k < n) and
(max_val == a[j] for some j, 0 <= j < n)
```

Now we're getting somewhere. This is exactly what we want to be true after the loop, because it's the postcondition for the function. So establishing this assertion to be, in fact, a loop invariant will be sufficient to establish that if we ever get to the end of the loop, our function will work correctly. We'll address the second issue—getting to the end of the loop—in a moment.

Establishing the
Loop Invariant   In order to establish the loop invariant to be true, we need to show two things: that the invariant is true the first time the loop is entered and that if it is true on any given iteration it remains true on the next.[5] When we enter the loop the first time, i == 1, therefore the invariant can be written this way:

```
(max_val >= a[k] for 0 <= k < 1) and
(max_val == a[j] for some j, 0 <= j < 1)
```

Because max_val == a[0], these expressions hold true for k == 0 and j == 0.

Now suppose that the invariant holds true on some iteration. We'll use the letter i to represent the value of the loop counter on that iteration. This is illustrated in Figure 3-1. The value in a[i] is either bigger than max_val, or it's not. Look at the if statement in the loop. In the first case, max_val will get the value of a[i], so the invariant will continue to hold; likewise, if a[i] is smaller than the old value of max_val, the invariant will continue to hold without changing max_val. In either case, the invariant is maintained.

---

5. You may recognize this as a form of proof by induction.

Figure 3-1   *Illustrated loop invariant for function* max

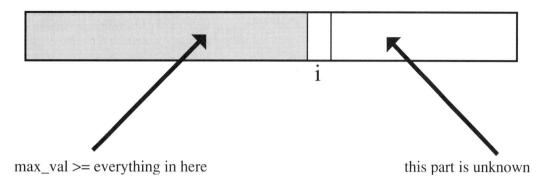

max_val >= everything in here   this part is unknown

Proving
Termination   How do we know that we ever get to the end of the loop? Because the loop control variable, i, starts at one and increases by one on each pass through the loop, it has to eventually get to n, no matter what value n has. So for this loop, ***proving termination*** is quite easy.

Steps for Analyzing a
Loop   This example illustrates an approach to loop invariants that works for a wide range of problems. Normally a loop processes some sequence of data elements (at this point, this is always an array, but later on we'll see other kinds of sequences that can be processed with loops). When the loop begins, none of the array will be processed; during the iterations of the loop, part of the array will be processed and part will not; and at the end, the entire array will be processed. Thus, to analyze a loop, we look at the problem as follows:

1. *Establish the precondition.* This sets up conditions for processing in the loop.

2. *Find the invariant.* The invariant will describe the (partial) solution.

3. *Establish the postcondition.* When the loop is exited, the invariant should assure that the entire array has been processed.

4. *Prove termination.* Determine that the loop will always terminate.

Sum ***Function with***
Invariant   Before going on to harder stuff, let's take a look at another very simple algorithm; summing up the items in an array. We start with the following function specification:

```
int sum(int a[], int n)
// precondition: a is an array of ints ranging from 0 to n-1
// postcondition: none
// returns: a[0] + a[1] + ... + a[n-1]
```

In this case, the precondition for the loop is simply the precondition for the function. Now think about what a partial solution would look like: some of the numbers have been summed, and some have not. We need a variable to hold the partial solution—we'll call it total—and at our intermediate step in the algorithm total will hold the sum of a portion of the array. It really doesn't matter which direction we go, but let's assume that when we begin step i, we have already added up the items a[0] through a[i-1]; then in the ith step, we add in a[i]. Stated as a loop invariant:

```
// loop invariant: total = a[0] + a[1] + ... a[i-1]
```

Now, where do we start total and i? One way to go is to set total to the value of a[0], and i to 1. Then, certainly, when we enter the loop the invariant will be true, since it will state that total = a[0] + a[1] + ... a[0], that is, total = a[0]. But there's a problem: we've actually created a hidden, additional precondition, *because if* n = 0, *our program has a bug.* When n = 0, the sum is certainly defined—it's zero—but a[0] is not. A better choice is to set total to 0, and i to 0. Then the invariant states that

```
total = a[0] + a[1] + ... + a[i-1] = a[0] + a[1] + ... a[-1]
```

In other words, the value of total is equal to the sum of the array elements from 0 to -1! Looks strange, but does it make sense? Such conditions arise frequently in loop invariants, and they're often quite useful. A statement about an empty set, or an empty array range in this case, is referred to as **vacuous** and is always considered true. Vacuous statements often work well in establishing the initial state of a loop invariant.

What about when we leave the loop? After the last pass i = n, so the loop invariant states that total = a[0] + a[1] + ... + a[n-1], which is just what we want. Furthermore, if we start with i equal to 0 and increment it on each pass through the loop, using the loop condition i < n assures that the program *will* leave the loop, since i has to get to n eventually. Applying our loop invariant and the initial values as discussed above leads to Code Example 3-4.

Code Example 3-4   sum *function*

```
// cx3-4.cpp
// Code Example 3-4: sum function

int sum(int a[], int n)
{
    // Precondition: a is an array with subscripts ranging from 0 to n-1
    int i;
    int total(0);
```

```
for (i = 0; i < n; i++)
    // Loop invariant: total = a[0] + a[1] + ... + a[i]
    total += a[i];
// Postcondition: total = a[0] + a[1] + ... + a[n-1]
return total;
}
```

Next, we apply invariants to the problem of sorting.

Exercise 3-18   Write a function int min(int a[], int n) that finds the smallest item in array a. Use an appropriate loop invariant, and prove termination.

Exercise 3-19   Write a function int maxpos(int a[], int n) that returns the position of the largest item in the array. Use an appropriate loop invariant, and prove termination.

3.3.4   Insertion Sort

As you already know, sorting is the process of ordering data so that each item is less than (or greater than) the item preceding it (assuming that all elements are unique). There are many sorting algorithms; insertion sort is one of the simplest. Simple though it is, it's still useful to develop it using an invariant to assure that it will work correctly. The fundamental idea of ***Insertion Sort*** is this: move items from the set of unprocessed elements to a sorted list one at a time; as each item is moved, it is placed in the proper position in the sorted list. In order to place the new item, some items may need to be moved out of the way. Figure 3-2 illustrates this idea.[6]

The first observation is that we can do this ***in place***; that is, we can divide the array to be sorted into a sorted portion and an unprocessed, or unknown, portion and move items from unknown to sorted, without using any extra storage. Now we can envision our loop invariant as shown in Figure 3-3.

How do we get started? When the loop begins, the first item in the array will be in the sorted part—after all, a single item by itself is certainly sorted, as shown in Figure 3-4. In order to reestablish the invariant in each step, we insert the item at position *i* into its proper position in the sorted part of the array; the function insertNextItem will be responsible for this. The function based on these invariants appears in Code Example 3-5. The proof of termination for this loop is left as Exercise 3-20

---

6. As is customary, we will use integers for our model of sorting. The algorithm will work for any data for which the notion of "less than" or "greater than" makes sense, including strings.

Figure 3-2   *Basic idea of Insertion Sort*

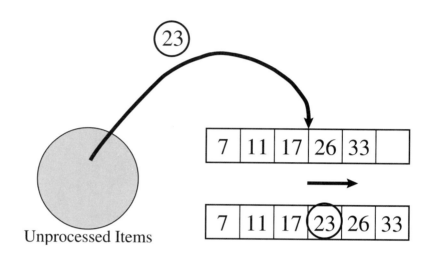

Unprocessed Items

Figure 3-3   *Loop invariant illustrated for Insertion Sort*

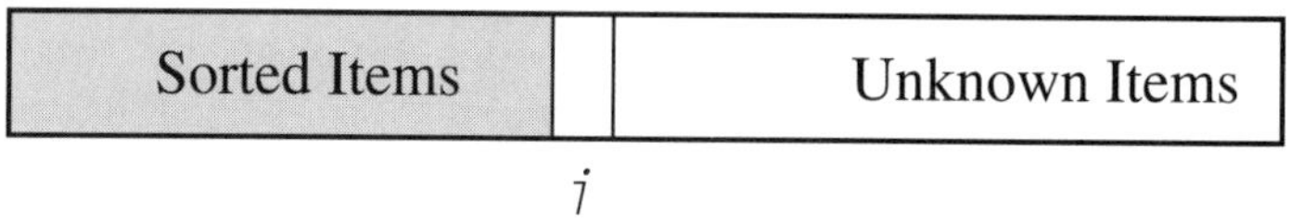

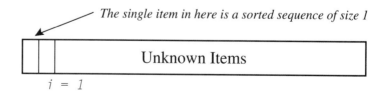

Figure 3-4   *State of Insertion Sort loop invariant on the first iteration*

The single item in here is a sorted sequence of size 1

Unknown Items

$i = 1$

Code Example 3-5   *Insertion Sort*

```
// cx3-5.cpp
// Code Example 3-5: Insertion Sort

void insertNextItem(int 0[], int i) // in cx3-6.cpp
void insertionSort(int a[], int n)
{
    // Precondition: a is an array with subscripts ranging from 0 to n-1
    int i;
    for (i = 1; i < n; i++)
        // Loop invariant: items in range from 0 to i-1 are sorted;
        //      items from i to n-1 have not yet been examined.
        insertNextItem(a, i); // see cx3-6.cpp
    // Postcondition: array a is sorted
}
```

InsertNextItem   Next we write the subfunction insertNextItem. The insertNextItem function needs to take the item at position i (see Figure 3-3) and put it into its proper position in the sorted portion of the array; this will cause the number of sorted items to increase by one. This function starts with the precondition that the array is sorted up to the position of the item to be inserted, which is at index i. Where does this precondition come from? It's our loop invariant. The function insertNextItem starts at the end of the sorted portion of the array and "slides" items to the right to make a space for the new item, eventually inserting it in the proper place. This function is shown in Code Example 3-6.

Code Example 3-6   InsertNextItem

```
// cx3-6.cpp
// Code Example 3-6: insertNextItem (used by Insertion Sort)

void insertNextItem(int a[], int i)
{
    // Precondition: array a is sorted from 0 to i-1
    int newItem(a[i]), insertPos(i);
    for ( ; insertPos && newItem < a[insertPos-1]; insertPos--)
        // Loop Invariant: newItem <= a[insertPos+1] .. a[i] &&
        //                  a[insertPos+1] .. a[i] are sorted
        a[insertPos] = a[insertPos-1];
    a[insertPos] = newItem;
    // Postcondition: array a is sorted from 0 to i
}
```

To understand the loop invariant for insertNextItem, observe that we want the loop to continue sliding elements to the right until we find the proper position for newItem. In other words, we only want items to end up on the right of newItem if they are larger than newItem. We can express that with the loop invariant:

```
newItem <= a[insertPos+1] ... a[i] &&
a[insertPos+1] ... a[i] are sorted
```

This is certainly true initially, since the range a[insertPos+1] ... a[i] is empty. On each iteration of the loop, insertPos goes down by one, but only if newItem is less than a[insertPos]; furthermore, we are sliding each element one step to the right, so the invariant is maintained.

Proving termination is slightly different here; now, the loop control variable is decreasing instead of increasing. Furthermore, there's more than one way to exit the loop because the loop condition contains two parts; the loop will continue to execute as long as insertPos > 0 or newItem < a[insertPos-1]. In order to prove termination, it's enough to show that one of these two parts eventually becomes false. Because insertPos decreases by one each time through, then as long as i starts out greater than 0 the loop will terminate when insertPos gets to 0.

When the loop is exited, note that the loop condition guarantees one of two things: either insertPos == 0, or newItem >= a[insertPos-1]. In the first case, the loop invariant tells us that newItem <= a[1] ... a[i], so the 0 position is the right place to insert the element. In the second case, a[0] ... a[insertPos-1] <= newItem <= a[insertPos+1] ... a[i], so insertPos is the right place to insert newItem, and the rest of the items remain sorted. These conditions can be used to prove that we have met the postcondition.

Using Examples to Understand Invariants

In principle, you can take the loop invariant and prove that the program works correctly and be done with it. But most people can understand the process of a loop better by looking at an example to see how it relates to the invariant. Let's suppose that on some particular call to insertNextItem, a = {1, 4, 15, 19, 8, 3, 20, 11}, and i = 4. First, let's check the precondition, which claims the array is sorted from 0 to i-1, in this case from 0 to 3. Looking at a, we can see that the precondition has been met. Now the value of newItem gets set to a[4], which is 8, and we initialize insertPos to 4. Upon entry to the loop, is the loop invariant in fact true? The loop invariant refers to the array range a[insertPos+1] ... a[p], which when we enter the loop is a[5] ... a[4], a nonexistent region of the array; hence the claims a[insertPos+1] ... a[p] are true vacuously.

Now let's execute the line a[insertPos] = a[insertPos-1] within the loop—update insertPos, and check the next iteration of the loop. The shifting assignment leaves the contents of a looking like {1, 4, 15, 19, 19, 3, 20, 11}, and the new value of insertPos is 3. The loop control clause, insertPos && newItem < a[insertPos-1], has the value 3 && 8 < a[3]. Because a[3] is 19 the statement is true, and the loop continues. You can verify that the loop invariant, which is 8 <= a[3] && a[4] ... a[4] are sorted, holds at this point.

Once again, the program will execute the body of the loop and update the value of insertPos, leaving a = {1, 4, 15, 15, 19, 3, 20, 11} and insertPos = 2. However, the loop will now terminate, because newItem < a[insertPos-1] is false. Hence we know that the statement a[insertPos] = newItem will put the new value, 8, into the second position, yielding a = {1, 4, 8, 15, 19, 3, 20, 11}.

Looking at examples doesn't substitute for working through the invariants. I suggest you use the examples to help understand the invariants, but really understanding the invariants and why they work will give you the strongest evidence that you've built the program correctly. We will use loop invariants throughout the rest of the book to help us "get loops right." In the next chapter, we'll see how we can use preconditions and postconditions to give well-defined specifications for the operation of data structures.

Exercise 3-20   Prove the termination of the loop in Code Example 3-5.

Exercise 3-21   Suppose the insertNextItem function (Code Example 3-6) is called with a negative value of i—does the loop terminate? Explain. Can we be certain that i is always positive?

Exercise 3-22   Trace the operation of insertionSort for a = {17, 3, 9, 6, 14, 25, 2}. As you work, check with the actual numbers to make sure that the loop invariants really *are* invariant.

Exercise 3-23   Use your driver from Exercise 3-12 to test insertionSort.

Chapter Summary

- Computer scientists and software engineers have a moral and ethical responsibility to apply techniques that lead to reliable software.
- Software errors can be categorized by the source from which they arise.
- Systematic testing procedures, including the use of test plans, can help find software errors and improve reliability.
- You can use drivers and stubs to help with unit testing.

- Applying program correctness techniques to software development can reduce errors and improve reliability.

- Preconditions and postconditions provide a precise specification of the operation of a function.

- Loop invariants and proving loop termination can help us avoid errors when writing loops.

- The Insertion Sort algorithm can be derived using loop invariants.

Programming Laboratory Problems

Lab 3-1   Write a test driver that can be used to test sorting routines. The driver should read a sequence of integers from standard input, call a sorting routine, and then check for the following:

1. The array of data contains the same items before and after the sort. (Of course, the order will probably be different.)

2. The items are in sorted order.

Step 2 is quite easy to check; Step 1 is trickier—you will want to think carefully about how you will do this.

Use your test driver to test the insertion sort algorithm from this chapter. Be sure to use the guidelines in the chapter to develop a test plan that you then use to guide your testing.

Deliverables: Test plan, driver, and results of all tests.

Lab 3-2   Write a function `median` with the following specificiation:

```
int median(int a[], int n)
```

Precondition: a is an array indexed from 0 to n-1.

Postcondition: None.

Returns: the median of a; that is, an element of a such that the number of elements in a less than (or equal to) the median is equal to the number of elements in a greater than (or equal to) the median. (When n is even, return the average of the two elements closest to the median.)

For example, the median of 1, 3, 5, 6, 8 is 5, and the median of 1, 3, 5, 7, 9, 20 is 6. (Note, however, the inputs will not necessarily be in sorted order.) The easiest way to compute the median is to sort the list first (use the `insertionSort` code, Code Examples 3-5 and 3-6) and then pick the middle element or elements from the array.

1. Write a test plan for `median`.

2. Write a driver for `median`.

3. Compile and run your driver using the stub in Code Example 3-2.

4. Write the `median` function, and test it using your test plan.

Deliverables: Test plan, driver, `median` function, and results of executing your test plan.

Lab 3-3 Consider the function `countChars` with the following specification:

```
int countChars(const string & s, char c)
```
[7]

Precondition: None.

Postcondition: None.

Returns: The number of appearances of the `char` c in the string s.

1. Write a test plan for `countChars`.

2. Write a stub for `countChars`.

3. Write a test driver for `countChars`. Compile and run the driver with the stub.

4. Implement `countChars`, using a *useful* loop invariant. (Note: some string libraries provide a function that can do the whole thing; for the purposes of this exercise, implement `countChars` yourself with a loop.)

5. Test `countChars` using your test plan.

Deliverables: Test plan, stub, driver, `countChars` function (including a loop invariant), results of executing test plan.

Lab 3-4 Consider the function `remDups` with the following specification:

```
void remDups(int a[], int & n)
```

Precondition: a is an array of integers, indexed from 0 to $n-1$.

Postcondition: a is an array of integers containing the same values as the original array except that any adjacent duplicated elements in a_{pre} have been replaced by a single element in a_{post} and n has been set to the length of a_{post}.

For example, if a_{pre} = {1, 3, 4, 4, 3, 3, 2} and n_{pre} = 7, then a_{post} = {1, 3, 4, 3, 2} and n_{post} = 5.

1. Write a test plan for `remDups`.

2. Write a stub for `remDups`.

3. Write a test driver for `remDups`. Compile and run the driver with the stub.

---

7. If possible, use the string class library provided by your compiler. If your compiler doesn't include a string library, you can get one from the Web page for this book. For more information, see Section 4.6.2.

4. Implement `remDups`, using a *useful* loop invariant.

5. Test `remDups` using your test plan.

Deliverables: Test plan, stub, driver, `remDups` function (including a loop invariant), results of executing test plan.

Lab 3-5 Write a function `longestIncreasingSequence` with the following specification:

```
int longestIncreasingSequence(double a[], int n)
```

Precondition: a is an array of `doubles`, indexed from 0 to $n-1$.

Postcondition: None.

Returns: The length of the longest continuous increasing sequence in the array a.

For example, if a = `{1.1, 2.2, 3.3, 1.0, 2.0, 7.5, 7.6, 7.6, 6.5, 6.1}`, then the value returned is 4, since the sequence `1.0, 2.0, 7.5, 7.6` is the longest continuous increasing sequence. Note that 0 is a valid answer when there is no increasing sequence in the array. Write a careful test plan, use a loop invariant to write the function, and use a test driver to carry out your test plan.

Deliverables: Test plan, function with loop invariant, test driver, results of test plan execution.

Lab 3-6 In a *Caesar cipher*, each letter in a message is encoded by the letter that appears k positions later in the alphabet, for some parameter k. For letters near the end of the alphabet, you wrap around to the beginning. To simplify things, we'll use only capital letters and spaces (with spaces remaining unencoded). For example, suppose we encode the following:

> Something tells me it's all happening at the zoo.

First, we convert everything to upper case and throw out the punctuation, giving

> SOMETHING TELLS ME ITS ALL HAPPENING AT THE ZOO

Then for $k = 3$, S gets encoded as V, since V is 3 letters past S in the alphabet, and O becomes R. Because Z is at the end of the alphabet, we wrap back around to the beginning and use C to encode Z. The complete message then becomes

> VRPHWKLQJ WHOOV PH LWV DOO KDSSHQLQJ DW WKH CRR

Write a function `encodeCaesar` with the following specification:

```
encodeCaesar(string & s, int k)
```

Precondition: s is a string containing uppercase letters and spaces.

Postcondition: s_{post} contains the string representing the results of encoding s_{pre} as a Caesar cipher with parameter k.

(Note: to decode, call the `encodeCaesar` function with a negative value of k.)

Write a test plan, the `encodeCaesar` function (using a loop invariant), and a test driver. Test your function thoroughly with positive and negative values of k.

Deliverables: Test plan, `encodeCaesar` function, driver, and results of executing test plan. (Note: in order to assure the reliability of your function, create the test plan by hand—using your `encodeCaesar` function to create the test plan may mask errors in your program.)

Lab 3-7   Write a function `merge` with the following specification:

```
void merge(int a[], int n1, int b[], int n2, int c[])
```

Preconditions: a is a sorted array of integers, indexed from 0 to n1-1;
         b is a sorted array of integers, indexed from 0 to n2-1.

Postconditions: c contains all the items from a, plus all the items from b, in sorted order, indexed from 0 to n1+n2-1; that is, the array c contains the merge of the items in a and b.

Your `merge` function should contain two loops. The first iterates as long as there are items in both a and b, picking the next item to put into c. Eventually you run out of items in one array or the other, at which time a second loop will take all the items from the array that still has data left and move them to c. (It may be convenient to write the code with three loops, although on any single pass you will only execute two of them.) For each loop in your program, write a loop invariant. Be sure to review Section 3.3.3, on loop invariants, so that you write a useful invariant that "captures" the essence of the loop.

You will need to write a test driver for the merge program and to test the program thoroughly.

Deliverables: The `merge` function (with loop invariants); driver; test plan; results of all tests.

Chapter Vocabulary

assertion	proving program correctness
beta testing	proving termination
black-box testing	real-time environment
client	run-time error
driver	stub
functional testing	system integration
glass-box testing	system testing
in place	syntax error
Insertion Sort	testing
logic error	test plan
loop invariant	unit testing
maintenance error	vacuous
multiprocessor system	validity error
postcondition	verification error
precondition	

Chapter 4 Abstract Data Types, Classes, and Objects

Overview

A discussion about how abstract data types (ADTs) simplify programming by hiding information, how the C++ class can implement ADTs, and how the principles of object-oriented programming start with the ADT.

Chapter Objectives

1. To understand ADTs, information hiding, and encapsulation.

2. To see how ADTs aid code reuse.

3. To explain the use of C++ classes to build ADTs.

4. To understand the role of ADTs in object-oriented programming.

4.1   Problem: Computing with Time

A friend with a part-time job in a doctors' office approaches you with the following problem. "The doctors are trying to improve their customer service, and I'm supposed to keep track of the amount of time patients wait before they are seen. They gave me a list of the times the patients arrived, and were seen by a doctor, and I'm supposed to figure out how long the average wait was. It's so tedious by hand—can you help?"

"Hey, sure, I can write a program to do that. No sweat," you reply. Of course, as usual, once you look more carefully you find it's not as easy as it seems. How can you figure out the waiting time for a patient that arrived at 11:48 A.M. and was seen at 12:10 P.M.? It's easy to do in your head but not so obvious how to do this in a program. You realize what you need is a way to manipulate "time" as if it were a built-in type in the C++ compiler. After all, to find the difference between two `int`'s, you simply subtract one from the other. If you could have variables of type "time" and could subtract one time from another, the program would practically write itself.

Like an `int`, which doesn't require you to worry about its exact representation in the computer, a Time type would require you only to think about the particulars of the problem and not about manipulating the Time values. As a convention, we capitalize these user-defined types to highlight the difference from built-in types. Your resulting program might look something like Code Example 4-1. In this chapter we will learn how to add new data types to C++. We often call these user-defined types *abstract data types* (*ADT*s). We'll also see that ADTs provide the foundation for *object-oriented programming*.

Code Example 4-1   *Patient waiting time*

```cpp
// cx4-1.cpp
// Code Example 4-1: Patient Waiting Times

#include <iostream.h>
// Somehow, the type "Time" gets defined up here
int main()
{
    int numberOfVisits(0), totalWaitingTime(0);
    char answer;
    do {
        Time arrival, seenByDoctor;
        cout << "Enter arrival time:";
        cin >> arrival;
        cout << "Enter time seen by doctor:";
        cin >> seenByDoctor;
        numberOfVisits++;
```

```
        // assume that subtracting one Time from another yields the
        // difference in minutes as an int
        totalWaitingTime += seenByDoctor - arrival;
        cout << "Done? Enter 'y' to quit, anything else to continue: ";
        cin >> answer;
    } while (answer != 'y');
    cout << "Number of visits: " << numberOfVisits << "\n";
    cout << "Total waiting time: " << totalWaitingTime << " minutes.\n";
    cout << "Average wait is " << totalWaitingTime/numberOfVisits
            << " minutes.\n";
    return 0;
}
```

Here's a sample of input and output from the patient waiting time program:

```
Enter arrival time: 12:17PM
Enter time seen by doctor: 12:25PM
Done? Enter 'y' to quit, anything else to continue: .
Enter arrival time: 1:10PM
Enter time seen by doctor: 2:02PM
Done? Enter 'y' to quit, anything else to continue: y
Number of visits: 2
Total waiting time: 60 minutes.
Average wait is 30 minutes.
```

Exercise 4-1   List six operations you would like a Time ADT to provide to you.

Exercise 4-2   List three different ways you could store a representation of the time of day. What would be the relative advantages of your representations?

4.2   Describing Data Types

4.2.1   What's an ADT and Why Use It?

The success of a software project often depends upon the choices made in the representation of the data. Object-oriented design methods emphasize this by focusing first on the data items in the problem domain, but it's of critical importance no matter what methodology is used. The proper choice of a data structure can be a key point in the design of many algorithms. Clearly, we need good ways to describe and talk about data.

How does the designer specify the data in a program? Traditionally, data structures were specified by the code or something very close to it. For example, suppose you were asked to describe your representation for time in a program. A possible answer would be "The time is represented by two integers, one representing the hours and the other the minutes." Programmers often use arrays to represent **aggregate data,** that is, collections of two or more individual data items. For example, suppose you asked a C programmer, "What is a string?" You would probably be told that a string is represented by an array of type `char`, with the end of the string indicated by the null character `'\0'`. In addition, you might be told that the `stdio` library recognizes this representation and that there is a C strings library containing functions to concatenate strings, return their lengths, and so forth.

In the past software engineers accepted such "low-level" specifications. But to think about all the data types in a program with low-level descriptions such as this means that you need to know too much detail in order to understand the operation of the program. This approach can also lead to bugs—for example, passing an array of `char` that lacks a null character to one of the string library functions can cause a program to crash because the library function has no other way to detect the intended end of the array. Specifying a data structure by the details of its implementation means that if you want to change the representation later, you have to find every line of code that manipulates strings, and make sure it corresponds to your new definition. Finally, mixing the abstract idea behind the data with the implementation reduces chances to *reuse* the code in other contexts.

With these notions in mind, we would like a way to specify data that is

1. *Abstract.* It should abstract the crucial features of the data without forcing the programmer to focus on implementation details, thus making the code (and the design) easier to understand and maintain.
2. *Safe.* It should allow control over the manipulation of the data representation so that errors can be prevented.
3. *Modifiable.* It should make it relatively easy for modifications in the representation to be made.
4. *Reusable.* It ought to be possible to reuse the representation and its implementation in other code.

This is the motivation behind **abstract data types** (ADTs). To create an ADT, we specify the data by its operation, rather than by its implementation. That is, we talk about what the data can "do" and how it is used but not about the details of the code that implements it. (See Definition 1.2, page 5, for a formal definition of ADT.)

We'll address the implications of this approach later on in the chapter, but first let's apply it to the example we started with.

4.2.2 A Time ADT

We now return to the problem of representing the quantity time. For this particular problem all times fall on the same day, so we don't have to worry about handling times from different days; that makes things somewhat simpler. We'll need a way to read a time in and a way to subtract one time from another and determine how many minutes apart they are. ADT 4-1 provides a minimal specification for a Time ADT.

ADT 4-1

Time

Characteristics:

- A Time consists of some number of hours and minutes and is either before noon (AM) or after noon (PM).
- Twelve Noon is 12:00 PM and Twelve Midnight is 12:00 AM.
- All Times are assumed to fall on the same day.

Operations:

Time readTime(bool & errorFlag)

Precondition: Standard Input has characters available.

Postconditions: Leading whitespace characters are ignored; readTime attempts to read, from standard input, a time in the format <HH>:<MM> <A>, where <HH> is an integer between 1 and 12, <MM> is an integer between 0 and 59, and <A> is either "AM" or "PM". If a properly formatted time can be read, errorFlag is set to false; otherwise, errorFlag is set to true.

Returns: If errorFlag is false, the Time read from Standard Input; otherwise, an arbitrary time is returned.

int subtractTimes(Time t1, Time t2)

Precondition: t1, t2 are well defined.

Postcondition: None.

Returns: The difference, in minutes, between Time t1 and Time t2. If t1 occurs before t2, this difference is negative.

Each time we create an ADT, we have to provide two categories of information. The ***characteristics*** describe the kind of data that the ADT stores. Each ADT will also include a number of ***operations*** that can be applied to items of the particular ADT. We specify, for each operation, a signature, or ***prototype***, that describes the type of each argument supplied to the operation and the type it returns. We also provide preconditions, postconditions, and a description of the return value. This documentation should give any user the information needed to use the ADT.

Given ADT 4-1, and defining Time as a type, we can rewrite Code Example 4-1 using these functions. Instead of using the built-in "<<" operator, we'd use the readTime function and check the error flag:

```
arrival = readTime(errorFlag);
while (errorFlag) {
    cout << "Time was incorrectly formatted; try again: ";
    arrival = readTime(errorFlag);
}
```

The subtraction would be performed by the function subtractTimes rather than the built-in "−" operator:

```
totalWaitingTime += subtractTimes(seenByDoctor,arrival);
```

In fact, you can implement an ADT using built-in operators such as "<<" and "−" for the user-defined type, via a C++ language feature called *operator overloading*. However, because you don't really need it to create an ADT and its use can be a bit tricky I've postponed the discussion of operator overloading until Section 7.7.

Code Example 4-2 contains the patient waiting time program, revised to be consistent with the Time ADT.

Code Example 4-2   *Patient waiting time program, revised for our implementation of Time*

```
// cx4-2.cpp
// Code Example 4-2: Revised Patient Waiting Time Program

#include "dslib.h"
#include <iostream.h>
// Somehow, the type "Time" gets defined up here
int main()
{
    int numberOfVisits(0), totalWaitingTime(0);
    char answer;
    do {
        bool errorFlag;
        Time arrival, seenByDoctor;
        cout << "Enter arrival time:";
        arrival = readTime(errorFlag);
        while (errorFlag) {
            cout << "Arrival time was incorrectly formatted; try again: ";
            arrival = readTime(errorFlag);
        }
        cout << "Enter time seen by doctor:";
        seenByDoctor = readTime(errorFlag);
        while (errorFlag) {
            cout << "Seen by doctor time was incorrectly formatted; try again: ";
            seenByDoctor = readTime(errorFlag);
        }
```

```
      numberOfVisits++;
      // assume that subtracting one Time from another yields the
      // difference in minutes as an int
      totalWaitingTime += subtractTimes(seenByDoctor, arrival);
      cout << "Done? Enter 'y' to quit, anything else to continue: ";
      cin >> answer;
   } while (answer != 'y');
   cout << "Number of visits: " << numberOfVisits << "\n";
   cout << "Total waiting time: "<< totalWaitingTime << " minutes.\n";
   cout << "Average wait is " << totalWaitingTime/numberOfVisits
           << " minutes.\n";
   return 0;
}
```

By now, you may be starting to feel like there's some magic going on behind the scenes. We started out with a potentially messy problem—manipulating times—and hid it "behind the ADT curtain." But the problem hasn't gone away; you're still going to have to write the code that figures out the difference between two times, aren't you? Well, maybe yes and maybe no, as we discuss in Section 4.3.1. But in any case, we have greatly reduced the complexity of the original problem by partitioning it into two parts: one part that manipulates Time as an abstract quantity and another part, which we haven't yet seen, that contains the representation of Times and knows how to manipulate them. Our example demonstrates information hiding. We have hidden the information about the details of the Time implementation from the program that uses Time as an ADT. We'll explore the idea of information hiding further in Section 4.4, but first let's see where the implementation comes from.

Exercise 4-3   To ADT 4-1, add definitions of an operation that will add an int (representing some number of minutes) to a time and one that will print the times. Specify preconditions, postconditions, and return values.

Exercise 4-4   Propose two different methods of representing a time, consistent with ADT 4-1. Will it be easier to implement the ADT with one representation than with the other?

Exercise 4-5   Define an ADT, USDollars, that can be used to represent money values as dollars and cents. Can you see any advantages to such an ADT over using ints or floats?

Exercise 4-6   Define an ADT, Zip9, that can store a nine-digit zip code.

Exercise 4-7   Define an ADT, SSN, that can store a U.S. Social Security number (nine decimal digits).

Exercise 4-8   Define an ADT, TelephoneNumber, that can store a telephone number including the area code.

Exercise 4-9   Define an ADT, Date, that can represent a date between January 1, 1901, and December 31, 2099.

Exercise 4-10   Define an ADT, Videotape, that can store the attributes of a videotape from the video rental system described in Chapter 2.

Exercise 4-11   As we approach the year 2000, there's a crisis in certain segments of the software industry because of programs that were written using two digits for the year (e.g., 98 to represent 1998). Suppose that a system did not hard-code two-digit dates but was instead designed to use a Date ADT. How might this have changed the impact of the turn of the century on these programs?

4.3   ADT Implementation and Code Reuse

4.3.1   Code Reuse: Don't Reinvent the Wheel

Now that we've specified the behavior of the Time ADT, we should begin to implement it—or should we? After all, many programs have come before that need to treat time as a fundamental quantity. Perhaps someone else has written a Time ADT already, and we can use it. Electrical engineers typically find the components they need to build devices by looking in a handbook or a catalog; why not software engineers?

Traditionally, many programmers have had a strong bias toward only using code they have written themselves. However, constantly "reinventing the wheel" can greatly reduce programmer efficiency and drive up costs. Today, software development is in the midst of a revolution in technique, a strong movement toward *code reuse*. Before writing our own Time ADT, it makes good sense to search at our school or our company and via the Internet for software components that can help us solve our problems. After all, it's not just the time required to write the software that matters, there's also the time needed to thoroughly test and debug. Even if we have to buy a Time ADT from somewhere, it may still be more cost effective than building one from scratch.

In many cases when searching for an ADT we will find something that nearly meets our requirements but needs some modification. If we can get the source code and change it, we may be able to save some time and money, although there's always a risk of introducing a bug. Object-oriented programming provides a technique for creating new ADTs from old ones—inheritance—that we'll introduce in Section 4.7. Right now, we're learning about ADTs so it makes sense to go ahead and create an implementation for the Time ADT. But you should remember that your first thought when you encounter the need for an ADT should not be "How do I implement it?" but rather, "Can I get an implementation from somewhere else?" Only after a reasonable effort at finding reusable code should you consider implementing the code yourself.[1]

4.3.2   Implementing a Time ADT

Adopting the ADT approach frees the programmer to choose the most advantageous internal representation for the ADT. The functions that use the ADT don't have to know anything about the way we've implemented the ADT—that's what we mean by information hiding. Careful consideration of the advantages and disadvantages of various approaches will pay big dividends in program efficiency and ease of maintenance.

In the case of the Time ADT, converting everything to minutes makes manipulating time values almost trivial. We know that all times lie in a range from midnight to midnight, so we can count 12:00 A.M. (midnight) as 0 minutes, 12:01 A.M. as 1 minute, 1:00 A.M. as 60, and so forth. Thus any time can be converted into an `int` ranging from 0 to 1439 (11:59 P.M.). We use this approach in the code shown as Code Example 4-3.

Code Example 4-3   Implementation of Time ADT

```
// cx4-3.cpp
// Code Example 4-3: Implementation of Time ADT

typedef int Time;
#include "dslib.h"
Time readTime(bool & errorFlag)
{
    // The time must be formatted as <HH>:<MM><AMorPM>, where
    // <HH> is an int in the range 0 to 12, <MM> is an int in
    // the range 0 to 59, and <AMorPM> is either AM or PM.

    enum AM_PM {AM, PM} AM_or_PM;
    int hour, minute;
    const char delimiter = ':';

    // Assume that the format is bad -- once valid data is extracted,
    // reset errorFlag to false
    errorFlag = true;
    // formatted input -- fail if not an int
```

---

1. Of course, if your instructor asks you to write some code for an assignment, the expectation is usually that you will write it yourself! At the very least, you must include a reference indicating any time you are reusing software, just as you would reference a quote in a term paper; otherwise, you are guilty of plagiarism.

```cpp
    if (!(cin >> hour))
        return 0;
    if (hour < 0 || hour > 12)
        return 0;
    char c;
    cin >> c;
    if (c != delimiter)
        return 0;
    if (!(cin >> minute)) // formatted input
        return 0;
    if (minute < 0 || minute > 59)
        return 0;
    cin >> c;
    if (c == 'A' || c == 'a')
        AM_or_PM = AM;
    else if (c == 'P' || c == 'p')
        AM_or_PM = PM;
    else
        return 0;
    cin >> c;
    if (c != 'M' && c != 'm')
        return 0;

    // if the program gets here, the data was correctly formatted --
    // so compute the time.
    errorFlag = false;
    Time returnTime;
    if (hour == 12)
        returnTime = minute;
    else
        returnTime = hour*60 + minute;
    if (AM_or_PM == PM)
        returnTime += 60*12;
    return returnTime;
}

int subtractTimes(Time t1, Time t2)
{
    return t1 - t2;
}
```

If you are unfamiliar with any of the C++ syntax in the example, such as enum or formatted input, consult Appendix A for more details.

One approach to using an ADT would be to simply copy the implementation in Code Example 4-3 and paste it into Code Example 4-1, enabling the use of the Time ADT. However, we're going to take advantage of the facilities of the language C++ to implement ADTs in a more sophisticated way, using C++ classes. Before we get to classes, we consider the broader context in which the ADT lies.

Exercise 4-12	Write a test plan for the Time ADT, and test the ADT thoroughly using a driver.
Exercise 4-13	Implement the additional operations specified by Exercise 4-3.
Exercise 4-14	Implement the ADT USDollars defined in Exercise 4-5.
Exercise 4-15	Implement the ADT Zip9 defined in Exercise 4-6.
Exercise 4-16	Implement the ADT SSN defined in Exercise 4-7.
Exercise 4-17	Implement the ADT TelephoneNumber defined in Exercise 4-8.

4.4   Information Hiding, Encapsulation, and Views

Let's define some of the terms we've encountered so far.

Definition 4-1   The program that uses an ADT is referred to as a ***client*** of that ADT.

For example, the main function in Code Example 4-1 is a client of the Time ADT. Each ADT can be viewed from two distinct viewpoints. The client views the ADT strictly as the functionality it provides. The implementor views the ADT's implementation directly. This dichotomy is illustrated in Figure 4-1.

Figure 4-1   *Two views of an ADT, using the Time ADT as an example*

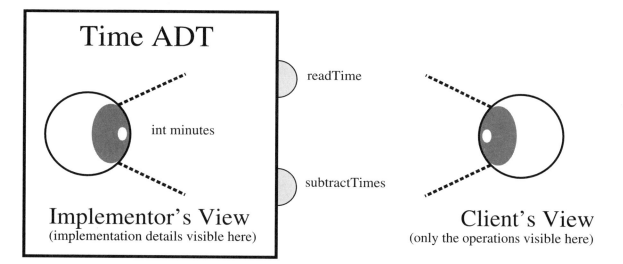

Definition 4-2   The principle that a client can use an ADT with no knowledge of its implementation is called ***information hiding.***

Some programming languages, including C++, allow information hiding to be enforced; that is, even if the programmer writing the client knows about the implementation, he or she *cannot* violate information hiding. This is called encapsulation, defined below. You can think of the black box around the Time ADT in Figure 4-1 as a "capsule" that prevents the client from any direct access to the implementation.

Definition 4-3   When a programming language allows the creation of an ADT in which the client has no access to the underlying implementation, we say that the language supports ***encapsulation.***

C++ uses a construct called the ***class*** to provide encapsulation. In the next section, we'll discover how to use a class to implement an encapsulated ADT.

4.5   Creating Encapsulated ADTs Using the C++ Class

You can (and should) use the idea of an ADT in any programming language, but some provide better support than others. In C++, we'll restrict ourselves to using the C++ class to implement ADTs. A class groups data and operations into a single package that a C++ program can manipulate. It provides a description of the ADT and allows the client program to create as many variables of that type as the program needs. When a C++ program contains a definition of a class, we refer to the variables of that class as objects. In other words, a type provides a definition for variables, while a class defines objects.[2] We can describe the relationship between an object and a class by saying that the object is an instance of its class. For example, time1 is an instance of the Time class.

Like many C++ features, the language allows programmers a lot of flexibility in how they implement classes. Rather than demonstrate all the features of C++ classes, we're going to concentrate on a particular format for creating classes. This restricted format lets you do everything you need and want to do to create an ADT. I strongly recommend that you stick closely to this format and follow the models in the book in order to avoid the pitfalls that can come from a less disciplined approach to creating classes.

---

2. In fact, since there's mostly a technical distinction between a type and a class (a type is built into the language, a class is built on top of the language) some authors choose to refer to both variables and objects as objects. While my terminology is more traditional, I can't see any objection to using the label *object* in both cases.

4.5.1   Declaring the Time Class

In our approach to creating classes, the parts of the class correspond directly to the parts of an ADT. First, let's consider the *class declaration*. For starters, Code Example 4-4 contains a declaration of ADT 4-1.

Code Example 4-4   *A class declaration for the Time ADT*

```
// cx4-4.h
// Code Example 4-4: Definition of Time Class

#include "dslib.h"

class Time {
public:
    void readTime(bool & errorFlag);
    int subtractTimes(Time t);
private:
    int minutes;
};
```

Before we get into the detailed meaning of this declaration, let's focus for a moment on the syntax. There are three new C++ keywords: `class`, `public`, and `private`. Each class declaration begins with the `class` keyword, followed by the name of the class, which we always capitalize to make it clear that it represents the name of an ADT. Enclose the rest of the declaration within brackets, and terminate the declaration with a semicolon. Make a mental note of the semicolon; forgetting the semicolon will cause the compiler to give you an error with a message that, in many cases, is rather difficult to decipher.

You'll also note that Code Example 4-4 contains a line `#include "dslib.h"`. This file is provided with the source code distribution for this book and includes certain definitions that make it easier to provide code that will work the same way on many different platforms. More details about this file will be provided in Section 7.3.1.

"Public" and "Private"   The first line within the brackets contains the keyword `public`, denoting the beginning of the public part of the declaration. If you refer back to Figure 4-1, you'll recall that the public view of an ADT is the part on the outside of the box—the part that the client sees. The `public` part of a class declaration lists exactly the information that the client needs: a list of prototypes for the operations provided by the ADT. In Code Example 4-4, the class declares two operations, `readTime` and `subtractTimes`. Because these functions are declared as part of a class, they are known as ***class member functions*** (often referred to simply as ***member functions***) or **methods.** The term *method* comes from object-oriented programming. In the context of C++, *class member function, member function,* and *method* are synonymous terms, and we'll use them interchangeably.

The keyword `private` precedes the definitions that the class needs internally to represent the ADT. In Code Example 4-4, this consists of a single item, an `int`, named `minutes`. The data fields for a class are referred to as its **class data members** or often just **data members.**[3] The Time class has just one data member, but we'll see lots of examples that require several data members. As the label `private` suggests, the client cannot access the contents of the private part of the C++ class; C++ encapsulates the implementation.

Class Header Files   We will store each class declaration in a header file that the client will include with the `#include` preprocessor command. When you create your own ADTs, you may want to give the header file the same name as the class (and the ADT). However, in order to keep track of the programs in the book, we name the files based upon their numbering within the book. In this case, Code Example 4-4 should be stored in a file called `cx4-4.h`. Then the client will contain the line:

```
#include "cx4-4.h"
```

While the data part of the implementation appears in the declaration, we put the actual code that implements the class in a separate, `.cpp` file.[4] This corresponds to our notion of information hiding — the client doesn't have to see, or know, the implementation of the data structure.[5] What it does need, the prototypes for the class functions, is contained in the `.h` file. In addition, we'll include the full specification of the ADT in the `.h` file, since that provides exactly the documentation that the programmer needs when writing the client function. Please note that the class specification declares the class and doesn't normally create any objects of that class. The file `cx4-5.h`, including the specification, appears in Code Example 4-5.

---

3. Data members are also called instance variables.

4. We use the DOS/Windows convention for the name of a C++ source file, `.cpp`. In the Unix environment, `.C`, `.cc`, and `.cxx` are more commonly used, although some Unix compilers now accept `.cpp` as well. Most Macintosh compilers also recognize `.cpp`.

5. Of course, having the data fields that implement the class appear in the `.h` file doesn't really correspond very well with our notion of information hiding. The design of C++ puts a high premium on efficiency, and there's no simple way for the compiler to generate efficient code without knowing about the class variables at compile time. Thus we are forced to compromise our notion of information hiding in this case.

Code Example 4-5   *Full definition file for Time ADT*

```
// cx4-5.h
// Code Example 4-5: full definition of class Time

#include "dslib.h" // standard header file for this book

class Time {
//
// Characteristics:
//
//   A Time consists of some number of hours and minutes, and is either before noon
//   (AM) or after noon (PM).
//
//   Twelve Noon is 12:00 PM and Twelve Midnight is 12:00 AM.
//
//   All Times are assumed to fall on the same day.
//
public:
   void readTime(bool & errorFlag);
//   Precondition: Standard input has characters available.
//   Postconditions: Leading whitespace characters are ignored;
//       readTime attempts to read, from standard input, a time in
//       the format <HH>:<MM><A>, where <HH> is an integer between
//       1 and 12, <MM> is an integer between 0 and 59, and <A> is
//       either "AM" or "PM". If a properly formatted time can be
//       read, errorFlag is set to false, and the value of the Time
//       variable is set to the time read; otherwise, errorFlag is
//       set to true.

   int subtractTimes(Time t);
//   Precondition: This Time variable contains a proper value.
//   Postcondition: None.
//   Returns: The difference, in minutes, between this Time and Time t.
//       If this Time occurs prior to Time t, the returned difference
//       is negative.

// **** the rest of the class declaration is private
private:
   int minutes;
};
```

4.5.2   Creating ADTs for C++ Classes

"This" Object   We'll have to make some small modifications to the Time ADT 4-1, shown below as ADT 4-2. In order to be consistent with the way class instances work, we have a new notion: *this* Time. Every call to a class function must be associated with a particular *class instance,* a Time **object.** "*This* Time" refers to the particular Time object connected with the class function call. For example, our new implementation will have the following line:

```
   arrival.readTime(errorFlag);
```

Assuming that the user formats the time properly, the program reads in a time, but where does it put it? The object `arrival` is the destination for the time that's read in. All calls to class functions will be in this "dotted notation" form:

```
<classInstanceName>.<classFunction>(<arguments>)
```

The particular class instance, or object, specified by `<classInstanceName>`, will be "*this* Time."

The way you call `readTime` seems pretty natural, but the call to `subtract-Times` tends to look a little strange at first. Remember, every call to a class function has to specify an object, so instead of calling `subtractTimes` with two Times as arguments, one Time must appear before the "dot," like this:

```
seenByDoctor.subtractTimes(arrival)
```

The Time that appears before the dot is "*this* Time," the Time object associated with this particular call to `subtractTimes`. Our ADT has been rewritten from this perspective.

ADT 4-2   Time ADT revised consistent with class syntax

Characteristics:

- A Time consists of some number of hours and minutes and is either before noon (AM) or after noon (PM).
- Twelve Noon is 12:00 PM and Twelve Midnight is 12:00 AM.
- All Times are assumed to fall on the same day.

Operations:

void readTime(bool & errorFlag)

Precondition: Standard Input has characters available.

Postconditions: Leading whitespace characters are ignored; readTime attempts to read, from standard input, a time in the format <HH>:<MM><A>, where <HH> is an integer between 1 and 12, <MM> is an integer between 0 and 59, and <A> is either "AM" or "PM". If a properly formatted time can be read, errorFlag is set to false; otherwise, errorFlag is set to true.

If errorFlag is false, the value of this Time is the time read from Standard Input; otherwise, the value of this Time remains unchanged.

int subtractTimes(Time t1)

Precondition: t1 is well defined.

Postcondition: None.

Returns: The difference, in minutes, between this Time and Time t1; that is, this Time − t1. If this Time occurs before Time t1, this difference is negative.

4.5.3   Creating Clients for C++ Classes

Given that we need to use the dotted notation whenever we refer to member functions, we need to revise the client code accordingly, as shown in Code Example 4-6.

Code Example 4-6   *Patient waiting times program, revised for C++ class notation*

```
// cx4-6.cpp
// Patient Waiting Times program, revised for C++ Class notation

#include <iostream.h>
#include "cx4-5.h"
int main()
{
    int numberOfVisits(0), totalWaitingTime(0);
    char answer;
    do {
        bool errorFlag; // arrival, seenByDoctor are instances of Time class
        Time arrival, seenByDoctor; cout << "Enter arrival time:";
        arrival.readTime(errorFlag);
        while (errorFlag) {
            cout << "Arrival time was incorrectly formatted; try again: ";
            arrival.readTime(errorFlag);
        }
        cout << "Enter time seen by doctor:";
        seenByDoctor.readTime(errorFlag);
        while (errorFlag) {
            cout << "Seen by doctor time was incorrectly formatted; try again: ";
            seenByDoctor.readTime(errorFlag);
        }
        numberOfVisits++;
        // assume that subtracting one Time from another yields the
        // difference in minutes as an int
        totalWaitingTime += seenByDoctor.subtractTimes(arrival);
        cout << "Done? Enter 'y' to quit, anything else to continue: ";
        cin >> answer;
    } while (answer != 'y');
    cout << "Number of visits: " << numberOfVisits << "\n";
    cout << "Total waiting time: "<< totalWaitingTime << " minutes.\n";
    cout << "Average wait is " << totalWaitingTime/numberOfVisits
            << " minutes.\n";
    return 0;
}
```

4.5.4   Implementation for C++ Classes

Next we'll look at the implementation, shown in Code Example 4-7. In order to tell the compiler that the routines `readTime` and `subtractTimes` are part of the `Time` class, we precede the names of the routines with "`Time::`". The double colon—"`::`"—is called the **scope operator**. The compiler then treats identifiers in these routines as part of our declaration of the class. For example, whenever the identifier `minutes` appears, the compiler considers it a reference to the data member `minutes`. Note that you should always `#include` the header file for the class; this assures that both client and implementor use the same declaration for the class.

Code Example 4-7   *Implementation of the Time class*

```
// cx4-7.cpp
// Code Example 4-7: Implementation of the Time Class

#include "cx4-5.h"

void Time::readTime(bool & errorFlag)
{
    // The time must be formatted as <HH>:<MM><AMorPM>, where
    // <HH> is an int in the range 0 to 12, <MM> is an int in
    // the range 0 to 59, and <AMorPM> is either AM or PM.

    enum AM_PM {AM, PM} AM_or_PM;
    int hour, minute;
    const char delimiter = ':';

    // Assume that the format is bad -- once valid data is extracted,
    // reset errorFlag to false
    errorFlag = true;
    // formatted input -- fail if not an int
    if (!(cin >> hour))
        return;
    if (hour < 0 || hour > 12)
        return;
    char c;
    cin >> c;
    if (c != delimiter)
        return;
    if (!(cin >> minute)) // formatted input
        return;
    if (minute < 0 || minute > 59)
        return;
    cin >> c;
```

```
   if (c == 'A' || c == 'a')
      AM_or_PM = AM;
   else if (c == 'P' || c == 'p')
      AM_or_PM = PM;
   else
      return;
   cin >> c;
   if (c != 'M' && c != 'm')
      return;
   errorFlag = false;
   if (hour == 12)
      minutes = minute;
   else
      minutes = hour*60 + minute;
   if (AM_or_PM == PM)
      minutes += 60*12;
}

int Time::subtractTimes(Time t)
{
   return minutes - t.minutes;
}
```

At first glance, the syntax of the `subtractTimes` function may seem strange—what's the difference between "`minutes`" and "`t.minutes`"? Both identifiers refer to the `minutes` variable in the `Time` class, *but for different instances of the class*. Consider the call to `subtractTimes`, shown in Code Example 4-6:

```
totalWaitingTime += seenByDoctor.subtractTimes(arrival);
```

In this particular case, `seenByDoctor` is "*this* Time," so `minutes` refers, implicitly, to the `minutes` field for the object `seenByDoctor`, while `t.minutes` refers, explicitly, to the `minutes` field for the object `arrival`.

Exercise 4-18 Reimplement the ADT USDollars from Exercise 4-14, using C++ class syntax.

Exercise 4-19 Reimplement the ADT Zip9 from Exercise 4-15, using C++ class syntax.

Exercise 4-20 Reimplement the ADT SSN from Exercise 4-16, using C++ class syntax.

Exercise 4-21 Reimplement the ADT TelephoneNumber from Exercise 4-17, using C++ class syntax.

4.6 Using Standard C++ Class Libraries

The current standard for C++ includes a rich set of **standard class libraries** that each C++ compiler should use. Because the international C++ standards committee agreed upon the details of the libraries relatively late in the game, you will find some deviations and omissions from the libraries I describe here. Over time, you can expect that compiler vendors will bring their products into compliance with the standard. Just in case you're stuck with an older version of C++, the software distribution for this book includes versions of certain libraries. If you can, use the standard libraries provided with your compiler, but where necessary you can substitute the versions provided with the book.

Class libraries required by the C++ standard include the following:

- Libraries for handling input and output, including <iostream> (for keyboard and screen I/O) and <fstream> (for file I/O).
- A string manipulation library <string>.
- Complex numbers <complex>.
- Bit manipulation <bitstring>.
- Dynamic arrays <dynarray>. Dynamic arrays can grow and shrink during the execution of a program.
- The Standard Template Library <stl>, which contains implementations of many of the data structures and algorithms discussed in this book.
- The Standard C Libraries. Generally, you'll want to use the newer C++ libraries wherever possible, but the C Libraries still have certain uses and also make it easier to convert old C code to C++.

We'll take a quick look at the I/O libraries, which you've certainly used already in your C++ programming, and then we'll examine the <string> library a bit more closely.

4.6.1   Using C++ Libraries for Input and Output

You might not have thought much about it, but `cin` and `cout` are objects. When you include a line like

```
cout << "Hello, Mom!";
```

in a program, the compiler generates a call to a member function for the object `cout`. The `cout` object is an instance of the class `ostream`..

Where's the declaration for the `ostream` class? It's contained within the header file `<iostream.h>`. That's why you get a syntax error if you try to compile a C++ function that contains I/O and forget to include the line

```
#include <iostream.h>
```

Now, just like our own classes we discussed in Section 4.5, the complete definition of the `ostream` class doesn't necessarily reside in the header file. Somewhere else on the system will be a compiled library that contains all of `iostream`. Generally the linker figures out where to find the standard library and links in any code that is needed to complete the class in the final, executable module. One syntax reminder—the angle brackets around the name of the header file tell the compiler to look for the file `iostream.h` in the location where the system keeps "standard" header files. When you use a header file that you or your team has created, you'll generally enclose the name in quotes (e.g., `"cx4-5.h"`). Each compiler has its own rules for searching for header files, rules that the user generally can modify; see the documentation for your compiler to learn how this works.

In general, you use the following format for calling a class function:

```
<objectName>.<functionName>(<arguments>)
```

Why doesn't a call to the I/O library, like

```
cin >> c
```

follow this format? Because the ">>" and "<<" operators are examples of overloaded operators, as mentioned above in Section 4.2.2. In fact, the following forms are equivalent:

```
cout << 'a';    cout.put('a');
```

So we can think of *operator overloading* as a convenient and expressive shorthand for the standard class function notation.

When you work with standard I/O, you'll generally use the predefined objects `cout` and `cin`. But when you use file I/O, you will need to declare objects yourself. For example, suppose you want to send output to a file. The standard C++ libraries include file output routines specified by the header file `fstream.h`. For each output file you want, you declare an instance of the class `ostream`. The syntax for creating the object requires you to give the name for the output file in a form compatible with the particular system on which you're creating the file. Let's look at an example:

```
ostream outfile("file.out");
```

The first part of the expression, "`ostream`," is the name of the class. The second part, "`outfile`," is the name that the programmer has given to the particular `ostream` object. The last part, "`("file.out")`," will tie the file name "`file.out`" to the object "`outfile`."

Constructors   We use the term *construction* to refer to the creation of a new instance of a class. When the compiler sees the declaration of the object `outfile`, it generates a call to a *constructor function* (or *constructor* for short) for the `ostream` class. So we can see the string `"file.out"` as an argument that's passed to a function, in this particular case the constructor function, essentially in the same way as any other argument. Every time the execution of a program reaches a declaration of an object, the appropriate constructor gets called. Classes primarily use constructors to initialize objects; in fact some people have suggested that *initializer* would really be a better term than *constructor.*

What about the built-in types, like `int`? You can view an expression like

```
int i(0);
```

as a call to the constructor function for `int`, passing the value 0 as the initial value of the variable `i`. Now, for efficiency reasons, C++ compilers generally treat the declarations of built-in types differently from declarations of class objects, but from the programmer's point of view there's no significant difference. That's why we chose to use the form `int i(0)` rather than the equivalent `int i = 0`.[6]

Encapsulation and Documentation

If you've been programming in C++ for a while, you've probably used `iostream` classes, particularly `cin` and `cout`, without thinking about how they're implemented. Generally, you want your program to perform input and output, and you don't much care about the details of implementation or how these details might vary from one operating system to another. That is, the program you write is the client of stream classes. Without knowing it, you've been using information hiding to reduce the complexity of your programs. (If you're familiar with programming in an assembly language, you can really appreciate how much the availability of I/O routines simplifies a program.) The C++ class has encapsulated the implementation of stream input and output.

You've probably never looked at the code for streams, so how do you know how to use them? You've used documentation in the form of textbooks, instructors, and perhaps the system documentation that came with your compiler. Looking at the implementation of the stream classes only confuses the issue; the external documentation available to you is the best way to learn about the use of the stream classes.

There are two lessons to be learned from this:

1. When you learn to use a new class, use the documentation for the class and not its implementation. Understanding the implementation will require you to acquire a lot of complex and irrelevant information; worse, you may try to use information about the implementation in your client, and implementations should always be viewed as "subject to change."

---

6. Some older C++ compilers will only accept the later form for initializing built-in types.

2. When you create your own classes, you will have an obligation to provide documentation so that others can use them without examining the implementation. No matter how carefully you may *design* your classes for reuse, you can be sure that without proper documentation they won't *be* reused.

We'll explore the documentation required by a class implementation in Section 4.7.

4.6.2 Using the C++ String Library

You may have already learned the technique of creating a string by using an array of `char`'s, terminated with the null character `'\0'`. This type of string was inherited from the original C language, and hence we'll refer to it as a *C string*. The advantages and disadvantages of a C string closely mirror those of C itself: the C string is straightforward and efficient, but it's also "low level" and in some cases dangerous. The C string can be dangerous because the compiler doesn't have any way to control the use of the string or guarantee that it's properly terminated. Using a C string and forgetting to mark the end with a null string, or failing to allocate the proper amount of memory for the number of characters in the string, can lead to run-time errors and unpredictable behavior. In one famous case, careless use of C strings created a security weakness in the Unix operating system that helped make possible an "Internet worm" that effectively shut down the Internet for a couple of days (Neumann, p. 133).

Unfortunately, the lack of a standard for a String class has delayed the general adoption of a class-based approach to strings in C++; much software and many books depend upon the "old-fashioned" C string. However, with the C++ community on the verge of adopting a standard `<string>` library, and with many String class implementations readily available, C strings can be abandoned for nearly all uses and replaced with a more powerful, more abstract, and more reliable class-based approach. In this section we'll learn about writing clients of the String class.[7]

Code Example 4-8 illustrates the use of the String class.

---

7. The examples of a String class in this section are based on an implementation of the String class specified by the draft C++ standard. Students should use the standard C++ String class provided by their compilers, if available; otherwise, my String class, supplied with the book, can be used until an up-to-date compiler is available. Note that I've based my class on the most recent version of the standard available when the book went to press, that my implementation is a proper subset of the most useful functions, and that I've emphasized portability and simplicity over efficiency.

Code Example 4-8   Using the C++ String class

```
// cx4-8.cpp
// Code Example 4-8: example client for string class

// include the C++ string library. If your compiler is not compliant with the
// ISO/ANSI C++ Standard, you may have to change the following line in
// order to include a compatible String Class

#include <string>
#include <iostream.h>
int main()
{
    string s1, s2, sarray[5];
    string s3("xyzzy");
    cout << "Enter a couple of strings... ";
    cin >> s1 >> s2;
    cout << "You entered " << s1 << " and " << s2 << ".\n";
    cout << "s1 + s3 is " << (s1 + s3) << "\n";
    int len = s3.length();
    s2 = s3.substr(1,len-2);
    cout << "The middle of string " << s3 << " is " << s2 << endl;
    cout << "Enter 5 strings for an array...";
    int i;
    for (i = 0; i < 5; i++)
        cin >> sarray[i];
    cout << "\nYour strings are: ";
    for (i = 0; i < 5; i++)
        cout << sarray[i] << '\t';
    s1 = sarray[0];
    cout << "\ns1 is " << s1 << endl;
    cout << "\nResult of s1.compare(sarray[0]): " << s1.compare(sarray[0]) << endl;
    return 0;
}
```

Just as with other classes, use of the String class requires the appropriate include: #include <string>.[8] Code Example 4-8 creates a total of eight strings; s1, s2, and s3 are single string objects, while sarray contains five string objects in an array. Every declaration of a string object generates a call to a string constructor. Because the declarations of s1, s2, and sarray have no arguments they call a constructor with no arguments. Most classes will include a no-argument constructor, called the ***default constructor.*** The declaration of s3 passes a string constant to the string constructor, and the string stores this constant as its initial value. The String

---

8. Some compilers use <string> to distinguish the C++ standard string library from an older C header file of the same name (string.h); your compiler may use a different convention.

class knows how to convert string constants—sequences of `chars` surrounded by quotes—so they can be used to initialize and set the value of string objects.

Next we see that the string class overloads the ">>" operator to handle input to a string object; the line

```
cin >> s1 >> s2;
```

will cause two strings from standard input to be stored in the string objects `s1` and `s2`. Likewise, in the next line these strings will be sent to standard output. For technical reasons, the functions that overload ">>" and "<<" are not implemented as part of the String class, but they are provided along with the class for the convenience of the client.

The following line includes the interesting expression `(s1 + s3)`. The string class library includes a declaration that overloads the "+" operation to perform *string concatenation.* That is, the expression `(s1 + s3)` returns a new string that contains the characters in string `s3` attached to the end of the characters in string `s1`.

The next two class functions use the standard dotted notation. The expression `int len = s3.length()` will call the `length` function on the object `s3`, returning the number of characters in `s3` and storing it in the variable `len`. Then, the `substr` function creates a substring of `s3`. Just like standard arrays in C++, string objects are indexed from 0 to `n-1`, so the expression `s3.substr(1,len-2)` returns the string in `s3` with the first and last characters stripped off.

The following section of code demonstrates the use of an array of string objects—and shows that an array of string objects is really no different from an array of a built-in type such as `float`. The line

```
s1 = sarray[0];
```

causes `s1` to become a copy of the string in `sarray[0]`. The overloading of the assignment operator—"="—supports this copy operation, which is again analogous to the way that other objects work.

Finally, the class function `compare` gives the client a way to determine the relative "dictionary" order of two strings. The format of `compare` was designed to be similar to comparable C language functions, which accounts for its rather unintuitive interface. A call of the form `s1.compare(s2)` compares the strings `s1` and `s2`. If `s1` is less than `s2`, that is, `s1` comes before `s2`, then the `compare` function returns some negative number; if `s1` is greater than `s2`, a positive number is returned; and if the two strings are identical, `compare` returns a 0. The asymmetry of the format `s1.compare(s2)` can't be avoided since a class function must be called for some particular object, in this case `s1`.

Exercise 4-22   Determine which version(s) of the C++ string library are available to you. If necessary, get an implementation from the Web page for this book or some other source. Write a program that reads a string and processes it using several of the operations available in the string class.

Exercise 4-23   Write a program that creates an array of strings, reads words into the array and sorts them. Use whatever sorting algorithm you like. Allow for up to 100 words.

4.7   ADTs, Objects, and Object-Oriented Programming

Now that we've examined the use of classes to create ADTs, it's time to clear up the relationship between classes, objects, and abstract data types. Implementing an ADT is one important use for a class, but a class can do more than that—classes can also overcome a significant limitation of ADTs. To illustrate this limitation, and the way in which a class can overcome this limitation, let's reconsider our video rental system discussed in Chapter 2.

Suppose that we want to expand the video rental system to allow the rental of video game cartridges, in addition to the rental of tapes. A video game has attributes that are essentially the same as a videotape—for example, a title—and it has attributes that are completely different — for example, the type of gaming system (Sega, Nintendo, etc.) on which the game runs. An implementation of the video rental system would probably include an ADT "Videotape." When adding the new ADT, "Video Game Cartridge," we would like to reuse as much as possible the code that implements the Videotape ADT.

How can we reuse an ADT? Programmers often make a copy of the source code for an ADT and then apply changes to it. So you could copy the Videotape ADT, modify it, and create a Video Game Cartridge ADT. While this beats starting over from scratch it has at least three significant problems:

1. While we may save time in coding, we have to test the new ADT completely, since once we modify the old code we can't rely on the testing that's gone before.

2. If we find a bug or need to make a change in the way we handle rentals, we may have to make separate changes in the code for both ADTs. Furthermore, future maintenance may cause the two ADTs to diverge—changes may be applied to one and not the other, leading to inconsistencies.

3. Any code that handles both videotapes and video game cartridges will have to be modified to check each rental items, determine which type of item it's handling, and act accordingly.

Now suppose that later on another type of rental item—say, video disks—gets added to the system. The problems listed here get worse exponentially with each new ADT.

Object-oriented programming provides a different and better way to create reusable ADTs. Observe that videotapes, video game cartridges, and video disks, as well as other items the store might want to handle, can all be considered particular kinds of "rental item." We would like our design, and our code, to handle the relationship shown in Figure 4-2 (the arrows point from each subtype to a parent type that has attributes common to all).

When a programming language allows us to create ADTs with a type-subtype relationship, we say that it supports **inheritance**. The Videotape ADT *inherits* characteristics (both data and behavior) from the Rental Item ADT. When you add inheritance to encapsulated ADTs, you get what's called **object-oriented programming** (OOP). Typically the name "ADT" is dropped and is replaced by "object" or "class."

Figure 4-2   *Subtype relationship for rental items*

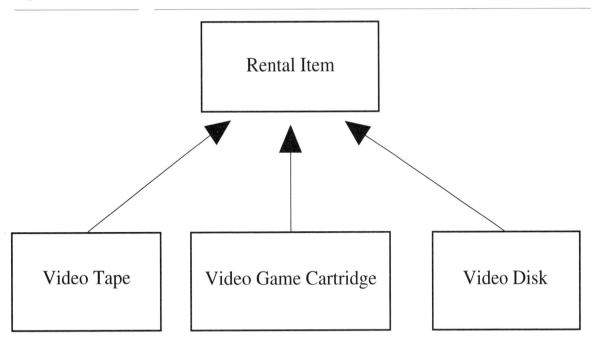

Along with inheritance, OOP languages generally provide one more extremely useful feature: ***polymorphism.*** This is a big word for a simple idea. Our video rental system will need to handle videotapes, video games, and video disks, but since these are all rental item objects, we can write code that manipulates "rental items." The compiler will keep track of these rental items and execute the appropriate code for each one. For example, suppose we have a routine that prints a list of rental items on loan to a particular patron. In traditional programming, the print routine would have to check each rental item, determine what kind of item it is, and execute the appropriate print routine. With object-oriented programming, we associate a print routine with each rental item subtype. Then when the "print a list" routine runs, it will call the print function for a rental item, and the compiler will automatically call the correct routine depending on whether the particular item is a videotape, game, or disk.

The big payoff to polymorphism comes when you add another type of rental item, say CD-ROMs. In a traditional program, you would have to find every piece of code that manipulates rental items and change it so that it can now handle CD-ROMs. But in OOP, you tell the system that CD-ROM inherits from rental item, write the code for handling CD-ROMs, and the compiler will now call the appropriate CD-ROM code for all rental items that are CD-ROMs.

To summarize then, an object is an ADT that lets you use inheritance and polymorphism. C++ classes make it easy to create objects, and object-oriented programs. I recognize that this will seem vague to you at this point. For much of this course, programming with ADTs will provide everything you need, but later on you will learn to use inheritance and polymorphism in C++. Once you actually use OOP, you'll start to see what all the fuss is about and why OOP has created a revolution in programming and software engineering.

Chapter Summary

- Abstract data types provide a powerful tool for organizing software.
- Code reuse makes programmers more efficient.
- Information hiding and encapsulation lead to simpler and safer software.
- You use a class to create an encapsulated ADT in C++.
- Standard C++ libraries provide an important source of reusable code.
- Using inheritance and polymorphism with encapsulated ADTs is called object-oriented programming.

Programming Laboratory Exercises

Lab 4-1 Write a program that prompts the user for a start time, a stop time, and a distance travelled (in miles) and computes the speed in miles per hour. Use the Time ADT. Output the result rounded to the nearest tenth of a mile.

Lab 4-2 Write a program that takes as input a list of song titles and lengths and determines whether the proposed song list will fit on a 45-minute cassette tape. Allow for a 5-second gap between songs. Your output should list the songs, the time for each, and the total time required for the tape. You will need to modify the Time ADT in order to add a function that can add two times together and give a new time.

Lab 4-3 In "Pig Latin," you modify words by moving any initial consonants to the end of the word and adding *ay;* if the word starts with a vowel, you just add *ay* to the end. For example, the sentence "All good programmers use objects" would be rendered in Pig Latin as "Allay oodgay ogrammerspray useay objectsay." Write a program that reads in a sentence and converts it to Pig Latin. (Of course, you should use the strings library.)

Lab 4-4 Implement a simple version of the Unix utility "uniq"; uniq reads lines from standard input and outputs the same lines to standard output, except that repeated lines are omitted. For example, if the following input is read:

```
line one
line two
line two
line three
```

the output should be

```
line one
line two
line three
```

Lab 4-5 Design and implement (as a C++ class) a Date ADT that can represent any date between January 1, 1901, and December 31, 2099. Remember that every fourth year is a leap year that includes February 29 as a valid date (*including* the year 2000). Your operations should include the following: date input and output, finding the difference between two dates (as an int representing the number of days), and adding some number of days to a date to give a new date. If you think carefully about how you represent your date internally, you can save yourself a lot of work. Test your ADT thoroughly.

Deliverables: A description of the Date ADT in a format like ADT 4-1; header file date.h; implementation file date.cpp; test plan; driver; test results.

Lab 4-6   Using a Date ADT (either the one written in Lab 4-5 or one obtained from another source) write a program that, given any date in the range allowed by the Date ADT, determines the day of the week for that date.

Lab 4-7   Define an ADT IntVector that can be used to store a vector (i.e., a one-dimensional array) of `int`s. Operations should include `v.put(i,j)`, which puts the value `j` into position `i` in the vector (analogous to `v[i] = j`), and `v.at(i)`, which returns the value located at position `i`. The constructor for the IntVector class should specify the number of elements to be stored in the array; you can require that it be less than or equal to 100. Your vector class should perform range checking; that is, if the first argument to *put* or *at* is not between 0 and one less than the size of the array, an error message should be printed and the value 0 returned. (If you know how to throw exceptions in C++, you can do that instead.)

Deliverables: `intvect.h`, `intvect.cpp`, test plan, driver, test results.

Lab 4-8   Modify the ADT IntVector class described in Lab 4-7 so that the constructor can specify starting and ending bounds of the array. For example, the line

```
IntVector v(10, 20);
```

would specify an array of length 11, indexed from 10 to 20. Negative bounds are allowed, but the first argument must be less than or equal to the second. The put and at operators must continue to assure that the argument is in the appropriate range.

Lab 4-9   Using the specifications in Section 2.2, create an ADT Videotape that can store a representation of a videotape. Test your program by writing a program that creates an array of video tapes, lets the user add tapes to the array, and then prints out all the tapes in the array.

Lab 4-10   Specify a USDollars ADT, including operations that

- allow the client to add and subtract two USDollars objects

- multiply or divide USDollars objects by doubles (e.g., compute $2.75 * 2.4)

- add or subtract percentages to a USDollars object (e.g. compute $9.95 + 10% of $9.95)

- return USDollars as a string properly formatted with a dollar sign (e.g., "$17.95" or "$1,750.00" or "($350.95)" for a negative value)

Note that to be precise you don't want to implement a money ADT using floating point because rounding may result in unpredictable results. For example, there is no exact binary representation of .01. Instead, the internal representation of the USDollars ADT should be stored as an `int` (or `long int`, depending upon your compiler) representing the number of cents for the value. Test your ADT by writing a driver that calls all the functions in your ADT.

Chapter Vocabulary

abstract data type (ADT)

ADT characteristics

ADT operations

aggregate data

c string

characteristic

class

class data member

class declaration

class instance

class member function

client

construction

constructor

data member

default constructor

encapsulation

information hiding

inheritance

instance (of a class)

member function

method

object

object-oriented programming (OOP)

operation

operator overloading

polymorphism

prototype

scope operator

standard class libraries

string concatenation

Chapter 5 Efficiency

Overview   An introduction to analyzing the efficiency of algorithms, illustrated through sorting and
searching.

Chapter Objectives

1. To begin to understand methods for analyzing
   the efficiency of algorithms.

2. To understand and analyze the Linear Search
   and Binary Search algorithms.

3. To understand and analyze the Selection Sort
   and Bubble Sort algorithms.

5.1   Selecting Good Algorithms

A key step in the design of a software system is the selection of the algorithms used in the system. An *algorithm* is simply the list of steps required to solve some particular problem in the system. Computer scientists create algorithms as abstractions of the processes carried out by computer programs. Examples include algorithms used for sorting or for determining whether a student qualifies for financial aid. In some cases, there may be only a single known algorithm for a problem, and in others (such as the financial aid calculation) the steps may be so straightforward that there's no need to consider anything other than the obvious. But other problems, such as sorting or finding the best highway route between two cities, have many known algorithms. Certainly, the designer and implementor want to use a "good" algorithm; the question is, what makes one algorithm better than another?

Traditionally, computer scientists have focused on the following two questions:

1. How fast does the algorithm run?

2. How much memory does the algorithm require?

These are not the only considerations. For example, one algorithm might be quite straightforward and easy to implement, while another is delicate and complicated. To take a specific example, suppose you want to find the median item in a list.[1] A straightforward approach requires sorting the list and returning the item in the middle. But there is an algorithm that is guaranteed to run faster, at least for large lists. This method, called the Linear Selection algorithm, requires a good understanding of recursion and is not so easy to follow without some thought. If your program only occasionally needs to find the median, and if your lists aren't too long, you might not want to use the Linear Selection algorithm, even if it might be faster. The run time saved may not be that much, and the implementation time will be greater because of the need to understand and code a complicated algorithm.

For the moment, we'll put this important software engineering consideration aside and instead concentrate on our two algorithm efficiency concerns: speed and memory. The reader should understand that the needs of the software system should drive the choice of the algorithm, not the other way around. A "good" algorithm is often the most efficient, but not always.

Exercise 5-1   Based on the discussion above, and upon your own insights, list the considerations that can be used to evaluate the desirability of an algorithm.

---

1. If x is the median of a list, then half the items in the list are greater than or equal to x, and half are less than or equal to x.

5.2   The Many Faces of Program Efficiency

In the early days of computer science, the efficiency of an algorithm was often reported by measuring the time required to solve some particular problem. For example, a research paper might report something like "Our new algorithm, SuperDuper Sort,[2] can sort a list of 1000 random integers in 14.2 seconds, while Bubble Sort requires 42.1 seconds. The authors tested the code on an IBM 701 with 16k of core." Looks pretty good: SuperDuper Sort seems to be about three times as fast as Bubble Sort. But there are many variables here: perhaps the speed of SuperDuper Sort depends on some special feature of the IBM 701, and the results can't be duplicated on a different computer. Or perhaps the author did a careful job of coding SuperDuper Sort and used a poor implementation of Bubble Sort. Furthermore, would the 3 to 1 ratio hold for 10,000 items, or 100,000? For these reasons and others, the computer science community began searching in earnest for ways to compare algorithms in a manner independent of the implementation hardware, programming language, or even the skill of the programmer. That is, the goal was to compare *algorithms*, not *programs*. From these efforts came the field known as the ***analysis of algorithms.***

Generally, the larger the problem is, the longer it takes to compute the answer. That is, sorting 10,000 items ought to take longer than sorting 1000. Thus the efficiency of an algorithm is always stated as a function of the problem size. Usually, the variable n represents the problem size; you can think of n as suggesting the "number" of things to process. For example, we might find that SuperDuper Sort requires $0.025n^2 + 0.012n + 0.005$ seconds on a Power Macintosh 7500. To find out how fast the sort will work for a particular input, just plug in a value for n.

Critical Operations   What we really want, though, is an expression that can apply to any computer, not just to one in particular. To do this, we'll state the efficiency in terms of one or more ***critical operations*** performed in the course of the algorithm. We pick the critical operation so that it serves as a stand-in for everything else the algorithm does. As we shall see, the critical operation for many sorting algorithms is the number of times two items are compared with one another; for example, we might find that Super-Duper Sort requires $2n^2 + n$ comparisons. The time that one computer requires to perform a comparison may of course be faster or slower than the time required by another, but measuring the algorithm by comparisons will give us a good guide to the relative performance of different algorithms, which is what we really care about.

But what is the most important aspect of an efficiency function? We can make things simpler by focusing on the ***rate of growth*** of the function. Suppose you have two

---

2. As far as I know, there is no such thing as SuperDuper Sort; I made up the name to use as an example.

functions, $f(n) = 1000n$ and $g(n) = n^2 + n$. When n is small, $f(n)$ is certainly the bigger function; (e.g., $f(10) = 10,000$ and $g(10) = 110$). But as n gets larger, there comes a point ($n = 1000$) at which $g(n)$ will be bigger than $f(n)$; after that, $g(n)$ keeps getting further and further from $f(n)$, and will always be larger. That's what we mean when we say that $g(n)$ grows faster than $f(n)$.[3] When do we care the most about the efficiency of an algorithm? *When* n *is large!* This leads us to Definition 5-1.

Definition 5-1   The **asymptotic efficiency** of an algorithm describes the relative efficiency of an algorithm as n gets very large.

With the speed and memory size of processors continuing to double roughly every two years, it's become clear that the asymptotic efficiency of an algorithm is *the* critical factor. Continuing with our SuperDuper Sort, we would say that the asymptotic efficiency of SuperDuper Sort is "of the **order**" n^2 —which happens to be the same as Bubble Sort. So SuperDuper Sort may be faster than Bubble Sort in some situations, but in terms of their asymptotic efficiencies they appear roughly equal. That doesn't guarantee that a more careful analysis might show that one is better than the other, but if we can find an algorithm with a lower order of asymptotic growth, we can say with some confidence that it will run faster than either of these sorting algorithms, at least when the problems get large enough.

Sometimes we'll need to refer to functions that *don't* grow with n. For example, suppose you write a program that starts by printing instructions. For this program, no matter what size problem it solves, the amount of work taken to print the instructions stays the same. We can describe this amount of time, therefore, as a **constant function.** In arithmetic terms, a constant function looks like $f(n) = k$, where k is just a constant

Asymptotic analysis also can be applied to the memory used by an algorithm. We'll see some examples later, but asymptotic analysis is often not as useful for analyzing memory requirements as it is for speed. That's because the exact details of memory usage are often quite critical. If our analysis of the running time is off by a factor of two, then we might have to run the program twice as long as expected, but that will often be acceptable. However, if our analysis of the memory needed is off by a factor of two, the program may simply not fit into main memory, and we won't be able to run it at all.

---

3. If you've studied differential calculus, you recognize that this situation is described by the expresssion: $\lim\limits_{n \to \infty} \dfrac{g'(n)}{f'(n)} = \infty$.

Now we'll take a look at some common algorithms for searching and sorting and see how the tools of algorithm analysis can be applied to compare their performance. Later on in the chapter we'll consider other techniques that can be applied to improve program efficiency.

Exercise 5-2   Rank the asymptotic orders of the following functions, from highest to lowest. (You may wish to graph some or all of them.)

$$3n^3 + 2n + 1000 \qquad 30n + 20n + 10n \qquad 60n$$

$$100 \qquad\qquad n^2 + 100 \qquad\qquad n\log n$$

$$2^n + n^2 \qquad\qquad n + \log n$$

5.3   Algorithms for Searching

Whether or not you've programmed a search algorithm before, you've certainly used them. When you look up a friend's number in the phone book, you are using a search algorithm. You use your friend's name and your knowledge of the organization of the book to search for the phone number. In computer science terms, we refer to the name as the **key**—the information used to organize the search. You use the key to find the data you want, which in this case is a telephone number. Generally, we can organize the data in a list into a key and the other data; together, we refer to each item in the list as a **record**.[4] Figure 5-1 illustrates a record.

Figure 5-1   *Sample record format*

Because the key is the most important element for searching, we typically drop the data part of the record and focus on searching for the key in a list. But you should keep in mind that when you turn the algorithm into a program you may also have to include some data that's associated with the key.

---

4. The term *record* refers to a specific construct in some programming languages, including Pascal and COBOL, but we're talking about something more abstract and general here.

5.3.1   Linear Search

The algorithm you use to find a number in the phone book is practical and efficient for humans, but not so good for computers. It's neither precise nor consistent, qualities needed for an algorithm. On the other hand, the speed of the computer means that a simple repetitive algorithm may be practical. Let's look at a different sort of search problem that's closer to the computer's method of searching.

Imagine for the moment that you have a pile of index cards containing the names of a company's customers. The pile is organized in no particular way. You want to find out whether Susan Cheng is a customer. You pick up the cards one by one and compare the name on each card with your *target key,* Susan Cheng. If you find the target, you stop; otherwise you continue until you've looked at every card, at which point you know that your target is not in the pile. We call this algorithm *Linear Search,* shown in Algorithm 5-1.

Algorithm 5-1	*Linear Search algorithm*

For each item in the list,
    if the item's key matches the target,
        stop and report "success"
Report "failure"

To turn this into a computer program, we'll assume that the items to be searched are stored in an array indexed from 0 to $n-1$. As we discussed above, we'll use records consisting of a key alone, without any other data. Finally, we'll use integers as the keys; the algorithm is the same for other types of keys, but the process of comparing two keys will vary. The function will return the position of the target within the array, if found; so if the target is in the search array, the value returned will be in the range $0...n-1$. We use the value -1 to indicate that the target was not found. The calling program can either use the returned index to find the targeted record, or it can simply check whether the value is positive or negative to indicate whether the target was found. With these simplifications in mind, we can write a linear search function as shown in Code Example 5-1.

Code Example 5-1	*Linear Search*

```
// cx5-1.cpp
// Code Example 5-1: Linear Search

int linearSearch(int a[], int n, int target)
{
    int i;
    for (i = 0; i < n; i++)
```

```
    if (a[i] == target) // key comparison
        return i;
    return -1; // use -1 to indicate failure
}
```

We will analyze the speed of this algorithm by counting the number of **key comparisons** required. The only key comparison in the program is in the line

```
    if (a[i] == target) // key comparison
```

Note that there may be other places in the algorithm where comparisons are performed. In particular, the clause i < n is a comparison, but it's not a comparison of *keys*, so we don't count it. We've now reduced the problem of analyzing Code Example 5-1 to the question: How many times is the key comparison performed as a function of *n*?

Unfortunately, the question is still too vague, because the number of key comparisons depends on where, or whether, the target key appears in the list. Let's look at the extremes. If the target key happens to be the first one in the list (a[0] == target) then the function returns after a single key comparison, no matter how big *n* is. On the other hand, if the target is not in the array a, the function compares all *n* items in a to the target before giving up, so the number of comparisons is *n*. These extremes are referred to as the **best case** and the **worst case.** Which is really the relevant case? For most purposes, the worst case is more important. After all, the worst case gives us a bound on how long the function might have to run; if it's faster, that's fine. So for linear search, the best case performance is one comparison, and the worst case is *n*. Recall that we want to state the performance of the algorithm as a function of *n*; so if $f(n)$ stands for "the worst case performance of Linear Search," then $f(n) = n$. If you plot this function you get a straight line; hence the name *Linear* Search.

Of course, it's possible that both the worst and best cases are relatively unusual, and what we really want to find is a "typical" case. Because the typical case occurs "on average," it's generally called the **average case.** Average case analysis requires some theory about the relative likelihood of various possible inputs. You might collect some information about real-world data to develop this theory, or you might simply propose a likely scenario. For a simple searching algorithm, our model of the input would be pretty simple, and the analysis straightforward; for more complicated algorithms, finding the right model is quite difficult, and a good knowledge of probability theory is required to analyze the algorithm.

Let's consider the performance of Linear Search under the following set of assumptions:

1. The target has a 50-50 chance of being in a,

2. If the target is in a, then it's as likely to be in one position as in any other.

Because of the first assumption, half the time the target is not in the search array, and thus the worst case occurs—the search looks at every item in the list, finally giving up when it gets to the end, and n comparisons are required. The other half of the time, the target is found somewhere between position 0 and position $n-1$, so on average the algorithm has to compare the target with half the items: $n/2$. Combining these two possibilities together and multiplying each by the chance that it happens— 50%, or $1/2$—yields Equation 5-1:

Equation 5-1
$$\frac{1}{2}n + \frac{1}{2} \cdot \frac{n}{2} = \frac{n}{2} + \frac{n}{4} = \frac{3}{4}n$$

While Equation 5-1 is relatively simple and easy to interpret, we'll see later that the functions for many algorithms are messy and confusing. What we really want is a method to describe the *essence* of an algorithm's performance. One good way to get a feel for the performance of an algorithm is to plot its function on an *x-y* graph. On our graph (Figure 5-2), the *x* axis represents *n*, the size of the problem; and the *y* axis is $f(n)$, the number of comparisons for a problem of size *n*. One particular data point is illustrated: when the size of the search list is 100, the average number of comparisons is 75. You can obtain this number by plugging $n = 100$ into Equation 5-1.

Recall that any equation that looks like Equation 5-1 is called a ***polynomial*** and that it is made up of **terms.** The simplified polynomial (the part to the right of the equals sign) has one term: $(3/4)n$. In any polynomial, we call the fastest growing term the **high-order term.** For the average case of linear search, there's only one term, $(3/4)n$; so the high-order term is the product of *n* and a constant. Any polynomial in which the highest power of *n* is 1 is called a ***linear function;*** hence, the name linear search. The following expressions:

$$100n + 1000 \qquad\qquad 75n + 10\log n - 17 \qquad 0.001n - n^{0.5}$$

are also linear—for each of them, the high-order term is a product of *n* and a constant.

Because the high-order term represents the most important part of the analysis function, we refer to the rate of its growth as the **order of magnitude** of the function, or just *order* for short. Linear search can then be referred to as an *order n* algorithm, in both the worst and average cases. We often use the notation $O(n)$, known as **big-O** *notation,* to mean "order n." Later on, we'll see examples of algorithms that are $O(n^2)$, $O(\log n)$, $O(n\log n)$, and others.

Figure 5-2   *A graph of the average case performance of Linear Search*

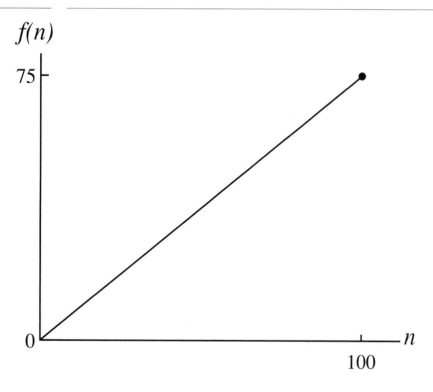

Next, we'll see an alternate search method, Binary Search, that's nearly always much faster than Linear Search.

Exercise 5-3   For the following formulas, identify the high-order term and indicate the order of each using big-O notation.

$$3n + 4 \qquad\qquad n - n^{3/4} \qquad\qquad n - n^{3/2}$$

$$n + n\log n \qquad\qquad n^2 - n\log n + 75 \qquad\qquad 2^n + n^2$$

$$n^{1/2} + 10^{20} \qquad\qquad n^3 + 2^n \qquad\qquad \log n + n$$

Exercise 5-4   The standard Linear Search algorithm assumes that the items being searched are static, that is, each item remains in the same position for every search. Suppose you are allowed to move the data around while you're searching—can you suggest a method for making the search more efficient?

Exercise 5-5   Write a driver for the function `linearSearch` (Code Example 5-1) that creates a large array and fills it with random data.[5]

Exercise 5-6   Analyze linear search under the following assumptions:

1. The target item is found 90% of the time.

2. The target item is found every time.

For these assumptions, is linear search still $O(n)$? Are there any assumptions about the probability of finding the target item that would make linear search anything but linear? Explain.

Exercise 5-7   Design and implement a driver similar to the one in Exercise 5-5, but make sure that the search data never contains a duplicated element.

Exercise 5-8   Using the C++ standard String class, modify your driver and the `linearSearch` function to perform a search of strings instead of `int`s. (Because the strings take more room than the `int`s you may need to reduce the size of your test array.)

5.3.2   Binary Search

The idea of **Binary Search** is quite simple, although the implementation can be trickier than you might think (see, for example, *Programming Pearls* by Jon Bentley, Chapter 4). First of all, we need to start with items stored in an array *in sorted order.*[6] We begin by comparing the key to the "middle element"; that is, to the item in the array halfway between the beginning and end. Of course, if there's an even number of items in the array, there's no middle element, so we use either one of the items that straddle the middle. Again, we start with an array `a` indexed from *0* to *n* – 1. Let `a[mid]` represent the middle element, and `key` be the search key. We now compare `a[mid]` and `key` for equality—if they match, we're done. Otherwise, the key must be larger or smaller than `a[mid]`. If the key is smaller, then if it's in the array it must be to the left of `a[mid]`; likewise, if the key is larger, then the element can only be found to the right. So assuming we don't find the key on the first try, we eliminate half the array as a potential location for the key. We refer to the portion of the array that can still potentially contain the key as *live*. We repeat the search process on the live half—find a new midpoint, compare the key, and so on. Eventually, one of two things has to happen: either we get a match, or the live portion of the array becomes empty, in which case we know that the key is not in the array.

---

5. The size of a "large" array depends upon the operating environment in which you're working. If possible, use arrays of size 100,000 elements or larger.

6. Note that sorted order can be *ascending* or *descending*. We'll assume ascending when we refer to sorted order, unless otherwise specified.

Exercise 5-9   Make a list of, say, 20 items, and practice Binary Search. Try items in the list and items not in the list.

How Fast Is Binary
Search?   Before we get to the implementation, let's analyze the algorithm. We'll count the number of times the key is compared to an element of the array. Obviously, whenever the key is found in the array, the algorithm terminates, so the worst case is searching for an item that's not in the array. Each time we don't match, the size of the live portion of the array is cut in two; so if we use n as the size of the array, the number of elements under consideration proceeds in a series: $n, n/2, n/4, \dots$. How far can this go? Eventually, there's only one possible element, which is compared with the key. At that point, we always have the answer one way or the other. So the entire series has to look like this: $n, n/2, n/4, \dots, 1$. Each item in the series corresponds to one comparison, so if we can figure out how many items are in the series we'll know the number of comparisons.

You may already know that if you take an integer and keep dividing by 2 until you get to 1, the number of divisions is approximately $\log_2 n$; but if you don't, how could you figure it out? I find it's easier to turn the series around: start with one and keep multiplying by 2 until you get to n. Certainly the length of this series is the same as starting with n and dividing by 2 to get to 1. (Well, maybe not exactly the same, if n is not a power of 2, but it will be close enough for our purposes.) Our multiplicative series goes like this: $1, 2, 4, \dots, k \geq n = 2^0, 2^1, 2^2, \dots, 2^c \geq n$. The length of this series is $c + 1$; we can bound the value of c by observing that $2^c \geq n > 2^{c-1}$ and by using the base-2 log ($\log_2$) of all terms, as shown in Equation 5-2:

Equation 5-2 $2^c \geq n > 2^{c-1}$ implies (by taking the base-2 log of all terms) that

$$\log_2 2^c \geq \log_2 n > \log_2 2^{c-1} \text{ implies (by evaluating the base-2 log) that}$$

$$c \geq \log_2 n > c - 1 \text{ implies (by addition) that}$$

$$\log_2 n + 1 > c \geq \log_2 n$$

This shows that the length of the series, c, is bounded by the base-2 log of n and thus that binary search is an $O(\log n)$ algorithm.[7]

Before getting into the details of the implementation, let's get a feel for the difference between a linear algorithm and an $O(\log n)$, or **logarithmic,** algorithm. Table

---

7. In the big-O notation, we can omit the base of the logarithm. That's because of a fundamental fact about logarithms: you can convert a logarithm in any base b to a logarithm in base a by multiplying by the constant $\log_a b$. Since multiplying by a constant doesn't change the order of the equation, the base is customarily omitted in big-O notation.

Table 5-1   *The growth of the base-2 log function*

n	n (as a power of 2)	$\log_2 n$
16	2^4	4
256	2^8	8
4,096	2^{12}	12
65,536	2^{16}	16
1,048,576	2^{20}	20

5-1 shows the comparative rates of growth for linear and logarithmic algorithms. We can also look at the shapes of linear and logarithmic curves, as shown in Figure 5-3. Either way you look at it, you will see that logarithmic functions grow very slowly—and that's good, because it means that even very large problems can be solved quickly if a logarithmic algorithm is available. To search a million items with linear search may take a million comparisons; but if we can use Binary Search, only about 20 comparisons will be needed. Suppose that on a particular system we can perform 10,000 comparisons per second. Then each linear search will require nearly two minutes, while binary search will take just 2/1000 of a second. A dramatic difference indeed!

Implementing
Binary Search—
Correctly   The idea of Binary Search is simple, but implementing a Binary Search is deceptively tricky. Consider Code Example 5-2, which *claims* to perform a Binary Search but actually contains a bug. Can you see what's wrong?

Code Example 5-2   *Defective Binary Search*

```cpp
// cx5-2.cpp
// Code Example 5-2: Defective Binary Search -- Do Not Use!

int binarySearch(int a[], int n, int target)
{
    // Precondition: array a is sorted in ascending order from a[0] to a[n-1]
    int first(0);
    int last(n - 1);
    int mid;
    while (first <= last) {
        mid = (first + last)/2;
        if (target == a[mid])
```

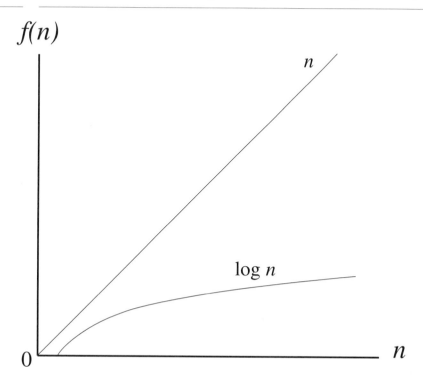

```
        return mid;
    else if (target < a[mid])
        last = mid;
    else // must be that target > a[mid]
        first = mid;
    }
    return -1; // use -1 to indicate item not found
}
```

What happens if you call the function `binarySearch` in Code Example 5-2? As long as `target` is in the search array, the function works correctly. But if you search for an item that's not there, the code falls into an endless loop. Instead of trying to fix the implementation directly, let's instead look at the problem in terms of invariants and derive a correct program without the defects in Code Example 5-2.

Once again, we need to find something that's true every time through the loop, something that captures something important about the behavior of the loop. If we're still in the loop, we're still searching; if we're still searching, we haven't found the target yet. When the target is found, the function returns immediately from inside the loop, so if the loop terminates normally, we want to be certain that the target is not in the array. Each time through the loop, the portion of the array under consideration must get smaller, otherwise we might get stuck. (Perhaps this is related to the bug in Code Example 5-2?)

Figure 5-4   *Illustrated invariant for Binary Search*

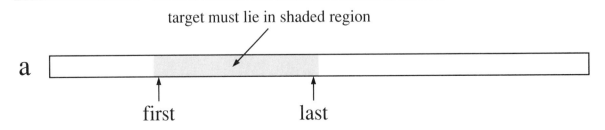

In Figure 5-4, we see a snapshot of the operation of Binary Search. The region that still may contain the target lies between `first` and `last` and is shaded in the figure. We've given up on the rest of the array. Stated as an invariant, it looks like this:

```
a[first] <= target <= a[last]
```

What assumption does this invariant make? It assumes that the list does contain the target, but that's not necessarily true. More correctly, we should say:

```
if target in a, then a[first] <= target <= a[last]
```

Since, initially, `first` and `last` represent the extreme values of the list (0 and n–1) this is certainly true when we first enter the loop. Once the precondition is established for the initial entry into the loop, we have to determine whether the logic in the loop maintains the precondition. Suppose `target < a[mid]`; then since `a[first] <= target <= a[last]` upon entering the loop, `target < a[mid]` implies that `a[first] <= target < a[mid]`. Since `last` on the next pass is going to be equal to `mid` on this pass, the invariant is maintained. You can make the mirror argument when `target > a[mid]`. So the function *does* maintain the invariant, but still, it doesn't work.

Up to this point we've concentrated on maintaining the loop invariant as the key to program correctness arguments. But there's a second consideration in the correctness of a loop: *termination*. If the loop works correctly, but never terminates, we certainly have a problem! What do we need in order to prove a loop will, eventually, halt? One way is to show that on every pass through the loop, something happens to "move us closer" to the termination condition for the loop. Because the loop in the binary search continues as long as `first <= last`, the termination condition is `first > last`. So if we can show that on each pass, `first` either increases or last decreases, we can prove the loop correct. Is this true—does first increase or last decrease every time?

Let's look at an example. Suppose the search list is a[] = {2, 3, 7, 9, 13}, and target = 5. Then the first four passes of the loop yield the trace shown in Table 5-2.

Table 5-2   *Trace of Code Example 5-2*

Pass	First	Last	Mid
1	0	4	2
2	0	2	1
3	1	2	1
4	1	2	1

Look at what happened on the third pass. Because $first = 1$ and $last = 2$, $mid = (1+2)/2 = 1$.[8] Then the if test in the loop will determine that, since target(5) > a[mid](3), last is set to mid. In fact, whenever $first = last$, $mid = (first + last)/2 = last$. That means that the line last = mid leaves last unchanged. Ah ha! If last never changes, then the loop keeps checking the same value over and over again and we have an endless loop. To fix this, note that there's no reason to leave mid within the range under consideration, because we've already tested it against the target. Instead, we either add 1 to mid (when using the right-hand partition) or subtract 1 from mid (when using the left-hand partition). Code Example 5-3 is the revised, corrected, and approved version of binary search.

Code Example 5-3   *Verified Binary Search*

```
// cx5-3.cpp
// Code Example 5-3: Corrected Binary Search

int binarySearch(int a[], int n, int target)
{
    // Precondition: array a is sorted in ascending order from a[0] to a[n-1]
    int first(0);
    int last(n - 1);
    int mid;
    while (first <= last) {
        // Invariant: if target in a, then a[first] <= target <= a[last]
```

---

8. Recall that with integer division the fractional part of a number is discarded.

```
        mid = (first + last)/2;
        if (target == a[mid])
            return mid;
        else if (target < a[mid])
            last = mid - 1;
        else // must be that target > a[mid]
            first = mid + 1;
    }
    return -1; //use -1 to indicate item not found
}
```

Because Binary Search is so effective, can we now discard Linear Search? No, because Binary Search requires a sorted array, while Linear Search can be used on any array. Furthermore, for a very short list, Linear Search is plenty good enough. Finally, as we shall see later, Binary Search requires a way to jump to the middle of the list, which is not practical for all data structures.

Exercise 5-10　　Write a driver for `binarySearch`, and test it with the defective Binary Search in Code Example 5-2. Give an example of an input where it returns an answer and an input where it goes into an endless loop.

5.4　Analysis of Some Simple Sorting Algorithms

We've already looked at one simple sorting method, Insertion Sort, in Section 3.3.4. As we discussed for search problems, sorting often requires that a sequence of records containing several fields are put into order using their key fields. Since it's the key that plays the "key role" in the sorting algorithm, we'll focus on records consisting of a key field alone, and we'll let the key be an integer. In the exercises you'll have a chance to extend these ideas to records containing multiple fields.

Computer scientists and software engineers need to know how to code and use sorting algorithms, not only because sorting a list is a frequently occurring operation, but also because sorting is an important subpart of many other algorithms. Furthermore, sorting provides an excellent set of examples for illustrating the analysis of algorithms. In this section, we'll consider some simple and not particularly efficient sorting algorithms. As our data structures knowledge becomes more sophisticated, we'll see that more complicated, but more efficient, sorting algorithms are needed when the data to be sorted is large and the speed of the sort is important.

5.4.1　Selection Sort

To understand how *Selection Sort* works, imagine that you start with two arrays, one containing the initial data, and another that starts out empty but ends up containing the sorted array. The fundamental operation for Selection Sort is select the largest (or smallest) element from the unsorted array and move it to the sorted array. When we've moved all the elements, we're done. You can either choose to move the smallest items first, or the largest, as long as you put them into the right order. You don't really need two arrays because you can use a single array and break it into two parts, one representing the sorted part and the other the unsorted, and move the items from one side to the other.

Finding the Position of the Max
The routine requires finding the largest (or smallest) element in an array. First, some terminology. If you have a list of items from a total order, and sort them, each item will have some position within the sorted list. (If there are duplicate items in the array, the exact position is ambiguous—to simplify the discussion, we'll assume every item is unique.) An item's position in the sorted array is called its ***rank.*** Note that even if you don't sort a list, each item still has a rank: the position it would end up in if you chose to sort. In particular, the first item in the sorted list has rank 1, and the last item in the sorted list of length n has rank n. The item with rank 1 is the *minimum*, abbreviated *min*; the item with rank n is called the *maximum* or *max*. The item in the middle, with rank $n/2$, is called the *median*. In general, algorithms designed to find an element with a particular rank are called ***selection algorithms.***

We're not going to solve the general selection problem here; instead, we just need an algorithm to find the max. We looked at a Max algorithm in Chapter 3, but we're going to do things slightly differently here because we need to find the position of the largest element rather than its value. Algorithm 5-2 is the **Max Select** algorithm we need here.

Algorithm 5-2   *Selection of max element*

```
max position ← position of first item in the array
current position ← position of second item in the array
while current position is not past the end of the array do
        if item in current position is greater than item in max position then
                max position ← current position
        current position ← position of next item in the list
return max position
```

We can easily translate this algorithm into a max selection function for arrays. We can also use Algorithm 5-2 to analyze the running time of max selection. Starting with the second item in the list, there is a comparison performed for each item in the list to the end. So for a list of size n, there are $n-1$ comparisons. Thus the Max Selection algorithm is $O(n)$.

Exercise 5-11   Write and analyze a Min Selection algorithm.

The implementation of maxSelect for an array, Code Example 5-4, will likely look quite familiar to you. You should convince yourself that it corresponds closely to the high-level description, that the loop invariant given has the desired effect of proving that the final result is correct, and that the loop will always terminate.

Code Example 5-4   *The* maxSelect *function*

```
// cx5-4.cpp
// Code Example 5-4: Max Select function

int maxSelect(int a[], int n)
{
    int maxPos(0), currentPos(1);

    while (currentPos < n) {
    // Invariant: a[maxPos] >= a[0] ... a[currentPos-1]
        if (a[currentPos] > a[maxPos])
            maxPos = currentPos;
        currentPos++;
    }
    return maxPos;
}
```

Now we're prepared to complete the implementation of Selection Sort for an array. The sorted list is built up one item at a time by repeating the following process: find the largest element, move it to the end of the list. In the middle of the process of Selection Sort, the array being sorted can be viewed as shown in Figure 5-5.

Figure 5-5   *The operation of Selection Sort*

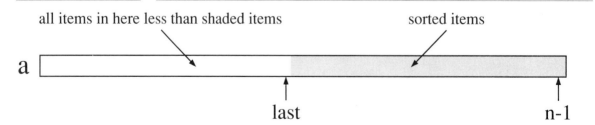

Let last be the position of the last unsorted item in the array. We can now state the basic step of selection sort as find maxPos, exchange the item at maxPos with the item at last, subtract 1 from last. Initially, last is set to n-1; the process continues until last becomes 0, at which point there's nothing left to sort. We can summarize the operation of selection sort by the following loop invariant:

a[last+1]...a[n-1] *is sorted, and*
everything in a[0]...a[last] <= *everything in* a[last+1]...a[n-1].

If we write a loop that maintains this invariant until last == 0, then we're guaranteed to have a sorted list; substitute last == 0 into the invariant to confirm this. Code Example 5-5 implements Selection Sort based on these ideas.

Code Example 5-5   *Selection Sort*

```
// cx5-5.cpp
// Code Example 5-5: Selection Sort

void swapElements(int a[], int maxPos, int last);
int maxSelect(int a[], int n); // see cx5-4.cpp
void selectionSort(int a[], int n)
{
    int last(n-1);
    int maxPos;

    while (last > 0) {
    // invariant: a[last+1] ... a[n-1] is sorted &&
    //    everything in a[0] ... a[last] <= everything in a[last+1] ... a[n-1]
        maxPos = maxSelect(a, last+1); // last+1 is length from 0 to last
        swapElements(a, maxPos, last);
        last--;
    }
}
```

The function swapElements takes an array and two indices as arguments and exchanges the elements at those indices.

Exercise 5-12   Write swapElements.

We need to verify the loop invariant. When last == n-1, the portion of the array from last+1 to n-1 is empty. Whenever you have a statement about the contents of an empty set, it's true by definition; in this case, we say the invariant is true **vacuously.** To see that the invariant is maintained, observe that a[maxPos] is greater than or equal to everything else in the unsorted portion, by the operation of maxSelect, and that it's less than or equal to everything in the sorted portion, by the invariant. Thus when we move a[maxPos] to position last, using swapElements, it will be in the correct position to maintain the invariant after last is decremented by the expression last--.

Finally, let's analyze the running time of Selection Sort. The loop is executed $n-1$ times; the only operation within the loop that is not constant time is the call to the maxSelect function. As discussed above, each call to maxSelect requires $n-1$

comparisons to take the max of a list of length n. The first time it is called, the max is found for a list of length n; the second time, the list is length $n-1$, and so forth down to 2. Thus the number of comparisons performed by Selection Sort is

Equation 5-3
$$(n-1) + (n-2) + \ldots + 1$$

An additive sequence of this form can be expressed by summation notation as

Equation 5-4
$$\sum_{1}^{n-1} i$$

A well-known relationship called Gauss's formula states the following relationship:

Equation 5-5
$$\sum_{1}^{x} i = \frac{x(x+1)}{2}$$

Substituting $n-1$ into Equation 5-5 gives us

Equation 5-6
$$\frac{(n-1)((n-1)+1)}{2} = \frac{(n-1)n}{2} = \frac{1}{2}n^2 - \frac{1}{2}n$$

To express Equation 5-6 with big-O notation, pull out the largest order term, which is n^2. Thus we finally conclude that Selection Sort is an $O(n^2)$ algorithm. A function in which the high-order term is a square (a power of 2) can be referred to as *quadratic*, so we call Selection Sort a **quadratic algorithm.** Because of its operation, Selection Sort requires $O(n^2)$ comparisons in the worst, best, and average cases. It is possible to do better, as we shall see; however, Selection Sort is perfectly acceptable for sorting small lists. Next, we'll look at an alternative sorting method and use analysis to compare it with Selection Sort.

Exercise 5-13   Use Gauss's formula (Equation 5-5) to simplify the following expressions:

$$1 + 2 + \ldots + \frac{k}{2} \qquad\qquad 1 + 3 + \ldots + 99$$

$$n + (n-1) + \ldots + 1$$

Exercise 5-14   Use algorithm analysis to determine the efficiency of Insertion Sort (Code Example 3-5). How does Insertion Sort compare with Selection Sort?

5.4.2 Bubble Sort

Bubble Sort also moves items one at a time into a sorted region of the array. We refer to the process that puts a single item in its place as a *phase*. We shall see that in addition to increasing the size of the sorted region, each phase also has the opportunity to make the remaining portion "more sorted." The algorithm can exploit this to terminate sooner and thus can be more efficient in some cases than Selection Sort.

Figure 5-6   *Example of one phase of Bubble Sort*

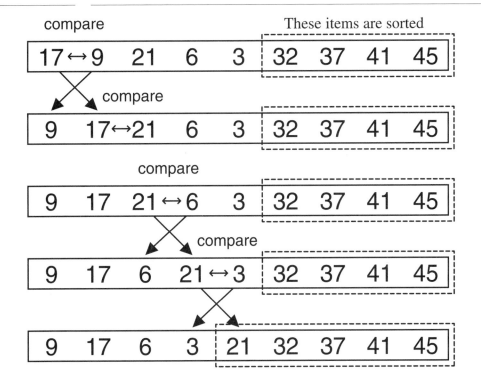

Each phase of the algorithm consists of "passing through" the unsorted portion of the array, comparing adjacent pairs of items, and exchanging the positions of the items in pairs that are out of order. Take a look at the example in Figure 5-6. Before the phase begins, the last four elements have already been placed in position; after the phase is completed, five elements lie in the sorted region. Note that in addition to moving 21 into its correct, final, position, the values 3, 6, and 17 have also moved closer to their correct positions, even though they don't end up in the sorted region, while 9 has moved away. This tendency to move many items "toward" their final positions can be exploited to improve Bubble Sort; you can explore this idea in Exercise 5-16, below. The name "Bubble Sort" comes from the motion of the smaller, or "lighter" elements toward the "top" of the array. (In the diagram, the top of the array is on the left.)

The function shown in Code Example 5-6 performs one phase of Bubble Sort. The index `last` represents the index of the last item in the unsorted region.

Code Example 5-6   BubbleSortPhase

```
// cx5-6.cpp
// Code Example 5-6: Bubble Sort Phase

void swapElements(int a[], int maxPos, int last); // see Exercise 5-12
void bubbleSortPhase(int a[], int last)
{
    // Precondition: a is an array indexed from a[0] to a[last]
    // Move the largest element between a[0] and a[last] into a[last],
    // by swapping out of order pairs
    int pos;
    for (pos = 0; pos < last; pos++)
        if (a[pos] > a[pos+1]) {
            swapElements(a, pos, pos+1);
        }
    // Postconditions: a[0] ... a[last] contain the same elements,
    // possibly reordered; a[last] >= a[0] ... a[last-1]
}
```

It's pretty easy to analyze `bubbleSortPhase`. There is one comparison on each pass through the loop, and the number of iterations of the loop depends only on the value of `last`. So the number of comparisons is a linear function of `last`, $O(last)$. Using `bubbleSortPhase` makes it very simple to write the function `bubbleSort`, as shown in Code Example 5-7.

Code Example 5-7   BubbleSort

```
// cx5-7.cpp
// Code Example 5-7: Bubble Sort

void bubbleSortPhase(int a[], int last); // see cx5-6.cpp
void bubbleSort(int a[], int n)
{
    // Precondition: a is an array indexed from a[0] to a[n-1]
    int i;
    for (i = n - 1; i > 0; i--)
        bubbleSortPhase(a, i);
    // Postcondition: a is sorted
}
```

Now we're ready to complete our analysis. Function `bubbleSort` makes $n-1$ calls to `bubbleSortPhase`. The number of comparisons depends on the value of i, which starts at $n-1$ and goes to 1; so once again we have

$$n-1+n-2+\ldots+1 = \sum_{i=1}^{n-1} i = O(n^2)$$

Equation 5-7

I implied above that Bubble Sort might be faster than Selection Sort, at least in some cases, but our analysis suggests that the two appear to be about the same. That's because we're not taking advantage of the fact that Bubble Sort moves items closer to their sorted positions as it works. However, as you'll see if you do the analysis, in the worst case Bubble Sort is still no faster than Selection Sort. In order to find faster algorithms, it helps to become comfortable with the tool covered in the next chapter: recursion.

Exercise 5-15 Add a loop invariant to Code Example 5-7 that can be used, along with the operation of `bubbleSortPhase`, to argue for the correctness of the postcondition.

Exercise 5-16 We can improve the average performance of Bubble Sort by using the following observation: if we make a complete pass through `bubbleSortPhase` without swapping any items, then the array must be in sorted order. Explain.

Exercise 5-17 Using the observation in Exercise 5-16, modify `bubbleSortPhase` and `bubbleSort` so that the sort terminates as soon as it knows that the array is sorted, rather than completing all $n-1$ passes.

Exercise 5-18 How does the modification you made in Exercise 5-17 affect the worst-case performance of Bubble Sort?

Chapter Summary

- Computer scientists use analysis techniques to compare algorithms based on how fast they run and how much memory they use.
- Asymptotic analysis is a useful technique for comparing the performance of algorithms.
- The Linear Search algorithm requires $O(n)$ comparisons to search a list of size n, in the worst case.
- Binary Search can search a sorted list of size n with only $O(\log n)$ comparisons.
- Selection Sort and Bubble Sort each require $O(n^2)$ to sort a list of size n, although Bubble Sort may be faster in some cases.

Programming Laboratory Problems

Lab 5-1   Using a driver and the corrected Binary Search (Code Example 5-3), test the number of key comparisons performed by binary search. To do so, you'll need to modify the `binarySearch` function to keep track of the number of comparisons performed and return this number each time it's called. Make sure you catch every key comparison! Perform 50 tests on different random targets (in each case, use an array in which `a[i] = i`) for the following values of *n:*

10
100
1000
10,000
100,000
1,000,000 (if possible on your system)

Graph the results and compare them to the hypothesized asymptotic analysis curve shown in Figure 5-3.

Lab 5-2   Write a driver using the Timer class[9] that records the elapsed time required by calls to the `binarySearch` function. Record the time required by 50 searches for 10^1 through 10^7 (if possible). If you have a very fast processor and a very crude clock (such as that provided by DOS) you may need to increase the number of searches to get meaningful results. Graph the times and compare them to the results from Lab 5-1 and to the hypothesized asymptotic analysis curve shown in Figure 5-3.

Lab 5-3   Modify `binarySearch` to search for strings using the C++ strings library. Record the times required by the searches. (You may have to settle for fewer searches because of the extra time and space required by the strings.) Graph the results and compare with the results from previous labs, if done, and to the hypothesized asymptotic analysis curve as shown in Figure 5-3.

Lab 5-4   Using the Timer class, compare the running times of the original Bubble Sort to Bubble Sort as modified in Exercise 5-17. Use arrays of size from 10^1 up to 10^5 and at least 50 randomly generated arrays for each size.[10]

Lab 5-5   Using the Timer class, compare the running times for (modified) Bubble Sort, Selection Sort, and Insertion Sort. Which algorithm appears to be the fastest? How do the shapes of the performance graphs for the three sorts differ?

---

9. See the software distribution for this book.

10. If you have a slower system, you might have to stop at a lower power of 10.

Lab 5-6   *Interpolation Search* is a variant of Binary Search that can be faster on data that's "evenly distributed."[11] In standard Binary Search, the middle element is chosen using this formula:

$$mid = \frac{(last - first)}{2}$$

Suppose you are searching an array of integers for the target item 47, with $a[first] = 43$ and $a[last] = 785$. Certainly if the integers were evenly distributed, you'd expect that it's likely that 47 is closer to the first position than to the last position, but the standard Binary Search doesn't take advantage of this. Interpolation Search works just like binary search, but it uses the following formula for choosing the middle value:

$$mid = \frac{target - first}{last - first}$$

Perl et al. proved in 1978 that Interpolation Search requires $O(\log\log n)$ comparisons, which is somewhat faster than Binary Search.

Modify the Binary Search program to create an Interpolation Search function, and compare it to Binary Search. Generate your search arrays using the following method.

For an array of size n:

1. Pick each element in the range from 0 to $10n$.

2. Sort the array.

3. Pick the target by choosing a random value i between 0 and $n - 1$ and using the value in $a[i]$.

Using a version of Interpolation Search that keeps track of the number of comparisons performed, run the search on ten randomly chosen arrays, using ten random targets (for a total of 100 runs per value of n), for the following values of n:

10
100
1000
10,000
100,000

---

11. The correct term in probability theory is *uniformly distributed*.

Run Binary Search for the same randomly chosen data. Plot the results. Did Interpolation Search do better than Binary Search for your data? (They will probably be quite close in performance.)

Lab 5-7   Linear Search with Move to Front (LSMF) works as follows: each time you search, move the key that's found one step closer to the front of the array. For example, suppose your array contains the following:

    10   2   7   9   14   11   5

and you search for 14. After you find it, you move it one step toward the front by exchanging it with 9; so the array will now look like this:

    10   2   7   14   9   11   5

The potentially good thing about LSMF is that if some items are much more commonly retrieved, they end up clustering near the front of the array, where they can be found quickly, while rarely retrieved items move toward the back.

1. Analyze the time complexity of LSMF: how many comparisons does it require in the worst case?

2. Implement LSMF, along with a test driver that creates random lists for searching. You'll also need a sort routine to prepare the list used by LSMF. Use a separate array for each search, of size 2^{10}=1024 elements. Fill the list with random numbers between 0 and 30,000. Add a counter to the LSMF function that will count the number of comparisons performed. Thoroughly test your algorithm by selecting random search keys and calling the LSMF function.

3. Now compare LSMF to standard Linear Search. LSMF only works well if certain items are accessed more frequently than others (why?) To evaluate LSMF, we'll use the following procedure:

   - $n = 1024$

   - Fill the array with random numbers (in the range 0 to 1,000,000)

   - Find ten numbers that are in the array—you can use the numbers at 100, 200, 300, ... Call these the "hot numbers"—the ones that will be accessed frequently. In some searches, you will look for numbers randomly, while in others you will only look for the hot numbers.

   - First trial: 50% of the time, select (randomly) a hot number; 50% of the time, choose any number at random.

   - Second trial: 90% of the time, select a hot number; 10% of the time, choose any number at random.

   - Run each trial 100 times. Be sure to completely reset everything and pick new random numbers each time.

   - Describe your results. How does LSMF compare to Linear Search? How does the first trial compare to the second trial? When is LSMF a good algorithm to use?

Chapter Vocabulary

algorithm

analysis of algorithms

asymptotic efficiency

average case

best case

big-O notation

Binary Search

Bubble Sort

constant function

critical operation

high-order term

key

key comparison

linear function

Linear Search

logarithmic algorithm

Max Select

order (of function)

order of magnitude

phase

polynomial

quadratic algorithm

rank

rate of growth

record

selection algorithm

Selection Sort

target key

terms (of a polynomial)

vacuously true

worst case

Chapter 6 Recursion

Overview | A discussion of the use of recursion as a problem-solving tool.

Chapter Objectives

1. To understand, evaluate, and implement simple recursive functions.
2. To apply recursion to searching and sorting problems.
3. To understand and analyze Quicksort
4. To begin to understand how the computer evaluates recursive programs.

6.1 Solving Problems with Recursion

6.1.1 A Very Simple Example

Let's suppose you needed to compute 2^5. No problem, right? You pick up a calculator. But bear with me for a minute, and let's look at how you could write a program to do it. OK, you say, it's a simple loop—2^5 is just 2 multiplied by itself five times. But there's another way to look at the problem. Note that $2^5 = 2 \times 2^4$; so if you knew the value of 2^4, you could find 2^5 by a simple multiplication. So we've taken the problem of computing 2^5 and turned it into two subproblems; compute 2^4, then multiply by 2. You know how to multiply by 2, of course; so now we need a way to compute 2^4. Why not apply the same method? $2^4 = 2 \times 2^3$, and so on. We can take this algorithm and turn it into a set of functions, one for each power of 2. Of course, eventually we get to 2^0, which is, by convention, equal to one. Your program might look like Code Example 6-1.

Code Example 6-1   *One way to compute 2^5*

```
// cx6-1.cpp
// Code Example 6-1: Computing 2 raised to the 5th, without recursion.

#include <iostream.h>

int twoRaisedTo0()
{
    return 1;
}
int twoRaisedTo1()
{
    return 2 * twoRaisedTo0();
}
int twoRaisedTo2()
{
    return 2 * twoRaisedTo1();
}
int twoRaisedTo3()
{
    return 2 * twoRaisedTo2();
}
int twoRaisedTo4()
{
    return 2 * twoRaisedTo3();
}
int twoRaisedTo5()
{
    return 2 * twoRaisedTo4();
}
```

```
int main()
{
    cout << "2 to the 5th is " << twoRaisedTo5() << "\n";
    return 0;
}
```

Surely there's got to be a method less tedious than Code Example 6-1! It looks like we're doing the same thing in each function, except for the `twoRaisedTo0` function. The only difference is the number at the end of the name of each function. So let's make that into a parameter. Of course, since 2^0 is a special case, we'll have to test for it in the function. If we did this, we would end up with Code Example 6-2.

Code Example 6-2   A better way to compute 2^5

```
// cx6-2.cpp
// Code Example 6-2: Recursively computing powers of 2

#include <iostream.h>

int twoRaisedTo(int n)
{
    if (n == 0) // special case
        return 1;
    else
        return 2 * twoRaisedTo(n-1);
}

int main()
{
    cout << "2 to the 5th is " << twoRaisedTo(5) << "\n";
    return 0;
}
```

Not only is Code Example 6-2 a better way to compute 2^5, it's much more general because it can be used to compute any power of 2. And the (perhaps) amazing thing is, it really works! The function `twoRaisedTo` is a function that calls itself; it is a **recursive function**. Like all modern programming languages, C++ accepts recursive functions and computes them correctly.

There's no question that a loop would have worked just fine for this particular problem. But, as we shall see later in the chapter, there are other problems for which the recursive program is much simpler than the nonrecursive program for the same algorithm. It will take us a little while to get there, but I promise the examples will get more interesting as we go along.

6.1.2 The Nature of Recursion

Ever since you started formal instruction in writing computer programs, you've probably been told that a good approach to problem solving is to take a large problem and break it into smaller ones. When you turn this into a program, you get a top-level program (in C++, the `main` function) that calls subfunctions to handle the various pieces of the problem to be solved. By now, you should be comfortable writing functions that call other functions to get their work done. The idea of recursion derives from the following insight: *sometimes the best way to solve a problem is to solve a smaller version of the exact same problem first.* When you turn this into a program, you end up with functions that call themselves.

Many (but not all) students find it difficult to get a handle on recursion. It seems to offend their sense of how the world ought to work to see a program call itself. Often they get bogged down in trying to understand exactly what the computer does when this happens. Unfortunately, those of us teaching recursion make the problem worse because in an attempt to present simple examples, we generally present examples that are rather useless. Consider these warnings cautionary, not predictive. You *can* understand recursion and learn to use it as an effective tool. With a little patience and a little work, you can get "over the hump," and, once you get there, you'll look back and wonder what the big deal was.

6.2 Recursive Definitions

We can take the function `twoRaisedTo` and write it down as the following mathematical function:

Equation 6-1
$$f(n) = \begin{cases} 2 \times f(n-1) & \text{when } n \geq 1 \\ 1 & \text{when } n = 0 \end{cases}$$

Equation 6-1 looks a little different from most function definitions you're probably familiar with. The lines to the right of the "{" should be read as follows: if $n \geq 1$, use the top line as the definition of the function. If $n = 0$, use the bottom line. Since the function f appears on both sides of the "=," Equation 6-1 is an example of a ***recursive definition*** of a function.[1] Note that for a recursive definition to be meaningful, there has to be one or more lines that are nonrecursive—a ***base case.*** This is one of the keys to making recursion work; you can define f in terms of itself, but at some

---

1. These are sometimes known as *recurrence relations*.

point you have to get to something that's *not* defined in terms of *f*, or your computation can never terminate. Thus every complete recursive definition needs one or more base cases.

It's often (but not always) the case that there are equivalent, nonrecursive definitions; Equation 6-1 and Equation 6-2 define exactly the same function.[2]

Equation 6-2
$$f(n) = 2^n, \; \forall n \geq 0$$

An equation that is not defined recursively is sometimes called a ***closed form***. Typically you can prove that a recursive definition and a closed form define the same function using induction.

Evaluation by Substitution

As we saw in Code Example 6-2, it's generally pretty easy to turn a recursive definition into a recursive program. It's also useful to be able to evaluate recursive definitions by hand. Let's look at evaluating $f(5)$ using Equation 6-1. The first step is to use the equation to expand $f(5)$; plugging in the top line in Equation 6-1 yields $f(5) = 2 \times f(4)$. This process is called ***substitution***. You can keep substituting values until you get to something that is evaluated without recursion. At this point your work would like something like Equation 6-3.

Equation 6-3
$$f(5) = 2 \times f(4)$$
$$f(4) = 2 \times f(3)$$
$$f(3) = 2 \times f(2)$$
$$f(2) = 2 \times f(1)$$
$$f(1) = 2 \times f(0)$$
$$f(0) = 1$$

Now that we've gotten to the nonrecursive line at the bottom, we can use its value on the line above it and so forth. This is called ***back substitution***. Applying back substitution to Equation 6-3 gives us Equation 6-4.

---

2. The symbol "$\forall$" means "for every"; in other words, Equation 6-2 states that this relation holds for every value of *n* as long as $n \geq 0$. Also, recall that $2^0 = 1$, by definition.

$$f(5) = 2 \times f(4) = 2 \times 16 = 32$$
$$f(4) = 2 \times f(3) = 2 \times 8 = 16$$
$$f(3) = 2 \times f(2) = 2 \times 4 = 8$$
$$f(2) = 2 \times f(1) = 2 \times 2 = 4$$
$$f(1) = 2 \times f(0) = 2 \times 1 = 2$$
$$f(0) = 1$$

Equation 6-4

You can apply this method to any recursive definition to find its value for a particular argument.

Factorial Function   Let's look at another example. Equation 6-5 defines the factorial function, $n!$, without using recursion.

Equation 6-5 $$n! = n \times (n - 1) \times (n - 2) \times \ldots \times 1$$

By definition, $0! = 1$. Using recursion, we can write the equivalent definition shown in Equation 6-6.

Equation 6-6 $$f(n) = \begin{cases} n \times f(n - 1) & \text{when } n \geq 1 \\ 1 & \text{when } n = 0 \end{cases}$$

Exercise 6-1   Using Equation 6-6 and substitution, evaluate $f(6)$.

Exercise 6-2   Use Equation 6-6 to write a program that computes the factorial function.

A Combinatorial Function   Our next example comes from the mathematical field known as **combinatorics,** or counting. To illustrate our problem, suppose that Bonnie, a disk jockey, works for a radio station with a rigid "classic rock" format. In each hour, the deejay selects 10 different songs to play from 40 available records. How many different one-hour shows can she program? Or, in general, given 40 different things, how many different sets of size 10 can be chosen?

Because this problem arises commonly when computing probabilities, it has a standard name—**n choose k**—and a standard notation:

$$\binom{n}{k}$$

For our radio station example, we want to find the value of the expression

$$\binom{40}{10}$$

There's a standard, closed form definition for n choose k, shown in Equation 6-7.

Equation 6-7
$$\binom{n}{k} = \frac{n!}{k!(n-k)!}$$

Without knowing Equation 6-7, you can use the ideas of recursion to derive, directly, a recursive definition for n choose k. Let's go back to the deejay, Bonnie. In any given hour, she can either include, or not include, the song "Stairway to Heaven." All the possible sets she can include are the sum of the sets that include "Stairway to Heaven" and the sets that *don't* include "Stairway to Heaven." This is summarized in Equation 6-8.

Equation 6-8 Total number of sets = Sets with "Stairway" + Sets without "Stairway"

Now we can figure out the number of sets that include "Stairway to Heaven." Since 1 of the 10 songs has been selected, she has to pick 9 more from the 39 remaining. For the sets that don't include "Stairway to Heaven," she selects 10 songs from all the other songs, that is, 39 choose 10. Now, there's nothing special about which recording we use to make this argument—the same logic would hold. This suggests that we can write Equation 6-9:

Equation 6-9
$$\binom{40}{10} = \binom{39}{9} + \binom{39}{10}$$

If we abstract this equation to the general case, we can derive a partial definition of the n choose k function shown in Equation 6-10.

Equation 6-10
$$\binom{n}{k} = \binom{n-1}{k-1} + \binom{n-1}{k}$$

It may be a little hard to see at first, but this is a (partial) recursive definition. If we rewrite it using the notation $c(n,k)$ to mean n choose k, as shown in Equation 6-11, it looks rather more like our definitions above.

Equation 6-11
$$c(n, k) = c(n-1, k-1) + c(n-1, k)$$

It does look somewhat different, because it is a function of two parameters, and we've been referring to it as a *partial* definition because there is no nonrecursive line. To complete the definition, we need to determine the conditions under which the recursive definition makes sense and when to apply a nonrecursive equation.

In order for n choose k to be meaningful, it's clear that n must be at least as big as k, since you can't choose 10 things from a set of size 8. Furthermore, when $n = k$, there's only 1 way to choose. Finally, for the selection to be meaningful, k must be at least 1, and when k is 1, there are n ways to choose; for example, there are 10 ways to pick 1 item from 10. This gives us the recursive definition shown in Equation 6-12.

$$\textit{Equation 6-12} \qquad c(n,k) \;=\; \begin{cases} n & \text{when } k \;=\; 1 \\ 1 & \text{when } n \;=\; k \\ c(n-1,k-1) + c(n-1,k) & \text{when } n > k \text{ and } k > 1 \end{cases}$$

Because this definition has three clauses, two nonrecursive and one recursive, it translates into a C++ function with three paths, as shown in Code Example 6-3.

Code Example 6-3   *The choose recursive function*

```
// cx6-3.cpp
// Code Example 6-3: The n choose k function

int choose(int n, int k)
{
    if (k == 1)
        return n;
    else if (n == k)
        return 1;
    else // recursive case: n>k and k>1
        return choose(n - 1, k - 1) + choose(n - 1, k);
}
```

Exercise 6-3   (Exercise for the mathematically inclined.) Use mathematical induction to prove the equivalence of Equation 6-7 and Equation 6-12.

Exercise 6-4   In any programming language that uses integers bounded within a fixed range, a straightforward implementation of Equation 6-12 can be used for larger values of n and k than a straightforward implementation of Equation 6-7. Explain.

Exercise 6-5   Evaluate Equation 6-12 for small values of n and k, say 5 and 2.

If you did the Exercise 6-5, you probably noticed that certain calls to c, such as $c(3,2)$, appear more than once. Generally, the runtime for C++ doesn't notice that it has previously computed an answer for these values, and it does the work over, which really slows things down for larger values of n and k. To compute the answer for our original example, $c(40, 10)$, took nearly three minutes on a pretty fast work-station (an SGI Indy R4000SC). (By the way, the answer is 847,660,528.) You can improve this by keeping track of all values of the function that have been computed previously and returning these values instead of recomputing, but this is easy to say, and not so easy to implement.

6.3   Applying Recursion to Sorting and Searching Problems

The recursive problems we've looked at so far have all been described as recursive functions. However, recursion as a problem-solving approach has a wider applica-tion. We'll use the name ***recursive routines*** to distinguish these solutions from re-cursive function definitions. In this section we find recursive routines for the now-familiar problems of searching and sorting.

6.3.1   Recursive Search Algorithms

Linear Search   We can use the recursive problem-solving approach with searching to derive recur-sive versions of Linear and Binary Search. Suppose you face the common problem of finding a target in an array a of length n. To apply recursion to this problem, we need to figure out a way to solve the complete problem given a solution to a smaller version of the same problem. To help yourself understand what's going on here, look at a picture (Figure 6-1). Let's assume that the calling signature for Linear Search will be the same as it was in Chapter 5:

```
int linearSearch(int a[], int n, int target)
```

Now, it's possible that our target element is located at the end of the list—that is, `target == a[n-1]`. That's easy enough to check, and if it's true we've found our answer. Otherwise, we want to use recursion to solve a smaller problem: to search the list from `a[0]` through `a[n-2]`, that is, `linearSearch(a, n-1, target)`.

There are only two things that can happen from this call. If the target was located somewhere in position 0 through n-2, you will get its position; you're done, and you can simply return it. Otherwise, if the target was not found, the value -1 will be returned, indicating that the search failed to locate the target. If you put these ideas together, you are nearly ready to write the function recursively. Like a recursive function definition, a nonrecursive course of action is necessary to prevent an infi-nite regression. Suppose you are asked to search for the target in an empty array—

Figure 6-1   *Visualization of recursive Linear Search*

use recursive call `linearSearch(a, n-1, target)` for this part

```
                    a[0]  through a[n-2]
```

a[n-1]

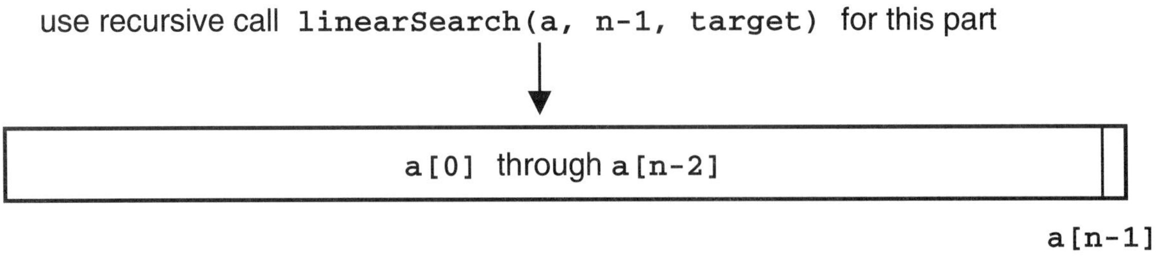

what do you do? Because the target *can't* be in an empty array the program returns -1. What does an empty array look like? Well, if n is the size of the array, then when n is less than or equal to 0, the calling function requests the search of an empty array. Using these ideas yields Code Example 6-4.

Code Example 6-4   *Recursive Linear Search*

```cpp
// cx6-4.cpp
// Code Example 6-4: Recursive Linear Search

int linearSearch(int a[], int n, int target)
{
    // Recursive version of linear search
    // Precondition: a is an array indexed from 0 to n-1
    if (n <= 0) // an empty list is specified
        return -1;
    else {
        if (a[n-1] == target) // test final position
            return n-1;
        else // search the rest of the list recursively
            return linearSearch(a, n-1, target);
    }
    // Postcondition: If a value between 0 and n-1 is returned,
    //                a[returnValue] == target;
    //                Otherwise, if -1 is returned, target is not in a
}
```

You can trace the operation of a recursive routine in a manner similar to that used for recursive function definitions, although it can be a bit trickier to keep track of the operation. For example, suppose a = {17, 6, 9, 21}. We will trace the call `linearSearch(a, 4, 6)`:

```
linearSearch(a, 4, 6)

   n == 4; target == 6. Since a[3] != target, return linearSearch(a, 3, 6)

   linearSearch(a, 3, 6)

      n == 3; target == 6. Since a[2] != target, return linearSearch(a, 2, 6)

      linearSearch(a, 2, 6)

         n == 2; target == 6. Since a[1] == target, return 1
```

We suggest that you work through the following exercises carefully and systematically; understanding recursion gets easier with practice.

Exercise 6-6   For an array a = {22, 11, 13, 81, 5}, trace linearSearch(a, 5, 11).

Exercise 6-7   For an array a = {22, 11, 13, 81, 5}, trace linearSearch(a, 5, 50).

In order to analyze the running time of the recursive version of Linear Search, you have to determine the number of times the recursive function is called and multiply it by the number of comparisons in each call. The function linearSearch has several comparisons, but only one key comparison—the line:

```
   else if (a[n-1] == target) // test final position
```

Thus we've reduced the problem to counting the number of calls to the function. Examining your trace above, you'll see that for a list of size n, the number of calls is $n+1$; however, the last call never gets to the key comparison, so the worst case number of comparisons is n. In other words, the asymptotic efficiency of the recursive and nonrecursive versions is the same. That doesn't necessarily mean, of course, that one can't be faster than the other on a particular machine or in a particular implementation; we'll come back to the issue of the efficiency of recursion in Section 6-4.

Binary Search   It's quite natural to describe Binary Search as a recursive algorithm. The first step of Binary Search is to examine the middle element; assuming we don't find the key, we then use binary search recursively to search the appropriate half of the array. Algorithm 6-1 details recursive Binary Search.

Algorithm 6-1   *Recursive Binary Search*

Preconditions: a is an array sorted in ascending order,
first is the index of the first element to search,
last is the index of the last element to search,
target is the item to search for.

```
if first > last
        return failure
mid ←(first+last)/2
if a[mid] is equal to target
        return mid
else if target < a[mid]
        return result of recursive search of a from first upto mid-1
else
        return result of recursive search of a from mid+1 upto last
```

Postcondition: Value returned is position of target in a, otherwise return failure.

We can easily turn Algorithm 6-1 into Code Example 6-5. We indicate "failure" by returning the value -1.

Code Example 6-5   *Recursive Binary Search*

```cpp
// cx6-5.cpp
// Code Example 6-5: Recursive Binary Search

int binarySearch(int a[], int first, int last, int target)
{
    // Preconditions: a is an array sorted in ascending order,
    //     first is the index of the first element to search,
    //     last is the index of the last element to search,
    //     target is the item to search for.
    if (first > last)
        return -1; // -1 indicates failure of search
    int mid = (first+last)/2;
    if (a[mid] == target)
        return mid;
    else if (target < a[mid])
        return binarySearch(a, first, mid-1, target);
    else // target must be > a[mid]
        return binarySearch(a, mid+1, last, target);
    // Postcondition: Value returned is position of target in a,
    // otherwise -1 is returned
}
```

Exercise 6-8   For an array a = {1, 6, 15, 22, 37, 45, 52}, trace binarySearch(a, 0, 6, 37).

Exercise 6-9　For an array `a = {1, 6, 15, 22, 37, 45, 52}`, trace `binary-Search(a, 0, 6, 40)`.

Correctness of Recursive Functions

When we developed the original, nonrecursive binary search, we used loop invariants to argue for the correctness of the program. What about the correctness of recursive programs? Recursion is closely related to the method of mathematical induction, so we create an argument for the correctness of a recursive program using ***proof by induction.*** We'll sketch the idea of such a proof here; the mathematically inclined student is invited to turn this into a formal proof.

In proof by induction, we always have one or more base cases; each base case corresponds to a nonrecursive path through the procedure. We ask the question, Does the program work correctly in the base (nonrecursive) case? For Binary Search, the base case occurs when `first > last`, that is, when the portion of the array to be searched is empty. Since in this case the program reports that the target was not found, the algorithm works for the base case. To prove that the recursive part works, we make an ***inductive hypothesis:*** the program works for problems smaller than size *n*. In the case of Binary Search, we take it as a given that a search in an array of size smaller than *n* works correctly and ask, if that's the case, does the program work overall? Suppose that `a[mid] == target` — then we've found what we're looking for, and the program certainly works. In the other cases, we call Binary Search on the only parts of the array in which the target can possibly be; by our inductive hypothesis, the program works when it searches these smaller intervals. Thus, the program appears to be correct. As we cautioned above, this is only an informal outline of the proof, but it does give some insight into how and why the program works.

6.3.2　Quicksort: A Recursive Sorting Algorithm

Quicksort was discovered and named by an English computer scientist, C. A. R. Hoare, and first published in 1962. Here's the basic idea:

1. Pick one item from the array to be sorted, and call it the ***pivot.***

2. Partition the items in the array around the pivot; that is, reorganize the array so that every item smaller than the pivot lies in the partition to the left of the pivot, and every item larger than the pivot is in the partition on the right. (We'll put items equal to the pivot on the left.)

3. Use recursion to sort the two partitions.

Figure 6-2 illustrates the condition of the array after applying step 2. We've labelled the partitions "partition 1" and "partition 2" for convenience. Note that the pivot doesn't necessarily end up in the middle; in fact, it's always possible that one of the partitions is empty, for example, when the pivot is the smallest item in the array. A minute of reflection may convince you that after step 2, the pivot is in the position it should occupy when the sort is complete. This is the justification for sorting the two partitions independently—if we put each partition into the proper order, the entire array will be sorted. If you convince yourself of these facts, you'll see why Quicksort works.

Figure 6-2   *Quicksort: The array after one partition step*

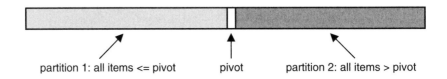

partition 1: all items <= pivot   pivot   partition 2: all items > pivot

Partitioning the array elements around the pivot is the trickiest part of the algorithm to understand. Using a top-down approach, we can go ahead and turn our algorithm into a program; we'll hide the complexity of the partition process in a subroutine, as shown in Code Example 6-6.

Code Example 6-6   *The Quicksort function*

```
// cx6-6.cpp
// Code Example 6-6: Quicksort
// Note: this quicksort function depends upon the partition function in cx6-7.cpp
int partition(int a[], int first, int last);
void quicksort(int a[], int first, int last)
{
    // precondition: a is an array;
    //    The portion to be sorted runs from index first to index last inclusive.
    if (first >= last) // Base Case -- nothing to sort, so just return
        return;

    // Otherwise, we're in the recursive case.
    // The partition function uses the item in a[first] as the pivot
    // and returns the position of the pivot -- split -- after the partition.
    int split(partition(a, first, last));

    // Recursively, sort the two partitions.
    quicksort(a, first, split-1);
    quicksort(a, split+1, last);
    // postcondition: a is sorted in ascending order
    // between first and last inclusive.
}
```

The initial call to the `quicksort` function looks like this:

```
quicksort(a, 0, n-1);
```

Now we develop the partition function. Obviously there's going to be some kind of loop moving the items into their proper positions within the array. We'll develop the algorithm by stating the pre- and postconditions and by trying to find an appropriate loop invariant. Refer again to Figure 6-2, which illustrates what we want the array to look like when we're done. We'll use `split` to denote the position of the pivot; thus we can write the postcondition this way:

$$a[first]...a[split-1] \le a[split] \ \&\& \ a[split+1]...a[last] > a[split]$$

Note that there's a less than or equal to condition here, since there might be more than one element with the same value as the pivot. It doesn't really matter which partition the equal elements go into as long as we're consistent.

Let's imagine that we're somewhere in the loop, partitioning the items in the array around the pivot. One possibility is that our partial solution looks like Figure 6-3. Then each pass through the loop would move one item from the unknown region into either partition 1 or partition 2 and adjust the `split` accordingly. I've included some sample numbers to help illustrate what's going on.

Figure 6-3   *First attempt at a loop invariant for partition*

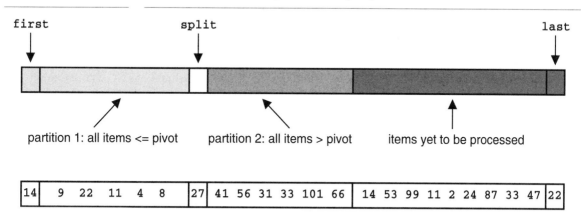

You could implement this, but it's unnecessarily messy because of the need to move the pivot around. A better approach is to leave the pivot in its initial position at a[first], build the two partitions, and then move the pivot into the correct spot as the final step. Our revised loop invariant looks like Figure 6-4. We'll use the label lastSmall for the last item in partition 1. Our loop index, i, will indicate the item we're currently in the process of moving into one of the two partitions. In the numeric example, a[first] == 27, a[lastSmall] == 8, and a[i] == 14.

Figure 6-4   *Better loop invariant for partition*

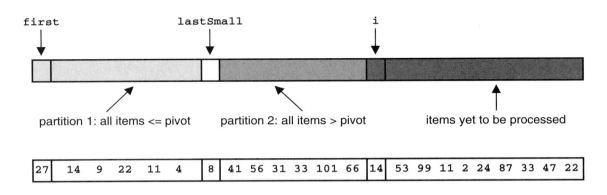

Using Figure 6-4 as a guide, we can now write our loop invariant this way:

a[first+1]...a[lastSmall] ≤ a[first] && a[lastSmall+1]...a[i–1] > a[first]

The first time through the loop, we want both partitions to start out empty; this works by setting i to first+1 and lastSmall to first. To maintain the invariant, the program examines the item at position a[i]. If a[i] is larger than the pivot, that is, a[first], then there's nothing to do—partition 2 will be expanded on the next pass through the loop, with a[i] located in the appropriate position. But if a[i] is smaller than the pivot, it needs to be moved into partition 1. The easiest way to do it is to swap it with the first item in partition 2, a[lastSmall+1], then increment lastSmall because the size of partition 1 has grown. Actually, when I wrote the code, I incremented lastSmall first and then swapped a[i] and a[lastSmall], which amounts to the same thing. We use the function swapElements, described in Section 5.4.1, which exchanges two items in an array. Figure 6-5 illustrates the results after swapping the items and updating lastSmall and i.

There's one more detail: after the loop has done its work, the pivot has to be moved into the proper position. This is illustrated in Figure 6-6. If you put all these pieces

Figure 6-5   *Partition example after* swapElements *update of* lastSmall *and* i

| 27 | 14 | 9 | 22 | 11 | 4 | 8 | 14 | 56 | 31 | 33 | 101 | 66 | 41 | 53 | 99 | 11 | 2 | 24 | 87 | 33 | 47 | 22 |

together in a C++ function, you get Code Example 6-7. If you'd like to see the partition and quicksort functions combined into a single file, take a look at Supplemental Example 6-1 (sx6-1.cpp), included in the software distribution for this book.

Figure 6-6   *Getting the pivot into its proper location*

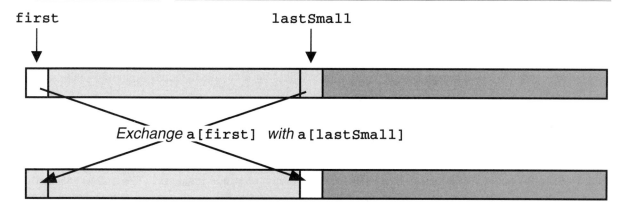

Code Example 6-7   *The partition function for Quicksort*

```
// cx6-7.cpp
// Code Example 6-7: Partition function (for quicksort, cx6-6.cpp)

void swapElements(int a[], int first, int last) // see Exercise 5-12
int partition(int a[], int first, int last)
{
    int lastSmall(first), i;
    for (i=first+1; i <= last; i++)
        // loop invariant: a[first+1]...a[lastSmall] <= a[first] &&
        //    a[lastSmall+1]...a[i-1] > a[first]
        if (a[i] <= a[first]) { // key comparison
            ++lastSmall;
            swapElements(a, lastSmall, i);
        }
    swapElements(a, first, lastSmall); // put pivot into correct position
    // postcondition: a[first]...a[lastSmall-1] <= a[lastSmall] &&
    //    a[lastSmall+1]...a[last] > a[lastSmall]
    return lastSmall; // this is the final position of the pivot -- the split index
}
```

Exercise 6-10   For the array a = {17, 22, 91, 11, 4, 50}, trace partition(a, 0, 5).

Exercise 6-11   For the array a = {11, 21, 19, 44, 56, 51, 95, 45} trace partition(a, 4, 7).

Exercise 6-12   For the array a = {72, 19, 25, 26, 19, 44, 91, 88, 11}, trace quicksort(a, 0, 8).

Analyzing Quicksort   Let's consider the efficiency of Quicksort, starting with the worst case. All the key comparisons take place in the partition function, at the line noted by the comment key comparison (see Code Example 6-7). The partition function performs a comparison for each iteration of the loop, and there are last - first iterations. So to analyze the performance of Quicksort, we need to figure out how many times partition is called and with what values of first and last. To visualize the operation of this recursive algorithm, we'll draw a picture called a ***recursion tree.*** In a recursion tree, we show each call to the recursive function, with arrows indicating the direction of recursive calls.

Let's start with an example. Use Quicksort to sort the array

     a[] = {67,58,38,81,90,57,54}

The recursion tree for this input array is shown in Figure 6-7. The dashed lines represent the operation of the partition function, while the solid lines indicate the recursive calls to quicksort. Note that, as shown in Code Example 6-6, there are two recursive calls for each call to quicksort, except for the nonrecursive or terminal cases. When the list consists of only one or no elements, there is no recursive call; this is indicated in the figure by a box around the array elements. (Empty brackets shown in the tree as "[ ]" indicate an empty partition, i.e., first > last.)

Exercise 6-13   Draw a recursion tree to illustrate the operation of Quicksort on the following inputs:

     1. a[] = {4,2,3,1,6,5,7}
     2. a[] = {7,6,5,4,3,2,1}

Quicksort in the Worst Case   The two inputs in Exercise 6-13 illustrate extremes of the efficiency of Quicksort. The worst case occurs when the input array is either sorted or "reverse-sorted" order, that is, sorted in the reverse direction to the desired output. The recursion tree for a sorted array will have the form shown in Figure 6-8. I omitted the partition call from the diagram to emphasize the shape of the tree.

Figure 6-7   *Example recursion tree for Quicksort*

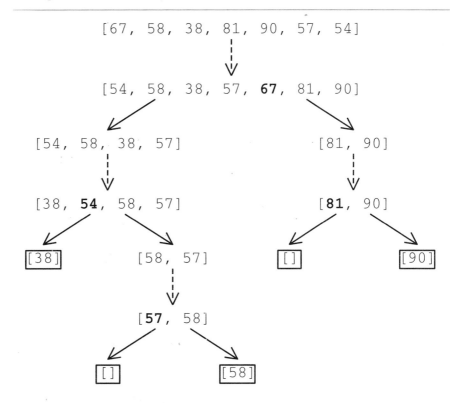

Let's look at the calls to partition. The first time it's called, first=0 and last=6, so partition performs 6 comparisons. The next time, first=1 and last=6, for 5 comparisons; 4 comparisons on the next, and so on. Therefore, if you start out with *n* items to sort, in the worst case the number of comparisons is shown in Equation 6-13. Note that we're again applying Gauss's formula, Equation 5-5.

Equation 6-13 $$(n-1) + (n-2) + \ldots + 1 = \sum_{i=1}^{n-1} i = \frac{n(n-1)}{2} = O(n^2)$$

Looking at Equation 6-13 might make you wonder whether Quicksort is misnamed; after all, we've just shown that in the worst case, the performance of Quicksort is similar to that of the other sorts we've already seen, such as Insertion Sort and Bubble Sort. But if you use Quicksort to sort some big lists and keep track of the number of comparisons and then compare the results with, say, Bubble Sort, you'll find that

Figure 6-8   *A worst case recursion tree for Quicksort*

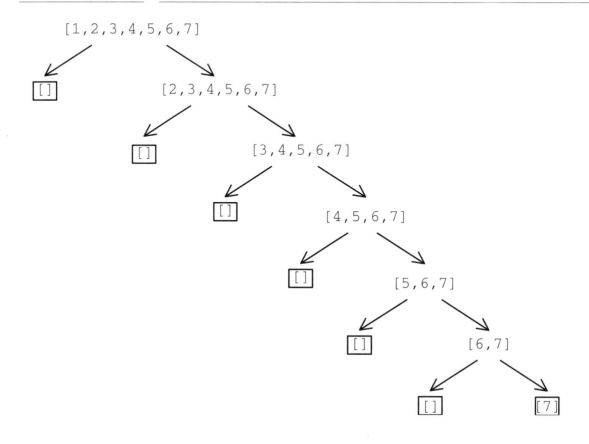

Quicksort seems to be much more efficient. We did just such a comparison; the re-sults are shown in Table 6-1.

Table 6-1   *Bubble sort and Quicksort: Sample comparison counts.*

n (as power of 2)	n	Quicksort Comparisons[a]	Bubble Sort Comparisons
2^3	8	9	28
2^4	16	18	120

Table 6-1   *Bubble sort and Quicksort: Sample comparison counts.*

n (as power of 2)	n	Quicksort Comparisons[a]	Bubble Sort Comparisons
2^5	32	53	496
2^6	64	148	2,016
2^7	128	448	8,128
2^8	256	853	32,640
2^9	512	2,200	130,816
2^{10}	1,024	4,942	523,776
2^{11}	2,048	13,656	2,096,128
2^{12}	4,096	26,854	8,386,560
2^{13}	8,192	68,957	33,550,336
2^{14}	16,384	123,080	134,209,536

a. This represents the number of comparisons used by one randomly chosen run of Quicksort.

Quicksort in the
Best Case   To get an idea of why Quicksort seems to be so fast, even though it doesn't look that good from a worst case perspective, we'll now derive the best case performance. We mentioned in Chapter 5 that the best case often doesn't tell us much, but as we'll see, Quicksort is an exception. If you fiddle around with a few examples, you'll find that the best case for Quicksort occurs when the recursion tree is **balanced;** that is, when at each step, the elements are split in half. That was the case for Exercise 6-13, above. Figure 6-9 demonstrates what happens.

We can think about the size of a tree by considering the number of **levels** it has. If you count the initial call to the function as level 0, then all the recursive calls from level 0 are at level 1, and in general, the recursive calls placed at level i are at level $i + 1$. For example, in Figure 6-7, there's one initial call at level 0, two calls at level 1, and one at level 2, while in Figure 6-8, the last call is at level 6. In order to analyze Quicksort in the best case, we need to figure out how many levels this tree can have for a general value of n, and we need to determine the number of comparisons at each level. Then we can multiply these two values together to get the total number of comparisons. As we've seen, the first level requires $n - 1$ comparisons, or, in the tree shown in Figure 6-9, six comparisons. Take a look at the next level down, where

Figure 6-9   *A best case recursion tree for Quicksort*

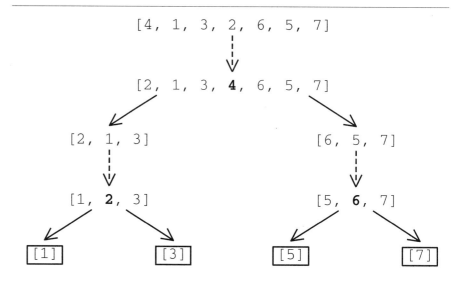

[1,2,3] and [6,5,7] are sorted. Each requires two comparisons, or four total; in the general case, $n-3$. It's kind of messy to keep track of this series, so we'll use n as an upper bound for the work at each level, which turns out to be good enough.[3]

Now we'll try to figure out how many levels there can be. Each time we go from one level to the next, the number of things to sort is cut in half. (Actually there's a bit less than half, but again we're trying to keep things simple.) When Quicksort has only one or zero things to sort, it stops making recursive calls, so the question is, If you have n things and repeatedly take half of them, how many times can you do this before you have only one? More formally, what is the length of the series

Equation 6-14 $$n, \frac{n}{2}, \frac{n}{4}, \frac{n}{8}, \dots ?$$

Try to turn the question around; suppose you start with 1 and double it, then double the result, and so forth; surely, this is the opposite of dividing by 2. How many times do you have to multiply by 2 before you get to some value of n? In other words, what is the value of 2^i such that $2^i \geq n > 2^{i-1}$? At this point, you need to recall

---

3. If you find a phrase like "turns out to be good enough" annoying and frustrating, good! You're encouraged to work it out more carefully to verify that you get the same final answer I get.

something about how exponents and logarithms work—they are inverse functions. So taking the logarithm, *base 2*, of both sides, works as follows:

Equation 6-15

$$n > 2^{i-1} \Rightarrow$$
$$\log_2 n > \log_2 2^{i-1} \Rightarrow$$
$$\log_2 n > i - 1 \Rightarrow$$
$$\log_2 n + 1 > i$$

Equation 6-15 tells us that the number of levels (i in the equation) is no more than the base-2 log of n. (Remember where else we saw a base-2 log?)

Now we're ready to put it together to get the best case performance of Quicksort. There are $\log_2 n$ levels, and for each level there are fewer than n comparisons; multiplying these together gives us $n\log_2 n$. So Quicksort is an $O(n\log n)$ algorithm in the best case, and an $O(n^2)$ algorithm in the worst case. That's a big gap; for example: $1024 \times \log_2 1024 = 2^{10}\log_2 2^{10} = 1024 \times 10 = 10,240$, while $1024^2 = 1,048,576$. Where does the average performance of Quicksort lie in this gap?

Quicksort on Average

Perhaps surprisingly, the average case performance of Quicksort can be shown to be the same order of magnitude as the best case, that is, $O(n\log n)$. The average case analysis is not terribly difficult, but it's outside the scope of this book (see, for example, Cormen et al.). Instead, here's an informal argument that should give you a feel for why the performance of Quicksort is so good. Let's assume that when we pick the pivot, it's just as likely to split the array in any one position as in any other. This assumption of **uniform likelihood** cannot be as easily justified as one might like, so we'll come back to it later, but it will serve us for now. Because the pivot split is equally likely to fall anywhere between first and last we expect that about half the time it will fall somewhere "near the middle," as illustrated in Figure 6-10.

Figure 6-10   *Uniformly distributed pivot splits near the middle half the time*

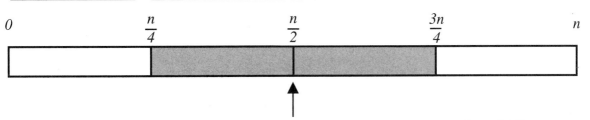

about half the time, the pivot falls in the shaded area around the middle

Recall that a pivot near the middle is "good" and a pivot near the end is "bad." Let's be pessimistic and assume that the pivots near the middle are actually at the $n/4$ position (or $3n/4$, it makes no difference) and that the pivots not near the middle are as bad as possible and fall right at the end of the range. If that's the case, then every other split is going to partition the array into pieces of size $(1/4)n$ and $(3/4)n$ or better, or to put it another way, we eliminate a fourth of the items at every other level in the tree (at level 2, 4, 6, ...). Now we ask, how deep can this tree be? In other words, how long can the sequence in Equation 6-16 run until you have only a single element?

Equation 6-16
$$n, \frac{3}{4}n, \left(\frac{3}{4}\right)^2 n, \left(\frac{3}{4}\right)^3 n, \ldots$$

Using the same logic as Equation 6-15, we can turn this around and ask how many times we have to multiply $4/3$ by itself to get up to n, as shown in Equation 6-17.

Equation 6-17
$$\left(\frac{4}{3}\right)^i \le n \Rightarrow \log_{4/3}\left(\frac{4}{3}\right)^i \le \log_{4/3}n \Rightarrow i \le \log_{4/3}n$$

Compare this to Equation 6-15. In both cases we have a log of n, but with different bases. However, as we discussed back in the note 7 of Chapter 5, a logarithm in one base can be converted to any other base by multiplying by a constant; in other words, the base doesn't affect the fundamental *shape* of the function curve. Thus we can conclude from this rather informal argument that Quicksort is, on average, an $O(n\log n)$ algorithm, which explains the outstanding run times in Table 6-1.

Remember, though, that we made a big assumption:

The pivot position is uniformly distributed; that is, it's equally likely to split the array at any position.

Is this reasonable? Well, consider the worst case example in Exercise 6-13, when the array is in sorted or reverse-sorted order, Quicksort requires $O(n^2)$ comparisons. But sorted order is hardly random; there might be certain environments in which such an ordering occurs frequently, and for these environments the performance of Quicksort would be disappointing. In Exercises 6-15 through 6-18, we'll look at alternative methods for picking the pivot that avoid this problem.

Exercise 6-14   Create a recursion tree for Quicksort when the input array is [7,6,5,4,3,2,1], that is, in reverse-sorted order.

Exercise 6-15 As we saw above, if the partition function always picks the first element as the pivot, then a sorted or reverse-sorted list yields the worst case. In many situations, the sorted or reverse-sorted lists may come up more often than you would expect if the orders are random, so you could argue that it's a bad idea to pick the first element as the pivot. Instead, you could pick the middle element: `a[(last - first) / 2]`. Trace the operation of a Quicksort with the pivot chosen as the middle element to verify that a reverse-sorted list no longer results in worst case performance.

Exercise 6-16 Picking the middle element as the pivot, as discussed in Exercise 6-15, eliminates the reversed-sorted list as the worst case, but there still exists an $O(n^2)$ worst case input. Show an input of size 7 that has worst case performance when picking the middle element.

Exercise 6-17 Suppose you pick the pivot at random rather than from a fixed position. Then as long as all the input elements are distinct, that is, as long as none of the integers occurs more than once, no input will always result in the worst case performance. After all, a "randomized" algorithm will behave differently each time. Modify the partition function to create a randomized Quicksort. Can you see any *disadvantage* to this approach?

Exercise 6-18 The strategy discussed in Exercise 6-17 works to prevent the worst case when all elements are distinct. However, suppose that the input consists of an array that contains all the same number. Can you suggest a modification to Quicksort that will prevent poor performance in this case?

6.4 How Is Recursion Implemented?

So far we've been treating recursion like magic—if you get the logic right and translate it into a C++ program, it works! You really *don't* need to understand how the compiler handles a recursive program in order to use the technique, but most students have a rather uneasy feeling about the whole thing until they get a good understand of how recursion is implemented. In this section, you'll get the rough idea; once you've learned about an ADT called the *stack*, covered in Chapter 8, we'll return to the topic in more detail.

6.4.1 What Happens When a Function Is Called?

Let's start by reviewing what happens when one function calls another in C++, or any other similar language such as Pascal or Ada. We'll illustrate this with the useless Code Example 6-8. What happens when function b calls function a, in the line with the comment // ***? Because the computer has to stop executing function b and start executing function a, but come back to function b later, it needs to store everything about function b that it's going to need. In particular, it must store the values stored in any local variables or parameters—in this case, x, y, and z—plus the place to start executing upon return, which is the assignment of the return value of function a to the variable y. Then it has to **bind** a value to the parameter for function a; in this case, the parameter x in function a is bound to the value of the variable z in function b. Finally, control is transferred to function a, which is executed to completion. At this point, all the old values of the parameters and variables in function b are restored, the return value from function a is placed into the variable y, and the computation continues with the next line of function b. Sounds complicated, but by now you have a pretty good idea that this is going on; otherwise, you would have a lot of trouble writing programs with functions that call other functions.

Code Example 6-8   *Sample program to illustrate function calls*

```
// cx6-8.cpp
// Code Example 6-8.cpp: function calls

int a(int x)
{
    return x+x;
}

int b(int x)
{
    int z(x + 3);
    int y(a(z)); // ***
    z = x * y;
    return z;
}
```

6.4.2   What Happens When a Recursive Function Is Called?

Now let's compare what happens when a simple recursive program executes. You might want to start by tracing Code Example 6-9 with various values so that you can understand what it does. Just like a regular function call, a recursive function call requires that the computer store everything about the current state of execution: the values of the local variables and parameters and the line to return to when execution is complete.

Code Example 6-9   *Sample program to illustrate recursive calls*

```
// cx6-9.cpp
// Code Example 6-9: Recursive function call

int f(int x)
{
```

```
    int y;
    if (x == 0)
        return 1;
    else {
        y = 2 * f(x-1);
        return y + 1;
    }
}
```

To help you visualize the operation of a recursive call, take a look at Figure 6-11, which traces the call f(3). Each box represents one of the recursive calls; f(3), f(2), f(1), and f(0). When the computer reaches the recursive call, it stores the state, suspends execution of the function, and transfers to what is, in effect, a new copy of the recursive function. Except for the fact that the calling and called functions have the same name, you can see that there is really no difference between recursive and nonrecursive function calls. Once you become comfortable with this idea, the "magic" nature of recursion starts to fall away, and you can use it as a tool without a second thought.

6.4.3   Is Recursion Inefficient?

While nobody disputes that recursion is the best way to describe many algorithms, such as Quicksort, there is some controversy about whether recursive functions belong in quality software. Any recursive algorithm can be written as a nonrecursive program, although the conversion of an algorithm like Quicksort to a nonrecursive form is hardly trivial. My position is that modern systems generally execute recursive routines efficiently, so that there is no reason, in most cases, to remove recursion from programs. For example, I compared recursive and nonrecursive versions of binary search, compiled on an SGI Indy R4000SC running Irix 5.2. Over many runs of the program, the performance of the two versions was very similar; in some cases, the recursive version actually executed faster than the nonrecursive routine. On average, the recursive program was about 2% slower than the nonrecursive program, a difference that will be virtually undetectable in most environments.

However, there are situations in which a recursive routine can be extremely slow. We saw an example in Code Example 6-3, which computed the *choose* function. When this program runs, certain values of the function are called many times, leading to much redundant computation and a very inefficient approach. It's the redundancy that's the problem, not the recursion itself.

Figure 6-11   *Execution of Code Example 6-9 for* `f(3)`

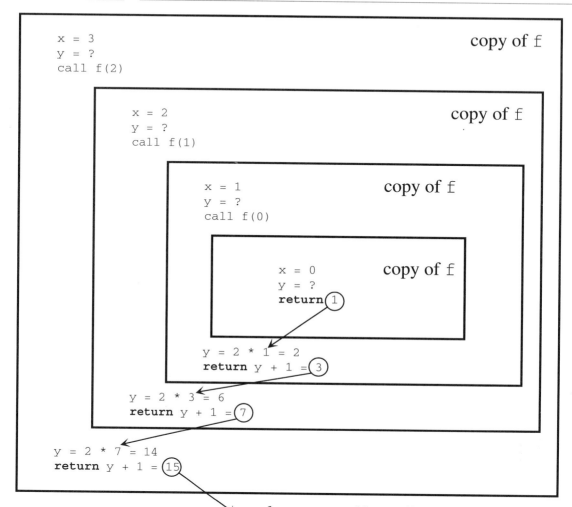

value returned by call is 15

The programmer must also recognize that recursive routines may require more RAM than non-recursive programs.[4] That's because space is required to store the information about the state of the function at the point where the recursive call is

---

4. This is generally true for languages such as C++, C, Pascal, Java, and Ada, but not for the language Scheme, which is optimized for recursion and which consumes no more memory for a properly formed recursive routine than would be required by a loop.

made. If the recursion tree is deep, if there is a lot of local information to maintain, and if space is an important consideration—as it often is on a microprocessor—the programmer may need to look carefully at this issue and in some cases may need to look for a non-recursive alternative.

In general, therefore, you can't say that recursion is inefficient. However, the programmer must have a good understanding of the potential downfalls of redundant computation and excessive memory consumption when using a recursive program. I'd suggest that you use the following rule of thumb:

> *If you have a recursive algorithm, try the recursive program and test its performance. Only if there appears to be a problem should you worry about looking for a nonrecursive alternative.*

In the remainder of this book you'll use recursion frequently in the design and implementation of data structures.

Exercise 6-19   Trace Code Example 6-9 for the call f(4).

Exercise 6-20   Find a closed-form expression for the function f in Code Example 6-9.

Chapter Summary

- A recursive solution to a problem is stated in terms of a smaller version of the same problem and a nonrecursive base case.
- Functions can be defined by recursive definitions, which can be translated directly into recursive programs.
- Recursion can be used to create Linear Search and Binary Search algorithms.
- Quicksort is a recursive sorting algorithm with $O(n\log n)$ average case performance.
- Compilers implement recursive function calls in much the same way they implement nonrecursive ones.

Programming Laboratory Problems

Lab 6-1   Modify the recursive binarySearch function so that each time it's called it prints the values of first and last. Create a driver that creates a large (at least 10,000 elements) array of ints and calls your modified binarySearch. Try searching for targets in the list and targets not in the list.

Lab 6-2　　Add code to Quicksort to keep track of the number of comparisons, and write a driver that calls Quicksort with random data. Build a table of the comparisons performed by Quicksort, similar to Table 6-1. How do your results compare with mine? Graph the number of comparisons. How does your graph compare to the predicted average performance of Quicksort?

Lab 6-3　　Using the Timer class[5] and your driver, experiment with the recursive and nonrecursive versions of Binary Search on your system. You should use a fairly big list (say, 10,000 items) and a reasonable number of searches (say, 1000). How does the relative performance of the two searches compare?

Lab 6-4　　MergeSort is an algorithm that sorts an array with $O(n\log n)$ worst case performance. (For a proof, see an algorithms book such as Cormen et al.) MergeSort consists of two parts:

1. A recursive part that breaks the array into two subparts, makes recursive calls to sort each of the two subparts, and then calls a merge function to merge them back together.

2. A merge, that takes two sorted subarrays and merges them into a single sorted array

The MergeSort algorithm is shown in Algorithm 6-2.

Algorithm 6-2　　　　*MergeSort*

```
MergeSort(a, first, last)
Precondition: Input is an array, a, and two indices first and last.
if (first >= last)
        then there's nothing left to be sorted, so just return
else
        mid = (first + last)/2;
        MergeSort(a, first, mid)
        MergeSort(a, mid+1, last)
        Merge(a, first, mid, last)
Postcondition: Array a is sorted from index first to index last.
```

To sort an array of *n* elements, you call `MergeSort(a, 0, n-1)`.

To complete the MergeSort project:

1. Write a Merge function with the following specification:

```
void merge(int a[], int first, int mid, int last)
```

---

5. See the source code distribution for this book.

Preconditions: a is an array with the items from `first` up to `mid` sorted, and the items from `mid+1` up to `last` are sorted.

Postconditions: a_{post} contains the same items from a_{pre} and is sorted from `first` up to `last`.

Note that there may be other parts of the array between 0 and `first-1` and between `last+1` and the end of the array, but the merge function should leave these elements undisturbed.

For example, suppose a = {1, 3, 6, 2, 8, 9}, `first`=0, and `mid`=2. Then after calling merge, a = {1, 2, 3, 6, 8, 9}.

2. Write a test plan for merge, and a driver, and test your merge function thoroughly.

3. Write the `mergeSort` function:

```
void mergeSort(int a[], int first, int last)
```

4. Write a test plan for `mergeSort`, and a driver, and test your `mergeSort` function thoroughly.

Lab 6-5 Write a recursive function, `binPrint`, with the following specification:

```
void binPrint(int i, int length)
```

Precondition: i is an integer whose binary representation is `length` digits long.

Postcondition: None.

Side Effect: Prints the binary representation of i, including leading zeros.

For example, `binPrint(14,5)` would print out: 01110.

Use the following observations to create the recursive function: if `length == 0`, then you do nothing. If `length > 0`, then you first print the results of `binPrint(i/2,length-1)` and then print either a 0 or 1 depending on the last digit in i. For example, using `binPrint(14,5)`, you first (recursively) print `binPrint(7,4)`, which is 0111, and then print, in this case, a 0. Write the `binPrint` function, a test plan, and a test driver and test your `binPrint` function thoroughly.

Lab 6-6 A *Gray Code* is a sequence of binary numbers in which each number differs in exactly one digit from the number before it. For example, a Gray Code of size 3 is: 000, 001, 011, 010, 110, 111, 101, 100. You can write a recursive program for computing Gray Codes by using the following observations:

- A Gray Code of size 1 is 0, 1.

- A Gray Code of size *i* can be computed by computing a Gray Code of size *i*–1, then adding first a 0 to the beginning of each number (using the original order for the *i*–1 code) and then adding a 1 to the beginning of each number (reversing the order for the *i*–1 code). For example, a Gray Code of size 2 is: 00, 01, 11, 10. To get the Gray Code of size 3, you first add a 0 to the front of each item, giving 000, 001, 011, 010, then a 1 (with the items reversed), giving 110, 111, 101, 100. This gives you the Gray Code of size 3 that you see above.

Write a function grayCode with the following specification:

```
void grayCode(int a[], int n)
```

Precondition: None.

Postcondition: a contains the items in a Gray Code of length n.

Write grayCode and a driver. The driver has to allocate an array big enough to store the final result. A Gray Code of length *n* has 2^n items. Note that the results are ints, so if you simply print them you won't see them in binary. If you have a bin-Print function such as described in the last project, you can use it to print the results in binary.

Lab 6-7 The Towers of Hanoi puzzle consists of a set of graduated disks and three pegs, as shown in Figure 6-12. The goal is to move all the disks one at a time from peg 1 to peg 3, using peg 2 as necessary and without ever putting a larger disk on top of a smaller disk.

Figure 6-12   *The Towers of Hanoi, initial configuration*

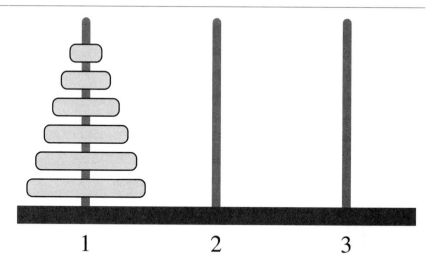

The recursive algorithm works like this. First, move every disk except the largest from peg 1 to peg 2 (using the same recursive algorithm, but for a smaller problem). Then, move the largest disk to peg 3. Now, again using the recursive algorithm, move all the disks from peg 2 to peg 3.

Write the following function:

```
void towers(int n, int fromPeg, int toPeg)
```

that prints the moves required to move n disks from the `fromPeg` to the `toPeg`. For example, `towers(1, 1, 2)` will print

```
move disk from peg 1 to peg 2
```

and `towers(3, 1, 3)` will print:

```
move disk from peg 1 to peg 3
move disk from peg 1 to peg 2
move disk from peg 3 to peg 2
move disk from peg 1 to peg 3
move disk from peg 2 to peg 1
move disk from peg 2 to peg 3
move disk from peg 1 to peg 3
```

Chapter Vocabulary

back substitution	pivot
balanced tree	proof by induction
base case	Quicksort
bind	recursion tree
closed form	recursive
combinatorics	recursive definition
inductive hypothesis	recursive routine
level (of a tree)	substitution
n choose k	uniform likelihood

Chapter 7 Lists

Overview

An introduction to the List ADT and its uses, dynamic memory allocation, and programming with linked lists.

Chapter Objectives

1. To understand and apply the List ADT.
2. To implement a List class using an array.
3. To implement a List class using a linked list.
4. To use dynamic allocation and pointers in C++.
5. To understand variations on the linked list.
6. To create a class with overloaded operators.

7.1   Problem: A Membership Management Program

At the last meeting of the Saturday Social Society, the membership chair asked you to put together a program to keep track of the members. "With all the time you spend on that data structures course, this ought to be a snap for you!" After a brief discussion of the requirements for the program, you head off to the lab to start coding it up in C++. But before you get there, the nagging voice of your instructor breaks through: "Design first, code later!" You decide it's worth it to stop for some refreshment while you think about how to write the program.

You could describe this sort of program as data processing. You realize that a key design decision is the representation of the list of club members. You also realize that you still have a big assignment due in Data Structures, not to mention 200 pages to read for History and a French vocabulary test on Tuesday. Maybe poking around first on the Internet to see whether someone else has already written such a program would make more sense than writing your own code. But you *are* interested in writing the program; it will give you a chance to put some of the new stuff you've learned into practice. It occurs to you that you might be able to find components or ADTs you can reuse to build the program.

Finding a Membership List ADT seems unlikely; it's too specialized. But you vaguely recall that there was something about lists in your textbook. And you can use that string class the professor gave out to store the names of the members. Instead of going to the lab next, you decide to head back to the dorm and look under your bed for that data structures book and check out the chapter on the *List ADT.*

7.2   The List ADT

You are probably already familiar with programs that include the representation of a list. For example, consider a program that maintains a list of names and phone numbers. You might have written such a program, using an array of names and a parallel array of phone numbers, or an array of records or perhaps an array of objects. In fact, you might have gotten the idea that a (one-dimensional) array and a list are more or less the same thing. In this chapter, we'll take a more abstract view of the list and see that an array is only one possible implementation of a List ADT. Furthermore, we'll look at variations on the List ADT and analyze the operations that we wish to perform upon them.

What operations are needed to define a list? Certainly we need a way to put things into the list and a way to look at the list to see what's in it. Depending upon the application, we might need to be able to remove things from the list. Many other operations, such as checking the size of the list, could be defined. To keep things simple, let's start with a small set of operations, which we can expand upon as needed.

ADT 7-1

List ADT

Characteristics:

- A List L stores items of some type, called ListElementType.

Operations:

void L.insert(ListElementType elem)

Precondition: None.
Postcondition: $L_{post} = L_{pre}$ with an instance of elem added to L_{post}.

bool L.first(ListElementType &elem)

Precondition: None.
Postcondition: If the list is empty, none. Otherwise, the variable elem contains the first item in L; the "next" item to be returned is the second in L.
Returns: True if and only if there is at least one element in L.

bool L.next(ListElementType &elem)

Precondition: The "first" operation has been called at least once.
Postcondition: Variable elem contains the next item in L, if there is one, and the next counter advances by one; if there is no next element, none.
Returns: True if and only if there was a next item.

List Traversal The process of accessing each item in a list is called **list traversal**. The `first` and `next` operations provide a method of list traversal. The rigorous computer scientist would find the postconditions for `first` and `next` to be excessively informal; I encourage you to write a formal description of `first` and `next`. It turns out that it's a lot easier to use these operations than to define them. Later on we'll write the membership program using `first` and `next`. In the meantime, here's a code fragment illustrating their use:

```
void printList(List L)
{
  ListElementType elem;
  bool avail; // was there a "next" element available?
  avail = L.first(elem);
  while (avail) {
    cout << elem << endl;
    avail = L.next(elem);
  }
}
```

Those who prefer the more compact idiom of C++ would write the loop this way:

```
for (avail = L.first(elem); avail; avail = L.next(elem))
    cout << elem << endl;
```

Exercise 7-1   Define some additional operations that might be useful for a List ADT.

7.3   Implementing Lists

7.3.1   A Header File for the List ADT

In order to share the definition of the List ADT with its client functions, store the declarations of all the operations for the list in a header (.h) file. These declarations, or prototypes, will need to have a definition for `ListElementType`. By modifying the definition of `ListElementType` we can vary the type that the list can store. We call an ADT that can store elements of various types **generic.** C++ has a more flexible method for creating generic ADTs using templates; however, because the syntax for templates is rather tricky and distracting we've deferred it until Chapter 8. The contents of the header file, `cx7-1.h`, are shown in Code Example 7-1. We've omitted, for the moment, portions of the header file that depend specifically upon the way in which we choose to implement the list; we'll come back and fill those in later.

Code Example 7-1   *List ADT header file, with implementation-specific lines omitted*

```
// cx7-1.h
// Code Example 7-1: List ADT header file

#include "dslib.h"

// the type of the individual elements in the list is defined here
typedef int ListElementType;

// implementation specific stuff here

class List {
public:
    List();
    void insert(const ListElementType & elem);
    bool first(ListElementType & elem);
    bool next(ListElementType & elem);
private:
    // implementation specific stuff here
};
```

Changing the type in the `typedef` line will change the base type for the List ADT. The header file as shown doesn't tie us to any particular implementation of List—a `.cpp` file will contain the data structures and algorithms that implement the list. Both the client and the implementation will include `cx7-1.h`, ensuring that the declarations are consistent.

Formal Parameters for Classes

You might notice that we've declared the parameter to `insert` as a "constant reference." That is, the ampersand (&) before the formal parameter `elem` indicates that `elem` should be passed by reference. The keyword `const` tells the compiler (and the programmer reading the header file) that the `insert` function is not allowed to modify the contents of `elem`. Recall that call-by-value—passing a copy of the actual parameter—is the default scheme for C++. Although making a copy of a simple variable such as an `int` or a `char` works fine, consider what happens when you pass a more complicated object, such as a string. Copying a string requires, at the minimum, a call to a special class function called a ***copy constructor***. Sophisticated class design requires every class to have a copy constructor, which defines how to copy an object. As the designer of the list class, you have no way of knowing how much work the copy constructor does, but you can avoid it in the parameter passing by using ***reference parameters***, which pass the address of the object rather than making a copy of it. Hence, from now on we'll always use reference parameters with our classes.

However, if you just use a reference parameter, the client has no assurance that you will not *change* the contents of the object that it passes to your class function. If you have no intention to change the object—which is the case for the `insert` function — you can make this explicit with the keyword `const`. To summarize, we'll use the following rules for parameters to class functions:

1. Use value parameters only for simple, built-in types like `int` or `char`; otherwise, use reference parameters.

2. Use `const` for parameters that the class will not change; omit the `const` only when you wish to indicate that the class may change the contents of the passed object.

Using this form to declare your parameters should have no effect on the underlying implementation. However, if you have a parameter declared `const` and you have code within your function that can modify the object, the compiler will complain. But then, if you're going to modify the object, you shouldn't declare it `const`, so the compiler's just keeping you honest.

dslib.h

The header file `dslib.h` contains code that allows us to simplify and standardize the code examples in the book. Among other things, certain compiler and platform dependencies are dealt with in `dslib.h`, so that a single version of the code will work the same on these various compilers and platforms. For example, current com-

List constructor

pilers define a ***boolean type***, `bool`, that we use throughout the book. For older compilers, the `dslib.h` file defines the type `bool`. The `dslib.h` file also provides some conveniences, such as including `<iostream.h>`, since we nearly always need it. We'll use `dslib.h` along with most of our ADTs.

You probably noticed that there's an extra function in the class definition in Code Example 7-1, called `List`, that we didn't include in the ADT description. The `List` function is a constructor, originally introduced in Chapter 4. Recall that a constructor function gets called one time when a class instance—in this case, a particular list—is created. The `List` constructor will be quite useful in our implementation.

Exercise 7-2

Even though passing the argument to `insert` eliminates one call to the copy constructor, a call to `insert` will still require copying the object when it runs. Why?

7.3.2   Implementation via Arrays

The simplest implementation of a List ADT is also the most obvious: the elements of the list correspond one-to-one with entries in an array. This implementation is called a ***linear list*** or ***contiguous list***.[1] The linear list consists of three parts: the array for storing the entries (`listArray`), a counter that keeps track of the number of items in the list (`numberOfElements`), and a counter to track the "next" item to be returned (`currentPosition`). These variables will be incorporated within the `private` section of the class definition. In addition, our initial implementation of the list will require us to specify a fixed size for the array that stores the entries; the constant `maxListSize` serves this purpose. The completed header file and implementation file are shown in Code Examples 7-2 and 7-3.

Code Example 7-2   *Header file for List implemented as an array*

```
// cx7-2.h
// Code Example 7-2: header file for list implemented with an array

#include "dslib.h"

// the type of the individual elements in the list is defined here
typedef int ListElementType;

// the maximum size for lists is defined here
const int maxListSize = 1000;
```

---

1. *Contiguous* literally means "touching"; in computer terms, two data items are contiguous if they are next to each other in memory.

```cpp
class List {
public:
    List();
    void insert(const ListElementType & elem);
    bool first(ListElementType & elem);
    bool next(ListElementType & elem);
private:
    ListElementType listArray[maxListSize];
    int numberOfElements;
    int currentPosition;
};
```

Code Example 7-3   *Implementation file for List as an array*

```cpp
// cx7-3.cpp
// Code Example 7-3: implementation file, list implemented with an array

#include "cx7-2.h"

List::List()
{
    // initialize to an empty list
    numberOfElements = 0;
    currentPosition = -1;
}

void List::insert(const ListElementType & elem)
{
    assert(numberOfElements < maxListSize);
    listArray[numberOfElements] = elem;
    numberOfElements++;
}

bool List::first(ListElementType & elem)
{
    if (numberOfElements == 0)
        return false;
    else {
        currentPosition = 0;
        elem = listArray[currentPosition];
        return true;
    }
}

bool List::next(ListElementType & elem)
{
    // with proper use, currentPosition should always be
    // greater than or equal to zero
```

```
   assert(currentPosition >= 0);
   if (currentPosition >= numberOfElements - 1)
      return false;
   else {
      currentPosition++;
      elem = listArray[currentPosition];
      return true;
   }
}
```

The `List` constructor function sets up the initial values of `currentPosition` and `numberOfElements`. The `insert` function puts a new element at position `numberOfElements` in the list. Note that when there are, for example, 5 elements in the list, they will be stored in array positions 0 through 4. That's why when `numberOfElements` is 5, the right place to put the next element is at position 5.

Iterator Functions　The variable `currentPosition` maintains a position within the list, used by the implementations of `first` and `next`. Each time an item is returned, `currentPosition` is incremented by 1. We refer to `first` and `next` as ***iterator functions***, and the variable `currentPosition` as a ***cursor***. Later on, we'll see a more sophisticated and flexible approach using iterator *classes,* but you can go a long way with the simple implementation given here.

There is one unfortunate wrinkle in the implementation that doesn't correspond to the abstract notion of a list. If a list is implemented as an array, there is a fixed maximum number of elements that can be inserted. If an attempt is made to insert an additional element, it will be stored in a memory location that the compiler has not allocated for the array `listArray`. To guard against this we'll use the `assert` function, to enforce the precondition that the size of the list is at most `maxListSize`. Specifically, if the addition is to succeed, the value of `numberOfElements` has to still be less than or equal to `maxListSize` after the new element is added, yielding the condition in the assert below:

```
   assert(numberOfElements < maxListSize);
```

Code Example 7-4 shows a simple client to illustrate the use of the List ADT. Note that this client would work not only with the linear list we've just defined but also with the various linked lists implementations we discuss later, all of which implement a List ADT.

Code Example 7-4 *Simple client for a List ADT*

```cpp
// cx7-4.cpp
// Code Example 7-4: simple List client

#include "cx7-2.h" // header for Linear List; ListElementType is int

int main()
{
    List l;
    ListElementType i; // header file defines this to be int
    cout << "Enter items to add to list, add 0 to stop: ";
    cin >> i;
    while (i != 0) {
        l.insert(i);
        cin >> i;
    }
    cout << "Here are the items in the list.\n";
    ListElementType elem;
    bool notEmpty(l.first(elem));
    while (notEmpty) {
        cout << elem << endl;
        notEmpty = l.next(elem);
    }
    return 0;
}
```

In the next section, we develop techniques that will permit us to eliminate a fixed size limitation on the list.

Exercise 7-3 Compile Code Example 7-3 and Code Example 7-4, link them, and run the resulting executable with various data.

Exercise 7-4 Write a program that creates a list, inserts the integers 1 through 10, and then iterates through the list twice, printing its contents.

Exercise 7-5 Write a program that creates two lists, L1 and L2, puts the characters 1 through 25 into L1, iterates through list L1 and copies its contents into list L2, and then iterates through list L2 and prints its contents.

Exercise 7-6 Make a copy of Code Example 7-2, and modify it so that it uses char rather than int. Make any changes required to Code Example 7-4 in order to work with the char type, then compile, link, and run.

Exercise 7-7 Experiment with your compiler to find out the approximate largest size you can specify for the constant maxListSize. Does it make a difference how many objects of type List you declare? Now change ListElementType to double; how does this affect the bounds on maxListSize?

Exercise 7-8   Using the String class and the List class, create a list of strings. Use the list to store
                  the names of the months (in the language of your choice); print them to verify that it
                  works.

7.3.3   Implementation via Linked Lists

The exact correspondence between logical and physical structure means that you
can implement a list with an array in a straightforward way. However, the requirement that array elements be stored in physically contiguous memory means that the
program must preallocate all the space that might be required; if 100 elements are
assigned to the array and the program needs space for 101, there is usually no good
solution, since the next memory location after the end of the array is typically allocated for some other use. This means that programs may need to allocate more space
than they really need and even then may fail when memory requirements grow. In
Section 7.6, we'll see that rather than specifying the array size when *compiling* the
program, we can let the program choose the size while it's *running*, but the point remains that, once chosen, the size remains fixed.

Certain types of insertion operations cause other problems for arrays. As long as we
always add new items to the end of an array, the insert operation is quite efficient; in
fact, it requires constant time regardless of the size of the list ($O(1)$). However, to
add an element to the *beginning* of the list without changing the order of the other
items in the list requires moving every element one position to the right, as illustrated in Figure 7-1. Because in the worst case every item in the list might have to be
moved, an insert operation of this kind is $O(n)$ —a lot worse than $O(1)$. For some
lists, such as the Inorder List in Section 7.4, we need to be able to make insertions
anywhere in the list, quickly.

Figure 7-1   *Inserting an item at beginning forces items to shift to the right*

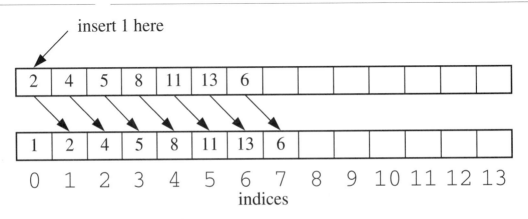

We can overcome these limitations by separating the logical from the physical, allowing the items in a list to be stored at various locations in memory. When adding a new item to the list, we can use any memory location that is available. Thus as long as the program has adequate memory available, it can extend the list. Note, however, that now that we are not storing the list items one after another in memory, we must have some way of figuring out how to get from one item to the next. We do this by keeping, along with each list item, the location of the next item in the list. This special pointer to the next item is called a **link**, analogous to a link in a chain. Hence the name **linked list**.

Before we get into the details, it helps to strengthen your intuitive understanding of linked lists with some pictures. In Figure 7-2, we present the list (7, 12, 5) in abstract form. Each box represents a single item and its corresponding link. The arrows, of course, are the links. The slash through the last link box indicates the end of the list. Note that we draw the linked list in its logical order, regardless of the order the items are actually stored in the system's memory; as we shall see, we normally don't concern ourselves with the actual memory locations; instead, we visualize the list using figures like Figure 7-2.

Figure 7-2   *Abstract representation of a linked list*

While the links allow us to navigate through the list from one element to the next, there's an important detail we've omitted: how does a program find the first item in the list? Each linked list has a special **external** or **head link**. We call it an external link because it is not stored in the list. For now, we'll extend the abstract notation to show the external link; the details will come later. Another bit of terminology: we refer to each data/link pair as a **node**. This list has three nodes. Figure 7-3 illustrates the list with the external link, which we label *head*.

Figure 7-3   *Linked list with external link*

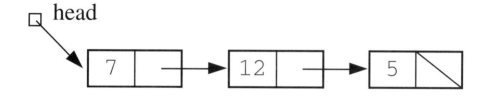

Adding a Node to a
Linked List   Now let's look at what happens when an element is added to this list. Recall that for *this* definition of the List ADT order is not important, so a new element can be added wherever is most convenient for the implementation. You might find it natural to add the element to the end of the list, but a moment's reflection will show that this causes a problem. In order to add to the end, we need to change the link field for the last node in the list. Access to a node can be made only via a link; thus to get to the last node in the list we have to follow every link, starting with the external link. That may not seem too bad for a list with 3 nodes, but what about a list with 300, 3000, or 300,000 nodes? On the other hand, no matter how long the list, we can access the beginning immediately, and add a new node with just a few simple operations. Using the language of asymptotic complexity, adding a node at the beginning of the linked list is $O(1)$, while adding to the end is $O(n)$—exactly the reverse of the situation for the array implementation.

Adding a new node is a four-step process:

1. Create a new node. (The new node represents memory that's currently available; how this memory is found will be addressed later.)

2. Copy the data value into the new node.

3. Copy the external link into the link field of the new node so that the new node is linked to the old first node of the list.

4. Change the external link to point to the new node.

Figure 7-4 and Figure 7-5 illustrate these steps pictorially, for adding the data item "9" to the list.

Figure 7-4   *Adding an element: Steps 1 and 2*

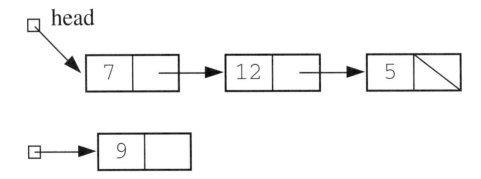

Figure 7-5 *Adding an element: Steps 3 and 4*

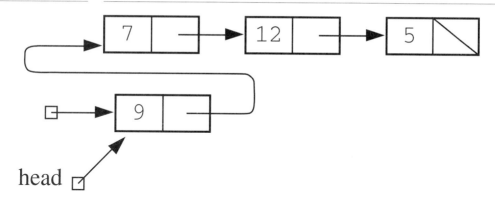

head

Adding to the End of the List

The process we've just presented adds an item to the front of the list, but what if you want to add at the end? Whenever you want to modify part of a linked list, you need to have a pointer to the part you want to modify. If you plan to add items at the end, you'll need to maintain a pointer to the end, or "tail," of a list. Without a tail pointer, you would have to follow through the links from the beginning to the end each time you want to add at the end. A list with a pointer to the beginning (the head pointer) and to the end (the tail pointer) is shown in Figure 7-6.

Figure 7-6 *Adding an element to the end of a list: Steps 1 and 2*

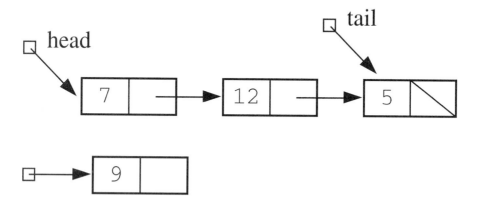

tail

head

When you add an item to the list, the first two steps are exactly the same as adding at the beginning. The next two steps are shown in Figure 7-7. The next pointer on the last item in the list is modified to point to the new final node, and the tail pointer is updated accordingly. Note also that you have to be sure to set the next field to mark the end of the list.

Figure 7-7   *Adding an element to the tail of a list: Steps 3, 4, and 5*

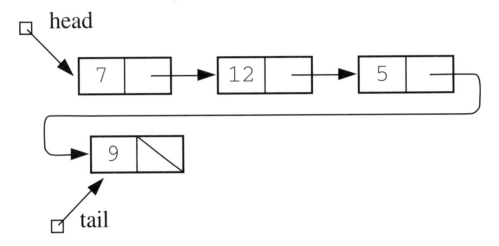

Here then are the steps required to add an item to the end of the list:

1. Create a new node.
2. Copy the data value into the new node.
3. Change the next field in the node pointed to by tail so that it points to the new node.
4. Mark the next field in the new node to indicate that it is the end of the list.
5. Move the tail pointer to point to the new node, which is now the last node in the list.

Traversing a Linked List

The process of examining each element of the list, whether to find a particular member or to implement our iterators, is straightforward. A temporary link variable—call it current—keeps track of the node currently under consideration. Initially, current gets a copy of the external link, so it points to the first node in the list. Then, as each node is processed, current is updated by getting a copy of the link to the next node. This is repeated until current is set to the special value that marks the end of the list. This value is called the ***null link***. The following pseudo-code expresses this procedure, called a ***list traversal***. The list traversal algorithm will reappear in many guises as we learn about linked lists.

Algorithm 7-1   *List traversal*

Comment: Assume that "head" is the name of the external link to the list.

current ← head;
while current is not NULL {
    process the node that current points to;
    current ← the link field of the node current points to;
}

Header File Now we examine the C++ code that implements a linked list. Each node will correspond to a `struct`; links are pointers to `struct`s. That is, a link is the location in memory of the node. The C++ compiler will assign these memory locations for us, so we will not manipulate them directly. We have to modify the header file, removing the constant `maxListSize`, which we no longer need, and changing the private section to include the definition of `Node`. The new header file is shown in Code Example 7-5.

Code Example 7-5   *Header file for linked list*[2]

```
// cx7-5.h
// Code Example 7-5: header file for list implemented with a linked list

#include "dslib.h"

// the type of the individual elements in the list is defined here
typedef int ListElementType;

class List {
// Use L to mean "this List"
public:
    List();
    // Precondition: None
    // Postcondition: L is an empty List
    void insert(const ListElementType & elem);
    // Precondition: None
    // Postcondition: Lpost = Lpre with an instance of elem added to Lpost
    bool first(ListElementType & elem);
    // Precondition: None
    // Postcondition: If the list is empty, none. Otherwise, the variable
    //     elem contains the first item in L; the "next" item to be returned
    //     is the second in L.
```

2. Some older C++ compilers will not permit you to nest a `struct` definition inside a class definition. In that case, you'll need to move the `struct` definition up ahead of the start of the List class.

```
    // Returns: true if and only if there is at least one element in L.
    bool next(ListElementType & elem);
    // Precondition: The "first" operation has been called at least once.
    // Postcondition: Variable elem contains the next item in L, if there is one,
    //     and the next counter advances by one; if there is no next element, none.
    // Returns: true if and only if there was a next item.
private:
    struct Node; // declaration without definition
    typedef Node *Link; // use declaration of Node
    struct Node { // now we define Node
        ListElementType elem;
        Link next;
    };
    Link head;
    Link tail;
    Link current;
};
```

The line with the comment "declaration without definition" may look strange to you. Its purpose is to introduce the name "Node" to the compiler so that it can be used in subsequent lines. Because a Link is part of the definition of struct Node and Link is also a pointer to a struct Node there is a circularity that is resolved by the declaration "struct Node;". A couple more points to note about the declaration of Node:

- No nodes or links are created here; the declaration just describes to the compiler what nodes and links will look like.

- The syntax "typedef Node *Link" means that a Link is defined to be a pointer to a Node.

Once we have declared Node and Link we can define objects of those types. Because we are going to add new items at the end of the list we define two external pointers, head and tail, as shown in the following lines:

```
    Link head;
    Link tail;
```

We'll also need a pointer to keep track of the element to return next when using the iterator functions, first and next—that's the purpose of the class variable current.

Null Pointer   For the implementation, let's first consider the constructor. The constructor demonstrates that we initialize the head and current to 0. Why 0? We need a way to specify a pointer that points to nothing—a Null pointer. The idea of a Null pointer, represented by a slash in our figures, is implemented by the integer 0 in C++. Note that 0 is the *only* constant we will ever assign to a pointer in this book. Unless you are a systems programmer with special knowledge about the location of data at particular memory locations, you will never need or want to assign a constant value to a pointer, except for the special case of a Null pointer. Note also that assigning a pointer to 0 doesn't necessarily refer to the memory at location 0, if indeed your particular system allows you to reference memory location 0; rather, it is reserved to indicate the special null pointer.[3] Our constructor is shown as Code Example 7-6.

Code Example 7-6   *Constructor function for List*

```
// cx7-6.cpp
// Code Example 7-6: Constructor function for linked list

#include "cx7-5.h"

List::List()
{
    // Initialize an empty list
    head = 0;
    tail = 0;
    current = 0;
}
```

`insert` *Function*   Code Example 7-7 shows the `insert` function for the linked list. For the moment, don't worry too much about what "`new Node`" does, we'll get to that in a minute. To refer to an item via a pointer, use the C++ symbol "`->`" which is typed as a minus sign followed by a greater-than sign. For example, the expression "`addedNode->elem`" tells the compiler: "use the pointer `addedNode` to find a node and then refer to the field `elem`." Using a pointer variable in this way is called ***dereferencing a pointer***.

Code Example 7-7   `Insert` *function for List*

```
// cx7-7.cpp
// Code Example 7-7: insert function for linked list

#include "cx7-5.h"

void List::insert(const ListElementType & elem)
{
    Link addedNode(new Node);
    assert(addedNode); // check to make sure node was allocated
    addedNode->elem = elem;
    if (head == 0) // list was empty -- set head
```

3. You may see C++ or C code that uses a special macro, NULL, to set pointers to 0. This is a carryover from C Language; in C++, 0 is the preferred way to designate a null pointer. See Plauger 1995, p. 33.

```
      head = addedNode;
  else
      tail->next = addedNode;
  tail = addedNode;
  addedNode->next = 0;
}
```

What happens when the first item is inserted into an empty list? Recall that the constructor set head to 0, so the line

```
      head = addedNode;
```

sets the head pointer to point to the first node in the list. For subsequent additions, the value of the tail pointer gets set to point to the addedNode, as shown in Figure 7-7. Other than the special case for the first item, the steps in the function correspond directly to the steps for adding a new node.

By the way, when you use pointer variables you have to make sure that you never use a Null or 0 pointer to try to refer to an item. If you're lucky, the program will crash! If you're not lucky, the program may corrupt memory, causing your program to crash later or perhaps even locking up a personal computer. One trick that will help you avoid corrupting pointers is to put the name of the pointer on the right when you compare it to zero, that is, use

```
      if (0 == p)
```

not

```
      if (p == 0)
```

What's the advantage? Suppose by mistake you use a single "="; in the first case, the code

```
      if (0 = p)
```

will not compile, while

```
      if (p = 0)
```

will assign the 0 value to the pointer p; later when you dereference p, your program will get into trouble.

Exercise 7-9   Draw a diagram illustrating a linked list containing the items 'a', 'b', 'c', and 'd'.

Exercise 7-10   Draw a sequence of linked list diagrams that illustrate each step in the insert function.

Exercise 7-11 Enter the following program into your system and test it to find out what happens when you dereference a Null pointer. *(WARNING: Depending on your system, this program could cause it to lock up or reboot, so be sure you've saved your work before you run this program.)*

```
int main()
{
   int * p(0); // p is a pointer to an int, initialized to 0
   *p = 1; // dereference it
   return 0;
}
```

Exercise 7-12 Enter the following programs to confirm that the code works as discussed above. The warning in Exercise 7-11 applies here as well.

```
// safe test of pointer with 0
int main()
{
   int * p; // p is a pointer to an int, initialized to 0
   if (0 = p) // obviously, == was intended
     cout << "zero pointer\n";
   else
     cout << "non-zero pointer\n";
   return 0;
}

// unsafe test of pointer with 0
int main()
{
   int * p; // p is a pointer to an int, initialized to 0
   if (p = 0) // obviously, == was intended
     cout << "zero pointer\n";
   else
     cout << "non-zero pointer\n";
   return 0;
}
```

7.3.4   Dynamic Memory Allocation

We now address the question, "Where do new nodes come from?" Somehow, there has to be a way to find out where free memory is available for the node and allocate it. You can write your own memory allocation routines, but it's difficult to do it right. Instead, C++ has a built-in operator, **new**, that requests the compiler to take care of this for us. The pool of memory available for allocation is called the *free store*. The new operator finds a block of free memory of the appropriate size, marks it so that it won't be used for something else, and returns a pointer to it.[4]

Consider for a moment what happens when you declare a global variable; for example:

```
int i;
```

The compiler has to allocate memory for the variable i. For any implementation of C++, an int occupies some fixed amount of memory, 4 bytes. So the compiler knows, when it compiles the program, that it must set aside the appropriate number of bytes for i. This is called *static memory allocation*. The term static is used, among those who work with programming languages, for any process that the compiler performs at compilation time, that is, before the program actually runs. By contrast, the creation of a node with new occurs during the execution of the program. This process is called *dynamic memory allocation*.

To use the new operator with the insert function, we use the following code:

```
Link addedNode = new Node;
```

As promised, we have eliminated the restriction that the size of the list be bounded by a fixed size. However, that doesn't mean that all lists will fit on all machines—after all, on any given machine, there is some limit to the amount of memory that a program can allocate. So while there is no fixed limitation, the maximum size of the list is still bounded, and we still have to be concerned about running out of memory. If the new operator successfully allocates memory for the node, it will return the location in memory; if no space is available, the value returned is 0.[5] Thus we can use assert and check the value of addedNode:

```
assert(addedNode)
```

If any memory has been allocated, addedNode will be non-zero, the assertion will be satisfied, and the insertion will take place. But if new fails to allocate memory, addedNode will be zero, the assertion will fail, and the program will halt with an appropriate message. Depending on the purpose of your program, simply halting the program may or may not be acceptable behavior, but it's *always* better than continu-

---

4. The C library function malloc is still available in C++, but it should *not* be used except by experts, because it will not work correctly with classes.

5. The current C++ standard requires that "new" will *raise an exception* when no memory is available. At this time, few compilers implement this.

ing with a bad pointer because attempting to use 0 as if it were a valid pointer leads to unpredictable results.

The complete code for the linked list implementation is presented in Code Example 7-8. Note that the interface for the two implementations—linear and linked—is exactly the same. Code that uses the List ADT will not need to be modified at all, except to choose the appropriate header file.

Code Example 7-8   *Linked list implementation of List ADT*

```cpp
// cx7-8.cpp
// Code Example 7-8: implementation file, linked list implementation of List ADT

#include "cx7-5.h"

List::List()
{
    // Initialize an empty List
    head = 0;
    tail = 0;
    current = 0;
}

void List::insert(const ListElementType & elem)
{
    Link addedNode = new Node;
    assert(addedNode); // check to make sure node was allocated
    addedNode->elem = elem;
    if (head == 0) // list was empty -- set head
        head = addedNode;
    else
        tail->next = addedNode;
    tail = addedNode;
    addedNode->next = 0;
}

bool List::first(ListElementType & elem)
{
    // After calling first, current points to first item in list
    if (head == 0)
        return false;
    else {
        elem = head->elem;
        current = head;
        return true;
    }
}

bool List::next(ListElementType & elem)
{
```

```
// with proper use, current should always be nonzero
assert(current);

// After each call, current always points to the item
// that next has just returned.
if (current->next == 0)
    return false;
else {
    current = current->next;
    elem = current->elem;
    return true;
}
}
```

Our iterators `first` and `next` can be used to implement a list traversal, as discussed above. The expression `current=current->next` updates the value of `current` so that it points to the next node in the list; hence, the current pointer is always ready to go for next time. Figure 7-8 illustrates the action of this statement.

Figure 7-8   *Advancing a temporary link from one node to the next*

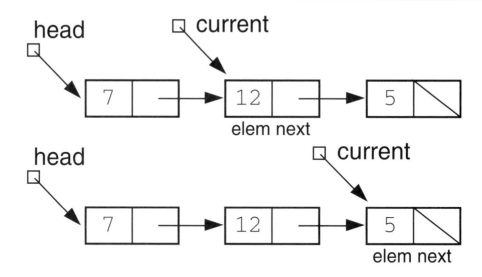

Exercise 7-13   Modify Code Example 7-4 so that it includes the header file for the linked list implementation (Code Example 7-5), compile the linked list code (Code Example 7-8), link these modules, and run the resulting executable. Verify that the linked list and linear list implementations give the same results.

7.4 The Inorder List ADT

Many applications and algorithms require that a list be maintained in some order. For example:

- a mailing list stored in alphabetical order or by zip code
- customer billing records kept in order by customer number
- a log of exceptional events on a Local Area Network, in order by the date and time of the event.

In each case, an Inorder List requires two things:

1. Some part of the information stored must be designated as a key. For example, the last name might serve as the key for a mailing list. Depending on the application, two data items might or might not be allowed to share the same key.

2. A rule for ordering the keys must be provided; that is, for any two keys k_1 and k_2, there must be a way to evaluate the expression $k_1 \le k_2$. For example, if the customer numbers are integers, then the usual less-than relationship works. Strings such as names are typically ordered using the rules by which words are placed in the dictionary—this is called **lexicographic order**. Any set of keys upon which such an ordering rule can be imposed is called a *total order*.

In typical use, the data in an *Inorder List* consists of a key plus additional, non-key data. But since the essence of the Inorder List can be captured by dealing with the key alone, we'll begin by using data consisting of a single integer. Later on, we'll show how this can be extended to accommodate any kind of data record.

The operations for an Inorder List ADT are the same as those for a standard list, except that the description of the iterators is changed to require that the elements are returned in the proper order. Plus we have something new: an ADT prerequisite. As we'll see later, our implementation of the Inorder List will require a way to compare elements in the List; thus, we require that `ListElementType` must work with the `<=` and `==` operators. Obviously, this isn't a problem for a simple built-in type like an `int`; later on, we'll see how user-defined objects can work correctly with an operator like `<=`.

ADT 7-2   Inorder List ADT

Characteristics:

- An Inorder List L stores items of some type (ListElementType) that is totally ordered.

- The items in the List are *in order*; that is, if a and b are elements of ListElementType, and $a < b$, then if a and b are in L, a will be before b.

Prerequisite:

ListElementType must work with the operations $<=$ and $==$.

Operations:

void L.insert(const ListElementType & elem)

Precondition:	None.
Postcondition:	$L_{Post} = L_{Pre}$ with an instance of elem added to the list.

bool L.first(ListElementType & elem)

Precondition:	None.
Postcondition:	If the list is empty, none. Otherwise, the variable elem contains the *smallest* item in L; the "next" item to be returned is the second smallest item in L.
Returns:	True if and only if at least one element in L.

bool L.next(ListElementType & elem)

Precondition:	The "first" operation has been called at least once.
Postcondition:	Variable elem contains the next item in L, in order, if there is one.
Returns:	True if and only if there was a next item.

This description of an Inorder List gives us considerable leeway in implementation. In particular, there is no requirement that we actually keep the items in order, only that the iterators produce them in order. For our implementation we choose to keep the items in order by keys so that printing the list will be simple.

We will use a modified version of our linked list. In this implementation, the `insert` function will add new nodes in order, so that the list will maintain the invariant that the data in every node is less than or equal to the data in the node it's linked to. To visualize this, examine Figure 7-9.

Figure 7-9   *Invariant for Inorder List implementation*

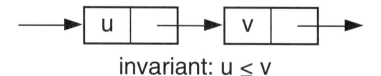

invariant: u ≤ v

Inserting in an
Inorder List Our goal is to write a new `insert` function that will maintain this invariant: that is, if we start with an Inorder List and insert a new element, we want to guarantee that the list is still ordered. The idea is simple, but we'll see that getting the code right turns out to be trickier than it sounds.

We start with an example of the general case. Let's suppose we're adding 9 to the list (3, 7, 12, 22, 35). Then we want to insert a node containing 9 between the nodes containing 7 and 12. An illustration of the situation before the insertion is shown in Figure 7-10

Figure 7-10　　　*In Order List before inserting the new node*

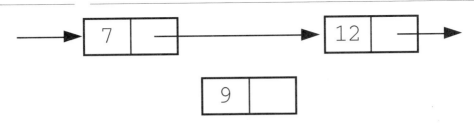

First of all, note that to insert the node containing 9 between 7 and 12, we have to change the `next` field in the node containing 7. We refer to one entry in a list that precedes another as the predecessor; hence in the final list 7 is a predecessor of 9, as shown in Figure 7-11.

Figure 7-11　　　*Inorder List after new node added*

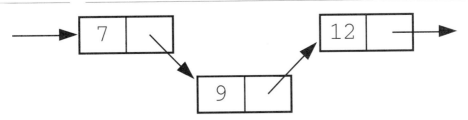

Because we will change the `next` field of the predecessor of the newly inserted node we will have to be able to access the predecessor node. All access is through pointers. So the situation we have to create in order to insert the new node will look like the picture in Figure 7-12. `Pred` is an external pointer to the predecessor; `addedNode` points to the newly created node, waiting to be inserted into the list.

Figure 7-12   *Pointers prepared for insertion of new node*

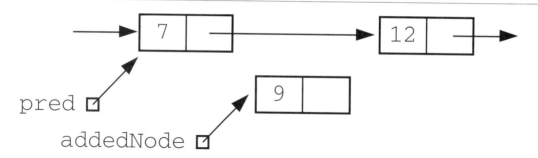

The invariant for the Inorder List allows us to make certain assertions about the state of the list before the insertion. In Figure 7-13, we illustrate the relevant conditions that hold prior to the insertion.

Figure 7-13   *Assertions holding before inserting new nodes[a]*

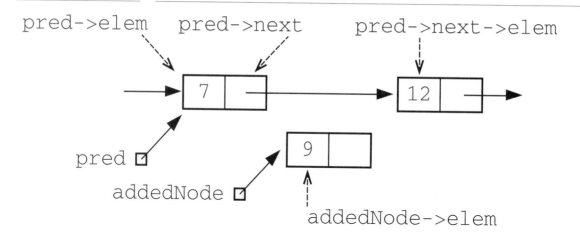

Assertion: pred->elem <= addedNode->elem &&
         addedNode->elem <= pred->next->elem

a. Dashed lines are labels; solid lines are links.

In order to assure that we have achieved the conditions shown in Figure 7-14, we will state them with some care and then figure out how to write a loop with the correct invariant. Recall that we reference the data element of a node by the notation ->elem so that, for example, pred->elem is equal to 12 in Figure 7-12. When the values of pred and addedNode are assigned correctly, the data in the predecessor node will be less than or equal to that in the new node; furthermore, the data in the new node will be less than or equal to that in the node that follows the predecessor node. More succinctly,

```
pred->elem <= addedNode->elem <= pred->next->elem.
```

That's not quite enough, because it's possible that the value for the new node is larger than any value already in the list, in which case we want to insert the new node after the last node in the list. For this insertion to work, pred should be pointing at a node whose next field is 0. We can express this with the more complicated condition

```
(pred->elem <= addedNode->elem <= pred->next->elem) ||
(pred->elem <= addedNode->elem && pred->next == 0)
```

Because the beginning of each of the two parts of the condition is the same the rules of logic let us simplify this expression slightly, giving us our goal assertion, which we'll label Assertion 7-1:

Assertion 7-1
```
(pred->elem <= addedNode->elem) &&
(addedNode->elem <= pred->next->elem || pred->next == 0)
```

Once this assertion is satisfied, we can insert the new node into the list with the code

```
addedNode->next = pred->next;
pred->next = addedNode;
```

If our original list was in order, it now must be the case that

```
pred->elem <= pred->next->elem
```

furthermore, either

```
pred->next->next == 0
```

or

```
pred->next->elem <= pred->next->next->elem
```

So if the list was in order to begin with, it must be in order now. The reasoning behind these statements is illustrated in Figure 7-14. In the figure, the assertions are simplified under the assumption that we're not inserting at the end of the list.

Exercise 7-14   Draw the corresponding diagram for an insertion at the end of the list.

Figure 7-14   *Assertions holding after inserting new node*

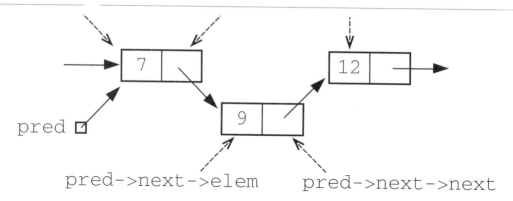

Assertion: `pred->elem <= pred->next->elem`
`<= pred->next->next->elem`

Hang on, we're getting close. Now we need to discover the loop invariant that will get us to the goal assertion, Assertion 7-1. We need an assertion that, when violated, that is, when we leave the loop, will guarantee that Assertion 7-1 is satisfied. Let's expand the sample list (3, 7, 12, 22, 35) and the insertion of 9. We start `pred` off at the head of the list; after all, access to the list is at the head. Then the loop will advance `pred` step by step toward its destination node, which is the node containing 7 (as shown in Figure 7-10). By examination we see that we want to keep advancing as long as

Assertion 7-2   `addedNode->elem > pred->next->elem`

If we leave the loop because we've violated this part of the invariant, we'll know that

`addedNode->elem <= pred->next->elem`

which will be adequate to satisfy the second part of the invariant. But there's another possibility suggested by the assertion—we might get to the end of the list without ever violating Assertion 7-2. In this case, `pred->next` will be 0; so we can use

Assertion 7-3   `pred->next != 0`

as the second part of the invariant.

What about the first part of Assertion 7-1, the claim that

`pred->elem <= addedNode->elem`

You might conclude, by looking at the example, that this is just always going to be true—but you would be wrong. If the new item is smaller than any item in the list, then

```
pred->elem > addedNode->elem
```

for every node in the list. We'll treat this as a special case—if the new item is smaller than anything in the list, we insert it at the beginning. We can also check to see if the existing list is empty, and handle these two cases together. Once we've eliminated these cases, we'll be able to assert that

```
pred->elem <= addedNode->elem
```

and at last all the pieces fall into place.

After all this work, the code itself is anticlimactic. But that's the way it's supposed to be. By working everything out in advance via assertions and invariants—a process that's not always easy—we make it easy to write correct code.

Code Example 7-9   *Inorder List insertion*

```
// cx7-9.cpp
// Code Example 7-9: insert function for an Inorder List ADT

#include "cx7-5.h"

void List::insert(const ListElementType & elem)
{
    // precondition: list is in order
    Link addedNode(new Node);
    assert(addedNode);
    addedNode->elem = elem;
    // Special case: if the existing list is empty, or if the new data
    // is less than the smallest item in the list, the new node is added
    // to the front of the list
    if (head == 0 || elem <= head->elem) {
        addedNode->next = head;
        head = addedNode;
    }
    else {
        // find the pointer to the node that is the predecessor
        // to the new node in the in-order list
        Link pred(head);
        // assertion: pred->elem <= addedNode->elem
        while (pred->next != 0 && pred->next->elem <= addedNode->elem)
            // loop invariant: pred->next != 0 && pred->next->elem <= elem
```

```
        pred = pred->next;
    // assertion 7-1: (pred->elem <= addedNode->elem) &&
    //      (addedNode->elem <= pred->next->elem || pred->next == 0)
    addedNode->next = pred->next;
    pred->next = addedNode;
    // assertion: pred->elem <= pred->next->elem &&
    //      (pred->next->elem <= pred->next->next->elem || pred->next->next == 0)
    }
    // postcondition: list is in order, with elem added in proper position
}
```

Exercise 7-15   Illustrate the process of adding 17 into an Inorder List previously containing 5, 10, and 20.

Exercise 7-16   Illustrate the process of adding 25 into an Inorder List previously containing 5, 10, and 20.

Exercise 7-17   What changes, if any, need to be made to the other functions in order to make a List ADT into an Inorder List ADT?

Exercise 7-18   What changes, if any, need to be made to a list client in order to work with an Inorder List ADT instead of a List ADT?

Exercise 7-19   In Code Example 7-9, the header file from Code Example 7-5 was included. This will work, but actually there's a small change that ought to be made to the header file to be consistent with the way we've implemented the Inorder List. What is it?

7.5   Variations on a Linked List

The basic idea of a linked list serves as the starting point for many useful variations. In this section we'll look at a few of them that have proven to be essential tools for the computer scientist and software engineer.

7.5.1   Dummy Head Nodes

In this section we'll make a some changes to the implementation of Inorder List, including the addition of a new operation, remove. An updated header file for this implementation is shown in Code Example 7-10. We'll be referring to this header file throughout this section.

Code Example 7-10   Header file for Inorder List with dummy head node implementation

```
// cx7-10.h
// Code Example 7-10: header file for list implemented with dummy head node

#include "dslib.h"

// the type of the individual elements in the list is defined here
typedef int ListElementType;

class List {
// Use L to mean "this List"
public:
    List();
    // Precondition: None
    // Postcondition: L is an empty List
    void insert(const ListElementType & elem);
    // Precondition: None
    // Postcondition: Lpost = Lpre with an instance of elem added to Lpost
    bool first(ListElementType & elem);
    // Precondition: None
    // Postcondition: If the list is empty, none. Otherwise, the variable
    //    elem contains the first item in L; the "next" item to be returned
    //    is the second in L.
    // Returns: true if and only if there is at least one element in L.
    bool next(ListElementType & elem);
    // Precondition: The "first" operation has been called at least once.
    // Postcondition: Variable elem contains the next item in L, if there is one,
    //    and the next counter advances by one; if there is no next element, none.
    // Returns: true if and only if there was a next item.
    void remove(const ListElementType & target);
    // Precondition: None
    // Postcondition: Lpost = Lpre with one instance of target removed
private:
    struct Node; // declaration without definition
    typedef Node *Link; // use declaration of Node
    struct Node { // now we define Node
        ListElementType elem;
        Link next;
    };
    Link head;
    Link current;
};
```

Our first variation, the ***dummy head node***, simplifies the code that manipulates linked lists by eliminating certain special cases. If you refer back to the linked list implementation of Inorder List in Code Example 7-9, you'll find that a big chunk of the code deals with the special case of the first node in the list. Since the pointer to the first node is in the head node, while all the other pointers are next fields in nodes, inserting and deleting the first node in a standard linked list is a special case.

We can get around this by never inserting or deleting the first node! That is, before we start working with the list, we put a single node on the list that is never used as a member of the list. All "real" nodes in the list follow the dummy head node, and the external head pointer for the list never points to a "real" node. Figure 7-15 shows an empty standard linked list and an empty linked list with a dummy head.

Figure 7-15   *Comparison of empty linked lists, standard and with dummy head*

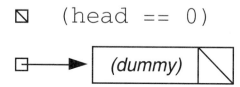

Figure 7-16 visually compares a list of two elements in the standard and dummy head representations.

Figure 7-16   *Standard and dummy head node representations of (7,4)*

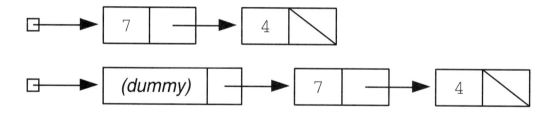

The dummy head node works quite nicely with the Inorder List ADT, so we'll use that as an example. Most of the routines in the implementation need to be modified slightly to reflect the dummy head node, and a new function needs to be added. Note that, as usual, our change of implementation has no effect on the user's view of an Inorder List. We make sure that the dummy head node is created by adding the code to the constructor function as shown in Code Example 7-11. The definition of a node didn't change when we added the dummy head. Note that when we create the dummy head in the constructor, we don't bother to assign a value to the data field—new->elem—since it's a dummy and we don't intend to use it for anything. If leaving it empty makes you nervous, feel free to put any value you like into the dummy node.

The implementation in Code Example 7-11 includes this new version of the constructor function, modifications to insert and first, plus a new operation, remove, which we discuss below.

Code Example 7-11   *Implementation of an Inorder List with a dummy head node*

```cpp
// cx7-11.cpp
// Code Example 7-11: Inorder List implemented with dummy head node

#include "cx7-10.h"

List::List()
{
    // Initialize an empty list
    head = new Node;
    assert(head);
    head->next = 0;
    current = 0;
}

void List::insert(const ListElementType & elem)
{
    // precondition: list is in order
    Link addedNode(new Node);
    assert(addedNode);
    addedNode->elem = elem;
    // find the pointer to the node that is the predecessor
    // to the new node in the in-order list
    Link pred(head);
    // loop invariant: pred->elem <= elem
    while (pred->next != 0 && (pred->next->elem <= addedNode->elem))
        pred = pred->next;
    // assertion 7-1: (pred->elem <= addedNode->elem) &&
    //      (addedNode->elem <= pred->next->elem || pred->next == 0)
    addedNode->next = pred->next;
    pred->next = addedNode;
    // postcondition: list is in order
}

bool List::first(ListElementType &elem)
{
    // After calling first, current points to first item in list
    assert(head); // if no head, something is very wrong!
    if (head->next == 0)
        return false;
    else {
        current = head->next;
        elem = current->elem;
        return true;
    }
}

bool List::next(ListElementType & elem)
```

```
{
    //·With proper use, current should always be nonzero
    assert(current);
    // After each call, current always points to the item
    // that next has just returned.
    if (current->next == 0)
        return false; // no next element available
    else {
        current = current->next;
        elem = current->elem;
        return true;
    }
}

void List::remove(const ListElementType & target)
{
    assert(head);
    Link pred, delNode;
    // pred starts out pointing at the dummy head
    for (pred = head; pred->next != 0 && pred->next->elem < target;
            pred = pred->next)
        ;
    // at this point, check to see if we've found target --
    // if so, remove it
    // Have to check carefully to make sure we don't
    // dereference a null pointer!
    if pred->next && (pred->next->elem == target) {
        // remove the next node in the list
        delNode = pred->next;
        pred->next = delNode->next;
        delete delNode; // return node to memory
    }
}
```

insert *Function*   The `insert` function is quite similar to that in Code Example 7-9, but with the special case removed. Note that the code, shown in Code Example 7-11, is not only simpler, but also slightly more efficient because there's no need to test for the special case.

first *Function*   We do need to make small changes to the `first` function in order to account for the dummy head node. The first item returned is now the second node in the list, since the first is the dummy.

remove *Function*   So far we've avoided adding an operation that removes items from the List ADT because it's particularly tricky in a standard linked list. However, using a dummy head node makes it relatively simple. First, we modify the ADT definition by adding a remove operation that removes one instance of a particular value, if it's found in the list.

void L.remove(ListElementType target)

Precondition: None.
Postcondition: $L_{post} = L_{pre}$ with one instance of target removed.
Returns: None.

One trick to the removal implementation is that we need a pointer to the node *preceding* the node to be removed; the state of the list before the removal, including a `pred` pointer, is shown in Figure 7-17.

Figure 7-17   *State of the list before a removal*

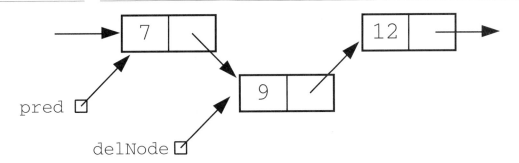

We need to write a loop that looks for elements equal to the target element, keeping track of the node that precedes each examined node so that it can be used to remove the target element. The removal process is illustrated in Figures 7-17 and 7-18. We'll use the link variable `pred` to point to the node preceding the target for removal, and the variable `delNode` to point to the node that we remove. Study the code for `remove` in Code Example 7-11 along with the figures to see how this fits together.

Figure 7-18   *State of the list after the removal*

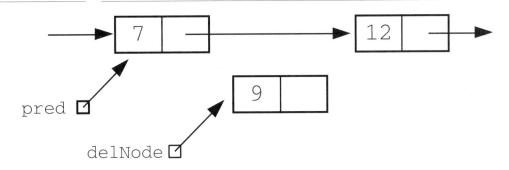

Exercise 7-20   How would you modify the `remove` function for a standard linked list, that is, one with no dummy head node?

The C++ Delete Operator

There's a new C++ construct in the `remove` function. The line

```
delete delNode;
```

returns the memory used by the node pointed to by `delNode` to the dynamic memory pool, so that it can be used by future calls to `new`. When you're writing your programs for a course such as this, it's unlikely you'll ever run out of dynamic memory, unless you have a bug. However, failing to return unused memory to the pool causes your program to have a *memory leak*; as your program continues to run, the available memory drips away until there is none left, even though the full capacity of memory is not in use. It's considered good practice to delete unused memory so that when you start to work on more complicated systems you will already be in the habit.

7.5.2   Circular Linked Lists

If you follow the pointers in a standard linked list from the beginning, you can get to every item in the list by following the "next" pointers; but when you get to the end of the list there's no way to get back to the beginning without examining the external "head" pointer again. As a result, we used two external pointers in our linked list implementation shown in Code Example 7-8. If you replace the null pointer at the end of the list with a pointer back to the beginning of the list, you can move through the list as many times as needed without ever looking at the head pointer more than once. Take a look at Figure 7-19 to see an example of a *circular linked list*.

Figure 7-19   A simple circular linked list

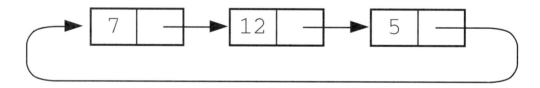

In Figure 7-19, we've omitted the external pointer. Obviously, we need an external pointer as a way to access the list; the question is, where should it point? It may not be too obvious to you now, but in many lists most access occurs at the ends. If we put the external pointer at the head, we can directly access the first item in the list, but to get to the last item we will have to traverse the entire list. On the other hand, a pointer to the end of the list will allow quick access to both ends, since we can follow the "next" pointer to get to the head. If you write this in C++ it looks like this (assuming that `tail` is the external pointer):

```
tail->elem // data field for the last node in list
tail->next->elem // data field for first node in list
```

The algorithms for list traversal, list insertion, and list removal have to be modified to take account of the circular nature of the list. A list traversal now has to examine the current pointer and compare it with `tail`, rather than looking for the null pointer.

Exercise 7-21   Starting with our first linked list implementation (Code Examples 7-5 and 7-8) rewrite the header file and the member functions as required for a circular list. (Note that you should not make any change in the definition of the List ADT; use ADT 7-1.) Test your new implementation using the client in Code Example 7-4.

7.5.3   Doubly Linked Lists

Our List ADT and Inorder List ADT both offer the iterators `first` and `next`, permitting the client to process the list from beginning to end. Suppose you wanted to add the following operation to the ADT:

bool previous(ListElementType &elem)

Precondition:	The *first* operation must have been executed.
Postcondition:	The current list position is backed up by one; in other words, the sequence: next(e); previous(e) puts the list back into the same condition it started in.
Returns:	True if there is a previous item, otherwise false.

With the *previous* operation, a client program can move forward and backward through the list.

It's a simple exercise to add the *previous* operation to array implementation, but adding it to a standard linked list is not so simple. A program can't "back up" in a linked list—there's no way, given a pointer to a node in the list, to access its predecessor without going back to the `head` pointer and working forward. But we can solve the problem by adding a predecessor link to every node, creating a ***doubly linked list***, as shown in Figure 7-20. Note that the list now has two Null pointers, because a program can reach the end of the list either moving forward or backward.

Because each node now has three parts—two links plus the data element—we need to change the declaration of `node`, yielding the new header file shown in Code Example 7-12. Please note that other than adding the *previous* operation, we've made

Figure 7-20   *An example of a doubly linked list*

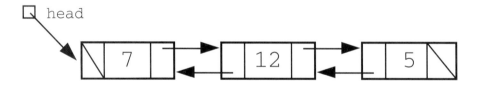

no change in the public interface defined all the way back in Code Example 7-1 on Page 164.

Code Example 7-12   *Header file for doubly-linked list*

```
// cx7-12.h
// Code Example 7-12: header file for doubly-linked list

#include "dslib.h"

// the type of the individual elements in the list is defined here
typedef int ListElementType;

class List {
public:
    List();
    void insert(const ListElementType & elem);
    bool first(ListElementType & elem);
    bool next(ListElementType & elem);
    bool previous(ListElementType & elem);
private:
    struct Node; // declaration without definition
    typedef Node *Link;
    struct Node {
        ListElementType elem;
        Link next;
        Link prev;
    };
    Link head;
    Link current;
};
```

To insert a new item into the list requires changing a forward (next) link and a backward (prev) link. The insert for the List ADT, with the added lines marked with comments, appears as Code Example 7-13.

Code Example 7-13   insert *function for a doubly linked list*

```
// cx7-13.cpp
// Code Example 7-13: insertion into a doubly-linked list

#include "cx7-12.h"

void List::insert(const ListElementType & elem)
{
    Link addedNode = new Node;
    assert(addedNode);
    addedNode->elem = elem;
    addedNode->next = head;
    if (head) // test to see if there was a node in the list
        head->prev = addedNode;// if so, it needs to point back to the new node
    addedNode->prev = 0;
    head = addedNode;
}
```

The `previous` function, in Code Example 7-14, is quite simple—just follow the `prev` pointer.

Code Example 7-14   previous *function for a doubly linked list*

```
// cx7-14.cpp
// Code Example 7-14: previous function for a doubly linked list

#include "cx7-12.h"

bool List::previous(ListElementType &elem)
{
    assert(current);
    if (current->prev == 0)
        return false;
    else {
        current = current->prev;
        elem = current->elem;
        return true;
    }
}
```

Double links simplify the insertion and removal operations, so why not use them all the time? Doubling the links doubles the amount of storage overhead required by the linked list. If you really don't need the ability to move backward and forward in the list, then most programmers would prefer to use the more space-efficient singly linked list. But a doubly linked list is always preferred when there's a need to traverse the list in both directions.

Exercise 7-22   What changes, if any, need to be made to `first` for a doubly linked list?

Exercise 7-23   Write the `previous` function for the array implementation of a List ADT. (The header file is Code Example 7-2, and the implementation is in Code Example 7-3.)

Exercise 7-24   Implement a doubly linked list with a dummy head node.

Exercise 7-25   Draw a picture of a circular, doubly linked list. What should the `prev` pointer for the first node contain?

Exercise 7-26   Create a new ADT, 2-Way List, based on ADT 7-1, that can be traversed in two directions. To the three operations in ADT 7-1, define operations `last` and `back`, that work like `first` and `next` in reverse.

7.6   A Dynamic Linear List

As we mentioned in Section 7.3.3, there's a way to create a linear list that, while fixed in size, can be created using a size chosen at runtime rather than when writing the program. While a dynamic linear list lacks the flexibility of a linked list, it does offer a nice compromise for many applications. In order to understand this approach, it helps to know a bit about the way arrays work in C++, which it inherited from C. Unlike some languages, a C++ array is really nothing more than a fixed pointer to an area of reserved memory. When your program contains a declaration like

```
char a[1000];
```

the compiler reserves room for 1000 `char`s, with a pointing to the first `char`. In fact, the two notations `*a` and `a[0]` are equivalent: both mean "the `char` pointed to by `a`." Likewise, the notation `a[375]`—the 376th element of the array `a`—refers to exactly the same item as `*(a+375)`—the item stored at memory location a plus 375. Conversely, if you have a pointer, you can use array notation to access the memory it points to. So if you declare a to be a pointer, and then allocate memory using `new`, you can use a just as if it were declared as an array but with the advantage that you can pick the size of the list just before you use it, rather than fixing a size in advance. Furthermore, the client program can create lists of various sizes, as appropriate.

The header file containing the declaration of the dynamic linear list is shown in Code Example 7-15, and the implementation of the constructor and the size function (which returns the actual size of the list) is shown in Code Example 7-16. The constructor allocates memory for the array, using `new`. The rest of the List code remains as shown in Code Example 7-3.

Code Example 7-15   *Declaration for a dynamic linear list*

```cpp
// cx7-15.h
// Code Example 7-15: header file for dynamic list

#include "dslib.h"

// the type of the individual elements in the list is defined here
typedef int ListElementType;

class List {
public:
    List(int lSize);
    void insert(const ListElementType & elem);
    bool first(ListElementType & elem);
    bool next(ListElementType & elem);
    int size();
private:
    ListElementType * listArray;
    int numberOfElements;
    int currentPosition;
    int listSize;
};
```

Code Example 7-16   *Partial implementation for dynamic linear list*

```cpp
// cx7-16.cpp
// Code Example 7-16: partial implementation of dynamic list

#include "cx7-15.h"

List::List(int lSize)
{
    assert(lSize > 0);
    listSize = lSize;
    listArray = new ListElementType[listSize];
    assert(listArray); // make sure memory was successfully allocated
    numberOfElements = 0;
    currentPosition = -1;
}

List::size()
{
    return listSize;
}
```

An excerpt from a sample client is shown in Code Example 7-17. Note that you have to pass an argument that tells the constructor the size you want each list to be.

Code Example 7-17   (Partial) client for dynamic linear list

```
// cx7-17.cpp
// Code Example 7-17: (partial) client for the dynamic list

#include "cx7-15.h"

int main()
{
    int list1size, list2size;
    cout << "Enter size of the first list: ";
    cin >> list1size;
    List list1(list1size);
    cout << "Enter size of the second list: ";
    cin >> list2size;
    List list2(list2size);
    // . . . and so on . . .
```

Exercise 7-27   Compare the advantages and disadvantages of (static) linear lists, dynamic linear lists, and linked lists. Consider execution speed and memory overhead.

Exercise 7-28   Note that since the constructor requires an argument, there's no (obvious) way to declare an *array* of the lists when using the class declared in Code Example 7-15. However, you can use the correspondence between pointers and arrays to get around this. Essentially, you have to use the same trick in the client that we demonstrated in Code Example 7-16. Use this to write a client that declares an array of 10 lists, each of size 50.

Exercise 7-29   Write the preconditions, postconditions, and returns for the List function *size*.

7.7   The Membership Management Program Revisited

Whew! Okay, we know something about lists, and we're ready to tackle that membership list problem we started with. Before you're ready to start writing the code, you need to have a specification to work from. After some discussion and exchange of e-mail with the membership chair, you agree on the following description of the problem:

Specification   The Saturday Social Society membership list program will keep track of club members, who number about 100. The membership chair needs to be able to do the following:

1. Add new members to the list.

2. Look up individual members to get information about them.

3. Remove members from the list.

4. Print out a membership roster, listing all members and associated information in alphabetical order by last name.

For each member, the following information must be stored:

1. Last name.

2. First name.

3. Mailing address (two lines should be sufficient).

4. Telephone number (three-digit area code plus seven-digit phone number, stored as characters).

5. Expected year of graduation (an integer between 1998 and 2050).

Let's begin our design process by considering the type of list to use. We know that we will, on occasion, need a list of the members sorted by last name. While we don't *have* to use an Inorder List—we could sort the list when we need it—we've got an Inorder List ADT handy and it will make things easy. So we'll go with the Inorder List, ADT 7-2, supplemented with the *remove* operation.

Data storage   Next we'll consider how to store the information for each member. Naturally, it makes sense to make this an object, represented by a class, which we'll call Club-Member.[6] Each of the six items of information (including two lines of address) will be a member variable. In order to preserve the encapsulation of the class, we'll need a "set" function for each field, and a "get" function for each field, plus we've added a function to set all fields at once. Most of the fields will be stored as String, except the graduation year which can be made an int. Code Example 7-18 contains the header file for the ClubMember class.

Code Example 7-18   *Declaration for ClubMember class*

```
// cx7-18.h
// Code Example 7-18: header file for ClubMember class

// string is the standard C++ string class library
#include <string>

class ClubMember {
public:
    ClubMember();
    void setName(const string & fn, const string & ln);
```

---

6. We call it ClubMember instead of Member to avoid confusion between a member of the club and the object-oriented programming term *member*, i.e., a member function.

```
    void setAddress(const string & ad1, const string & ad2);
    void setTelnum(const string & tn);
    void setGradYear(const int gy);
    void setClubMemberData(const string & fn, const string & ln,
        const string & ad1, const string & ad2, const string & tn,
        const int gy);
    string getFirstName() const;
    string getLastName() const;
    string getAddrOne() const;
    string getAddrTwo() const;
    string getTelnum() const;
    int getGradYear() const;
private:
    string firstName;
    string lastName;
    string addrOne;
    string addrTwo;
    string telNum;
    int gradYear;
};
```

const *member functions*

If you examine Code Example 7-18, you'll find a new use of the C++ const keyword. For example, the getFirstName member function is declared as

```
    string getFirstName() const;
```

This use of the const keyword tells the compiler that the getFirstName() member function may be applied to a ClubMember object that's declared to be a constant. At first glance you might wonder why we would ever declare a ClubMember object to be constant—the answer is that it occurs implicitly whenever a ClubMember object is passed to a function where the parameter is a constant. For example, suppose you wanted a function printMember that takes a ClubMember object as an argument to be printed and wrote it like this:

```
    void printMember(const ClubMember &member)
    {
      cout << member.getFirstName();
      ... and so on
```

Now, suppose that getFirstName was *not* declared as a const member function. When the compiler processes the function call, member.getFirstName(), it has no way to know whether or not the getFirstName function might change the contents of the object for which it's being called. Because this object, member, is declared to be a const parameter, the compiler will refuse to accept this code.[7] However, since the `getFirstName` function, as well as others used to access information from the ClubMember object, are declared `const`, the compiler knows that they can be safely used with a `const` parameter, and the code is legal. Of course, to complete the bargain, the code for `getFirstName` must not make any changes to the fields in the `ClubMember` object that receives the call — if it tries, the C++ compiler will reject the code.

Member functions that retrieve information from an object without changing the state of the object are called *accessors*. Generally, you should declare accessor functions to be `const` member functions.

Operator
Overloading   There's an important addition we need to make this class work effectively with our Inorder List. The Inorder List will have to be able to compare ClubMembers using the "`<=`" operator. Furthermore, retrieving individual members requires the "`==`" operator to work on ClubMembers. We can add this functionality to our class using *operator overloading*. Operator overloading lets us redefine how operators like "`<=`" and "`==`" work for objects from a user-defined class. The return type and argument type(s) for a function are referred to as its *signature*. When overloading an operator, we have to match the built-in signature for the operator, except we use one or more of our classes as opposed to the built-in types. Here's the declaration for the `<=` operator:

```
int operator<=(const ClubMember &, const ClubMember &);
```

The declaration uses the new C++ keyword **operator** to indicate our intention to overload an operator. In this case, our operator function will be passed two objects, and we have to decide how to compare them. Our approach will be to first compare the last names—if they differ, the result comes from comparing the two last names; if the last names are the same, the result depends upon the first name. The code could look like Code Example 7-19. This code depends upon the overloading of the definition of "`<=`" to work with the String class.

Note that we've been negligent in documenting our Inorder List class, because the client has to know about the internal design of the class in order to know that the operator definitions for "`==`" and "`<=`" are required. We'll examine this issue in the next chapter, and develop a standard for documenting dependencies of this kind.

---

7. Some older compilers may accept this, or issue a warning, but the current C++ standard does not allow such code to be compiled.

Code Example 7-19   Definition of `operator<=` *for ClubMember class*

```
// cx7-19.cpp
// Code Example 7-19: Implementation of <= operator for members

#include "cx7-18.h"

// We'll use the names lhs -- short for left hand side -- as the
// formal parameter name for the argument on the left of an operator,
// and rhs -- right hand side -- for the name of the argument on the right.
int operator<=(const ClubMember & lhs, const ClubMember & rhs)
{
    if (lhs.getLastName() == rhs.getLastName())
        return lhs.getFirstName() <= rhs.getFirstName();
    else
        return lhs.getLastName() <= rhs.getLastName();
}
```

You should have enough information now to complete the membership list program by assembling all the pieces you've been given so far.

Exercise 7-30   Change the definition of `getFirstName` and `getLastName` in Code Example 7-18 so that they are not `const` member functions. What should now happen when compiling Code Example 7-19? Try it with your compiler and compare the results to your prediction.

Exercise 7-31   This section claims that you can't use the List class without defining "==" and "<=" for the list element type. Perform the following experiment: define a class that *doesn't* work with the equality and inequality operators, and attempt to compile a program that uses your class as the list element type. How does the compiler respond?

Exercise 7-32   You could add a member function to ClubMember that prints out the data for a ClubMember object. Discuss the pros and cons of including such a member function within the class definition.

Exercise 7-33   Is C++ the right tool to use for the ClubMember program? What are the pros and cons of using other tools you might be familiar with, such as a spreadsheet, a data base manager, a GUI-oriented language such as Visual Basic, or Unix tools such as AWK and Perl, rather than writing a program in C++?

Chapter Summary

- A List ADT represents items that can be retrieved in some order.
- Linear lists implement the List ADT using an array.

- Iterator functions can be used to retrieve items in a List.
- Linked lists provide greater flexibility by breaking the connection between the logical idea of a list and its implementation.
- Dynamic memory allocation allows a program to allocate memory at runtime.
- The Inorder List ADT maintains items in a specified order.
- Dummy head nodes, circular linked lists, and doubly linked lists provide alternative approaches to the implementation of a linked list.
- Client applications may need to implement particular functions for classes stored within another class.
- Operator overloading provides a way to make built-in operators meaningful for user-defined classes.

Programming Laboratory Problems

Lab 7-1 Complete the ClubMember List application. You will need to do the following:

- Write the definition of `operator==` for the ClubMember class. We'll treat `==` as indicating key equality; that is, two member objects are the same if they have matching first and last names, regardless of the rest of the information.
- Write a function that takes a ClubMember and adds it to an Inorder List.
- Write a function that removes a specified ClubMember from an Inorder List.
- Write a function that prints each ClubMember from an Inorder List of ClubMembers, nicely formatted.
- Using the functions above, write a main function with a menu to complete the membership list application.

Lab 7-2 Create a Videotape object that includes the following information:

- Name of the tape (string)
- Running time (double)
- Year released (int)
- Price (double)

Write a function that prompts the user for a series of videotapes, adds them to an Inorder List (in order by the name), and then prints out the list of tapes.

Lab 7-3 Write a program that creates an Inorder List of Strings, reads in each word from an input file, puts them into the Inorder List, and then prints a table of word frequencies, listing each word that occurs more than once.

For example, if the input were the previous paragraph, the output would be

```
Words appearing more than once:

word 3
a 2
an 2
each 2
of 2
that 2
Inorder 2
List 2
```

For ease of implementation, you may treat upper- and lower-case words as distinct.

Lab 7-4 To the standard linked list implementation (Code Examples 7-5 and 7-8) add the following functions:

1. `void L.append(List l)`: glues list l to the end of this list (L).

2. `List * L.copy()`: makes a copy of this list and returns a pointer to it.

Lab 7-5 Implement an Inorder List using a doubly linked list with a dummy head and dummy tail node. You'll find that the double links make the `insert` function simpler than the one in Code Example 7-9. Include a `remove` function in the implementation of this list.

Lab 7-6 Add a reverse operation to the standard list implementation (Code Examples 7-5 and 7-8). Implement the reverse operation recursively, using the following observation: to reverse an empty list, do nothing. To reverse a non-empty list, keep a pointer to the head of the list, reverse (recursively) the list consisting of the second through last nodes, and then add the old head node to the end of the reversed list.

Lab 7-7 Using the Selection Sort algorithm (discussed in Section 5.4.1) write a sort function and add it to the standard list implementation (Code Examples 7-5 and 7-8). (Why can't Quicksort be implemented with a linked list?)

Lab 7-8 Using the standard list implementation (Code Examples 7-5 and 7-8), add a `merge` function:

```
void L.merge(const List & mergeList);
```

Precondition: L_{pre} and mergeList are lists in sorted order.

Postcondition: L_{post} contains a merge of the items in L_{pre} and mergeList. (mergeList remains unchanged).

A merged list contains the items in each list in the proper order. For example, if L_{pre} is {1, 7, 21} and mergeList is {2, 19, 21, 23} then L_{post} is {1, 2, 19, 21, 21, 23}.

Lab 7-9   Using the merge function from Lab 7-8 (or one supplied by your instructor) add a sort operation to the standard list implementation (Code Examples 7-5 and 7-8), using the MergeSort algorithm described in Lab 6-4.

Chapter Vocabulary

accessor function

boolean type

circular linked list

`const` member function

`const` parameter

contiguous list

copy constructor

cursor (current pointer)

doubly linked list

dummy head node

dynamic memory allocation

external link

first operation

free store

generic ADT

head link

Inorder List ADT

iterator function

lexicographic order

linear list

link

linked list

List ADT

list traversal

memory leak

`new` operator

next operation

node

null link

`operator` (keyword)

operator overloading

reference parameter

signature (of a function)

static memory allocation

total order

Chapter 8 Stacks

Overview   A discussion of the specification, use, and implementation of the Stack ADT.

Chapter Objectives

1. To understand and apply the Stack ADT.
2. To implement the Stack ADT as a C++ class.
3. To implement a Stack using an array.
4. To implement a Stack using a dynamic list.
5. To implement an ADT with C++ templates.
6. To explore applications of the Stack ADT.

8.1   Problem: Robot Navigation

Suppose you want to program a robot to move across a room, such as the floor of a factory. To simplify the problem, we'll assume that the robot has a map of the room represented as a sequence of squares, rather like a chess board. The robot can move across certain squares and is blocked—by furniture, machinery, walls—from moving across others. In Figure 8-1, the letter **R** marks the initial position of the robot in the room, and the letter **T** marks the target: the position that the robot wants to get to. The dark gray squares stand for blocked space; the robot can navigate across the white squares.

Figure 8-1   *Initial conditions for robot navigation problem*

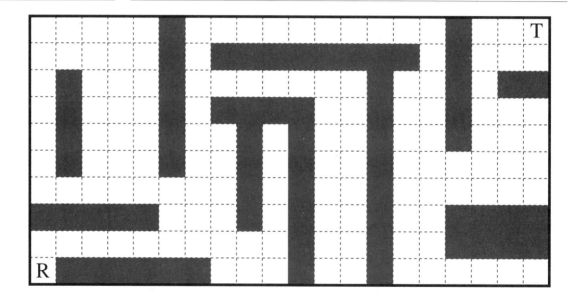

Let's suppose that we adopt the following basic strategy for the robot:

1. If possible, move in the direction of the target. (If there are two directions, both of which move the robot closer to the target, choose one arbitrarily.)

2. If the robot can't move toward the target, try any other move arbitrarily.

Following this strategy will get the robot to the position shown in Figure 8-2.

At this point, the robot has reached a dead end and has to back up. By following back through the positions previously occupied, the robot eventually reaches a position where there's another choice available. Note that, except for the squares reached

Figure 8-2   *The robot hits a dead end*

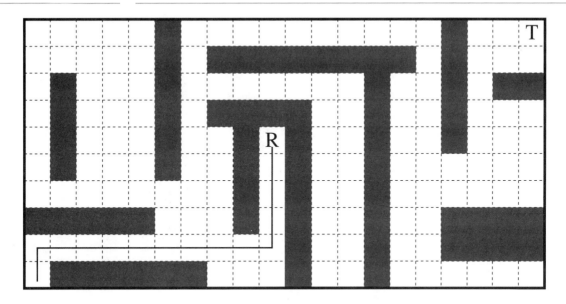

by this "backing up" process, there's never any reason for the robot to revisit squares that it has already been in—otherwise, the robot could get into an endless loop. Thus we assume that as the robot goes it leaves a mark in the squares it has visited, which we represent in the diagram by light-gray shading. To make the diagram easier to read we don't show the shading for squares in which we've indicated the "back-up" path for the robot with a solid line. Figure 8-3 illustrates the situation after backing up the first time.

Based on our discussion above, we add the following rules to our algorithm:

3. As the robot moves, it marks the squares so that the robot doesn't revisit them, except as indicated in rule 4.

4. When the robot reaches a dead end, it backs up through its previous positions until it finds an unexplored direction to try.

Eventually, after trying several dead ends, the robot will succeed in reaching the target, at least for this room. At this point the solid line represents a path that the robot can use to actually move from the initial position to the target, as shown in Figure 8-4. The light-gray squares represent all the positions the robot tried and abandoned.

The general strategy pursued to solve the robot navigation problem is called ***backtracking.*** In backtracking, we follow a path toward a solution as far as we can go, making choices about the direction to follow; once we reach a dead end, we back up

Figure 8-3   *The robot backs up and tries another direction*

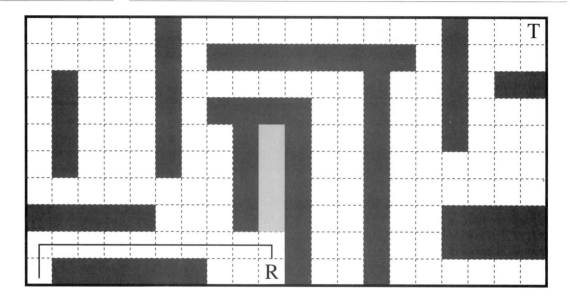

Figure 8-4   *The robot's path to the target*

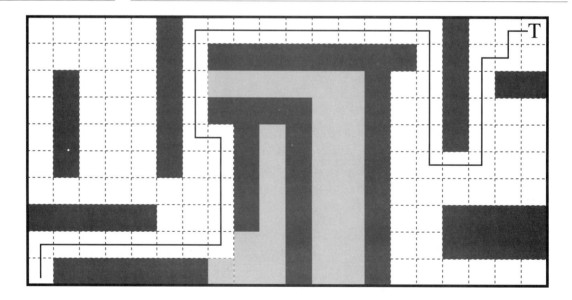

until we reach a decision point and try a different direction. While the robot navigation problem offers many interesting programming design problems, we're going to

focus on one particular issue: how to keep track of the path we're following so that we can back up. The Stack ADT provides exactly the mechanism we need to support backtracking algorithms, as well as other common algorithms. After we learn about the design and implementation of the Stack ADT, we'll return to the robot navigation problem to see exactly how the Stack ADT fits into the solution.

Exercise 8-1   At various decision points in the search traced above, the robot could choose to try "up" or "to the right" first. Which did it choose? Would it have made any difference in this case if it had used a different strategy?

8.2   The Stack ADT

A *container* is an ADT that can hold multiple objects. Each kind of container structures the objects in a different way. A *stack* is a container that stores items in *Last In, First Out (LIFO)* order. For example, if we have a stack of integers, and we add the number "1 2 3" to the stack and then ask the stack to return them to us, we receive them in the order "3 2 1." We use the *push* operation to add items to the stack, and *pop* to retrieve them.

In addition to push and pop, most Stack ADTs will include at least one other operation: a predicate that tests whether the stack is empty. It makes no sense to apply a pop operation to an empty stack; hence "Stack not empty" will be a precondition for pop. Therefore, the predicate isEmpty will be included as part of the definition of the Stack ADT. Another useful operation is top, which returns the value of the top item on the stack without the side effect of modifying the stack. Of course, top can be simulated by a pop followed by a push, but since top is quite easy to implement, it's often included. These operations define the Stack ADT as shown in ADT 8-1.

ADT 8-1   Stack ADT

Characteristics:

- A stack S stores items of some type (stackElementType) in Last-In, First-Out (LIFO) order.

Operations:

stackElementType S.pop()

Precondition:	! *S.isEmpty()*
Postcondition:	$S_{Post} = S_{Pre}$ with *top* removed.
Returns:	The item *x* such that *S.push(x)* was the most recent invocation of *push*.

void S.push(stackElementType)

Precondition:	None.
Postcondition:	Item *x* is added to the stack, such that a subsequent *S.pop()* returns *x*.

stackElementType S.top()

Precondition:	! *S.isEmpty()*
Postcondition:	None.
Returns:	The item *x* such that *S.push(x)* was the most recent invocation of *push*.

bool S.isEmpty()

Precondition:	None.
Postcondition:	None.
Returns:	*True* if and only if S is empty, i.e., contains no data items.

8.3 Implementing the Stack I: Array

Before jumping into the details of the code, let's consider a general strategy for implementing the Stack ADT operations. First, we need a data structure for storing the data items in the stack. Since the stack contains elements all of one type—it is a *homogeneous* data structure—an array seems reasonable.[1] The terms *stack* and *top* suggest something like a stack of books with the most recently "pushed" book on the top of the stack. The terminology was originally inspired by a spring-loaded tray holder in a cafeteria, from which the tray on top can be "popped." Thus one might try to model this directly in the array, by fixing one position, for example, the 0 element, as the top of the stack and allowing the elements to "ride up and down" within the array. This approach is illustrated in Figure 8-5: an initially empty stack is shown following two *push* operations. Study it for a minute to see why this isn't as good an idea as it first appears.

The problem is that if the data is moved up and down within the array, the push and pop operations will have to copy every element in the stack each time they are executed. That doesn't look too bad for a stack with two elements, but what about a stack with 100 or 1000 elements or more? In fact, it's easy to see that such an implementation would make both push and pop $O(n)$ operations, where *n* is the current size of the stack. By being a bit more clever, we can design the stack so that *push*

---

1. It's often desirable to implement a stack so that it can store items of various types—a *heterogeneous* stack. This requires more sophisticated C++ machinery.

Figure 8-5   *First attempt at stack implementation with array*

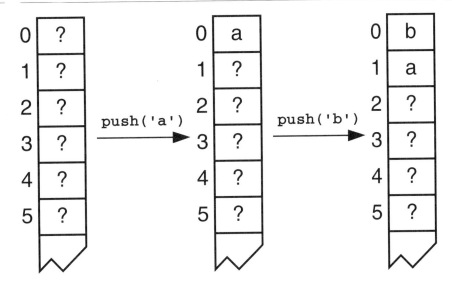

and *pop* are $O(1)$ operations. For all but the smallest stacks this makes a huge differ-ence.

The idea is that we can leave the data in place, and instead let the top of the stack float up and down. All we need to represent the top of the stack is an integer repre-senting the index of the current top element. Initially, top is set to –1, to indicate that there is no top element. Then each push increments top, and each pop decrements it. This is shown in Figure 8-6. Note that elements a and b are not in the same loca-tions as in the first implementation.

Implementing the
Stack in C++   Now we can write C++ code to implement the four operations. The stack requires two variables—we use stackArray to represent the array and topIndex to store the top. (We can't use top both as the name of the operation and also as the name of the index, since the two uses of the symbol top would conflict.) For the moment, we'll implement the stack to store values of type char; later, we'll look at ways to generalize the stack for other types.

Each push operation requires that topIndex be incremented and the new item be stored at stackArray[topIndex]; to pop, we return the top value and decre-ment topIndex. Note that there is no reason to clear the top memory location when performing a pop, since we'll never look at any value above topIndex. To implement isEmpty, we simply check topIndex to see whether it's equal to –1;

Figure 8-6   *Second stack implementation (floating top)*

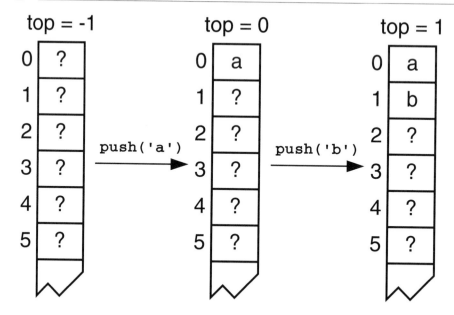

to implement top we return the value indexed by `topIndex`. The header file for our stacks appears in Code Example 8-1, with the implementation in Code Example 8-2.

Code Example 8-1   *Header file for stack implemented using an array*

```
// cx8-1.h Header File
// Code Example 8-1: Stack implemented using an Array

#ifndef __MB_CX8_1__
#define __MB_CX8_1__
#include "dslib.h"

const int maxStackSize = 1000;
typedef char StackElementType;

class Stack {
public:
   Stack();
   void push(StackElementType item);
   StackElementType pop();
   StackElementType top();
   bool isEmpty();
private:
   StackElementType stackArray[maxStackSize];
   int topIndex;
```

```
};

#endif
```

Code Example 8-1 uses some C++ syntax that may be new to you. The sequence of preprocessor statements:

```
#ifndef __MB_CX8_1__
#define __MB_CX8_1__
...
#endif
```

is designed to assure that the header file for the stack never gets included more than once. As we'll see later on in this chapter, it's common for header files to include header files. Problems can arise if the compiler encounters the same header file more than once—it will think that the programmer is trying to declare the same identifier more than once, and it will give an error. The idiom used above prevents this, by defining a preprocessor symbol. Here's how it works. The first time the compiler reads the code, the symbol __MB_CX8_1__ has not been defined. The preprocessor statement #ifndef means "if the symbol is not defined, then process the code from here to the next appearance of #endif. Because the symbol has not been defined the code in the header file is passed on to the compiler by the preprocessor. While processing this code, the preprocessor encounters the #define line, which defines the symbol __MB_CX8_1__. (It sets it to 1, but the value isn't important; what matters is that it's now defined.) If the compiler ever encounters the same code, the #ifndef __MB_CX_8_1__ will cause the compiler to skip over the header file. You'll find this idiom essential in creating header files for abstract data types. The name of the symbol, __MB_CX_8_1__, was chosen so that it's unlikely to be the same as any that might appear in the client program.

Code Example 8-2   *Implementation file for stack implemented using an array*

```
// cx8-2.cpp
// Code Example 8-2: Implementation file, stack implemented using an Array

#include "cx8-1.h"

Stack::Stack()
{
    topIndex = -1;
}

void Stack::push(StackElementType item)
{
    ++topIndex;
    // ensure array bounds not exceeded
```

```
    assert(topIndex < maxStackSize);
    stackArray[topIndex] = item;
}

StackElementType Stack::pop()
{
    // ensure array bounds not exceeded
    assert(topIndex >= 0);
    int returnIndex(topIndex);
    --topIndex;
    return stackArray[returnIndex];
}

StackElementType Stack::top()
{
    // ensure array bounds not exceeded
    assert(topIndex >= 0);
    return stackArray[topIndex];
}

bool Stack::isEmpty()
{
    return bool(topIndex == -1);
}
```

Note that violating the preconditions can cause serious problems with pop, since popping from an empty stack can cause a reference to memory that does not belong to stackArray. One strategy is to test each call to pop to assure that the precondition is met; however, in many uses of the stack the client program may be performing such a test, with the unfortunate result that every call to pop causes two tests of the stack. To be on the safe side, we use assert to make sure that we avoid the problem. This is a difficult design decision, and we have no general answer to offer here; it is essential, however, that the program designer be sensitive to this issue.

The Full Stack Furthermore, there is now a *new* precondition that was not part of the original abstract specification. The array stackArray will be of some fixed size, and if an attempt is made to push more items onto the stack than there are positions in the array, the program will write into memory that does not belong to stackArray. This can result in serious bugs that are difficult to diagnose. The implementation of a Stack ADT via an array forces us to add the following precondition to push:

> *Precondition: ! S.isFull()*

We'll add the following operation, which will permit the client program to test the precondition:

bool S.isFull()

> *Precondition:*   None.

> *Postcondition:*   None.
> *Returns:*   *True* if and only if the S is full, i.e., if a *push* operation is not allowed.

The `isFull()` operation can be implemented as follows. Note that the stack is full when `topIndex` equals `maxStackSize-1`, since a stack of size *n* is indexed from *0* to *n–1* in C++.

```
bool Stack::isFull()
{
   return bool(topIndex == maxStackSize-1);
}
```

Exercise 8-2   Suppose you have a stack *S*, containing various items, and an empty auxiliary stack *T*. Show how each of the following tasks can be performed using the stack operations:

1. Print out the contents of *S* in reverse order.

2. Count the number of items in *S*, returning *S* to its original state.

3. Delete every occurrence of a specified item from *S*, leaving the order of the remaining items unchanged.

Exercise 8-3   Create a client to test the Stack implementation in Code Example 8-2. Compile your client, link it with the Stack ADT, and run it.

Exercise 8-4   Using the dynamic array technique described in Section 7.6, modify the class definition and the Stack constructor so that the client can specify the maximum stack size, rather than being forced to use a compiled-in constant.

8.4   Creating Generic Classes with Templates

So far, we've been using a `typedef` to specify the type of item stored by the stack (and before that, the list.) The C++ language provides a more powerful technique, called ***templates,*** that accomplishes the same thing but has the advantage that you don't need to edit the code for your ADT when you change the type of the item in the container. Furthermore, templates make it easy to have containers that store more than one type; for example, you could have a client program that uses a stack of `int`s and a stack of strings. Note, however, that each templated class will store items of a single type; the containers continue to be homogenous. Thus, templates give us the ability to create ***generic classes,*** classes that can store any type that meets the preconditions for the class. As you'll recall, the Inorder List ADT requires that the type stored in the list must implement "`<=`" and "`==`" operators.

In a templated class, the type stored by the class becomes a parameter to the class. To declare a templated class, you use the new keyword `template` and indicate the type parameter within angle brackets. The Stack class declaration, rewritten with templates, appears in Code Example 8-3.

Code Example 8-3   *Stack declaration rewritten as a templated class*

```
// cx8-3.h
// Code Example 8-3: Stack declaration rewritten as a templated class

#ifndef __MB_CX8_3__
#define __MB_CX8_3__
#include "dslib.h"

const int maxStackSize = 1000;

template < class StackElementType >
class Stack {
public:
    Stack();
    void push(StackElementType item);
    StackElementType pop();
    StackElementType top();
    bool isEmpty();
    bool isFull();
private:
    StackElementType stackArray[maxStackSize];
    int topIndex;
};

#endif
```

As you can see, adding the template definition to a class is quite simple and easy. However, it's a bit tedious to add templates to the individual member functions. As shown in Code Example 8-4, the programmer has to add the template definition to each of the individual functions. In addition, each reference to the class Stack now must include `StackElementType` within angle brackets, because this type is now a parameter to the definition of the stack.

Code Example 8-4   *Definition of Stack member functions using templates*

```
// cx8-4.cpp
// Code Example 8-4: Definition of Stack member functions using templates

#include "cx8-3.h"

template < class StackElementType >
```

```
Stack < StackElementType >::Stack()
{
    topIndex = -1;
}

template < class StackElementType >
void
Stack < StackElementType >::push(StackElementType item)
{
    ++topIndex;
    // ensure array bounds not exceeded
    assert(topIndex < maxStackSize);
    stackArray[topIndex] = item;
}

template < class StackElementType >
StackElementType
Stack < StackElementType >::pop()
{
    // ensure array bounds not exceeded
    assert(topIndex >= 0);
    int returnIndex(topIndex);
    --topIndex;
    return stackArray[returnIndex];
}

template < class StackElementType >
StackElementType
Stack < StackElementType >::top()
{
    // ensure array bounds not exceeded
    assert(topIndex >= 0);
    return stackArray[topIndex];
}

template < class StackElementType >
bool
Stack < StackElementType >::isEmpty()
{
    return bool(topIndex == -1);
}

template < class StackElementType >
bool
Stack < StackElementType >::isFull()
{
    return bool(topIndex == maxStackSize - 1);
}
```

Rather than defining a stack, the template definition of a stack really defines an entire family of stacks. When we declare a particular stack, such as a stack of char or a stack of `int` or a stack of `string`, we refer to that declaration as an ***instantiation*** of a stack. That is, out of all the potential stacks the template defines, we are creating a class that is a particular *instance* of a stack. As you can probably guess, we instantiate a templated class by specifying its name along with the type that should be stored within the stack. As an example, to declare a stack of `char`, you would write

```
Stack < char > stack_of_char;
```

Because templated classes define an entire family of classes rather than one particular class, they pose special technical problems for the linker when it builds a program. Unlike a non-templated class, it's not possible for the compiler to create an object file directly from a templated class because the compiler doesn't know, for example, how much space to allocate for a variable of `StackElementType`. Rather than linking in a templated stack, the linker can only link a particular instantiation of a stack. The exact mechanism for handling this process depends upon the particular language environment in which you are working.

A syntax note: you don't really have to include spaces between the angle brackets and the type of the item in the Stack; that is, both

```
Stack < char > stack_of_char;
```

and

```
Stack<char> stack_of_char;
```

have the same effect. I recommend, however, that you include the extra space, because later on you will want to declare nested templates, which require extra spaces in order to avoid ambiguity.

Exercise 8-5   Write a client that instantiates a stack of `int`s. Compile, link, and test your client.

Exercise 8-6   Write a client that instantiates a stack of `string`s. Compile, link, and test your client.

Exercise 8-7   Given the definitions above, is it possible to create a stack of stacks? Why or why not? How about a stack of lists?

Exercise 8-8   Modify your dynamically sized stack (see Exercise 8-4) to use templates.

Exercise 8-9   Rewrite the implementation of the List ADT in Code Example 7-8 using templates.

8.5 Implementing the Stack 2: Dynamic List

Using an array to implement a stack is simple and efficient, but it has one major drawback: the maximum size of the stack is fixed at compile time (or when the stack is constructed) and cannot be adjusted afterward. Thus an array-based implementation can pose a problem if there is no bound on the stack size known in advance. In this situation, we can do better by basing the implementation on a linked list. We can build a linked list so that the stack can expand as long as there is memory available to the program; we can't hope to do better than that!

The declaration of the stack includes a structure declaration nested within the class. Since struct Node is declared as a private member of the class, it is a type that can be accessed only within the scope of the class. Note that the interface for the public member functions is exactly the same as for the array implementation; thus, a client can substitute the list stack for the array stack without any significant modification to the client. Code Example 8-5 presents the declaration of a stack using a linked list.

Code Example 8-5   *Declaration of a stack using a list*

```
// cx8-5.h
// Code Example 8-5: Declaration of a Stack using a list

#ifndef __MB_CX8_5__
#define __MB_CX8_5__
#include "dslib.h"

template < class StackElementType >
class Stack {
public:
    Stack();
    void push(StackElementType e);
    StackElementType pop();
    StackElementType top();
    bool isEmpty();
private:
    struct Node;
    typedef Node * Link;
    struct Node {
        StackElementType data;
        Link next;
    };
    Link head;
};

#endif
```

The implementation of push requires the allocation of a new node, which is inserted at the head of the list. The LIFO nature of the stack makes list implementation quite easy, since all access to the list is at the head. We provide the implementation of push in Code Example 8-6 and leave the remaining operations as an exercise for the student.

Code Example 8-6   *Definition of operations for the dynamic stack[2]*

```
// cx8-6.cpp
// Code Example 8-6: Declaration of push operation for dynamic stack

#include "cx8-5.h"

template < class StackElementType>
Stack < StackElementType >::Stack()
{
    head = 0;
}

template < class StackElementType >
void
Stack < StackElementType >::push(StackElementType e)
{
    Link addedNode = new Node;
    assert(addedNode);
    addedNode->data = e;
    addedNode->next = head;
    head = addedNode;
}
```

The precondition for pop is the same as it was before—the stack must not be empty. However, we treat the stack as if it can grow without bound and drop the notion of a "full stack." Just in case, we check to make sure that new nodes are allocated by adding the assert, which will cause the program to terminate if we ever run out of memory. This is reasonable in most environments, since if the stack runs out of memory there may not be a good way to recover. Be aware that in some critical environments it may be necessary to test the result of each new operation to assure that memory was allocated. In such a situation, it may be preferable to replace the standard new with a customized new that takes some appropriate action in the event that

---

2. A complete definition of the dynamic stack, including all the operations declared by the header file, can be found in Supplemental Examples 8-1 and 8-2 (sx8-1.h and sx8-2.cpp), included with the source code distribution for this book. The supplemental version also includes a clear operation, which empties the stack with a single call; we'll need this later on.

memory is depleted. Techniques such as this are outside the scope of this book, but all programmers should be sensitive to sources of runtime error.

Exercise 8-10   Implement `pop`, `top`, and `isEmpty`. Note that `pop` will require that the node from the head of the list be deleted. The other functions can each be implemented in one line if you let `head == 0` represent the empty stack.

Exercise 8-11   Create a stack client (or reuse your work from Exercise 8-3) to test the list implementation of the stack.

Exercise 8-12   Using the Timer class available with the source code distribution for this book, compare the performance of array-based and list-based classes. In order to see any differences, you should try something like the following process, repeated *X* times: push *Y* `int`s onto a stack, then pop them off the stack. For a typical environment, *X* = 1000 and *Y* = 10,000 is reasonable; depending on the speed of your system and the amount of RAM available, you might adjust these numbers up or down.

8.6   Applications of the Stack ADT

8.6.1   Building a Calculator with a Stack

An arithmetic calculator evaluates an expression such as $5 + 7 \times 3$ to determine that it's equal to 26. Expressions written in standard algebraic notation are known as *infix* because in an expression like $2 + 3$ the *operator*, +, is written between the two *operands,* 2 and 3. This is the notation that we're used to, and it's the notation used by most (but not all) programming languages, but it's not the only possible way to express arithmetic. One drawback to infix notation is that it is inherently ambiguous. For example, consider the expression $3 - 4 - 5 \times 3$, which has three operators and four operands. The value of the expression depends upon the order in which the operators are applied. For example, if we apply the operators from left to right, the expression would be evaluated this way:

$$3 - 4 - 5 \times 3 = -1 - 5 \times 3 = -6 \times 3 = -18$$

On the other hand, evaluating from right to left would yield 14. Of course, by the standard rules of algebraic expressions, we know that neither answer is "correct"—the expression's value is −16. This is because of the following *precedence rules:*

1. Evaluate expressions within parentheses first.

2. Within parentheses, apply $\times$ and $\div$ before applying + and −.

3. For a sequence of operators of equal precedence according to rule 2, apply the operators from left to right.

These rules are sufficient for any infix expression using the four operators +, −, ×, and ÷.

Precedence rules make it relatively difficult to write a program that evaluates infix expressions. However, expressions written using **Reverse Polish Notation (RPN)** or **postfix** notation, while less familiar, can be easily evaluated using a stack. The expression meaning add 2 and 2 is written 2 2 +; in other words, the two operands for a binary operator are written before the operator. More complicated expressions are best understood by examining the evaluation rules for RPN:

1. Evaluate expressions from left to right.

2. At each occurrence of an operator, apply it to the two operands to the immediate left and replace the sequence of two operands and one operator by the resulting value.

In RPN, the example expression above would be written 3 4 − 5 3 × −. The evaluation rules are applied as follows:

$$3\ 4 - 5\ 3 \times - = -1\ 5\ 3 \times - = -1\ 15 - = -16$$

While this might not be immediately apparent, using RPN eliminates the need for parentheses: any expression can be represented by the position of the operators. For example, consider the infix expression (3 − (4 −5)) ×3 which evaluates to 12; in RPN, this is 3 4 5 − − 3 ×. Later on we'll be looking at a procedure for converting infix expressions to RPN expressions, and we'll be able to prove that any infix expression can be represented in RPN without parentheses. To convince yourself that this seems reasonable, try converting expressions between the two notations.

The evaluation rules for RPN can be elegantly expressed using the Stack ADT. Each time an operand is encountered, it is pushed onto the stack; upon reaching an operator, the last two operands are popped off the stack, and the operator is applied. Note that in order to correctly simulate the rules above, the top of the stack is the right-hand operand, and the second item in the stack is the left-hand operand. Figure 8-7 illustrates the process for the expression above; the arrow points to the current point of evaluation.

In order to write a program to evaluate RPN expressions, we need a way to break up an input string into operands and operators. For example, the input "3 4 − 5 3 * −" contains the following constituent parts: 3 (operand), 4 (operand), − (operator), 5 (operand), 3 (operand), * (operator), − (operator). Each part of the input is called a **token**, and the process of "breaking up" the inputs is called **lexical analysis** or, more informally, **tokenization.** To simplify our explanation of the RPN evaluator, we'll as-

Figure 8-7   *Evaluation of an RPN expression using a stack*

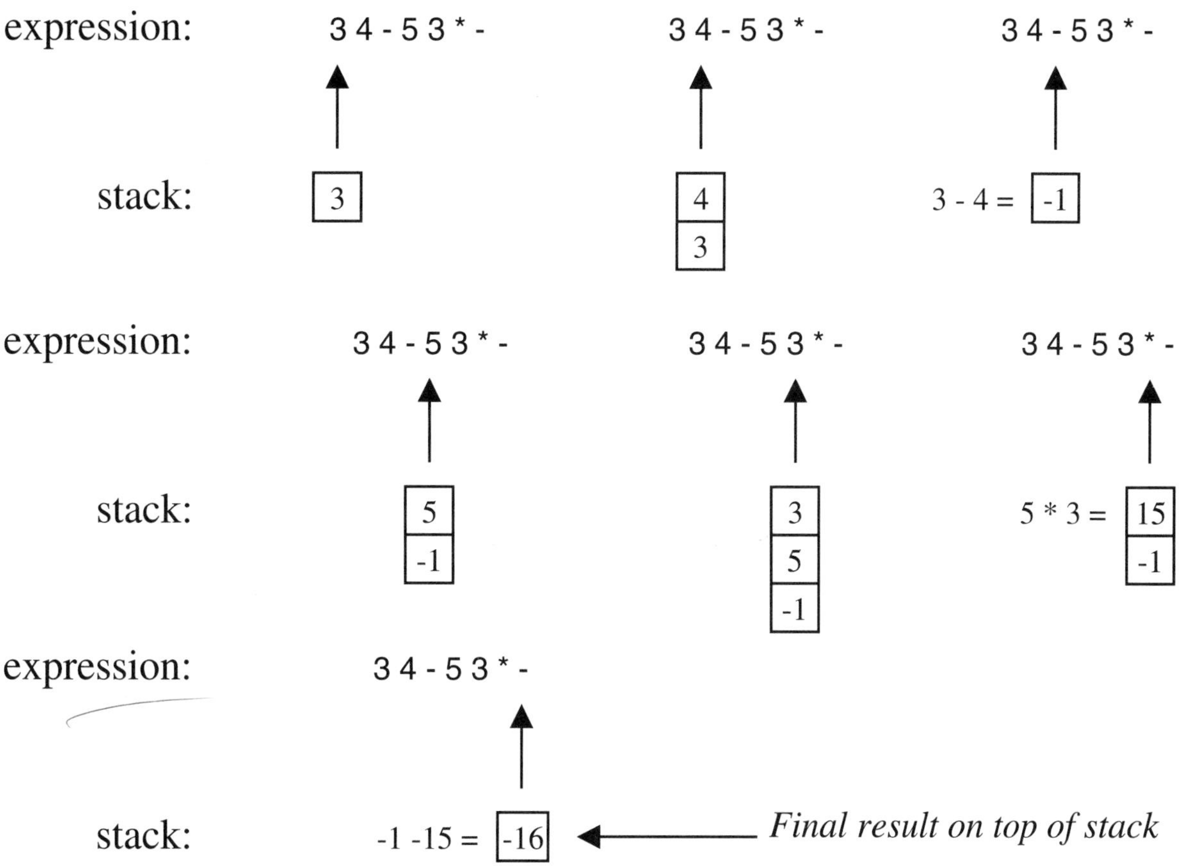

expression: 3 4 - 5 3 * -   3 4 - 5 3 * -   3 4 - 5 3 * -

stack: | 3 | | 4 | 3 - 4 = | -1 |
                                              | 3 |

expression: 3 4 - 5 3 * -   3 4 - 5 3 * -   3 4 - 5 3 * -

stack: | 5 | | 3 | 5 * 3 = | 15 |
                   | -1 | | 5 | | -1 |
                                              | -1 |

expression: 3 4 - 5 3 * -

stack: -1 -15 = | -16 | ◄——————— *Final result on top of stack*

sume that we have available a Token class that performs the tokenization for us.[3] We won't consider here the implementation of the Token class, but instead we'll examine it from the client's point of view.

The Token Class   The public interface of Token includes the following declaration:

```
enum tokenType {operandToken, operatorToken, eolToken,
                eofToken, badToken };
```

---

3. See Supplemental Examples 8-3 and 8-4 (sx8-3.h and sx8-4.cpp), provided with this book.

Each token will be one of the enumerated types. An operand will be an operand-Token; an operator will be an operatorToken. The end of a line and end of the input file will be signalled by the special eolToken and eofToken. Finally, if the tokenizer can't interpret the input, it will mark it as a badToken, leaving it to the client to respond appropriately.

The operators are classified using the following declaration:

```
enum operatorType {none, add, subtract, multiply, divide};
```

The none type is used if the client mistakenly requests the operator type for a token that's not an operator.

The code below contains the class declaration that defines the public interface for the Token class. You can see the complete declaration by looking at Supplemental Example 8-3 (sx8-3.h) in the code distribution, but be warned; it contains features of C++ that we don't cover in this book. In any case, you need only understand the public interface to use this class; you don't need to be able to read the implementation.

```
class Token {
public:
    tokenType nextToken(); // get next token stream
    operatorType getOperator();// return operator
    double getOperand();// return operand
```

The normal use for this class consists of calling nextToken() and then taking appropriate action depending on the type of the token. Using the Token and Stack classes we can implement the RPN evaluator using the algorithm described above. The complete code is shown in Code Example 8-7. We have chosen to use double as the type of the operands; thus, we will instantiate a stack that stores type double. The evaluator treats each input line as an expression—when the end of line is encountered (as signalled by an eolToken) the top of the stack, if any, will be displayed. To improve the robustness of the program, the stack is checked to make sure it's not empty each time an element is popped. This means that when processing an operator the stack must be checked twice, since two operands are needed from the stack. Note also that we have added a function to the stack: clear. This removes everything from the stack so that each line can start fresh.

Code Example 8-7　　*RPN evaluator*

```
// cx8-7.cpp
// Code Example 8-7: RPN Evalutator

#include "dslib.h"
#include "sx8-1.h" // Stack class, with "clear" operation added
```

```cpp
#include "sx8-3.h" // Token class definition
int main()
{
    Token t;
    Stack < double > s;
    double op1, op2;
    bool done(false);

    while (!done) {
        switch(t.nextToken()) {
        case operandToken:
            s.push(t.getOperand());
            break;
        case operatorToken:
            // op2 is the top of the stack, op1 is the next value down
            // first, have to make sure there are 2 items to pop
            if (s.isEmpty()  || (op2 = s.pop(), s.isEmpty()))
                cerr << "Not enough operands for operator!\n";
            else { // get op1, then apply appropriate operator
                op1 = s.pop();
                switch(t.getOperator()) {
                    case add: s.push(op1 + op2); break;
                    case subtract:  s.push(op1 - op2); break;
                    case multiply:  s.push(op1 * op2); break;
                    case divide:
                        if (op2 == 0)
                            cerr << "Division by zero!\n";
                        else
                            s.push(op1 / op2);
                        break;
                }
            }
            break;
        case eofToken:
            done = true;   // break intentionally omitted here
        case eolToken:
            if (!s.isEmpty()) // if there's something in stack, display it
                cout << "--> " << s.pop() << '\n';
            s.clear(); // clear the stack for the next line
            break;
        case badToken:
            cerr << "Input error!\n";
            break;
        }
    }
    return 0;
}
```

Now that you've seen how to create an RPN evaluator, you might ask, "What about evaluating standard (infix) expressions?" One approach is to convert an infix expression into the equivalent RPN expression, and then use an RPN evaluator. Tree-based data structures, discussed in Chapter 11, support a simple conversion algorithm.

Exercise 8-13   Using a Stack, trace the evaluation of the following RPN expressions:

```
7 3 15 * +
12 10 5 / 12 3 - * +
1 1 1 1 1 + - * / +
```

Exercise 8-14   Modify the Token class and the RPN evaluator to add the operation %, which yields the remainder of two operands. (In order to make this meaningful, the second operand needs to be converted to an `int`.)

8.6.2   How Is Recursion Implemented? Part 2

The Stack ADT gives us a framework for better understanding the implementation of recursion. The process of calling functions and returning occurs in LIFO order: if function A calls function B calls function C, then when function C completes its work the runtime will return to function B and then to function A. We can model this with a stack—each call corresponds to a push, and each return to a pop. Thus to implement function calls, including recursive function calls, the Stack ADT is just what we need.

Recall that each time a function is called it gets its own copies of the values of all local variables and formal parameters.[4] Additionally, when the recursive call (or any function call) is made, the runtime must remember the point in the calling program where the call occurred, so that it can return there when the called procedure ends. This information is collected into a structure traditionally called a ***stack frame*** or ***activation record.*** Using stacks and stack frames, we can express the process for calling a function as follows:

To *call* function g from function f:

1. Put the values of all local variables and formal parameters for function f, and the return address in function f, into a stack frame.

2. Push the stack frame onto the ***call stack.***

3. Bind the formal parameters for g to the actual parameters in the call.

4. Transfer control to the first instruction in function g.

To *return* to function f from function g:

1. Pop the top stack frame from the call stack.

2. Use the values in the stack frame to reinitialize the values for function f.

---

4. Remember that the formal parameters are the parameters in the declaration of a function, in contrast to the actual parameters, which are present in the call to a function.

3. Bind the return value for the call to *g*.

4. Transfer control to the return address in function *f*.

There is nothing in this procedure that precludes *f* and *g* from being the same function, so this process describes recursive calls as well as any other function calls. Of course, most people find it more confusing to understand in the recursive case. (Note that the code generated by the compiler has no such problem—it simply applies the rules without caring whether or not a particular call is recursive!)

The best way to get a feel for the interaction of the stack frames and the call stack is to trace through an example. We'll use a simple function that computes the integer power of a floating point number. The function is shown in Code Example 8-8. Note that we've written a rather verbose version of this function—everything within the block that follows the `else` could be written in one line—in order to aid our explanation of the recursive evaluation process.

Code Example 8-8   *Recursive power function*

```
// cx8-8.cpp
// Code Example 8-8: Recursive power function

double power (double base, int exponent)
{
    if (exponent < 1)
        return 1.0;
    else {
        int lower_exponent;
        double lower_power, result;
        lower_exponent = exponent - 1;
        lower_power = power(base, lower_exponent); // *1*
        result = lower_power * base;
        return result;
    }
}
```

Note that the parameters `base` and `exponent` are passed by value; thus, these parameters are treated similarly to local variables, and they need to appear in the stack frame. The stack frames for `power` could be organized as shown in Table 8-1.

Table 8-1

Empty stack frame for power

Label	Type	Value
exponent	int	
lower_exponent	int	
lower_power	double	
result	double	
returnAddress	(program counter)	

The function that calls power will also have a stack frame pushed onto the call stack (to simplify the example, we'll ignore this, but understand that there's at least one stack frame already on the call stack when our trace begins). We'll use "*1*" as the return address, as indicated by the comment in the code.

Now we're ready to begin the trace. Suppose that the function is invoked by the following:

```
cout << power(1.7, 3);
```

The first invocation of power begins with the following bindings:

```
base = 1.7
exponent = 3
```

The values of the other variables will be undefined until statements are executed that give them explicit values. When the code reaches the first recursive call, the stack frame will be in the state shown in Table 8-2.

Table 8-2

Frame 1

Label	Type	Value
base	double	1.7
exponent	int	3
lower_exponent	int	2
lower_power	double	??
result	double	??
returnAddress	(program counter)	1

The initial call to power is now suspended, and the new call begins execution with the following bindings:

```
base = 1.7
exponent = 2
```

Again, the if test is false, the else is executed, and another stack frame is pushed as illustrated in Table 8-3.

Table 8-3   *Frame 2*

Label	Type	Value
base	double	1.7
exponent	int	2
lower_exponent	int	1
lower_power	double	??
result	double	??
returnAddress	(program counter)	1

Two additional calls to power will be generated, yielding the stack frames shown in Table 8-4 and Table 8-5.

Table 8-4   *Frame 3*

Label	Type	Value
base	double	1.7
exponent	int	1
lower_exponent	int	0
lower_power	double	??
result	double	??
returnAddress	(program counter)	1

Table 8-5   *Frame 4*

Label	Type	Value
base	double	1.7

Table 8-5

Frame 4

Label	Type	Value
exponent	int	0
lower_exponent	int	??
lower_power	double	??
result	double	??
returnAddress	(program counter)	1

When the `power` function gets activated with the values shown in Frame 4 (Table 8-5), the bindings of the parameters will be

```
base = 1.7
exponent = 0
```

Hence, no recursion will occur, and `power` returns the value `1.0`. At this point, the call stack looks like Table 8-6.

Table 8-6

Call Stack when recursion bottoms out

Top:

Frame 4
Frame 3
Frame 2
Frame 1
(Frame for function that called `power`)

The execution of the return statement causes the compiler runtime system to

1. pop the top of the call stack

2. restore all variable bindings found in the stack frame that was popped—in this case, using Frame 4

3. replace the call to power with its return value (1.0)

4. continue execution at the spot indicated by the return address

At this point, the remaining computation of the power function can be summarized as

```
lower_power = 1.0;
result = lower_power * base = 1.0 * 1.7 = 1.7;
return 1.7;
```

Now the compiler runtime system pops the current top of the stack—Frame 3—and once again restores the variable bindings, supplies the return value, and continues at the appropriate return address. This process of unwinding the recursive calls will continue until finally control returns to the function that originally called the `power` function.

Exercise 8-15   Trace the stack frames and recursive execution for the following code:

```
cout << power(2.0, 4);
```

8.7   The Robot Navigation Problem Solved

As we discussed in Section 8.1, the backtracking technique can be used to solve the robot navigation problem. The very name *backtracking* suggests backing up when we get stuck, and this backing up will use a Stack. In addition to illustrating the use of a Stack, many other interesting issues arise in the design of a solution for this problem.

Let's start by considering the representation of the map upon which the robot moves. We can think of it as a maze, in which each position is marked by an *x-y* coordinate. We set up the coordinates in the standard geometric directions, as illustrated by Figure 8-8. So the position at the lower-left of the maze will be designated $(0, 0)$, *x* will indicate the column, and *y* will indicate the row.

Figure 8-8   *Directions in the x-y plane*

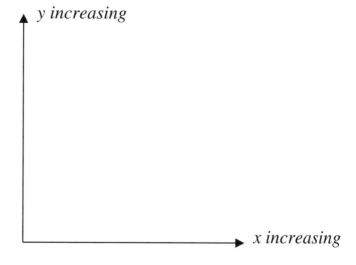

The maze will need to keep track of which squares contain a wall and which are clear. It's also convenient to have a way to mark the squares to keep track of where the robot has already been. Also, to illustrate the problem-solving path taken by the backtracking approach we'll mark the squares separately for forward moves and backward moves. The interface for the Maze class is shown in Code Example 8-9. The constructor for the Maze will take a file name and use it to read in a description of the maze. Remember that while the `private` section of the Maze class is shown in the example, you don't need to understand anything about the implementation in order to use it. Supplemental Example 8-5 (sx8-5.cpp) contains the full implementation of the Maze class so that you can compile and run the examples in this section.

Code Example 8-9   Maze class

```
// cx8-9.h
// Code Example 8-9: Maze class

#ifndef __MB_CX8_9__
#define __MB_CX8_9__

#include "dslib.h"
#include "cx8-10.h" // declaration for MazeCoordinate

enum SquareStatus {clear, blocked, markedForward, markedBackward,
      invalid_coordinate};

class Maze {
public:
    Maze(char * filename);
    int getRows();
    int getCols();
    void markSquareForward(const MazeCoordinate mc);
    void markSquareBackward(const MazeCoordinate mc);
    SquareStatus querySquare(const MazeCoordinate mc) const;
    void display();
private:
    int * * mazeBits;
    int mazeRows;
    int mazeCols;
};

#endif
```

Note that we've referenced a class called MazeCoordinate—this is a convenient way to handle *x-y* pairs that represent positions within the maze. The declaration of MazeCoordinate is shown in Code Example 8-10. The member function neighbor is particularly handy—it takes as an argument a direction in the maze and returns the coordinates of the neighbor in that direction. An enum defines the four valid directions for the maze:

```
enum MazeDirection {mz_north, mz_south, mz_east, mz_west};
```

All these items will be contained within a header file, maze.h, that the robot program will include. We're going to pass over the implementation details of the maze for now; you'll get a chance to look at the implementation if you do the exercises. The complete implementation file for the MazeCoordinate class can be found in Supplemental Example 8-6 (sx8-6.cpp). Note that in addition to declaring the class, the header file also declares an equality and inequality operator to use for comparing MazeCoordinate objects.

Code Example 8-10   MazeCoordinate class

```
// cx8-10.h
// Code Example 8-10: header file for MazeCoordinate class

#ifndef __MB_CX8_10__
#define __MB_CX8_10__

#include "dslib.h"

// MazeDirection represents all the possible directions that the robot can
// move in the maze. The values for the enums are convenient for representing
// the directions in a set

enum MazeDirection {mz_north = 1, mz_south = 2, mz_east = 4, mz_west = 8};

class MazeCoordinate {
public:
    MazeCoordinate();
    MazeCoordinate(int x, int y);
    void setX(const int x);
    void setY(const int y);
    MazeCoordinate neighbor(const MazeDirection dir);
    int getX() const;
    int getY() const;
private:
    int x_coord;
    int y_coord;
};

int operator==(const MazeCoordinate mc1, const MazeCoordinate mc2);

int operator!=(const MazeCoordinate mc1, const MazeCoordinate mc2);

#endif
```

The main function in the program, shown in Code Example 8-11, will cause construction of the maze and prompt the user for the start and target coordinates. It will also construct the stack that will be used for the backtracking. The declarations at the top of the example declare various functions that will be defined later on in this chapter. The main loop of the program will continue to attempt to move until the robot reaches the goal or is stuck in some position. The details of the move attempts are encapsulated within the function `moveAttempt`. Finally, the function `maze.display()` outputs the final maze, showing the path taken to the target. The type MazeCoordinateStack is defined by a `typedef` that uses template syntax to declare a stack of maze coordinates:

```
typedef Stack < MazeCoordinate > MazeCoordinateStack;
```

Code Example 8-11   main *function in robot navigation program*

```cpp
// cx8-11.cpp
// Code Example 8-11: main function in robot navigation program

#include "sx8-1.h" // stack declarations
#include "cx8-9.h" // maze

// A MazeCoordinateStack is a stack that stores objects of type MazeCoordinate
typedef Stack < MazeCoordinate > MazeCoordinateStack;

// defined in cx8-12.cpp
MazeCoordinate getXY(const Maze & maze);

// defined in cx8-13.cpp
bool moveAttempt(MazeCoordinate & currentPosition, const MazeCoordinate goal,
    Maze & maze, MazeCoordinateStack & posStack);


int main()
{
    // set up the maze and the initial positions
    Maze maze("cx8-11.dat"); // creates maze from data file
    // ask the user for the start and target positions
    cout << "Enter X, Y coordinates for start position: ";
    const MazeCoordinate start = getXY(maze);
    cout << "Enter X, Y coordinates for target position: ";
    const MazeCoordinate goal = getXY(maze);
    MazeCoordinate currentPosition(start);
    MazeCoordinateStack positionStack;
    while (currentPosition != goal) {
        if (!moveAttempt(currentPosition, goal, maze, positionStack)) {
            cerr << "Stuck at position: (" << currentPosition.getX() <<
                "," << currentPosition.getY() << ")\n";
            maze.display();
            return 1;
        }
```

```
    }
    cout << "Maze goal achieved.\n";
    maze.display();
    return 0;
}
```

The function GetXY, shown in Code Example 8-12, simply processes the input of an *x-y* pair, including a validity check. The program checks the proposed *x-y* value, inserted into a MazeCoordinate, by calling the querySquare member function for the maze.

Code Example 8-12   Function getXY

```cpp
// cx8-12.cpp
// Code Example 8-12: function getXY

#include "cx8-9.h" // declaration of the Maze (and MazeCoordinate)

MazeCoordinate getXY(const Maze & maze)
{
    int x, y;
    MazeCoordinate returnXY;
    while (1) {
        cin >> x >> y;
        returnXY.setX(x);
        returnXY.setY(y);
        switch(maze.querySquare(returnXY)) {
        case clear: return returnXY;
        case blocked:
            cout << "The position you've chosen is blocked by a wall.\n";
            break;
        case invalid_coordinate:
            cout << "The position you've chosen is not inside the maze.\n";
            break;
        default:
            cout << "There's something wrong with the maze!\n";
            assert(0);
        }
        cout << "Enter another X, Y: ";
    }
}
```

The key to the operation of the program is the function moveAttempt, shown in Code Example 8-13. The moveAttempt function tries three kinds of moves:

1. Attempt to move in the direction of the target.

2. If 1 fails, attempt to move in any other direction.

3. If 2 fails, back up using the stack.

The actual move gets made within the `tryMove` function, which we'll see in a moment.

Code Example 8-13   Function `moveAttempt`

```
// cx8-13.cpp
// Code Example 8-13: function moveAttempt

#include "sx8-1.h" // Stack declaration
#include "cx8-9.h" // Maze declaration

// A MazeCoordinateStack is a stack that stores objects of type MazeCoordinate
typedef Stack < MazeCoordinate > MazeCoordinateStack;

// defined in cx8-14.cpp
bool directionQuery(const MazeCoordinate pos, const MazeCoordinate target,
    const MazeDirection dir);

// defined in cx8-15.cpp
bool tryMove(Maze & maze, MazeCoordinate & currentPosition,
    const MazeDirection dir, MazeCoordinateStack & posStack);

// moveAttempt tries to make any move from the currentPosition;
// if a move is made, return true, otherwise return false (indicating
// that we're stuck with no valid moves).
// PRECONDITION: currentPosition is a valid position in the maze
// POSTCONDITION: maze, posStack, and currentPosition all updated to
// indicate the move
// RETURNS: true if a move was found, else false

bool moveAttempt(MazeCoordinate & currentPosition, const MazeCoordinate goal,
    Maze & maze, MazeCoordinateStack & posStack)
{
    // try all desirable directions
    if (directionQuery(currentPosition, goal, mz_north) &&
        tryMove(maze, currentPosition, mz_north, posStack))
        return true;
    else if (directionQuery(currentPosition, goal, mz_south) &&
        tryMove(maze, currentPosition, mz_south, posStack))
        return true;
    else if (directionQuery(currentPosition, goal, mz_west) &&
        tryMove(maze, currentPosition, mz_west, posStack))
        return true;
    else if (directionQuery(currentPosition, goal, mz_east) &&
        tryMove(maze, currentPosition, mz_east, posStack))
        return true;
    // if robot couldn't move in desired direction, try the rest
    if (!directionQuery(currentPosition, goal, mz_north) &&
```

```
      tryMove(maze, currentPosition, mz_north, posStack))
      return true;
   else if (!directionQuery(currentPosition, goal, mz_south) &&
      tryMove(maze, currentPosition, mz_south, posStack))
      return true;
   else if (!directionQuery(currentPosition, goal, mz_west) &&
      tryMove(maze, currentPosition, mz_west, posStack))
      return true;
   else if (!directionQuery(currentPosition, goal, mz_east) &&
      tryMove(maze, currentPosition, mz_east, posStack))
      return true;
   // no possible move -- can we back up?
   if (posStack.isEmpty()) // nope! we're stuck!
      return false;
   else { // back up
      maze.markSquareBackward(currentPosition);
      currentPosition = posStack.pop();
      return true;
   }
}
```

The function `directionQuery`, in Code Example 8-14, takes two coordinate positions and a direction and returns true if the proposed direction will take the robot closer to the target. For example, if the function call

```
directionQuery(currentPosition, goal, mz_north)
```

returns true, then moving north will take the robot closer to the target; otherwise, a move north will take the robot farther away.

Code Example 8-14   *Function* `directionQuery`

```
// cx8-14.cpp
// Code Example 8-14: function directionQuery

#include "cx8-9.h"

// directionQuery takes two positions and a direction, returning
// true if the proposed direction will take the robot in the direction
// from the first position to the second position, and false if the
// proposed direction will not

bool directionQuery(const MazeCoordinate pos, const MazeCoordinate target,
   const MazeDirection dir)
{
   switch(dir) {
   case mz_north: return bool(pos.getY() < target.getY());
   case mz_south: return bool(pos.getY() > target.getY());
   case mz_east:  return bool(pos.getX() < target.getX());
```

```
case mz_west:  return bool(pos.getX() > target.getX());
default: assert(0); // should never get here!
    return false;
}
}
```

We saw in function moveAttempt where the stack gets popped; items will get pushed in tryMove, in Code Example 8-15, which will actually perform the operation of a move if it can, including the push. In addition to pushing the current position onto the stack and updating the position, the function will also mark the square to indicate that we've been there and that we moved forward. This will prevent us from returning to this square (except when backing up), and it will also provide a record that we'll be able to view at the end when we display the maze.

Code Example 8-15   *Function* tryMove

```
// cx8-15.cpp
// Code Example 8-15: function tryMove

#include "sx8-1.h" // Stack declaration
#include "cx8-9.h" // Maze declarations

// A MazeCoordinateStack is a stack that stores objects of type MazeCoordinate
typedef Stack < MazeCoordinate > MazeCoordinateStack;

// tryMove takes a maze, a position in the maze, a direction, and a stack.
// If the dir represents a valid move, then push the currentPosition
// onto the stack, mark the currentPosition in the maze to indicate
// a forward move from that position, update currentPosition to move in
// that direction, and return true.
// Otherwise, return false.
// PRECONDITIONS: currentPosition is a valid position in maze
// POSTCONDITIONS: If a move can be made in direction "dir",
// the value of currentPosition is updated, the maze is marked to indicate
// the move, and the old position is pushed onto the stack.
// RETURNS: true if the proposed move was made, else false

bool tryMove(Maze & maze, MazeCoordinate & currentPosition,
    const MazeDirection dir, MazeCoordinateStack & posStack)
{
    MazeCoordinate tryCoordinate = currentPosition.neighbor(dir);
    if (maze.querySquare(tryCoordinate) == clear)  {
```

```
        posStack.push(currentPosition);
        maze.markSquareForward(currentPosition);
        currentPosition = tryCoordinate;
        return true;
    }
    else
        return false;
}
```

Exercise 8-16   As written, the function `moveAttempt` has some inefficiency because it will try all four directions every time. If the robot has already reached a position and then returns there from a stack pop, there's no reason to consider directions previously checked. Modify the program to store, in addition to the current position, a record of the directions already checked and use that information when returning to a position later.

Chapter Summary

- The Stack ADT is a LIFO data structure characterized by the operations push and pop.
- The Stack ADT can be implemented using an either array, which has a fixed maximum size, or a linked list, which can grow dynamically.
- Generic classes can be created using templates in C++.
- Reverse Polish Notation (RPN) expressions can be conveniently evaluated with a Stack ADT.
- The Stack ADT can be used to organize the stack frames used by a runtime to keep track of function calls, both recursive and nonrecursive.

Programming Laboratory Problems

Lab 8-1   Write a program that uses a stack to test for balanced bracket pairs. The input strings, all consisting of a single line less than 80 characters long, will include four types of brackets:

```
{ }, [ ], < >, ( )
```

In order for an expression to be parenthesized properly, each left bracket must be matched with a right bracket of the same type. For example, the expression

```
{A [B <C> <D> (E) F] (G)}
```

is correct, but

```
{A[B}]
```

is not, because the "}" after "B" pairs with a "[," which is not allowed.

Your program will read strings and determine whether they are properly parenthesized until it gets a string starting with a period ("."), at which point it will terminate. You will need to instantiate a Stack of `char`.

Lab 8-2   Use a stack to write a very simple adding machine program. The program will read in floating point numbers, push them onto a stack, add them together whenever a plus sign, "+," is entered and print the result. In addition, the adding machine will recognize the following instructions: a comma—","—means "cancel the last entry" and a period—"."—means "cancel all entries," that is, clear the stack. Note that you have to write the I/O portion of the program so that it can handle either a character or a number.

Lab 8-3   Operating systems generally use a stack to record the state of a computer system so that it can be restored later. As the system operates, it must respond to *interrupts* that are generated by various conditions. Consider what happens when you are typing on the keyboard. Each time you hit a key, the system must interrupt whatever its doing, store the character generated by the keypress in the appropriate memory location, and then return to whatever it was doing before. Furthermore, while processing one interrupt, another one may occur to "interrupt the interrupt." For example, the system may be receiving input from the keyboard, processing messages received via a network interface, handling disk I/O, and compiling a program all at the same time. (For a multi-user system such as a Unix server, the situation may be even more complicated.)

One strategy that operating systems use to keep track of the work they have to do is to use a context stack. Each item in the context stack will store a record of everything the system needs in order to restore the state of the system after an interrupt is handled. In this lab you will simulate a context stack. First, assume that the following information is sufficient to express the state of a system:

- PC: a 32-bit program counter

- registers 0–3: 4 registers, each containing 32 bits

- system flags: 32 boolean flags that express the state of the machine. (For example, one flag might mean that the system is running in user mode, i.e., that it has no special privileges, and another may indicate that a divide-by-zero has taken place. For the purposes of this assignment, the meaning of the system flags is not important, you will simply record them.)

Create a class Context that can store this information. Create a stack of Context. Test your system by writing a driver that uses the following algorithm:

1. Set the state of the system randomly.

2. Allow the user to enter either 'I' for Interrupt, or 'R' for Return from interrupt. Each time an interrupt is generated, the old context is pushed onto the stack, and a new context is created randomly. When a return is generated, the current context is thrown away, the top of the stack is popped and the state of the system is set from the context on top of the stack. (An attempt to return when nothing is on the stack is an error.)

3. Each time the state of the system changes, print out the current state so you can check that your system works. Output the data in hexadecimal, by using the hex output modifier:

```
cout << hex << pc;
```

Lab 8-4   A palindrome is a string of characters that's the same forward and backward. Typically, punctuation, capitalization, and spaces are ignored. For example, "Poor Dan is in a droop" is a palindrome, as can be seen by examining the characters "poordanisinadroop" and observing that they are the same forward and backward.

One way to check for a palindrome is to reverse the characters in the string and then compare them with the original — in a palindrome, the sequences will be identical.

1. Write a function `bool isPalindrome(string s)` that uses a stack to determine whether a string is a palindrome.

2. Write a program that reads in a string, removes spaces and punctuation, converts all the characters to lowercase, and then calls `isPalindrome` to check for a palindrome and reports the result.

Lab 8-5   An alternative to using a stack in a backtracking problem is to use recursion. As you now know, recursion will also depend upon a stack, but the stack is implicit rather than explicit. Rewrite the robot navigation program to use recursion, rather than a stack. (*Hint:* You will want to make a recursive call each time you move forward, and return from one each time you back up.)

Lab 8-6   Reimplement the Inorder List in Code Examples 7-10 and 7-11 to use templates. Test your code by instantiating Lists of `ints` and `strings`. Also, try to instantiate a List of stacks, and report the results.

Lab 8-7   A classic problem that can be solved by backtracking is called the Eight Queens problem, which comes from the game of chess. The chess board consists of 64 squares arranged in an 8-by-8 grid. The board normally alternates between black and white squares, but this isn't relevant for the present problem. The queen can move as far as she wants in any direction, as long as she follows a straight line, vertically, horizontally, or diagonally, as shown by Figure 8-9. The shaded squares represent all the positions that the queen, represented by the crown, can possibly move to. We say that the queen can *attack* the shaded squares.

Figure 8-9   *The queen's moves*

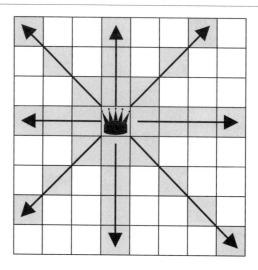

The Eight Queens problem is, How can you place eight queens on the board so that no queen can attack any other? The problem can by generalized to the *n* Queens problem, for an *n*-by-*n* board. To solve the problem, move from left to right and try to place a queen in each column. If, for example, you get to the fifth row and can't find a legal position, backtrack to the previous column and try the next legal position. Write a program that solves the *n* Queens problem. (*Hint:* Give some careful thought to the way in which you represent the board and the queens. Your first attempt will probably keep more information than you really need.)

Lab 8-8   The dynamic stack implementation in Section 8.5 is nice because it can grow and shrink as needed, but it has the disadvantage that you need a link for every item in the stack. For a large stack, this additional storage overhead could be substantial. An alternative is to combine features of the array-based stack and the list-based stack by creating a list of arrays! What you do is create a linked list in which each node contains, say, 100 elements instead of just 1. Each time you push, you attempt to add the new element to the existing array node if there's space available; otherwise, you allocate a new node that can store 100 elements and link it to the existing list. When you pop, you perform the reverse process—if a pop makes a node completely empty you delete it. Now your overhead is just a few extra bytes for each 100 elements. In fact, the size of the node can be a parameter passed to the constructor.

Implement and test a stack based on these principles. You can structure each node in the list like this:

```
struct stackNode;
typedef stackNode * stackNodePtr;
struct {
  StackElementType * elementArray;
  int current_top; // points to top in elementArray
  stackNodePtr next;
};
```

Then you allocate `elementArray` dynamically, using the technique discussed in Section 7.6. Note that when you `delete` the memory allocated for `elementArray`, you should use the following form:

```
delete elementArray[];
```

This informs C++ that the memory you want to delete was allocated as an array, that is, in the form

```
new elementArray[arrSize];
```

and therefore it will recover the memory correctly.

Chapter Vocabulary

activation record	operator
backtracking	pop
call stack	postfix
container	precedence rules
generic class	push
heterogeneous	Reverse Polish Notation
homogeneous	stack
infix	stack frame
instantiation	template
Last In, First Out (LIFO)	token
lexical analysis	tokenization
operand	top

Chapter 9 Queues

Overview   An introduction to the Queue ADT and its uses, including simulation.

Chapter Objectives

1. To understand and apply the Queue ADT.
2. To implement a Queue using an array and links.
3. To design and program simple simulations.

9.1   Problem: Computer Network Performance[1]

An important role of software is to simulate aspects of the "real world" so that alternative scenarios can be compared at low cost. As an example, we'll look at modeling a computer network under different conditions. Network modeling software lets us build a computer network on paper and analyze its performance before hardware is purchased and installed.

A widely-used standard for building computer networks is called Ethernet. Ethernet, developed by Xerox in the early 1980s, is not really a particular set of hardware and software. Rather, it is a set of rules, or a *protocol*, that describes exactly how devices can communicate with each other over a wire (or via radio). The standard IEEE 802.3 defines the protocol, called ***Carrier Sense Multiple Access with Collision Detection (CSMA/CD)***. In this chapter, we present a simplified description of the Ethernet protocol; for a more complete and accurate view, consult a computer networking text such as Tanenbaum (1996).

Figure 9-1 illustrates a typical Ethernet configuration. You're probably familiar with most of the things connected to the network, perhaps with the exception of the bridge—a bridge connects one network to another. On an Ethernet, every device has a unique identification (ID) number. Actual Ethernet ID numbers consist of six two-digit hexadecimal numbers; to simplify things here, we'll just assign each device an integer, as shown in Figure 9-1. For example, the printer is device 6 and the file server is device 1.

Figure 9-1   *A sample Ethernet configuration*

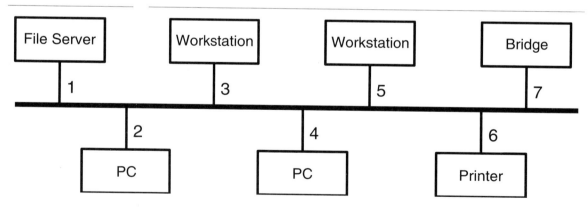

---

1. A discussion of this example first appeared in Berman (1996).

Figure 9-1 shows the *logical* connections between devices on an Ethernet. Depending on the type of wiring used, the actual connections might look quite different, but the algorithm is always the same. A device communicates with another device by putting messages out onto the Ethernet, preceded by the ID number of the device the message is intended for. For example, if a PC—device 2—wants to send a document to the printer—device 6—it puts the characters that make up the document out onto the network, preceded by a header indicating the data is intended for device 6. All the other devices on the network can look at the stream of characters that represents the document, but since they have ID numbers other than 6, they will simply ignore them. The printer, seeing a message for device 6, reads the characters and prints the document.

What happens if two devices want to send messages at the same time? This is the crux of the design of Ethernet. We'll look at this toward the end of the chapter, when we attempt a more complete simulation of an Ethernet; for right now, let's just look at the issues that arise when one device talks to another.

Device communication
Let's develop the example of device 2 talking to device 6 in more detail. We can envision the participants in the message as three: the PC, the printer, and the Ethernet itself. Conceptually, what happens is the PC passes the message to the Ethernet, and the Ethernet passes the message to the printer. What complicates matters is that these three players may each operate at different speeds. The Ethernet itself is very fast—10 million bits per second—so it can always keep up with the devices connected to it, but the converse is often not true. Let's suppose that the PC puts the document onto the Ethernet at 100,000 characters per second, but the printer can only process 10,000 characters per second. How can the printer make sure it doesn't miss any characters? At the interface between the Ethernet and the printer is a buffer. The operation of a buffer is illustrated in Figure 9-2. The buffer is special hardware that is fast enough to keep up with the Ethernet. Of course, a real buffer will contain thousands of characters. As characters enter the buffer, they are inserted on one end and removed from the other, as shown by the figure. The next character received via the Ethernet will be inserted next to the 'b'; the next character read by the printer will be '0'. This doesn't solve the whole problem—eventually, if nothing else is done, the buffer will overflow—but it is a critical piece of the puzzle.

The ADT that closely models the operation of a buffer is called a *queue*. The queue is a special kind of list in which all items are added from one end (the tail) and removed from the other (the head). Note the contrast with the stack, in which items are added and removed from the same end. While the stack reverses the order of items, the queue preserves the order; the queue is a First In, First Out (FIFO) data structure.

The queue also models the process of "waiting in line": as new people get on line, they go to the end; when it's time to serve a customer, the person at the head of the

Figure 9-2   *Operation of a buffer on an Ethernet*

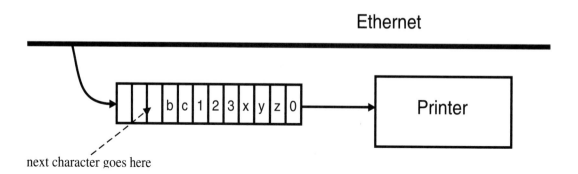

next character goes here

line is served. In fact, in most English-speaking countries other than the United States, the word *queue* is commonly used to refer to a waiting line. A queue can be used in any program that needs to keep track of items while preserving their order. Queues are ubiquitous in operating systems and network software; in fact, the mathematical theory that underlies such software is called queuing theory.

We'll take a more careful look at simulating the Ethernet at the end of this chapter. First, let's examine the Queue ADT and its implementation.

9.2 The Queue ADT

The Queue ADT illustrated in ADT 9-1 is structured quite similarly to the Stack, with the exception of the FIFO nature of adding and removing items. We use the term *enqueue* to mean "put an item on the rear of the queue" and *dequeue* to mean "take an item from the front of the queue."

ADT 9-1   Queue

Characteristics

- A Queue Q stores items of some type (queueElementType), with First-In, First-Out (FIFO) access.

Operations

queueElementType Q.dequeue()

Precondition: ! isEmpty()
Postcondition: $Q_{post} = Q_{pre}$ with front removed
Returns: The least-recently enqueued item (the front).

void Q.enqueue(queueElementType x)

Precondition: None.
Postcondition: $Q_{post} = Q_{pre}$ with item x added to the rear.

queueElementType Q.front()

Precondition: ! isEmpty()
Postcondition: None.
Returns: The least-recently enqueued item (the front).

bool Q.isEmpty()

Precondition: None.
Postcondition: None.
Returns: True if and only if Q is empty, i.e., contains no data items.

Let's look at a brief sample program that uses queues. We'll get to more interesting code when we return to the simulation problem at the end of the chapter. The program shown in Code Example 9-1 creates a stack and a queue, reads characters from input and adds them to the stack and queue, and then retrieves the characters from the stack and queue. You may want to get this program and run it, to get a better feel for the operation of stacks and queues.

Code Example 9-1   *Queue example*

```
// cx9-1.cpp
// Code Example 9-1: Queue example

#include "cx9-2.h" // queue declarations
#include "sx8-1.h" // stack declarations

int main()
{
    char c;
    Queue < char > q;
    Stack < char > s;

    // read characters until '.' found, adding each to Q and S.
    while (1) {
        cin >> c;
        if (c == '.') break; // when '.' entered, leave the loop
```

```
      q.enqueue(c);
      s.push(c);
   }
   while (!q.isEmpty()) {
      cout << "Q: " << q.dequeue() << '\t';
      cout << "S: " << s.pop() << '\n';
   }
   return 0;
}
```

Running this program will demonstrate that queues preserve order, while stacks reverse it; for example, if the input is "abc.", the output will be

```
Q: a   S: c
Q: b   S: b
Q: c   S: a
```

Let's now look at how we can construct a queue to meet this specification. Just like we did with stacks, we'll compare an array-based version to a linked list implementation.

Exercise 9-1   What is the output resulting from the following sequence, where q is an initially empty queue of int:

```
q.enqueue(1);
q.enqueue(3);
q.enqueue(2);
cout << q.front();
cout << q.dequeue();
cout << q.front();
if (q.isEmpty())
   cout << "empty\n";
else
   cout << "not empty\n";
```

9.3   Implementing a Queue 1: Array

While implementing a queue with an array is similar to implementing a stack, there is a complication with the queue that we didn't see with the stack. Unlike the stack, which had one significant end—the top—a queue is double-ended, with a front and rear. Figure 9-3 illustrates the process of enqueuing and dequeing elements from a queue built using an array of size 4. While it's unlikely you'd ever use such a small array, it illustrates the problem that arises with any fixed-size array. Let f mark the front, and r mark the rear element of the queue. Each time an item is enqueued, the rear of the queue moves one place to the right; each time an element is dequeued, the

Figure 9-3   *A sequence of enqueue and dequeue operations illustrated*

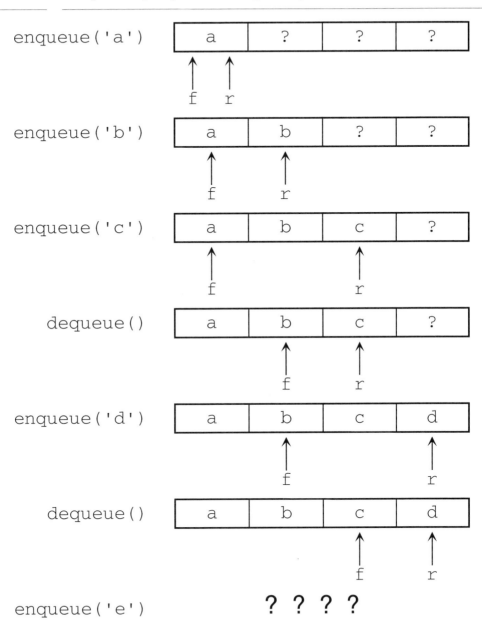

front moves one position to the right. Note that there's no particular reason to actual-ly remove the elements from the array, since the dequeuing operation depends upon the value of f, so a and b are still in the array after they're dequeued. The problem arises with the last operation: how should the enqueuing of e be handled? Clearly, the array has empty spaces in the first two positions, but there's no way to move r any further to the right.

The Circular Queue   The trick here is to think of the array as if the end wraps around to the front, like a circle; this is illustrated in Figure 9-4. Once we think of our array this way—as if the last element, in this case the item at index 3, is next to the first (0)—it's pretty easy to visualize how the queue should work. Instead of moving to the right, the queue migrates clockwise around the circle. Because we're treating the queue as a circle we won't run out of room when the contents of the queue get all the way to the highest elements in the array. This implementation is known as a ***circular queue***. Please note that there is no circular queue ADT; rather, the term *circular queue* describes a particular implementation of the Queue ADT.

Figure 9-4   *A Circular Queue*

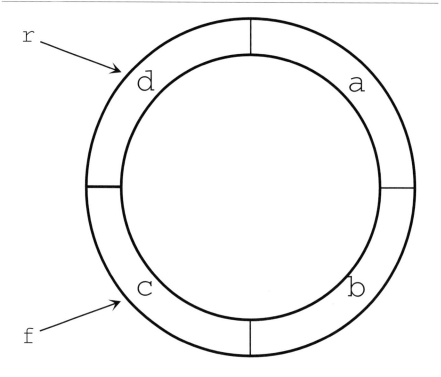

It's easy to visualize the queue as a circle, but what does this really mean for the implementation? We still have to work with arrays, not circles. In order for the first and last indices to work in a circular manner, they need to increase one element at a time until they get to the largest index in the array, which we denote as maxQueue-1, and then go to zero. One simple way to create this effect is to add 1 to the index and then compute the result "modulo maxQueue". That is, we take the remainder after dividing by maxQueue. Another possibility is to simply check each time we go to add 1—if the current value is equal to maxQueue-1, then go back to zero; this is the implementation we use here. Either way, the result is always in the range 0...maxQueue-1, giving us just the range we want. Because this operation occurs frequently we use an internal function nextPos to perform this calculation.

There's one more issue we have to address: where to start the values of f and r. The obvious implementation is for a queue with a single element to have f==r, but then r needs to start one step before f, so that adding the first element and incrementing r will result in f==r. For this implementation, the test for an empty queue would be nextPos(r)==f. The problem with this approach is that when the queue is full, nextPos(r)==f will also hold, thus leaving no way to distinguish between an empty queue and a full queue, as shown in Figure 9-5. This diagram illustrates a sequence of enqueue operations, from an empty queue to a full queue, showing that there's no way by looking at f and r alone to tell the two cases apart.

Figure 9-5
Queue implementation in which full and empty queues cannot be distinguished

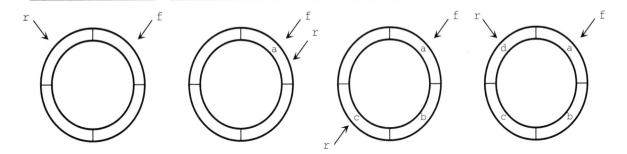

One approach is to let f==r indicate an empty queue. The cell pointed to by f is never used to contain queue data: the "real" data starts at nextPos(f). The queue is full when nextPos(r)==f. One cell in the array is "wasted," but this is unavoidable. Figure 9-6 illustrates the same sequence as Figure 9-5, using the approach described here. In Exercise 9-4 you can try out an alternative approach. The header file for a queue of chars appears in Code Example 9-2, while Code Example 9-3 shows the implementation file.

Figure 9-6   *Corrected queue implementation demonstrated*

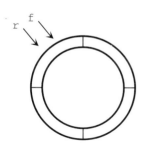 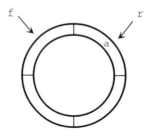 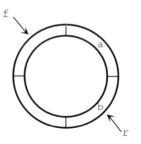 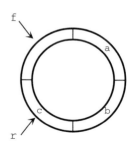

Code Example 9-2   *Header file for generic queue*

```cpp
// cx9-2.h
// Code Example 9-2: Header File for Queue

#ifndef __MB_CX9_2__
#define __MB_CX9_2__

#include "dslib.h"

const int maxQueue = 200;

template < class queueElementType >
class Queue {
public:
    Queue();
    void enqueue(queueElementType e);
    queueElementType dequeue();
    queueElementType front();
    bool isEmpty();
private:
    int f; // marks the front of the queue
    int r; // marks the rear of the queue
    queueElementType elements[maxQueue];
};

#endif
```

Code Example 9-3   *Implementation of a circular queue*

```cpp
// cx9-3.cpp
// Code Example 9-3: Implementation of a Circular Queue

#include "cx9-2.h"

int nextPos(int p)
{
    if (p == maxQueue - 1) // at end of circle
        return 0;
    else
        return p+1;
}

template < class queueElementType >
Queue < queueElementType >::Queue()
{
    // start both front and rear at 0
    f = 0;
    r = 0;
}

template < class queueElementType >
void
Queue < queueElementType >::enqueue(queueElementType e)
{
    // add e to the rear of the queue, advancing r to next position
    assert(nextPos(r) != f);
    r = nextPos(r);
    elements[r] = e;
}

template < class queueElementType >
queueElementType
Queue < queueElementType >::dequeue()
{
    // advance front of queue, return value of element at the front
    assert(f != r);
    f = nextPos(f);
    return elements[f];
}

template < class queueElementType >
queueElementType
Queue < queueElementType >::front()
{
    // return value of element at the front
    assert(f != r);
    return elements[nextPos(f)];
}
```

```
template < class queueElementType >
bool
Queue < queueElementType >::isEmpty()
{
    // return true if the queue is empty, that is,
    // if front is the same as rear
    return bool(f == r);
}
```

Exercise 9-2   Using a sequence of pictures similar to Figure 9-6, trace the state of an initially empty Queue of char, q, of size 4, for the following sequence of operations:

```
q.enqueue('c');
q.enqueue('a');
cout << q.dequeue();
q.enqueue('r');
cout << q.dequeue();
cout << q.dequeue();
q.enqueue('s');
```

Exercise 9-3   The circular queue can still fill up if too many items are added. Write a declaration
and the definition of the following function:

```
bool isFull()
```

that returns false if there's room to add another item to the queue and true otherwise.

Exercise 9-4   An alternative to leaving an empty cell in the array is to keep a count of the number
of elements in the queue. This size counter can be used to distinguish empty from
full queues. Modify the implementation of Code Example 9-3 using this idea.

9.4   Implementing a Queue 2: Dynamic List

Just as we did for the Stack ADT, we'll now examine implementing the queue with a
dynamic linked list. Because all the action in the stack takes place at one end a single pointer is all that is required. With the queue we have to keep track of a front and
a rear, requiring a pointer for each. Code Example 9-4 contains a header file with the
class definition for the queue. Note that the public portion is exactly as before, demonstrating the abstract nature of the queue definition.

Code Example 9-4   *Header file for queue implemented with a linked list*

```
// cx9-4.h
// Code Example 9-4: Header for Queue as Dynamic List

#ifndef __MB_CX9_4__
#define __MB_CX9_4__

#include "dslib.h"

template < class queueElementType >
class Queue {
public:
    Queue();
    void enqueue(queueElementType e);
    queueElementType dequeue();
    queueElementType front();
    bool isEmpty();
private:
    struct Node;
    typedef Node * nodePtr;
    struct Node {
        queueElementType data;
        nodePtr next;
    };
    nodePtr f;
    nodePtr r;
};

#endif
```

Now let's consider the implementation, as shown in Code Example 9-5. An empty queue will be represented by a linked list with no elements. Thus the constructor will initialize the queue by setting both front and rear pointers to 0.

Enqueuing a new item will require the dynamic allocation of a new node. The assert is used to ensure that if the allocation fails, the program terminates. The queue item is placed in the node, and the item added to the list, with special code required for the case of an initially empty queue.

Dequeuing reverses the process. In order to avoid a memory leak we keep a pointer to the original front of the list so that it can be deallocated with delete. We need to check and see whether we're deleting the last node in the list, in which case the value of r needs to be set to 0.

Code Example 9-5   *Implementation file for queue implemented with a list*

```cpp
// cx9-5.cpp
// Code Example 9-5: Implementation for Queue as Dynamic List

#include "cx9-4.h"

template < class queueElementType >
Queue < queueElementType >::Queue()
{
    // set both front and rear to null pointers
    f = 0;
    r = 0;
}

template < class queueElementType >
void
Queue < queueElementType >::enqueue(queueElementType e)
{
    // create a new node, insert it at the rear of the queue
    nodePtr n(new Node);
    assert(n);
    n->next = 0;
    n->data = e;
    if (f != 0) { // existing queue is not empty
        r->next = n; // add new element to end of list
        r = n;
    }
    else {// adding first item in the queue
        f = n; // so front, rear must be same node
        r = n;
    }
}

template < class queueElementType >
queueElementType
Queue < queueElementType >::dequeue()
{
    assert(f); // make sure queue is not empty
    nodePtr n(f);
    queueElementType frontElement(f->data);
    f = f->next;
    delete n;
    if (f == 0) // we're deleting last node
        r = 0;
    return frontElement;
}

template < class queueElementType >
queueElementType
Queue < queueElementType >::front()
{
```

```
    assert(f);
    return f->data;
}

template < class queueElementType >
bool
Queue < queueElementType >::isEmpty()
{
    // true if the queue is empty -- when f is a null pointer
    return bool(f == 0);
}
```

The relative advantages and disadvantages of the dynamic and static representations of a queue match those for the stack. The dynamic queue can grow to any size required, as long as dynamic memory is available, but it is generally slower due to the overhead of dynamic allocation. The choice between the two implementations depends upon what restrictions can be placed in advance on the growth of the queue.

Exercise 9-5   Implement a driver to test the performance of the Queue ADT. Design experiments to compare the relative performance of the array and linked list implementations.

9.5   Simulation: Modelling a Computer Network

We return to the subject discussed at the beginning of the chapter: using queues to simulate real-world objects, and in particular to model computer network performance. We will abstract from the operation of Ethernet in order to simplify the problem; some of the exercises will examine extensions that will make the simulation more realistic. Although the model used here is greatly simplified, it captures certain aspects of network performance and provides a good illustration of the use of the queue.

Each device on the Ethernet is connected to the net via special hardware called a ***controller***. We are going to model the performance of the Ethernet when two or more controllers try to send a message at the same time. Recall that the network consists, conceptually, of a single cable, to which multiple devices are attached. You can think of it like an old-fashioned speaking tube, in which people in different parts of a building or a ship communicate by shouting into the tube. Before you try to call someone, you first listen to make sure no one is speaking. But there's always a chance that two people listen at the same time, hear nothing, and then shout at the same time. Similarly, two (or more) controllers on the Ethernet may attempt to send a message at the same time. The network can only transmit one message at a time, so when two controllers start sending simultaneously, the message is garbled. The controllers listening to the network are able to detect the problem, so they ignore the garbled message; likewise, the two controllers trying to send will each notice that the message didn't go through. This condition is called a **collision**. When a controller detects a collision, it will back off and try again later. Randomness is used to prevent the two controllers from trying to send again at the same time.

A device connected to the network, such as a PC or a printer, is not expected to know anything about how the Ethernet works. All it should have to know is that it can send and receive data on the network. When a device sends data to the controller, the controller may or may not be able to send it right out to the network—after all, some other controller may be talking. Likewise, when information is being captured by the controller, the device may not be able to keep up with the speed of the Ethernet. So, as Figure 9-7 shows, the controller will have a queue at its interface with the device. (Actually, it will need two queues, one for each direction.)

Figure 9-7   *Device-controller interface*

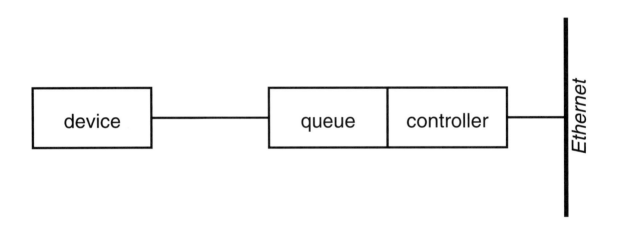

For the purposes of our simulation, we'll ignore the process of reading information off the network and instead will focus on sending. This will be sufficient to illustrate network collisions. By simulating the performance of the network under various assumptions about the number of devices, the frequency of messages, and the size of messages, we can estimate the frequency of network collisions. One performance characteristic of a network is its **effective bandwidth ratio**. This is a measure of the ratio between the amount of data actually transmitted and the maximum possible data. For example, if the network is transmitting data half the time and is idle half the time, its effective bandwidth ratio is .5. As the number of messages goes up on an Ethernet, the effective bandwidth ratio will go up; but when too many devices are trying to communicate at once, collisions will occur, and the effective bandwidth ratio will decline—after all, each time a collision occurs data is not transmitted.

Implementing controllers and devices

We will implement controllers and devices as C++ classes. The Controller class will be a client of queue. "Real" network controllers can, of course, send and receive simultaneously, but to simulate the controllers, we divide the process into two phases. First, we check with each controller to see whether it has data to send. If no controllers are sending, the network is quiet; if exactly one controller sends, the network contains the data sent by that controller. When two or more controllers try to send, a collision occurs. In the second phase, each controller receives the contents of the network. The values `netQuiet` and `netCollide` are special constants defined by an `enum` in `cx9-7.h` (shown in Code Example 9-7). The controllers either receive the data sent by one of the controllers, or else one of the special values. The code for the `main` function of the simulation is shown below. Note that the connections illustrated in Figure 9-7 are mirrored by the code—the top level (Code Example 9-6), which can be thought of as representing the whole network, knows only about the controllers. As we'll see in a moment, the code for the controllers calls the code for the devices.

Code Example 9-6   `Main` *function: Ethernet simulation*

```
// cx9-6.cpp
// Code Example 9-6: Main function: Ethernet simulation

#include "dslib.h"
#include "cx9-7.h"
#include <math.h>

int main()
{
    randomize(); // provide seed to random generator
    int steps;
    cerr << "Enter number of steps: ";
    cin >> steps;
    int maxCnts;
    cerr << "Enter max number of controllers: ";
    cin >> maxCnts;
    int cnts;

    for (cnts = 10; cnts <= maxCnts; cnts+=10)
    {
        Controller * ctrl[1000];
        int i;
        for (i=0; i < cnts; i++)
            ctrl[i] = new Controller;
```

```
    long int collisions(0), transmissions(0);
    int p;
    for (p = 0; p < steps; p++) {
        int senders(0);
        int netChar(netQuiet);
        int c;
        for (c = 0; c < cnts; c++) {
            int ch(ctrl[c]->phase1());
            if (ch != 0) {
                senders++;
                netChar = ch;
            }
        }
        if (senders > 1) {
            netChar = netCollide;
            collisions++;
        }
        else if (senders == 1)
            transmissions++;

        for (c = 0; c < cnts; c++)
            ctrl[c]->phase2(netChar);
    }

    cout << "---\nControllers: " << cnts << "\n";
    cout << "Collision count: " << collisions << "\n";
    cout << "Transmission count: " << transmissions << endl;
    for (i = 0; i < cnts; i++)
        delete ctrl[i];
}

    return 0;
}
```

The main loop of the program runs a sequence of simulations, with the number of controllers going up by ten each time. The code declares an array `ctrl` of Controller objects. Recall that the way C++ classes work, each Controller will have its own values for its variables. Thus different controllers will be in various states, but all this gets taken care of by C++. In other words, each controller has the same logic, but each operates independently. This illustrates one of the advantages of an object-oriented language.

Now let's consider the Controller. The interface file for the Controller is shown in Code Example 9-7. In phase 1, the controller starts by calling the update function for its associated device—if the device is trying to send data to the network, a value will be returned and stored in `inchar`; otherwise, 0 will be returned. This isn't too realistic, because it forces the controller and the device to operate synchronously, that is, at exactly the same rate, but it's good enough for our simulation. If a character arrives from the device, it is enqueued in outQ, which corresponds to the queue in Figure 9-7.

Code Example 9-7 *Header file for controller class*

```
// cx9-7.h
// Code Example 9-7: Controller Class

#include "cx9-4.h" // Queue declaration
#include "cx9-9.h" // Device declaration

enum {netQuiet = 0, netCollide = -100};
const long maxWait = 20;

class Controller {
public:
    Controller();
    int phase1();
    void phase2(int netchar);
private:
    enum state { Idle, Listen, Wait, Send };
    int currentState;
    Queue < char > outQ;
    Device dev;
    int waitTime;
};
```

Controller State Machine   The operation of the controller is described by a set of states: Idle, Listen, Wait, Send. We'll call each pair of calls to phase1 and phase2 a *step*. Each step begins in one of the four states and, depending on the results of calling the device and upon the contents of the queue, may stay in the same state or transit to another state. The operation of the controller is illustrated by the ***state diagram*** in Figure 9-8. The circles represent the four states, and the arrows represent the possible transitions. The text along the arrows summarizes the conditions under which a transition occurs.

The only transition that can occur in phase 1 is from the Idle state to the Listen state—if the controller is idle, and the device sends a character, the controller should now listen to the state of the network. Phase 1 communicates with the device, and also sends characters out to the network. A character is sent to the network only from the Send state; the character always comes from the outQ. In phase 2, the network sends to the controller its current contents—a character, or one of the special values netQuiet or netCollide. Note that in phase 2, the controller does not

Figure 9-8   *State diagram for network controller*

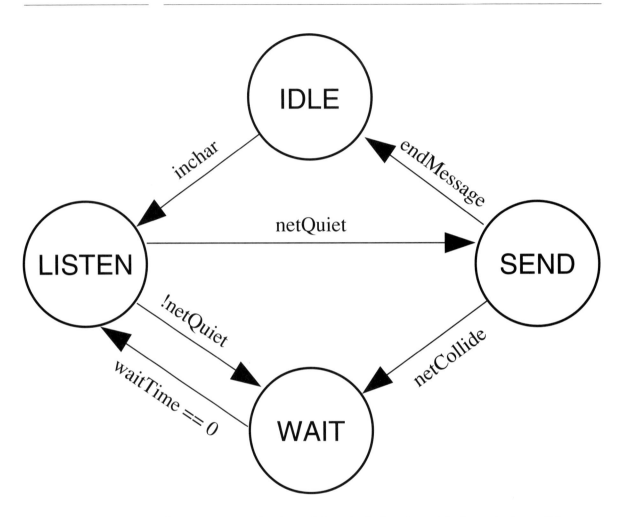

have any output. Another subtle point is that phase 1 looks at the front of the queue using the front function and doesn't dequeue the character, since phase 2 needs to examine the same character to determine whether it has reached the end of a message. (endMessage is a special value defined in cx9-9.h, which appears in Code Example 9-9.) The rest of the details can be found in Code Example 9-8.

Code Example 9-8 *Implementation of Controller class*

```cpp
// cx9-8.cpp
// Code Example 9-8: Controller Class

#include "cx9-7.h"

Controller::Controller()
{
    currentState = Idle;
}

int Controller::phase1()
{
    int inchar(dev.update());
    int outchar(0);
    if (inchar)
        outQ.enqueue(inchar);
    switch(currentState) {
        case Idle:
            if (inchar)
                currentState = Listen;
            break;
        case Listen:
        case Wait:
            break;
        case Send:
            if (outQ.isEmpty())
                currentState = Idle;
            else
                outchar = outQ.front();
            break;
    }
    return outchar;
}
void Controller::phase2(int netchar)
{
    int outchar;
    switch(currentState) {
        case Idle:
            break;
        case Listen:
            if (netchar == netQuiet)
                currentState = Send;
            else {
                waitTime = random(maxWait) + 1;
                currentState = Wait;
            }
            break;
        case Wait:
            if (waitTime > 0)
                waitTime--;
```

```
            else
                currentState = Listen;
            break;
        case Send:
            if (netchar == netCollide) {
                waitTime = random(maxWait) + 1;
                currentState = Wait;
            }
            else {
                outchar = outQ.dequeue();
                if (outchar == endMessage)
                    if (outQ.isEmpty())
                        currentState = Idle;
                    else {
                        waitTime = random(maxWait) + 1;
                        currentState = Wait;
                    }
            }
            break;
    }
}
```

Finally, we look at the code for the devices. Note that because each controller declares a device, there will be multiple device objects operating simultaneously, each using the same logic but potentially in different states. The device is either Idle or Send. An Idle device picks a random number between 0 and the constant avDelay-1. Each time a 0 comes up, the device moves to the Send state and returns nonzero values to the controller, finally ending with the special value endMessage, and then returning to the Idle state. The header file for the device class can be found in Code Example 9-9, and the implementation appears as Code Example 9-10.

Code Example 9-9   Header file for Device class

```
// cx9-9.h
// Code Example 9-9: Device Class

#ifndef __MB_CX9_9__
#define __MB_CX9_9__

#include <stdlib.h>
#include "dslib.h"

const int avDelay =  5000;
const int maxMsg = 10;
const int endMessage = -1;
```

```cpp
class Device {
public:
    Device();
    int update();
private:
    enum state { Idle, Sending };
    state currentState;
    int messageLength;
};

#endif
```

Code Example 9-10   Implementation of Device class

```cpp
// cx9-10.cpp
// Code Example 9-10: Device Class

#include "cx9-9.h"

Device::Device()
{
    currentState = Idle;
```

Phobias   664

Object of Fear	Phobia	Object of Fear	Phobia
itching	acarophobia	sex	erotophobia
lice	pediculophobia	sleep	hypnophobia
lightning	astrapophobia	slime	blennophobia
loneliness	autophobia	snakes	ophidiophobia
magic	rhabdophobia	snow	chionophobia
marriage	gametophobia	solitude	eremophobia
men	androphobia	speed	tachophobia
mice	musophobia	spiders	arachnophobia
mirrors	eisoptrophobia	stars	siderophobia
mobs	ochlophobia	string	linonophobia
money	chrematophobia	stuttering	laliophobia
names	onomatophobia	sun	heliophobia
needles	belonephobia	swallowing	phagophobia
night	nyctophobia	teeth	odontophobia
nudity	gymnophobia	thirteen	triskaidekaphobia
open places	agoraphobia	thunder	brontophobia
pain	algophobia	touch	haptophobia
people	anthropophobia	travel	hodophobia
pleasure	hedonophobia	water	hydrophobia
precipices	cremnophobia	waves	cymophobia
priests	hierophobia	wind	anemophobia
rail travel	siderodromophobia	women	gynophobia
rivers	potomophobia	words	logophobia
robbers	harpaxophobia	work	ergophobia
sea	thalassophobia	worms	helminthophobia

```
character out to the controller
  {

th + 32; // convert number to a printable digit


r to decide whether to start sending
e
  {
(maxMsg) + 1;
;
```

... e show sample data from running the network simulation. To collect ... we set the average delay between messages to 5000 and the average ... to 10. For each controller number, a trial of 100,000 steps was run, ... of transmissions and collisions are shown. As expected, the data ... number of controllers is increased, the amount of data (as indicated by the effective bandwidth ratio) goes up, until the growing number of collisions eats into the available bandwidth. The reader is encouraged to experiment with the simulation, which is included with the source distribution.

Figure 9-9   *Sample data from network simulation*

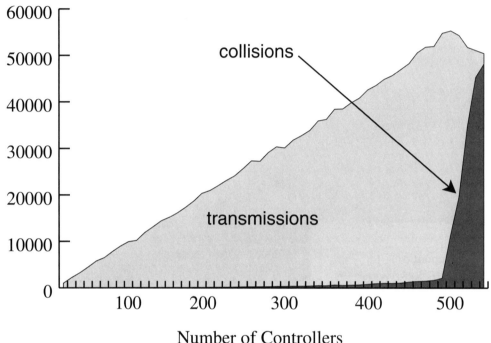

Number of Controllers

There are a number of modifications and improvements that can be made to this simulation in order to model more closely the real operation of an Ethernet. You should understand, however, that a simulation is by definition an abstraction from reality and that whenever possible the results of simulation must be confirmed by comparing with real-world data. The choice of which features to include in a simulation is quite difficult and requires judgement based upon experience.

Exercise 9-6   Run the simulation with various values of the average delay and average message length. How do your results compare with Figure 9-9? (Warning: Depending on your system environment, it's entirely possible that you may run out of memory during some experiments.)

Exercise 9-7   Modify the code for the controllers to keep track of the average delay between the time a message arrives at the controller and the time it is successfully sent across the net. Create a graph of the average (across all controllers) of the averages; compare this average delay graph with the bandwidth ratio graph in Figure 9-9 for a similar range of network load.

Chapter Summary

- The Queue ADT provides a container that stores its contents in First-In, First-Out (FIFO) order.
- A Queue can be implemented using an array by treating it in a circular manner.
- A Queue can be implemented by a linked list.
- Queues can be used to solve simulation problems, such as modeling an Ethernet.

Programming Laboratory Problems

Lab 9-1   The ***Deque ADT*** combines characteristics of the Stack and the Queue. The name "Deque" comes from "double-ended queue" and is usually pronounced "deck." Like the Stack and the Queue, a Deque permits elements to be accessed only at the ends. However, a Deque allows items to be added at either end and removed from either end. We can refer to the operations supported by the Deque as enqueueFront, enqueueRear, dequeueFront, and dequeueRear. Write a formal description of the Deque, implement it (using a dynamic, linked implementation), and test your implementation. (Note that once you have a Deque, you can use it to implement both the Stack and the Queue, thus achieving significant code reuse.)

Lab 9-2   The circular queue implementation in Code Examples 9-2 and 9-3 used a fixed-size array. Rewrite the queue to use a dynamically allocated array, as discussed in Section 7.6.

Lab 9-3   Modify the list implementation of the queue (Code Examples 9-4 and 9-5) to use a circular list.

Lab 9-4   Write an application that reads text from standard input, buffers it in a queue until the end of a sentence is reached (indicated by a word ending with '.'), and then writes out the complete sentence to standard output. Your program should continue to read sentences and write them out again until the input file is closed.

Lab 9-5   The Ethernet simulation makes the unlikely assumption that all devices have the same profile of messages. Redesign the simulation with at least four different types of devices, each with different characteristic delays and message frequencies. Run a large number of simulations, graph the results and compare with Figure 9-9.

Lab 9-6   Simulate the operation of a traffic light in an intersection, as illustrated in Figure 9-10. Cars arrive at random intervals and wait at the light until it's green. The simula-

Figure 9-10   *Traffic simulator*

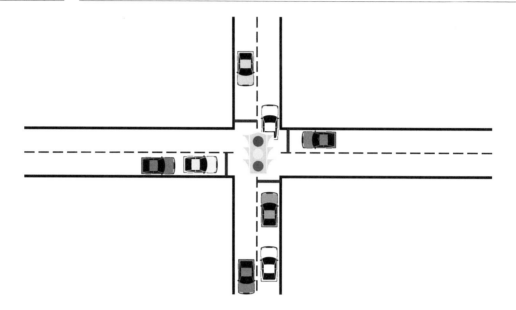

tion should keep track of the state of the intersection with a resolution of 1 second. Two variable parameters will drive the simulation:

1. The number of seconds between the light changing (assume that it stays red and green in each direction for the same amount of time).

2. The probability that at any given second, a new car arrives at the intersection

Assume that it takes exactly 3 seconds for each car to clear the intersection once the light turns green. The simulation should keep track of the number of cars that pass through the intersection and the average time that cars wait. Graph these two variables across a range of timing variables.

Keep a queue for each direction for entering the intersection, and add a car to the appropriate queue when it reaches the intersection. (Note that the way the simulation is set up, you don't really need to keep a queue, just a count, but this more general approach will be useful if you do the next project.)

Lab 9-7   Modify Lab 9-6 as follows:

1. Create three types of vehicles, say, cars, buses, and trucks. The relative probabilities and time taken to pass through the intersection should be different for each vehicle type.

2. Allow some percentage of the vehicles to turn left. Left-turning vehicles block the line until the light changes, as long as there's traffic in the opposite direction.

3. Modify the traffic light cycle to add a left-turn arrow. Compare the number of vehicles and average delays with and without the left-turn arrow.

Lab 9-8   In a ***priority queue***, items are enqueued along with a priority, and each dequeue returns the item with the highest priority. If two items have the same priority, they can be dequeued in either order. Priority queues are heavily used in computer system software—for example, when keeping track of jobs waiting to print on a printer.

Here's an example of how a priority queue works. Suppose the data elements are strings; then for the following sequence:

```
q.enqueue("hello", 7);
q.enqueue("goodbye", 5);
q.enqueue("you", 1);
q.enqueue("say", 2);
cout << q.dequeue() << " " << q.dequeue() << " ";
cout << q.dequeue() << " " << q.dequeue() << endl;
```

The output would be

```
you say goodbye hello
```

Implement a priority queue, using an Inorder List to store the items in the queue. Create a class that includes the data items (which should be templated) and the priority (which should be an `int`.) The Inorder List should contain these objects, with operator `<=` overloaded so that the items with highest priority appear at the beginning of the list (which will make it relatively easy to retrieve the highest item.)

Chapter Vocabulary

Carrier Sense Multiple Access with Collision Detection (CSCD/MA)	enqueue
circular queue	Ethernet
collision	First-In, First-Out (FIFO)
controller	priority queue
Deque ADT	protocol
dequeue	Queue
effective bandwidth ratio	state diagram

Chapter 10 **Tables**

Overview

A discussion of direct access to data via a key, through the Table ADT, implemented as a hash table.

Chapter Objectives

1. To describe how the Table ADT provides direct access to data indexed by a key.

2. To delineate the use of hashing techniques to support very fast retrieval via keys.

3. To explore two approaches to hash tables: linear probing and chained hashing.

10.1   A Data Structure to Support Retrieval by Key

10.1.1   The Routing Problem

In Chapter 9, we simulated an Ethernet, the physical layer of a ***Local Area Network (LAN).*** When connecting networks together to form the Internet, the most important protocol is called, not surprisingly, ***IP,*** the ***Internet Protocol.*** The Internet Protocol is responsible for getting packets of information moved from one network to another, via a process called ***routing.*** The IP protocol depends upon 32-bit addresses that uniquely identify each computer (called a ***host***) and network. For ease of use, the 32-bit addresses are written in four parts, separated by dots.

For example, suppose my IP address is 63.100.1.17, and your IP address is 33.44.10.5. Part of each address specifies the network, while the rest indicates the particular computer (for details, see Comer 1991). For our example addresses, the 63 and 33 indicate the networks, while the rest of the numbers specify particular computers. Now, how does a packet get from my computer to yours? When my computer wants to talk to yours, it knows that it can't talk to it directly because we're not on the same LAN, so it sends the packet to a special computer called a ***router.*** The purpose of a router is to figure out what to do with packets addressed to other networks. The operation of the router follows a very simple pattern: take a packet and look up in a table to determine where to send it next. For example, your LAN and mine probably aren't directly connected; so my router will take the packet and pass it on to a router on an intermediate network, where the process will be repeated. If everything's working, the packet arrives at your computer after passing through several intermediate networks, often in a small fraction of a second.

Routers present several interesting problems, in particular how to build the table of routing information so that packets get where they are supposed to go as fast as possible. For this chapter, we want to focus on one particular issue: how can the router, once given the number of a network, look it up very quickly so that it can send the packet on toward its destination? We'll call the network that the packet's intended for the ***destination network,*** and the network that the router will send it to next the ***forwarding network.*** What we need is a data structure that supports the rapid retrieval of information (the forwarding network number) given a key (the destination network number).

In general, tables support using a key to look up some associated data. The key may be an IP address, an employee number, an ISBN (International Standard Book Number), a social security number, or a variable in a computer program. Occasionally, we simply want to know whether or not a particular key is present, so the associated data is empty. In this chapter, we'll look at the use and implementation of the *Table* ADT.

10.1.2 Defining the Table ADT

We can take the informal description of a Table above and use it to write ADT 10-1 .

ADT 10-1 Table

Characteristics:

- A Table ADT T stores data of some type (tableElementType) with an associated key (tableKeyType).

Operations:

bool T.lookup(tableKeyType lookupKey, tableElementType & data)

Precondition:	None.
Postcondition:	If lookupKey equals a key in the table, the value of data is set to the data associated with that key; otherwise, the value of data is undefined.
Returns:	True if and only if lookupKey equals a key in the table.

void T.insert(tableKeyType insertKey, tableElementType insertData)

Precondition:	None.
Postcondition:	insertData and associated insertKey are stored in T, i.e., T.lookup(insertKey, data) == true, and the value of data will be set to insertData upon return.
Note:	The Postcondition implies that if insertKey duplicates an existing key within the table, the data associated with that key is replaced by insertData.

void T.deleteKey(tableKeyType deleteKey)

Precondition:	None.
Postcondition:	T.lookup(deleteKey, data) will return false.

As usual, we'll now look at how to implement the Table ADT.

Exercise 10-1 Make a list of other situations in which a Table ADT would be useful.

Exercise 10-2 Compare and contrast the Table ADT and the Ordered List ADT.

10.2   Implementing a Table

10.2.1   A Simple Implementation That Doesn't Quite Work

A straightforward implementation is obvious: simply store the key and data in an array, and perform a linear search for the lookup key. The interface file is shown in Code Example 10-1.

Code Example 10-1   *Interface file for table implemented with Linear Search*

```
// cx10-1.h
// Code Example 10-1: Interface File for Table Implemented with Linear Search

#ifndef __MB_CX10_1__
#define __MB_CX10_1__

#include "dslib.h"

// for an array implementation, need a max table size
const int MAX_TABLE = 100;

template < class tableKeyType, class tableDataType >
class Table
{
public:
    Table();  // Table constructor
    bool lookup(tableKeyType lookupKey, tableDataType & data);
    void insert(tableKeyType insertKey, tableDataType insertData);
    void deleteKey(tableKeyType deleteKey);
private:
    // implementation via an unordered array of structs
    struct item {
        tableKeyType key;
        tableDataType data;
    };
    item T[MAX_TABLE]; // stores the items in the table
    int entries;   // keep track of number of entries in table
    int search(tableKeyType key); // an internal routine for searching table
};

#endif
```

A few things to note: because an array stores the data we have to select a fixed size up front. Also, the class definition contains a declaration of a private, or internal, member function, search; this permits any member function within the class to access the function search, but outside the class this function is not accessible.

The search function proves useful in implementing all three of the operations provided by the table. Finally, the template definition needs to refer to both `table-KeyType` and `tableDataType`. With this in mind we're ready to look at our first table implementation, shown in Code Example 10-2.

Code Example 10-2   *Implementation file for Table implemented with Linear Search*

```cpp
// cx10-2.cpp
// Code Example 10-2: Implementation File: Hash Table

#include "cx10-1.h"

template < class tableKeyType, class tableDataType >
int
Table < tableKeyType, tableDataType >
::search(tableKeyType key)
{
    // internal routine for implementation --
    // searches in table for the key --
    // if found, returns its position;
    // else it returns the current value of
    // "entries" -- which is the index 1 past the
    // last item in the table
    int pos;
    for (pos = 0; pos < entries && T[pos].key != key; pos++)
        ;
    return pos;
}

template < class tableKeyType, class tableDataType >
Table < tableKeyType, tableDataType >::Table()
{
    entries = 0;
}

template < class tableKeyType, class tableDataType >
void
Table < tableKeyType, tableDataType >
::insert(tableKeyType key, tableDataType data)
{
    assert(entries < MAX_TABLE);
    int pos(search(key)); // set pos to search results
    if (pos == entries) // new key
        entries++;
    T[pos].key = key;
    T[pos].data = data;
}
```

```
template < class tableKeyType, class tableDataType >
bool
Table < tableKeyType, tableDataType >
::lookup(tableKeyType key, tableDataType &data)
{
    int pos(search(key)); // set pos to search results
    if (pos == entries) // not found
        return false;
    else {
        data = T[pos].data;
        return true;
    }
}

template < class tableKeyType, class tableDataType >
void Table < tableKeyType, tableDataType >
::deleteKey(tableKeyType key)
{
    int pos(search(key)); // set pos to search results
    if (pos < entries)  { // otherwise, it wasn't found, so do nothing
        // copy last entry into this position
        --entries;
        T[pos] = T[entries];
    }
}
```

Note that in the search function we compare values of type tableKeyType using the operator !=. Hence our implementation has the class invariant that tableKeyType understands the inequality operator.

The array-based implementation does meet the formal requirements of the ADT. However, such an implementation doesn't really meet the needs of most uses of the Table. The problem is efficiency. Typical use of a Table depends upon quick retrieval of data given the key. Ideally, we'd like the performance to be $O(1)$; that is, regardless of the size of the table, the retrieval (and insertion) times ought to be constant. Instead, an array and a Linear Search requires time $O(n)$. We can do better, as we'll see in Section 10.3.

Exercise 10-3   Consider using a List ADT to implement the Table. Does it work? What would the performance of the operations be in this case?

Exercise 10-4   Suppose you keep the array in sorted order and use Binary Search for lookup. How fast would each of the operations be in this case?

Exercise 10-5   Using the dynamic array technique in Section 7.6, rewrite the table so that the constructor specifies the size of the table rather than uses a constant.

10.3 Hash Tables for Fast Retrieval

10.3.1 Hash Functions

In order to understand the technique we're going to look at next, let's start with a thought experiment. Suppose you want to make a table of the employees of a large company, using their Social Security numbers (SSNs) as a key. An SSN consists of nine digits; nearly all combinations of these digits form valid SSNs, so there are 10^9 = 1,000,000,000 possible SSNs. Let's suppose that we could build an array with 1,000,000,000 elements. Now, of course we know that such an array would be several orders of magnitude too big for today's computers—each entry would need to contain many bytes of data, and you'd need a billion of them—but bear with me. Using this monster array, we could look up any employee's records directly, by using the SSN as an index, for example, `employeeTable[123456789]`. Because the array is direct access all operations on the table would require $O(1)$ time.

Figure 10-1 *Hash function map*

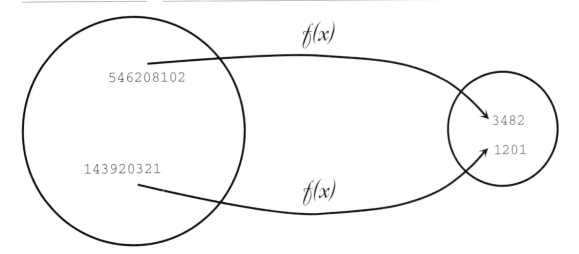

Domain: 1 ... 1,000,000,000   Range: 0 ... 9999

Well, we can't hope to build an array that big, at least for a few more years, and besides, a huge amount of space would be wasted. Suppose the company had 10,000 employees; then 10,000/1,000,000,000 = 0.000001 of the file would be used, and the rest would be empty. Somehow, we want to balance the efficiency of direct access with better space efficiency. The answer lies in coming up with what we call a ***hash function.*** Our hash function will take numbers in the domain of SSNs, and map them into the range 0 to 10,000. (Actually, as we'll see in a moment, we may want to use a slightly larger range.) Figure 10-1 illustrates the hash function map. The function $f(x)$ will take SSNs and return indexes in a range we can use for a practical array. Looking ahead a bit, the idea of hashing is to take our key in some large range, apply the hash function, and use the resulting value as an array index.

Issues in Hashing   You can see right away, however, that's it's not quite that simple. If you apply a function to a domain with a billion elements and map the results into a range of size ten thousand, you are going to have many elements in the domain that map into the same element in the range, as shown in Figure 10-2. So even though we're only *using* ten thousand of the possible SSNs, we really have no hope of picking a function that will map each of the SSNs to a different index. Each time two keys map to the same index we call it a ***collision.***

Figure 10-2   *A collision*

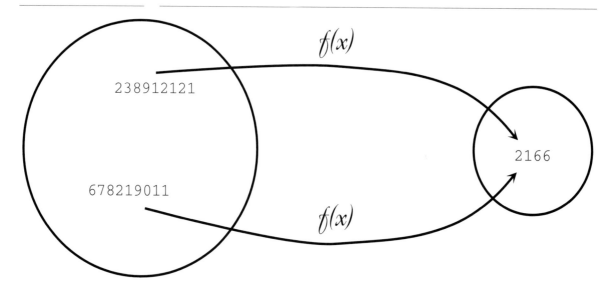

Thus there are two issues we must address:

1. We want to pick a hash function that minimizes the number of collisions. Even when we know little or nothing about the distribution of keys, there are certain principles that will help us pick a good hash function.
2. We need a strategy for handling the collisions that do occur.

We'll address these two issues in the following sections.

10.3.2   Picking a Good Hash Function

Ideally, we'd like to pick a hash function that "spreads" the values of $f(x)$ as evenly as possible throughout the range 0...9999. We say that such a function *randomizes* the keys. It's easiest to understand the notion of a good hash function by first looking at some bad ones. Here's one that's pretty bad for SSNs:

Equation 10-1

$$f(x) \;=\; int\!\left(\frac{x}{100,\,000}\right)$$

Assume that the `int` operator returns the integer portion of the results of the division. Equation 10-1 simply "chops off" the last five digits and returns the first four. What's wrong with that? The first digit of an SSN identifies the region of the country in which the number was issued. Because the company likely has many employees from certain regions, some of the digits will be much more common than others, and the hash function will yield more collisions than necessary.

A Rule for Hash Functions

The above example leads us to the following rule for choosing hash functions:

A good hash function depends upon the entire key, rather than just a part.

So clearly, a function that simply throws out some digits and keeps others doesn't meet this test.

Division Hashing

While dividing by a power of 10 doesn't work well, the idea of using division in the hash function is a good one—indeed, most hash functions use some form of division. However, in order to thoroughly "mix the bits," the best approach is to divide by a prime number and take the remainder. For example, taking our SSNs, dividing by 10,007 (the smallest prime number greater than 10,000) and taking the remainder yields integers in the range 0 to 10,006. The *modulo* operator—"%" in C++—expresses this process.

To summarize, *division hashing* can be performed as follows:

1. Pick a table size that's prime.

2. Compute the table index from the key using the hash function

```
index = key % tableSize;
```

Generally, division hashing provides excellent randomization, and for most purposes it's fast enough, although the exercises challenge you to find a faster method. However, no matter how well we randomize the hash function we're still going to have some collisions; Section 10.3.3 discusses what we do with them.

Exercise 10-6   Suppose the key is a string rather than an integer—propose a method for using division hashing in this case.

Exercise 10-7   Suppose the key is an integer, but it's very long, say 40 digits. How can the key be processed to permit it to be hashed?

10.3.3   Methods for Handling Collisions

We call the results of a hash function applied to a key the ***home address*** for that key. Collisions, then, occur when two keys have the same home address. Of the many approaches to collision resolution that computer scientists have discovered, we present just one here, leaving another to be explored in the exercises. We refer to each location in the table as a ***slot***. The basic idea is quite simple: try to put the key (and data) at the home address, but if it's in use, search forward through the table and store the key and data at the next free slot. When retrieving the data, we use the same technique—start at the home address, then search forward until we either find the data or give up when we hit an empty slot (because if the target item had been added to the table, it would have been stored at the first available slot). This technique goes by the name ***linear probing***. Note that you need to store the key along with the data, because that's the only way to tell whether a particular item you're looking at is really the one you want.

An Example   Let's work through an example. We'll use an unrealistically small table just so we can keep track of it. Let N be the size of the table; in this case, $N = 11$. So the home address for each key will be computed using the formula

Equation 10-2 $$\text{home address} = \text{key} \% 11$$

To simplify the example, we don't show any data with the keys, and we assume that the keys are integers, perhaps representing an employee number or a product code. Figure 10-3 shows the status of the table after the keys 321, 415, 330, 791, and 498 have been hashed.

Each of the keys added so far has been stored at its home address. However, let's suppose we now wish to add the key 365. Because $365 \% 11 = 2$ the home address for 365 is 2, but this spot is currently occupied by 321. The third location in the array is occupied as well; hence, we insert 365 in position 4, as shown in Figure 10-4. If later on we receive a request to look up key 365, we compute the home address—2—and try there first; failing to find it at home, we try locations 3 and, finally, 4, at which point we've found the target key.

What happens if we search for a key that's not in the table? For example, if we get a lookup request for 719, we compute its home address, which is 4. The search begins at location 4, which does not contain the target key; then we continue on to 5, but,

Figure 10-3   *Hash table after first five entries inserted*

0	330
1	
2	321
3	498
4	
5	
6	
7	
8	415
9	
10	791

finding it empty, we know that the target key is not in the table—if it were, we would have put it either in location 4 or location 5. So the lookup function returns false.

Wrapping Around We have three more issues to deal with here. First, what if we get to the bottom of the table and run out of spaces to check? For example, suppose the table looks like Figure 10-4, and we want to add 659. Its home address, 10, is already taken by 791, so we can't put it there, and there are no more slots to be found looking forward. We use a similar approach to the circular queue, and wrap back around to the beginning of the array. The 0 position is filled, so 659 gets added at position 1, as shown in Figure 10-5. Of course, we have to be sure we use the same strategy for lookups.

Handling Deletions Secondly, we have to consider carefully how we handle deletions from the table. Suppose the table's in the state shown by Figure 10-5, and we delete 321, yielding the table shown in Figure 10-6. Now a lookup request comes in for key 365. The home address for 365 is 2, and we begin searching there, find that location to be empty, and stop the search—even though if we had probed forward to location 4, we would have found 365 there. Clearly, we can't remove items from the table and leave empty spaces when we're using linear probing. Instead, we need to put a special marker of some kind to distinguish between deleted spaces and empty spaces. One approach to identifying the deletions is illustrated in the implementation, shown in Code Example 10-4.

Figure 10-4   *Hash table after 365 added*

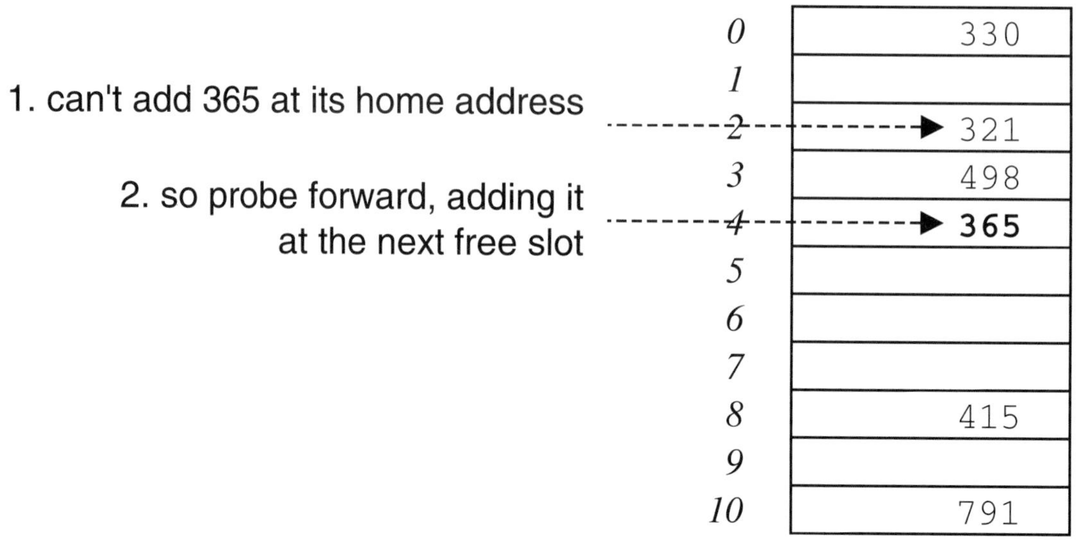

0	330
1	
2	321
3	498
4	**365**
5	
6	
7	
8	415
9	
10	791

1. can't add 365 at its home address

2. so probe forward, adding it
at the next free slot

Figure 10-5   *Hash table after 659 added*

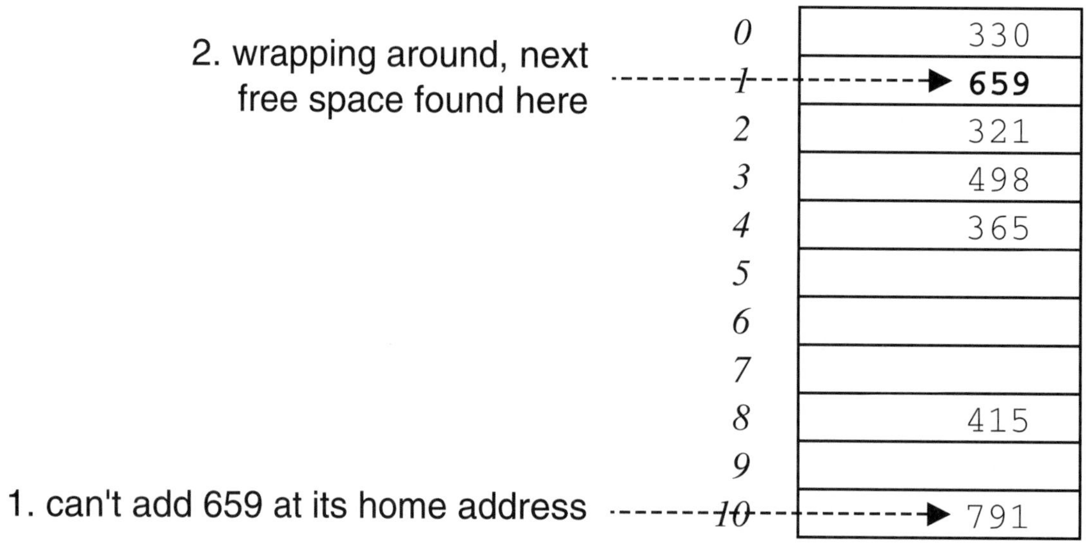

0	330
1	**659**
2	321
3	498
4	365
5	
6	
7	
8	415
9	
10	791

2. wrapping around, next
free space found here

1. can't add 659 at its home address

Figure 10-6   *Hash table after 321 deleted*

0	330
1	**659**
2	
3	498
4	365
5	
6	
7	
8	415
9	
10	791

Performance Finally, let's take a look at the performance. A careful analysis of the performance of hashing requires the application of some sophisticated machinery from the study of probability and is beyond the scope of this book. But it's easy to get a common sense idea of how it ought to work. If most keys end up stored close to their home addresses, then lookups will be quite fast. If, on the other hand, we end up putting many keys far away from the home address, the performance will be bad. In the worst case, the lookup performance could be as bad as $O(n)$.

Now we can see that there's a limitation on the density of the information stored in a hash table. If we have 10,000 employees and build a hash table of size 10,000, then every time we looked up a number that was *not* in the table, the lookup function would end up looking at every item in the table. (In fact, unless there's at least *one* empty space, the lookup function the way we wrote it would go into an endless loop!) So the table requires some empty slots, both to reduce the cost of the retrievals and also to make it possible to put most of the keys close to their home addresses. There's a trade-off here: more free slots will improve the performance, but at the cost of additional memory. Squeezing the data into a smaller table saves memory, but degrades the performance. In practice, typical hash table densities range from about 50% to 90%. In the exercises, you will have the chance to construct experiments to determine the performance of hash tables at different densities.

Clustering in Linear Probing

The efficiency of the hash table depends on getting items close to their home addresses and also on avoiding long blocks of filled-in slots, each of which has to be examined when searching for an item that's not in the table. What you want is everything to be nicely spread out, with empty slots evenly spaced. Unfortunately, linear probing will tend to cluster the items together, because each time an item finds another using its home address, it goes to the end of an existing cluster. If you were to take a "bird's-eye view" of the contents of a hash table after its been operating for a while, it might look something like Figure 10-7. As you can see, as the clusters get bigger, the chances that each new insertion will "hit" one of the existing clusters, and make it grow larger, goes up, until nearly every insertion will cause a cluster to grow. Methods for avoiding this tendency will be discussed in the exercises. Despite this weakness, simple linear probing works well enough for many applications.

Figure 10-7   *Used slots tend to cluster with linear probing*

Black areas represent slots in use; white areas are empty slots

10.3.4 A Complete Implementation

The interface file for our implementation of hashing appears in Code Example 10-3, and the implementation file in Code Example 10-4. We use a `struct` to represent each slot in the table, with each slot consisting of the key and the data, plus a special value of enumerated type `slotType`. We'll use `slotStatus` to distinguish between slots that are empty, deleted, or in use.

Code Example 10-3   *Interface file for hash table*

```
// cx10-3.h
// Code Example 10-3: Interface File: Hash Table

#ifndef __MB_CX10_3__
#define __MB_CX10_3__

#include "dslib.h"

// Implementing a Table via Hashing

// for an array implementation, need a max table size
```

```
const int MAX_TABLE = 11;

template < class tableKeyType, class tableDataType >
class Table
{
public:
    Table(); // Table constructor
    void insert(const tableKeyType & key, const tableDataType & data);
    // Precondition: None
    // Postcondition: data and associated key are stored in the Table,
    //    i.e., lookup(key,data) == true and returns the data
    // Note: If there was already data stored with this key, the insert
    //    call will replace it.
    bool lookup(const tableKeyType & key, tableDataType & data);
    // Precondition: None
    // Postcondition: if key is in the table, returns true and associated
    //    data is returned; otherwise, false is returned and
    //    data is undefined.
    void deleteKey(const tableKeyType & key);
    // Precondition: None
    // Postcondition: lookup(key,d) returns false
    void dump(); // print the contents of the hash table -- handy!
private:
    // implementation via a hash table
    enum slotType {Empty, Deleted, InUse};
    struct slot {
        slotType slotStatus;
        tableKeyType key;
        tableDataType data;
    };
    slot T[MAX_TABLE]; // stores the items in the table
    int entries; // keep track of number of entries in table
    int hash(const tableKeyType & key);
    // Precondition: none
    // Postcondition: none
    // Returns: the home address for key
    int probe(const int pos);
    // Precondition: pos is a slot between 0 and MAX_TABLE-1
    // Postcondition: none
    // Returns: the next slot, using wrapping (between 0 and MAX_TABLE-1)
    bool search(int & pos, const tableKeyType & target);
    // Precondition: pos is the hash address of target
    // Postcondition: if target is in the table, pos is set to its actual slot
    // Returns: true if target is in the table, else false
};

#endif
```

Implementation
Notes

There are a few things to note about the implementation in Code Example 10-4. First, we don't really *need* to make hash a separate function, but it does encapsulate it nicely so that if we decide to go back later and change to a different hash function we can find and update it without the chance of missing an occurrence somewhere in the code. The `probe` function encapsulates the notion "advance through the table, wrapping around when you reach the end."

The `search` function not only tells the calling function whether or not the target is in the table but also returns its actual slot index as a side effect. The caller will need this to get the data associated with the key or, in the case of the `insert` function, to use as the slot for the insertion. The constructor function has to initialize the values of `slotStatus` for every item in the table; hence it requires time $O(n)$.

The `insert` function hashes the key, then calls `search` to determine whether it's already in the table. If so, it uses the old position and simply updates the data. If not, it has to find a free slot—that is, one that is either empty or deleted and that follows the home address as closely as possible. The key gets inserted into this free slot. Because the hash table must have at least one free slot in order to work correctly the insert function asserts that the table has no more than `MAX_TABLE-1` entries before it starts its work.

The `lookup` function simply hashes the key and calls `search` to do the work. If search finds the target key, then it returns the relevant data. The `deleteKey` function is almost the same—if it finds the key, it marks its slot `Deleted`.

Code Example 10-4   *Implementation file for hash table*

```
// cx10-4.cpp
// Code Example 10-4: Implementation File: Hash Table

#include "cx10-3.h"

template < class tableKeyType, class tableDataType >
int
Table < tableKeyType, tableDataType >
::hash(const tableKeyType & key)
{
    return key % MAX_TABLE;
}

template < class tableKeyType, class tableDataType >
int
Table < tableKeyType, tableDataType >
::probe(const int pos)
{
    if (pos < MAX_TABLE - 1)
        return pos + 1;
```

```
        else
            return 0;
}

template < class tableKeyType, class tableDataType >
bool
Table < tableKeyType, tableDataType >
::search(int & pos, const tableKeyType & target)
{
    // search for target, starting at pos
    for ( ; T[pos].slotStatus != Empty; pos = probe(pos))
        if (T[pos].slotStatus == InUse && T[pos].key == target)
            return true;
    return false;
}

template < class tableKeyType, class tableDataType >
Table < tableKeyType, tableDataType >
::Table() // implementation of Table constructor
{
    entries = 0;
    int i;
    for (i = 0; i < MAX_TABLE; i++)
        T[i].slotStatus = Empty;
}

template < class tableKeyType, class tableDataType >
void
Table < tableKeyType, tableDataType >
::insert(const tableKeyType & key, const tableDataType & data)
{
    assert(entries < MAX_TABLE - 1);
    int pos(hash(key)); // find a position to insert the item
    if (!search(pos, key)) { // key was not in the table
        // starting at home address, find first free position
        pos = hash(key);
        while (T[pos].slotStatus == InUse)
            pos = probe(pos);
        entries++; // number of entries goes up
    }
    T[pos].slotStatus = InUse;
    T[pos].key = key;
    T[pos].data = data;
}

template < class tableKeyType, class tableDataType >
bool
Table < tableKeyType, tableDataType >
::lookup(const tableKeyType & key, tableDataType & data)
{
    int pos(hash(key));
    if (search(pos, key)) {
```

```
        data = T[pos].data;
        return true;
    }
    else
        return false;
}

template < class tableKeyType, class tableDataType >
void
Table < tableKeyType, tableDataType >::deleteKey(const tableKeyType & key)
{
    int pos(hash(key));
    if (search(pos, key)) {
        T[pos].slotStatus = Deleted;
        entries--;
    }
}

// the following function is handy for debugging
template < class tableKeyType, class tableDataType >
void
Table < tableKeyType, tableDataType >::dump()
{
    int i;
    for (i = 0; i < MAX_TABLE; i++) {
        cout << i << '\t';
        switch(T[i].slotStatus) {
        case InUse:
            cout << "In Use\t" << T[i].key << endl;
            break;
        case Deleted:
            cout << "Deleted\t" << T[i].key << endl;
            break;
        case Empty:
            cout << "Empty\t" << endl;
            break;
        }
    }
    cout << "Entries = " << entries << "\n\n";
}
```

You can go a long way with the straightforward implementation of linear probing, but computer scientists have found many ways to enhance, modify, and improve the basic probing approach. You can explore some of these ideas in the exercises that follow.

Exercise 10-8   Write a simple test driver that will allow you to hash records with the key an `int`, and the data a string (using a String class). Compile and run your driver to test the hashing implementation.

Exercise 10-9 You may have noticed in Code Example 10-4 that there's an inefficiency in the `insert` function because in some cases you will look at the same slot more than once. Rewrite the insert and search functions to eliminate this inefficiency.

Exercise 10-10 If you have many deletions from your table, you may end up with many items far away from their home addresses even though there may be a slot that was opened up by a deletion that's much closer. Devise an algorithm for updating the table to move items back closer to their home addresses if possible. After your update runs, all slots should be marked InUse or Empty, and none should be marked Deleted. Optional: Program and test your algorithm.

Exercise 10-11 The hash table will work with any `TableKeyType` that understands the "`%`" operator. While we've been assuming that this would be a simple modulo operator, as it's predefined for `int`s, you can use operator overloading to make the "`%`" operator work on other data types. Overload the "`%`" operator so that it works to hash strings in some reasonable way.

Exercise 10-12 If you have special information about the keys in use, you can make the hash table somewhat more space efficient by eliminating the `slotStatus` field from the slot. Suppose you knew that all keys were positive `int`s — how could you modify the hash table implementation to eliminate the need for the `slotStatus` field? What is the disadvantage, if any, of modifying the hash table in this way?

Exercise 10-13 As we saw with Lists, Stacks, and Queues, you can eliminate the need to "compile in" the size of the hash table and instead have the constructor allocate the memory. Modify the hash table so that the constructor creates the hash table at run time.

10.3.5 Chained Hashing

The hash table data structure may seem to you to be rather "static," leading you to consider whether there's something more like a linked list that might have the advantages of a dynamic data structure. On the one hand, hashing's performance depends critically upon the direct access nature of an array—trying to replace the array with a linked list doesn't yield a structure in which the key can be used to quickly reach a particular slot. On the other hand, once a slot is reached, we can use something like a linked list to store the items with a particular home address. For instance, in our example hash table with 11 nodes, keys 321 and 365 both have 2 as their home address. In ***chained hashing,*** a linked list stores all the items at a particular home address, as shown in Figure 10-8. Note that in the example, we only show the key, but in most cases a field would be provided for data. With chained hashing, there's no need for a probing technique. We also have the advantage that the number of items in the hash table is not limited by the number of home addresses, because we can allow the average length of the chains to grow to support greater densities. Of course, as the average chain gets longer, the performance goes down.

Figure 10-8   *Chained hashing*

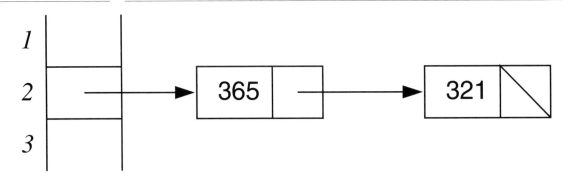

In Code Example 10-5, we present the header file for a hash table with chaining. Each slot now becomes something like a node from a linked list. The hash table stores the header link for the list of items that have each home address. The search routine now returns a pointer, rather than an index into the table.

Code Example 10-5   *Interface file for hash table with chaining*

```
// cx10-5.h
// Code Example 10-5: Interface File: Hash Table with Chaining

#ifndef __MB_CX10_5__
#define __MB_CX10_5__

#include "dslib.h"

// Implementing a Table via Hashing

// for an array implementation, need a max table size
const int MAX_TABLE = 11;

template < class tableKeyType, class tableDataType >
class Table
{
public:
    Table(); // Table constructor
    void insert(const tableKeyType & key, const tableDataType & data);
    // Precondition: None
    // Postcondition: data and associated key are stored in the Table,
    //    i.e., lookup(key,data) == true and returns the data
    //    Note: If there was already data stored with this key, the insert
    //          call will replace it.
    bool lookup(const tableKeyType & key, tableDataType & data);
    // Precondition: None
    // Postcondition: if key is in the table, returns true and associated
```

```
    //     data is returned; otherwise, false is returned and
    //     data is undefined.
    void deleteKey(const tableKeyType & key);
    // Precondition: None
    // Postcondition: lookup(key,d) returns false
    void dump(); // print the contents of the hash table -- handy!
private:
    // implementation via a hash table
    struct Slot;
    typedef Slot * Link;
    struct Slot {
        tableKeyType key;
        tableDataType data;
        Link next;
    };
    Link T[MAX_TABLE]; // table is an array of pointers to slots
    int hash(const tableKeyType & key);
    // Precondition: none
    // Postcondition: none
    // Returns: the home address for key
    bool search(Link & slotPointer, const tableKeyType & target);
    // Precondition: slotPointer points to the start of the chain for
    //     target's hash address
    // Postcondition: if target is in the chain, slotPointer points to it
    // Returns: true if target is in the table, else false
};

#endif
```

The implementation of the chained hash table, shown in Code Example 10-6, is quite straightforward. Deleting an item provides the greatest challenge. Recall that in order to delete a node from a linked list, you must have a pointer to the node that precedes the node you want to delete; this accounts for the relative complexity of the deleteKey function.

Code Example 10-6   *Implementation file for hash table with chaining*

```
// cx10-6.cpp
// Code Example 10-6: Implementation File: Hash Table with Chaining

#include "cx10-5.h"

template < class tableKeyType, class tableDataType >
int
Table < tableKeyType, tableDataType >
::hash(const tableKeyType & key)
{
    return key % MAX_TABLE;
}
```

```cpp
template < class tableKeyType, class tableDataType >
bool
Table < tableKeyType, tableDataType >
::search(Link & slotPointer, const tableKeyType & target)
{
    // search for target, starting at slotPointer
    for ( ; slotPointer; slotPointer = slotPointer -> next)
        if (slotPointer->key == target)
            return true;
    return false;
}

template < class tableKeyType, class tableDataType >
Table < tableKeyType, tableDataType >
::Table() // implementation of Table constructor
{
    int i;
    for (i = 0; i < MAX_TABLE; i++)
        T[i] = 0;
}

template < class tableKeyType, class tableDataType >
void
Table < tableKeyType, tableDataType >
::insert(const tableKeyType & key, const tableDataType & data)
{
    int pos(hash(key)); // find a position to insert the item
    Link sp(T[pos]);
    if (!search(sp, key)) { // key was not in the table
        // insert new item at beginning of list
        Link insertedSlot = new Slot;
        insertedSlot->key = key;
        insertedSlot->data = data;
        insertedSlot->next = T[pos];
        T[pos] = insertedSlot;
    }
    else  // found old record -- update the data
        sp->data = data;
}
```

```
template < class tableKeyType, class tableDataType >
bool
Table < tableKeyType, tableDataType >
::lookup(const tableKeyType & key, tableDataType & data)
{
    int pos(hash(key));
    Link sp(T[pos]);
    if (search(sp, key)) {
        data = sp->data;
        return true;
    }
    else
        return false;
}
template < class tableKeyType, class tableDataType >
void
Table < tableKeyType, tableDataType >::deleteKey(const tableKeyType & key)
{
    // need to find pointer to item preceeding the slot to delete
    int pos(hash(key));
    Link p;
    if (0 == T[pos]) // there's nothing here
        return;
    if (T[pos]->key == key) { // special case, for first item in chain
        Link deleteSlot(T[pos]);
        T[pos] = T[pos]->next;
        delete deleteSlot;
    }
    else
        for (p = T[pos]; p->next; p = p->next)
            if (p->next->key == key) {
                Link deleteSlot = p->next;
                p->next = p->next->next;
                delete deleteSlot;
                break;
            }
}
// the following function is handy for debugging
template < class tableKeyType, class tableDataType >
void
Table < tableKeyType, tableDataType >::dump()
{
    int i;
    for (i = 0; i < MAX_TABLE; i++) {
        cout << i << '\t';
        Link p;
        for (p = T[i]; p; p = p->next)
            cout << p->key << '\t';
        cout << '\n';
    }
    cout << '\n';
}
```

Exercise 10-14   Consider the relative advantages and disadvantages of hashing with probing and hashing with chains. Explain why hashing with probing may be somewhat faster in some environments.

Exercise 10-15   In our implementation of the chained hash table, we in effect reimplemented linked lists. Rewrite the chained table to reuse linked lists directly, using the version with a `remove` function. Discuss the relative advantages and disadvantages of reusing a linked list versus writing one from scratch.

10.4   Using Tables

We certainly know enough now about tables to handle the routing table problem presented at the beginning of the chapter. The details you'll need to solve this problem are explained in Lab 6.

Symbol Tables   Compilers and other programming tools commonly make use of hashing to create what's called a ***symbol table.*** A compiler must keep track of each variable and other user-defined identifier in a computer program. To keep it simple, let's just consider simple variables in a C++ program. We need to keep track of at least three pieces of information for each variable: its type, its scope, and the memory location where its value will be stored. Every time we encounter another variable in the program, we need to be able to check quickly to see where and how that variable is defined. A hash table provides the standard implementation of a symbol table; the name of the variable (possibly combined in some way with the name of the function in which they were defined) serves as the key, while the type and location information are the associated data.

Despite its utility, there's an outstanding weakness of the hash table in many situations. Suppose you want to list all the items stored in the hash table. Let's suppose that n represents the number of entries in the hash table, while N stands for the number of slots. In a hash table with probing, listing all the entries requires N steps rather than n, which could be a significant disadvantage. A chained hash table has even worse performance, $N + n$. (Why?) Furthermore, if you want to get the data in key order, you would have to first retrieve all the items and then sort them. For many situations, what you really want is a data structure that supports fast insertions and retrievals and also lets you get a list of the items sorted by key. We'll see in the next chapter that trees provide just what we need.

Chapter Summary

- The Table ADT supports insertion and retrieval via a key.
- A straightforward implementation of the table as an array doesn't have desirable performance characteristics.
- Hashing can be used to build tables with rapid insertion and retrieval.
- Division hashing is one approach to creating a hash function.
- Collisions result when two keys have the same home address.
- Probing techniques can be used to accommodate collisions.
- Chaining is an alternative to probing.
- Hashing is used for data processing, compilers, networking, and other applications.

Programming Laboratory Problems

Lab 10-1   Modify the ClubMember program (Section 7.7) to use a hash table. Note that you'll need to create a member number to use as a key. You will also need to modify the hash table to give you a way to print out all the members of the club. What are the relative advantages of a list versus a hash table for this particular problem?

Lab 10-2   As we discussed in "Clustering in Linear Probing," linear probing tends to cause clusters of used slots, which leads to inefficiency. To avoid these clusters, alternative probing methods have been devised, among them *quadratic probing.* Instead of looking forward one slot at a time, you use a quadratic function; so if h is the home address, you try: $h, h + 1, h + 4, h + 9, h + 16, \ldots$. Expressed as a quadratic equation, probe i uses slot $h + i^2$, except, of course, you want to wrap around the table just as you did with linear probing.

Modify the hashing implementation to use quadratic probing.

Lab 10-3   Modify the hashing code so that you can keep track of how many probes each lookup operation requires. Test the performance of a hash table of 1007 items at 50%, 70%, 90%, and 95% densities. Plot your results.

Lab 10-4   Create a SymbolTable class that could be used as part of a compiler. The SymbolTable class should implement the following ADT:

ADT 10-2   Symbol Table ADT

Characteristics:

- A Symbol Table ADT stores an object (from the SymbolTableEntry class) containing a string (the symbol) plus additional data associated with that string.
- No variable name can appear more than once in the table.

Prerequisites:

The SymbolTableEntry class must implement the member function symbol, which returns a string.

Operations:

bool T.insert(SymbolTableEntry e)

Precondition:	None.
Postcondition:	If there is no entry in the table with the same symbol as e, it is added.
Returns:	True if e was added to the table, false if it was not (because there was an existing entry with the same symbol).

void T.remove(string s)

Precondition:	None.
Postcondition:	Removes the entry with symbol s from the table.

bool T.retrieveEntry(string s, SymbolTableEntry & e)

Precondition:	None.
Postcondition:	If there was an entry in the table with symbol s, the associated entry is returned in e.
Returns:	True if an entry with symbol s was found, false otherwise.

You will need to implement a SymbolTableEntry class that meets the requirements of the SymbolTable. In addition to the symbol (stored by a string), the SymbolTableEntry should include a location (a long integer, representing the location of the symbol in the program) and a type (either `int`, `char`, `bool`, or `double`).

The SymbolTable should be implemented using the hash table in Section 10.3. Don't reimplement the code or copy it; instead, one of the data members in your symbol table must be a hash table.

Write a driver to test your symbol table. Since you don't have a real compiler to test it with, just make up arbitrary names, locations, and types.

Lab 10-5   While at any given time a hash table has a fixed size, you can devise methods that will allow the hash table to grow and shrink upon demand. What you have to do is allocate the memory for the table dynamically—see Section 7.6—reallocate a new hash table when you need to grow or shrink it, and then rehash all the data from the old table to the new. To rehash the data, take each item out of the old table, apply the new hash function, and insert the data into the new table. Once the data has been re-hashed, the old table can be deleted.

Modify the hash table implementation in Code Example 10-4 to support dynamic re-sizing of hash tables. The constructor should take an argument representing the smallest size the hash table is ever allowed to be; call this `MinTableSize`. The constructor should take a second argument, `MaxDensity`. The table starts out at the smallest prime larger than `MinTableSize`; whenever it reaches the maximum allowed density, the size of the table should be doubled and then increased to a prime number. When a key is deleted, if the density drops below **MaxDensity**/10, the size of the table should be reduced by half, except that it should never drop below `MinTableSize`.

Here's an example. Suppose `MinTableSize` is 100, and `MaxDensity` is .5. Then the table starts out with 101 entries (the smallest prime > 100) and, as long as the number of entries in the table stays below 51, the table size remains 101. Howev-er, when the 51st key is entered, the table size doubles to the next prime above 200, which is 211. Later on, when deletions drop the number of items in the table down to 19, the table would shrink to 101, and so on.

Lab 10-6   Use a hash table to simulate a routing table for an Internet router. The table consists of pairs of IP addresses. Each IP address is 32 bits long and is often written as a se-quence of 4 numbers in the range from 0 to 255. For example, one of the machines on my campus has the following IP address: 150.250.10.217. A number in the range 0 to 255 requires 8 bits to store, and hence this address can be stored in a single 32-bit variable.

It's easiest to understand the conversion if you treat each of the four chunks as a hexadecimal (base 16) number, since two hexadecimal digits can store numbers from 0 to 255. For example, the IP Address 150.250.10.217 can be written as 96FA0AD9, which requires 32 bits to store (each hex digit is 4 bits long).

Host IP Addresses consist of three parts—a Class Identifier (classid), a Network Identifier (netid), and a Host Identifier (hostid)—and are broken into three classes as follows (note that the bits are numbered from 0 on the left to 31 on the right):

1. Class A: classid is bit 0; netid is bits 1 through 7; hostid is bits 8 through 31.

2. Class B: classid is bits 0 and 1; netid is bits 2 through 15; hostid is bits 16 through 31.

3. Class C: classid is bits 0, 1, and 2; netid is bits 3 through 23; hostid is bits 24 through 31.

Furthermore, you can identify which Class an IP Address belongs to by looking at the classid bits—Class A starts with 0, Class B with 10, and Class C with 110 (all in binary). For example, the address 150.250.10.27, written in hex as 96FA0AD9, is written in binary as: 10010110011111010011011001. So we see that it's a Class B address (because it starts with 10); hence the netid is 01011011111010 binary = 16FA hex, and the hostid is 0AD9 (bits 16 through 31).

Build your solution from the following parts:

1. Write a function `readIP` that will read an IP address in the dotted notation form (e.g., 150.250.10.217) and return it as a single `unsigned long int` (this is generally a 32-bit integer in C++).

2. Write a function with the following prototype:

```
enum ipClass = {classA, classB, classC, badClass};
ipClass interpretIP( unsigned long int ipAddress,
            unsigned long int & netid,
                    unsigned long int & hostid);
```

`interpretIP` should return the class of the address (note that you could get an address with an invalid IP Address, e.g., starting with 1111, in which case return badClass), and it should set `netid` and `hostid` to contain the correct network identifier and host identifier.

3. Write a driver that can either take a pair of IP addresses, representing a destination/route pair and insert them into a table, or take a single IP address representing a destination and return a route. Note that only the `netid` portion of the address is relevant for routing—the rest should simply be padded with zeroes.

Chapter Vocabulary

chained hashing	linear probing
collision	Local Area Network (LAN)
destination network	quadratic probing
division hashing	randomize
forwarding network	router
hash function	routing
home address	slot
host	symbol table
Internet Protocol (IP)	table

Chapter 11 Trees

Overview   An introduction to trees, a flexible data structure useful for solving a wide range of problems.

Chapter Objectives

1. To describe how trees represent data in a hier-
    archical manner.

2. To define Binary Search Trees, which allow both
    rapid retrieval by key and in-order processing.

3. To outline how inheritance can be used to model
    "is-a" relationships and to support code reuse.

11.1 Introducing Trees

As we saw in the last chapter, lists, stacks, queues and tables each allow access to their data in a single manner. Lists support linear processing of their data, stacks and queues restrict access to either end, and tables let you go quickly to a particular key but aren't especially good if you want to process all the data. In order to get quick access by key, but also allow access to the entire list, we need a better data structure—the *tree*.

11.1.1 Talking About Trees

A tree represents data in a *hierarchical* manner. That is, you can visualize relationships within the tree in layers, with some parts of the tree "higher," and others "lower." Let's look at an example, as shown in Figure 11-1.

Figure 11-1   *A tree*

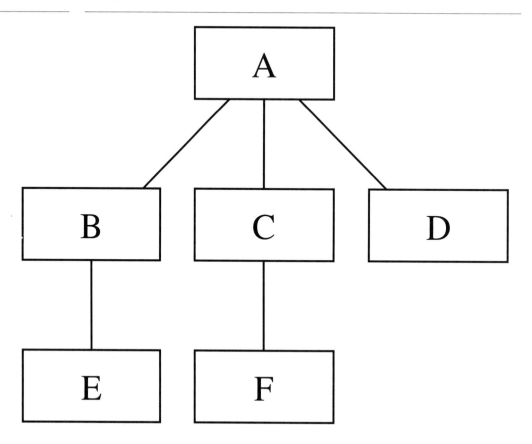

Tree Terminology   Let's go ahead and get some of the extensive (but useful) tree terminology out of the way. Each of the items in the tree, indicated in our diagram by a box, is a ***node.*** We call the node at the top of the tree the ***root;*** in Figure 11-1, the root contains "A." The relationships in the tree are traditionally described using family terms; for example, A is the ***parent*** of B, C, and D, and B, C, and D are ***children*** of A. We can extend this, for example, by calling F the ***grandchild*** of A, and A the ***grandparent*** of F. Furthermore, B, C, and D are ***siblings,*** as are E and F. The root, by definition, has no siblings.

More prosaically, we can discuss the ***levels*** in a tree. The root, by convention, is at level 0, and the level goes up by 1 as you go down the tree. Hence, B is at level 1, and F is at level 2. We also say that F has a ***depth*** of 2. Another way to look at it is that the depth of a node in the tree is the length of the path from the root to that node; if you trace a path from A to C to F, you pass along 2 "lines," hence F is at depth 2.

We can see that some of the nodes have children and others don't. We call the nodes with children ***internal nodes***; in Figure 11-1, the internal nodes are A, B, and C. Nodes with no children are called ***leaves;*** D, E, and F are the leaves in our example. The ***height*** of the tree is equal to the depth of the "deepest" leaf, so the tree in the example has a height of 2. We use the word ***degree*** to refer to the number of children of a node. Hence, A has degree 3, B has degree 1, and D has degree 0, as do all leaves. The degree of the tree is determined by the node with the highest degree; hence the tree in Figure 11-1 has a degree of 3.

11.1.2   Binary Trees

Most of our attention will focus on one particular class of tree, the ***Binary Tree,*** shown in Figure 11-2. A Binary Tree has degree 2—each node has at most two children. This makes binary trees particularly easy to implement. At the same time trees restricted in this way have a wide range of uses, as we shall see. In addition to limiting the degree to 2, we also consider the order of the children significant in a binary tree; hence each child node is either a *left* node or a *right* node. We formalize these notions in Definition 11-1.

Definition 11-1   A *Binary Tree* is either:

1. an ***empty tree;*** or

2. consists of a node, called a *root*, and two children, ***left*** and ***right,*** each of which are themselves binary trees.

Note that Definition 11-1 is recursive—we've defined a Binary Tree in terms of itself. The notion of an empty tree serves as the nonrecursive part of the definition. Note also that in this definition, all the internal nodes of a Binary Tree are themselves the roots of smaller Binary Trees. Looking at Figure 11-2, we find that the

Figure 11-2   *A Binary Tree*

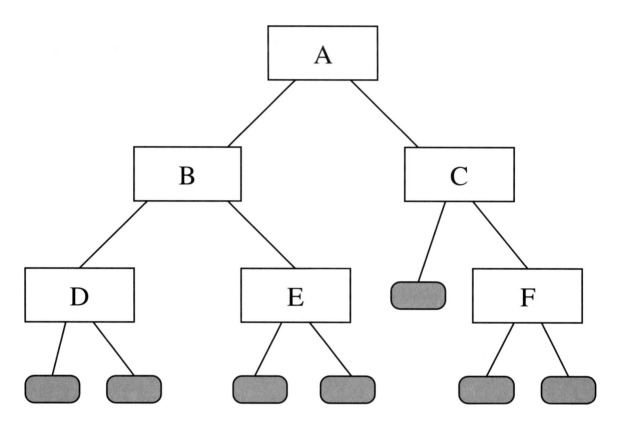

definition implies that every non-empty node has two children, either of which may be empty. The overall root A has two children: B is the left child of A, and C is the right child of A. C's left child is an empty tree (represented by the shaded oval) and its right child is F. Usually, we draw a Binary Tree without showing the empty trees.

Distinguishing Binary Trees

In a binary tree, you need to make a clear distinction between left and right children. For example, take a look at Figure 11-3. The two trees shown both contain three nodes, but they are structured differently—the tree on the left has a non-empty left subtree, and an empty right subtree, while the root on the right has just the opposite. (The empty trees for the leaves in the bottom row have been omitted.)

Figure 11-3   *Two distinct Binary Trees*

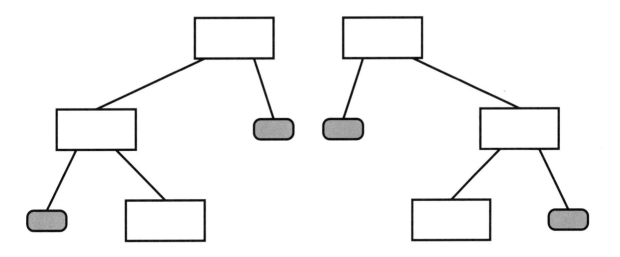

11.1.3   An Application: Expression Trees

We can use Binary Trees to represent arithmetic expressions. The tree representation makes it quite convenient to keep track of expressions within compilers and other software applications. Recall that the usual way we write arithmetic expressions is called *infix notation*. In infix notation, the operands (the numbers or variables) are separated by the operators (such as plus, minus, etc.). Most of the standard operators are binary—that is, they take two operands—so it's quite natural to model them as Binary Trees.

Let's start with an example. Suppose you have the following expression:

$$3 + 7 \times 2 - 1$$

By convention, we apply multiplication and division operators before we apply addition and subtraction, so the expression can be represented in fully parenthesized form as

$$((3 + (7 \times 2)) - 1)$$

In words, first multiply 7 by 2 giving 14, then add 3 giving 17, and finally subtract 1 yielding 16. To represent this as a tree, we make each parenthesized expression into a tree. Each internal node in the tree is labelled with an operator, and each leaf contains an operand. We've illustrated the *expression tree* for our example expression in Figure 11-4.

Figure 11-4　　　　　　*Expression tree for* $3 + 7 \times 2 - 1$

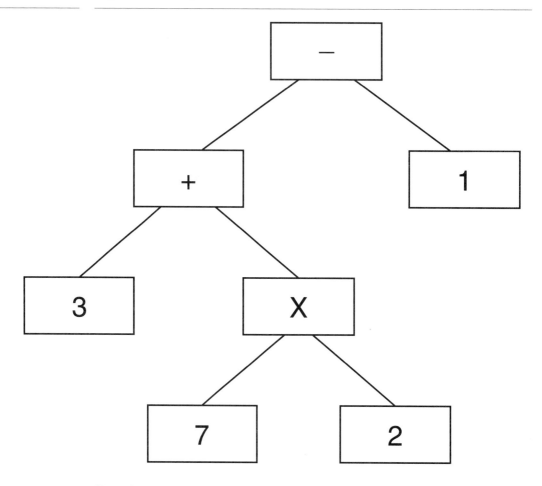

To evaluate the expression in the tree, choose a pair of leaves, apply the operator at their root, and replace the subtree with the result of the calculation. If you repeat this process, you'll end up with a tree with a single root, containing the value of the expression. We've illustrated the evaluation of our sample tree in Figures 11-5, 11-6, and 11-7.

Exercise 11-1　　There's only one possible empty Binary Tree, and one Binary Tree containing a single node. When you get to two nodes, there are two possible Binary Trees—a root with a left subtree, and a root with a right subtree. Draw the five possible Binary Trees with three nodes.

Exercise 11-2　　How many Binary Trees with four nodes are possible? with five nodes? Can you infer the formula for a tree with n nodes?

Figure 11-5   *Expression tree after first subtree evaluated*

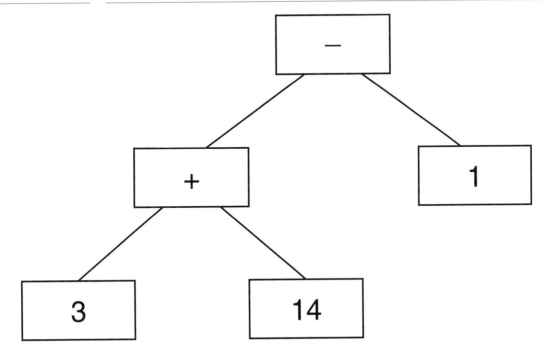

Figure 11-6   *Expression tree after second subtree evaluated*

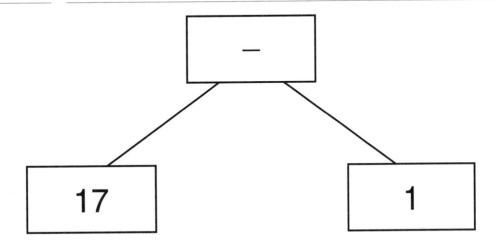

Figure 11-7   *Final value of expression tree*

$$\boxed{16}$$

Exercise 11-3   Create an expression tree for the following expression:

$$6 \times 4 \div 2 + 7 - 6 \times 3$$

Exercise 11-4   Evaluate the expression tree created in Exercise 11-3.

Exercise 11-5   Develop (recursive) algorithms

      a.   To determine the number of nodes in a tree.

      b.   To determine the degree of a tree.

      c.   To determine the depth of a tree.

Exercise 11-6   Explain the difference between a Binary Tree (as defined in Definition 11-1) and a tree of degree 2.

11.2   Building the Binary Tree

11.2.1   The Binary Tree ADT

Now we'll formalize our notions about Binary Trees by creating an ADT. Our Binary Tree ADT will support both creating Binary Trees by adding nodes and navigating through the tree by following children to the left and right. Our ADT definition will draw directly upon Definition 11-1.

ADT 11-1   Binary Tree

Characteristics:

    • A Binary Tree ADT T stores data of some type (btElement-Type), using a binary tree as defined in Definition 11-1.

Operations:

bool T.isEmpty()

Precondition:	None.
Postcondition:	None.
Returns:	True if and only if T is an empty tree.

btElementType T.getData()

Precondition:	!T.isEmpty()
Postcondition:	None.
Returns:	The data associated with the root of the tree.

void T.insert(btElementType d)

Precondition:	None.
Postcondition:	T.getData() == d

BinaryTree T.left()

Precondition:	!T.isEmpty()
Postcondition:	None.
Returns:	The left child of T.

BinaryTree T.right()

Precondition:	!T.isEmpty()
Postcondition:	None.
Returns:	The right child of T.

void T.makeLeft(BinaryTree T1)

Preconditions:	!T.isEmpty(); T.left().isEmpty()
Postcondition:	T.left() == T1

void T.makeRight(BinaryTree T1)

Preconditions:	!T.isEmpty(); T.right().isEmpty()
Postcondition:	T.right() == T1

11.2.2 Implementing a Binary Tree

We'll make a few enhancements to the ADT when implementing it as a C++ class. First, for efficiency sake, we'll pass around pointers to trees rather than the trees themselves. Otherwise, copies of the tree would have to be made as they are manipulated, which could be quite slow. We've also made judicious use of the const keyword and reference parameters. The header file is shown in Code Example 11-1. Recall that "this" means "the object for which the function was called."

Code Example 11-1   Interface file for binary tree

```
// cx11-1.h
// Code Example 11-1: Interface File: Binary Tree

#ifndef __MB_CX11_1__
#define __MB_CX11_1__

#include "dslib.h"

template < class btElementType >
class BinaryTree {
public:
    BinaryTree();
    bool isEmpty() const;
    // Precondition: None.
    // Postcondition: None.
    // Returns: true if and only if T is an empty tree
    btElementType getData() const; // getData is an accessor
    // Precondition: !this->isEmpty()
    // Postcondition: None
    // Returns: The data associated with the root of the tree
    void insert(const btElementType & d);
    // Precondition: none
    // Postconditions: this->getData() == d; !this->isEmpty()
    BinaryTree * left();
    // Precondition: !this->isEmpty()
    // Postcondition: None
    // Returns: (a pointer to) the left child of T
    BinaryTree * right();
    // Precondition: !this->isEmpty()
    // Postcondition: None
    // Returns: (a pointer to) the right child of T
    void makeLeft(BinaryTree * T1);
    // Precondition: !this->isEmpty(); this->left()->isEmpty()
    // Postcondition: this->left() == T1
    void makeRight(BinaryTree * T1);
    // Precondition: !this->isEmpty(); this->right()->isEmpty()
    // Postcondition: this->right() == T1
private:
    bool nullTree;
    btElementType treeData;
    BinaryTree * leftTree;
    BinaryTree * rightTree;
};

#endif
```

Implementation   To understand the implementation, refer back to Definition 11-1. Each binary tree is either empty or non-empty—the state of each particular Binary Tree will be indicated by the value of the boolean variable nullTree. When the tree is empty, the other data members are irrelevant; however, for a non-empty tree, treeData contains the data stored at the root of the tree, and leftTree and rightTree point to the children. Given these definitions, the implementation is quite straightforward, as illustrated in Code Example 11-2. The insert function proves to be the most subtle of the lot. When data is inserted into the tree, it's inserted at the root, which prior to the insertion was either empty or non-empty. If the root was not empty before, then the new data simply replaces the old data. However, if the root was empty, then it will now be nonempty, which means that two new empty children have to be created—this is how the tree grows.

Code Example 11-2   *Implementation file for binary tree*

```
// cx11-2.cpp
// Code Example 11-2: Implementation File: Binary Tree

#include "cx11-1.h"

template < class btElementType >
BinaryTree < btElementType > :: BinaryTree()
{
    nullTree = true;
    leftTree = 0;
    rightTree = 0;
}

template < class btElementType >
bool
BinaryTree < btElementType > :: isEmpty() const
{
    return nullTree;
}

template < class btElementType >
btElementType
BinaryTree < btElementType > :: getData() const
{
    assert(!isEmpty());
    return treeData;
}

template < class btElementType >
void
BinaryTree < btElementType >
:: insert(const btElementType & d)
{
    treeData = d;
```

```
    if (nullTree) {
        nullTree = false;
        leftTree = new BinaryTree;
        rightTree = new BinaryTree;
    }
}

template < class btElementType >
BinaryTree < btElementType > *
BinaryTree < btElementType > :: left()
{
    assert(!isEmpty());
    return leftTree;
}

template < class btElementType >
BinaryTree < btElementType > *
BinaryTree < btElementType > :: right()
{
    assert(!isEmpty());
    return rightTree;
}

template < class btElementType >
void
BinaryTree < btElementType >
:: makeLeft(BinaryTree * T1)
{
    assert(!isEmpty());
    assert(left()->isEmpty());
    delete left();
    leftTree = T1;
}

template < class btElementType >
void
BinaryTree < btElementType >
:: makeRight(BinaryTree * T1)
{
    assert(!isEmpty());
    assert(right()->isEmpty());
    delete right();
    rightTree = T1;
}
```

11.2.3   A Sample Client for the Binary Tree

Here's a sample client to illustrate the use of the BinaryTree class. The client, shown in Code Example 11-3, creates a representation of the tree shown in Figure 11-3. The btElementType for this example is char, and for convenience we use typedef to define charTree (for a BinaryTree containing char) and charTreePtr (for a pointer to a charTree). Figure 11-8 shows the

correspondence between the nodes in the tree and the pointers created in Code
Example 11-3. (The empty trees are omitted from the diagram.)

Figure 11-8   *The operation of Code Example 11-3*

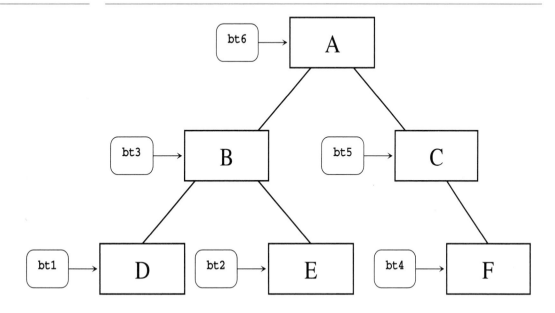

Code Example 11-3   *Sample client for binary tree*

```
// cx11-3.cpp
// Code Example 11-3: Simple Client for Binary Tree

#include "cx11-1.h"
#include <iostream.h>

int main()
{
    typedef BinaryTree < char > charTree;
    typedef charTree * charTreePtr;

    // Create tree from Figure 11-8

    // Create left subtree (rooted at B)

    // Create B's left subtree
    charTreePtr bt1(new charTree);
    bt1->insert('D');
```

```
// Create B's right subtree
charTreePtr bt2(new charTree);
bt2->insert('E');

// Create node containing B, and link
// up to subtrees
charTreePtr bt3(new charTree);
bt3->insert('B');
bt3->makeLeft(bt1);
bt3->makeRight(bt2);
// ** done creating left subtree

// Create right subtree

// Create C's right subtree
charTreePtr bt4(new charTree);
bt4->insert('F');

// Create node containing C, and link
// up its right subtree
charTreePtr bt5(new charTree);
bt5->insert('C');
bt5->makeRight(bt4);
// ** done creating right subtree

// Create the root of the tree, and link together
charTreePtr bt6(new charTree);
bt6->insert('A');
bt6->makeLeft(bt3);
bt6->makeRight(bt5);

// print out the root
cout << "Root contains: " << bt6->getData() << endl;

// print out root of left subtree
cout << "Left subtree root: " << bt6->left()->getData() << endl;

// print out root of right subtree
cout << "Right subtree root: " << bt6->right()->getData() << endl;

// print out leftmost child in tree
cout << "Leftmost child is: " <<
    bt6->left()->left()->getData() << endl;

// print out rightmost child in tree
cout << "Rightmost child is: " <<
    bt6->right()->right()->getData() << endl;

return 0;
}
```

11.2.4 Using the Binary Tree: Expression Trees Revisited

To illustrate a more significant use of our BinaryTree class, let's return to expression trees, first introduced in Section 11.1.3. We want to create BinaryTrees in which the node data type is some kind of object that can be either an operand (e.g., 4.3) or an operator (e.g., +). What we'll do is create a class, called evalNode, that includes a flag that distinguishes between operands and operators, and we'll make btElementType a pointer to evalNode. We show the relevant header file in Code Example 11-4.

Code Example 11-4 *Header file for expression tree*

```
// cx11-4.h
// CodeExample 11-4: Expression Tree: Header Files

#ifndef __MB_CX11_4__
#define __MB_CX11_4__

#include "dslib.h"

enum evalNodeType { evalOperator, evalOperand };

enum evalOperatorType { add, subtract, multiply, divide };

class evalNode {
public:
    evalNode(double d);
    evalNode(evalOperatorType op);
    evalNodeType getType() const;
    double getOperand() const;
    evalOperatorType getOperator() const;
private:
    evalNodeType nodeType;
    double nodeOperand;
    evalOperatorType nodeOperator;
};

typedef evalNode * evalNodePtr; // Pointer to an evalNode

#include "cx11-1.h" // binary tree header file

// An evalTree is a BinaryTree of pointers to evalNodes
typedef BinaryTree < evalNodePtr > evalTree;

typedef evalTree * evalTreePtr; // Pointer to an evalTree

double evaluateTree(evalTreePtr t);

#endif
```

One handy "trick" in the definition of evalNode is the way we've overloaded the constructor. If the client creates a node with a statement like this one:

```
evalTreeP t1(new evalNode(1.0));
```

C++ will call the constructor for an operand, setting the value of nodeType to evalOperand. Likewise, a statement of the form

```
evalTreeP t2(evalNode(multiply));
```

creates an evalOperator node. This is convenient, but more importantly, it prevents the client from setting the type wrong. Because the constructor code is the only place the nodeType flag gets manipulated we can be confident that it contains the appropriate value.

At the end of Code Example 11-4, you'll find a declaration for a function evaluateTree, which applies a simple recursive function:

• If the root is an operand, return its value.

• Otherwise, apply evaluateTree to the left and right subtrees, and apply the operator to the results.

Note that this is analogous to the "tree rewriting" method we discussed in Section 11.1.3, but it doesn't actually change the tree. The definitions for evaluateTree, and the member functions for evalNode, are shown in Code Example 11-5.

Code Example 11-5   Implementation file for expression tree

```
// cx11-5.cpp
// Code Example 11-5: Implementation file: Expression tree

#include "dslib.h"
#include "cx11-4.h" // header file for expression tree

evalNode::evalNode(double d)
{
    nodeType = evalOperand;
    nodeOperand = d;
}

evalNode::evalNode(evalOperatorType op)
{
    nodeType = evalOperator;
    nodeOperator = op;
}
```

```
evalNodeType
evalNode::getType() const
{
    return nodeType;
}

double
evalNode::getOperand() const
{
    assert(nodeType == evalOperand);
    return nodeOperand;
}

evalOperatorType
evalNode::getOperator() const
{
    assert(nodeType == evalOperator);
    return nodeOperator;
}

double evaluateTree(evalTreePtr t)
{
    assert(!t->isEmpty());
    evalNodePtr rootNodePtr = t->getData();
    if (rootNodePtr->getType() == evalOperand)
        return rootNodePtr->getOperand();
    else {
        double left(evaluateTree(t->left()));
        double right(evaluateTree(t->right()));
        switch(rootNodePtr->getOperator()) {
        case add:
            return left + right;
        case subtract:
            return left - right;
        case multiply:
            return left * right;
        case divide:
            assert(right);
            return left / right;
        }
    }
}
```

Given these definitions, we're now ready to set up and evaluate a tree. The code

```
new evalNode(...)
```

creates a new `evalNode` of the appropriate type and value, constructed depending upon the parameter. Thus to create, for example, a tree containing the operand 47, use something like the following:

```
evalTreeP et = new evalTree;
et->insert(new evalNode(47));
```

The first line creates a new tree (root); and the second inserts (a pointer to) a new `evalNode` representing the operand `1.0`. A complete program that builds and evaluates the expression tree for $3 + 7 \times 2 - 1$ (shown in Figure 11-4) appears as Code Example 11-6.

Code Example 11-6   *Code to create and evaluate an expression tree*

```
// cx11-6.cpp
// Code Example 11-6: Using the evaluation tree

#include "dslib.h"
#include "cx11-4.h" // Evaluation tree header file

int main()
{
    evalTreePtr et1(new evalTree);
    et1->insert(new evalNode(subtract));

    evalTreePtr et2(new evalTree);
    et2->insert(new evalNode(add));

    evalTreePtr et3(new evalTree);
    et3->insert(new evalNode(1.0));

    et1->makeLeft(et2);
    et1->makeRight(et3);

    evalTreePtr et4(new evalTree);
    et4->insert(new evalNode(3.0));

    evalTreePtr et5(new evalTree);
    et5->insert(new evalNode(multiply));

    et2->makeLeft(et4);
    et2->makeRight(et5);

    evalTreePtr et6(new evalTree);
    et6->insert(new evalNode(7.0));

    evalTreePtr et7(new evalTree);
    et7->insert(new evalNode(2.0));

    et5->makeLeft(et6);
```

```
et5->makeRight(et7);

cout << evaluateTree(et1) << endl;
return 0;
}
```

Exercise 11-7 Using Code Example 11-6 as a model, write and test a program to evaluate this expression:

$$6 \times 4 \div 2 + 7 - 6 \times 3$$

Exercise 11-8 Explicitly representing the empty trees in a Binary Tree requires extra space that is not really needed. In percentage terms, how much extra space is used? Describe in general how you could modify the implementation to eliminate this extra space. What would be the pros and cons of this alternate implementation?

11.3 Tree Traversal

11.3.1 Three Tree Traversal Algorithms

Back in Section 7.2, we saw that the process of visiting each element in a list is called list traversal. Likewise, we can define a similar process to *visit* the elements of a tree, called a *tree traversal.* However, unlike traversing the list, the best way to visit each item in a tree in an orderly fashion is not so obvious. Where should you start and how should you proceed?

The standard tree traversal schemes take advantage of the recursive nature of the tree and use a recursive traversal algorithm. The basic idea is this: when given a tree, visit the root directly and visit the children recursively. Given an empty tree, no action is required, so this serves as the base case for the recursion. Depending on when you visit the children, you can get three basic types of tree traversal, shown as Algorithm 11-1, Algorithm 11-2, and Algorithm 11-3.

Algorithm 11-1   *Preorder Traversal*

```
if the tree is not empty
    visit the root
    preOrderTraverse(left child)
    preOrderTraverse(right child)
```

Algorithm 11-2   *Inorder Traversal*

```
if the tree is not empty
        inOrderTraverse(left child)
        visit the root
        inOrderTraverse(right child)
```

Algorithm 11-3   *Postorder Traversal*

```
if the tree is not empty
        postOrderTraverse(left child)
        postOrderTraverse(right child)
        visit the root
```

Note that in principle you could get three more traversals by swapping the order of the left and right visits, but by convention we generally consider only the three shown here. The three traversals, ***preorder, inorder,*** and ***postorder,*** are nearly identical—the only difference is when the root is visited. Perhaps surprisingly in view of the similarity, these three traversal orders will visit the nodes in quite different orders for most trees.

Why the Traversals Work

Before you go any further, you ought to convince yourself that these algorithms really work, by applying an informal induction argument. By "works" we mean "visits each item in the tree exactly once." Take, for example, Algorithm 11-1, the Preorder Traversal algorithm. Certainly the algorithm works correctly for an empty tree, since traversing an empty tree requires doing nothing, and the algorithm certainly does that. Now, let's suppose that the algorithm works for trees of size k and consider those of size $k + 1$. Certainly visiting the root makes sense—we know we want to visit the root once. What about the subtrees? The subtrees are processed by recursive calls to our Preorder Traversal, and each subtree must be smaller than the entire tree, so it can't have more than k nodes, and we've hypothesized that the algorithm works for such trees. Thus we see that the algorithm visits the root, visits every node in the left subtree, and then visits every node in the right subtree, so we can conclude that it works. You can apply nearly the same argument to the other two algorithms.

Preorder Traversal

Now let's try applying these traversals to a sample tree, such as shown in Figure 11-9. For the purposes of our examples, we'll assume that we "print" each node as we visit it. We'll indicate that a node has been visited by putting a number in a circle next to it, indicating the order in which it was reached. Let's begin with a preorder traversal. The traversal begins at the root node, which is printed right away in a preorder traversal, and then proceeds to the left child. The traversal will work all the way down the left side of the tree, as shown in Figure 11-10.

Figure 11-9   *Sample tree to illustrate tree traversal*

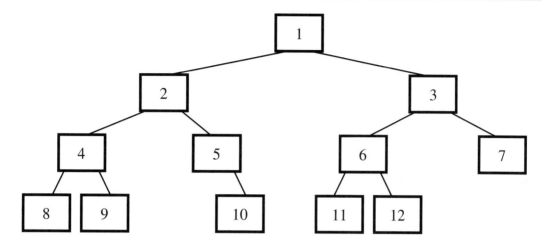

Figure 11-10   *Tree after four nodes visited in preorder traversal*

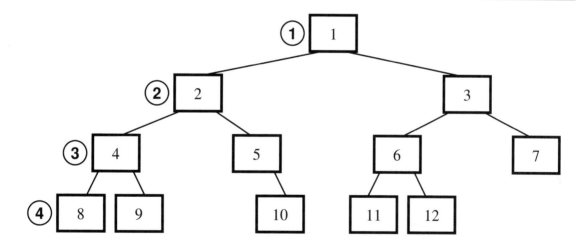

After labelling the left-most leaf, the recursion will back up to the node that contains a "4," and then visit its right child, which contains "9." At this point, the entire subtree rooted at "4" has been traversed, and the recursion backs up to the node labelled "2," and begins working on its right subtree. When this process has been completed, the tree will have been traversed as shown in Figure 11-11.

Figure 11-11   *Tree after left subtree of root visited using preorder traversal*

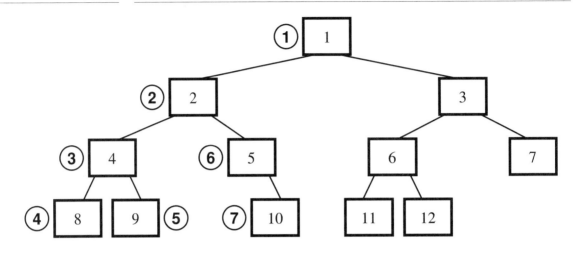

Figure 11-12   *Tree after completed preorder traversal*

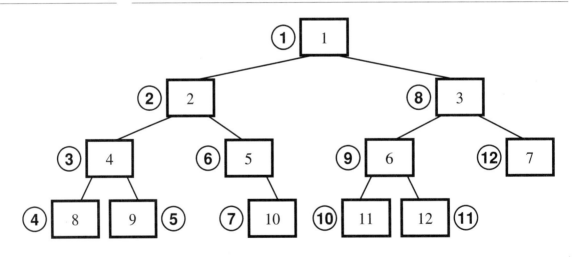

Following the traversal of the left subtree, the algorithm will traverse the right subtree, in the order shown by Figure 11-12. The final output from the preorder traversal will be

1 2 4 8 9 5 10 3 6 11 12 7

Inorder Traversal   Next, we'll look at an inorder traversal of the same tree. In the inorder traversal, the entire left subtree of each root is visited before the root is labelled, followed by a traversal of the right subtree. Note that in all three traversals, the nodes are traversed in the same order; the only difference is where in the process each node is "visited." An inorder traversal is shown in Figure 11-13. The final output from an inorder traversal will be

8 4 9 2 5 10 1 11 6 12 3 7

Figure 11-13   *Tree visited using inorder traversal*

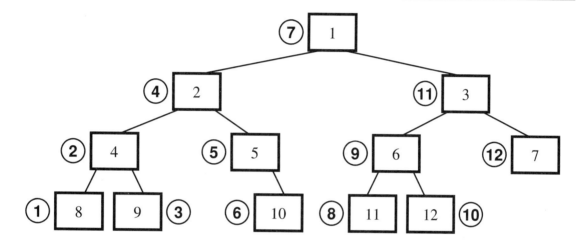

Postorder Traversal   Finally, we'll traverse the tree in postorder. In a postorder traversal, nodes are "visited" the last time the algorithm gets to the node. In other words, both the left and then the right subtrees are visited before the root. Using the postorder traversal yields the visit order shown in Figure 11-14. Visiting the nodes in postorder yields the following output:

8 9 4 10 5 2 11 12 6 7 3 1

11.3.2   Using Tree Traversals

The ordering of the tree elements yielded by the various traversals have some interesting and useful applications. We'll look at one here, involving expression trees, and another later on when we explore a related tree, the Binary Search Tree.

Let's suppose we have the expression tree for $3 + 7 \times 2 - 1$, originally encountered in Figure 11-4 and repeated in Figure 11-15. What happens when you traverse this tree in inorder and print out the sequence of nodes visited? Try it first before you look at the answer in the next paragraph.

Figure 11-14   *Tree visited using postorder traversal*

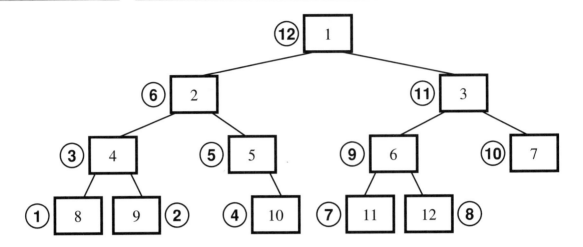

Traversing the tree in inorder and printing out the nodes as they are visited will give you the following:

$$3 + 7 \times 2 - 1$$

That is, traversing an expression tree in inorder gives you the expression represented by the tree. Nice, but perhaps not too surprising. Now try a postorder traversal. If you do it right, you will get the following sequence:

$$3 \ 7 \ 2 \times + 1 -$$

Does this sequence look like anything useful to you? If you spent some time learning about Reverse Polish Notation (RPN) in Section 8.6.1, then you may recognize that the expression above represents $3 + 7 \times 2 - 1$ in RPN, or postfix, notation. Now you can see that putting an expression in a binary tree and then traversing it provides an easy way to convert an expression from infix to postfix notation.

11.3.3   Implementing Tree Traversals

We're going to look at two approaches to programming a tree traversal. In our first approach, we get a very simple "single-purpose" traversal that can be programmed very easily but isn't particularly reusable; then we'll develop a slightly more sophisticated version that's a lot more flexible. In both cases, we're going to develop the traversal separately from the BinaryTree class, that is, as a client of it. Some designers might instead add the traversal as an element of the class, but the traversal really

Figure 11-15   ***Expression Tree for*** $3 + 7 \times 2 - 1$

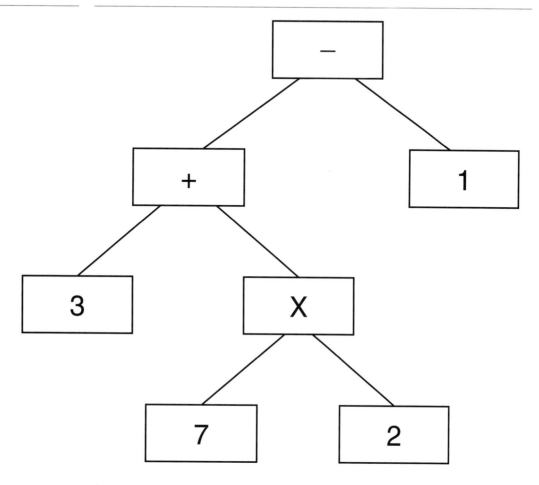

doesn't require any information about the internals of the class, so I'd argue that it makes the most sense to develop it separately.

In our first set of traversal functions, we hard-code an output statement to implement the notion of "visiting" a node. This provides a good test of the basic algorithm, but if you want the function to do anything else you have to recode the line that performs the visit. Using this approach, we can get the preorder and inorder traversals shown in Code Example 11-7. The postorder is left as an exercise.

Code Example 11-7   *Tree traversals: Version 1*

```cpp
// cx11-7.cpp
// Code Example 11-7: Binary Tree Traversals

#include "dslib.h"
#include "cx11-1.h"

typedef BinaryTree < int > btint;
typedef btint * btintp;

void preOrderTraverse(btintp bt)
{
    if (!bt->isEmpty()) {
        // visit tree
        cout << bt->getData() << '\t';
        // traverse left child
        preOrderTraverse(bt->left());
        // traverse right child
        preOrderTraverse(bt->right());
    }
}

void inOrderTraverse(btintp bt)
{
    if (!bt->isEmpty()) {
        // traverse left child
        inOrderTraverse(bt->left());
        // visit tree
        cout << bt->getData() << '\t';
        // traverse right child
        inOrderTraverse(bt->right());
    }
}
```

To initiate, for example, an inorder traversal as defined above, you would execute a statement like this:

```cpp
inOrderTraverse(bt);
```

where `bt` points to a Binary Tree.

The approach in Code Example 11-7 certainly works, but to make it do anything else you'd have to tinker with the code. A more flexible approach is to make `visit` a function, and pass it as a function pointer argument. The syntax takes a bit of getting used to, but the idea's quite simple—you add the function pointer argument to the traversal functions, you create a `visit` function that does whatever you want your visit to do, and then you pass a pointer to the `visit` function each time you call the traversal. The result is shown in Code Example 11-8, which has exactly the same effect as Code Example 11-7.

Code Example 11-8   *Tree traversals: Version 2*

```
// cx11-8.cpp
// Code Example 11-8: Binary Tree Traversal

#include "dslib.h"
#include "cx11-1.h"

typedef BinaryTree < int > btint;
typedef btint * btintp;

void preOrderTraverse(btintp bt, void visit(btintp))
{
    if (!bt->isEmpty()) {
        // visit tree
        (* visit)(bt);
        // traverse left child
        preOrderTraverse(bt->left(), visit);
        // traverse right child
        preOrderTraverse(bt->right(), visit);
    }
}

void inOrderTraverse(btintp bt, void visit(btintp))
{
    if (!bt->isEmpty()) {
        // traverse left child
        inOrderTraverse(bt->left(), visit);
        // visit tree
        (* visit)(bt);
        //traverse right child
        inOrderTraverse(bt->right(), visit);
    }
}

void visit(btintp bt)
{
    cout << bt->getData() << '\t';
}
```

Using Function Pointers

The syntax for passing and using *function pointers* may be unfamiliar to you, so let's take a look at it. In the declaration of `preOrderTraverse`, the second parameter can be recognized as a function pointer because it's a parameter with a return type—`void visit(btintp)`. Note that `visit` also has a type for a parameter. So putting it together, `visit` is a parameter that points to a function that returns `void` and takes a single argument of type `btintp`.

Each call to a traverse function will need to specify a `visit` function as an argument. For example, using the example function `printIt`, you could call a traversal function with the expression

```
inOrderTraverse(head, printIt);
```

The first parameter, `head`, must point to a Binary Tree, while the second `printIt` is (implicitly) a pointer to the function with the same name. What's really nice about this approach is the great flexibility it provides. Not only can you write a traversal function that can do almost anything you'd like, without any change to the code for the traversal, you can even have different calls to the traversal function do different things within a single program.

Within the traversal functions, the line

```
(* visit)(bt);
```

invokes the function. You need the "*" to dereference the pointer and get access to the function, and you need the first set of parentheses because of the C++ order of operations. The second set of parentheses are the same as those you'd find in any other function call. When this line is encountered in the program, the passed function is called, and `bt` is passed as the argument to the function.

In the rest of this chapter, we'll look at a variation on the Binary Tree that's quite useful and also expand our knowledge of object-oriented programming by using a feature called inheritance.

Exercise 11-9   Practice your three tree traversals, using the tree shown in Figure 11-16.

Exercise 11-10   Given an inorder traversal sequence, plus either a preorder or postorder sequence, it's possible to reconstruct the tree that has been traversed. For the following sequences, reconstruct the tree that they represent:

preorder: 3 2 1 5 4 8 7 6 9 10 13 12 11 14

inorder: 1 2 4 5 3 6 7 9 8 10 11 12 14 13

(*Hint:* You know that 3 is the head (why?), so the nodes 1 2 4 5 are in the left subtree, and the nodes following 3 are in the right subtree. Applying this recursively will give you the entire tree.)

Exercise 11-11   For the following expression:

$$17 \times 3 + 2 - (10 \times 9 \div 3) + 3 \times 4$$

Figure 11-16   *Sample tree for Exercise 11-9*

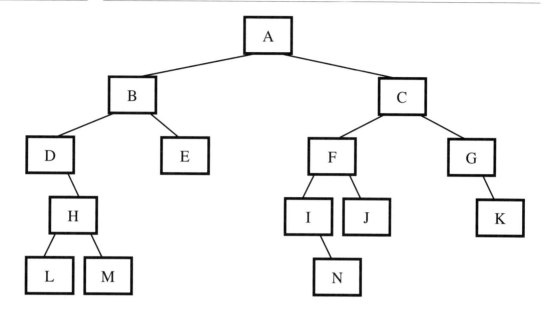

a. Draw the expression tree corresponding to the expression.

b. Convert the expression to prefix notation.

c. Perform a preorder traversal of the tree and confirm that it's the same as your prefix expression in part 2.

Exercise 11-12   Write a program that creates a small tree (with, say, 7 nodes), and then calls the traversal functions in Code Example 11-7 to print out traversals. Before you test the program, draw your tree and perform the traversals yourself, and compare the answers you get with the ones the program prints out.

Exercise 11-13   Add a function `postOrderTraversal` to Code Example 11-7. Write a driver to test your function for correct operation.

Exercise 11-14   Write a function that sends the data field of a tree to a disk file. Write a program that creates a small tree, calls the tree traversal from Code Example 11-8, and passes it a pointer to your function.

11.4   Binary Search Trees[1]

11.4.1   An Ordered Tree ADT

Back in Section 10.4, we promised that trees would give us a way to implement a data structure that can perform fast retrieval and insertion of individual elements, and also support sequential processing of the elements, unlike the table structures in Chapter 10. We're ready to deliver on that promise, by developing the ADT **Binary Search Tree (BST).** We'll begin with an abstract definition that can be implemented by a BST, and then we'll see how the BST can indeed perform the needed operations.

The definition of a BST starts with a version of the Binary Tree definition (Definition 11-1) but adds an ordering to the tree that can be used to retrieve and traverse the entries in order.

Definition 11-2   A *Binary Search Tree (BST)* is either

1. an *empty tree;* or

2. consists of a node, called a *root*, and two children, *left* and *right*, each of which are themselves BSTs. Each node contains a value, such that the value at the root is greater than the value in any nodes in the left subtree, and less than or equal to the value of any nodes in the right subtree.

We will refer to the ordering relationship—that the (value of) the nodes in the left subtree is less than the value at the root, which in turn is less than or equal to the nodes of the right subtree—as the **BST invariant.** As we work with BSTs, we must ensure that the program maintains the BST invariant, because otherwise the ordering of the tree will be confused and the algorithms won't work.

BST Examples and Counterexamples   Let's look at some examples and counterexamples. Figure 11-17 contains an example of a BST. You should check carefully that all conditions are met. However, Figure 11-18 is not a BST, even though the conditions appear to be met at the root, and even though both the left and right subtrees are correctly constructed BSTs. The problem is that the right subtree contains a value (15) that is less than the value of the tree root. Our final counterexample appears in Figure 11-19. In this tree, the BST conditions are met at the root, but there's a subtree in the lower right part of the tree, in which the root is 28 but the left child contains 31. Because this subtree does

---

1. A version of this implementation of Binary Search Trees first appeared in Berman and Duvall (1996).

Figure 11-17   **A Binary Search Tree**

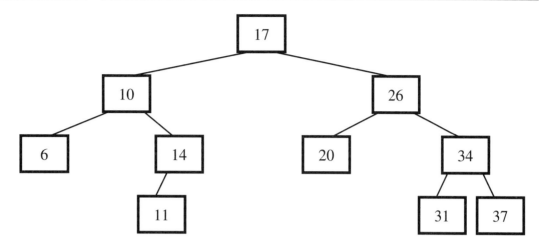

Figure 11-18   **A binary tree that is not a BST because BST invariant is violated**

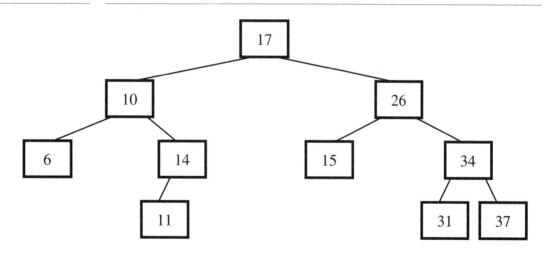

not meet the BST invariant the entire tree is disqualified and is not considered a BST.

We can derive an ADT (ADT 11-2) for the BST based upon Definition 11-2. Note that the BST invariant needs to be used as a pre- and postcondition for the operations that involve ordering of the tree, namely the insert and retrieve operations. This means that our retrieval operation is only guaranteed to work if we pass it a tree that meets the BST invariant.

Figure 11-19   *A binary tree that is not a BST because one subtree is not a BST*

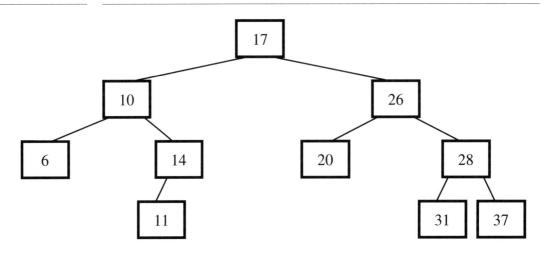

ADT 11-2   Binary Search Tree

Characteristics:

- A Binary Search Tree ADT T stores data of some type (btElementType), using a binary search tree as defined in Definition 11-2.

Prerequisites:

The data type btElementType must implement the < and == operators.

Operations:

bool T.isEmpty()

Precondition:	None.
Postcondition:	None.
Returns:	True if and only if T is an empty tree.

btElementType T.getData()

Precondition:	!T.isEmpty()
Postcondition:	None.
Returns:	The data associated with the root of the tree.

void T.insert(btElementType d)

Precondition:	T meets the BST invariant.

Postcondition: T.retrieve(d).getData() == d; T meets the BST invariant.

BinaryTree T.retrieve(btElementType d)

Precondition:	T meets the BST invariant.
Postcondition:	T meets the BST invariant.
Returns:	if T contains a node with data d, then T.retrieve(d).getData() == d; otherwise, T.retrieve(d).isEmpty().

BinaryTree T.left()

Precondition:	!T.isEmpty()
Postcondition:	None.
Returns:	The left child of T.

BinaryTree T.right()

Precondition:	!T.isEmpty()
Postcondition:	None.
Returns:	The right child of T.

BST Algorithms Before we get into the implementation, let's look at the algorithm for performing a retrieval. As the name "Binary Search Tree" suggests, you can use an algorithm analogous to Binary Search to retrieve elements from the tree.

For example, using the tree in Figure 11-17, let's suppose that we're searching for 31. Starting at the root and comparing 31 with 17, the BST invariant tells us that 31 has to be in the right subtree. Then we compare 31 with 26, determining that 31 is larger, so again we follow the right subtree. Next, we compare 31 with 34, follow to the left and finally arrive at 31.

On the other hand, suppose we attempt to retrieve 16, an item not stored in the tree. Because 16 is less than 17 we compare 16 to 10, and then to 14, where because 16 is larger than 14, we follow the right child of 14. If 16 were in the tree, it would have to be in the right subtree of 14, but this subtree is empty. At this point, because the retrieval algorithm encounters an empty tree we know that 16 is not stored in the tree.

Now let's consider the insertion algorithm. When you insert an item into a BST, you want to put it exactly where the retrieval algorithm would find it when it goes to search for that item. Hence, the beginning of the insertion algorithm will be the same as the retrieval algorithm—you search through the tree until an empty tree is encountered. Then, the new item becomes the item stored in that empty tree, and two new empty trees are created.

Figure 11-20   *A Binary Search Tree showing position where 12 would be inserted*

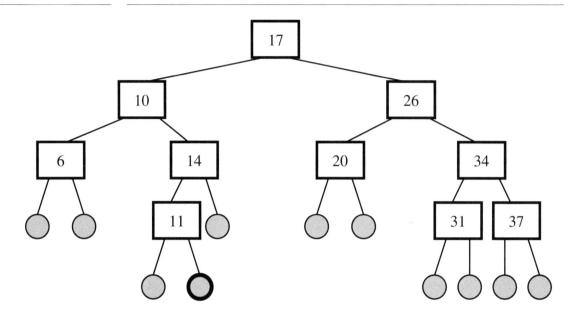

In Figure 11-20, we've repeated the tree from Figure 11-17, but this time we've included the empty trees. When we go to insert 12 into this tree, we'll visit the nodes containing 17, 10, 14, and 11, and we'll finally arrive at the empty tree with the dark circle around it. To insert 12, we convert the circled node into a non-empty root, with two empty children. Figure 11-21 shows the result following the insertion.

Finally, we promised that BSTs would provide a way to retrieve the tree data in order. Perhaps you've already realized that an inorder traversal of a BST will visit the tree data in order. You ought to try it on a couple of BSTs to convince yourself that it really works.

11.4.2   Implementing the Binary Search Tree

Now we'll turn these ideas into software. In the header file, Code Example 11-9, we've used quite similar techniques to those we used for the binary tree back in Code Example 11-1. For example, we make use of pointers to the trees, and call by reference, in order to get good performance. We'll see later, in Section 11.5, that we can exploit these similarities to minimize the amount of new code we need to create the BST; for now, we're going to provide a complete implementation of the BST. We are, however, going to postpone implementing the tree traversal algorithms until we can reuse our original tree traversals.

Figure 11-21   *The Binary Search Tree after 12 inserted*

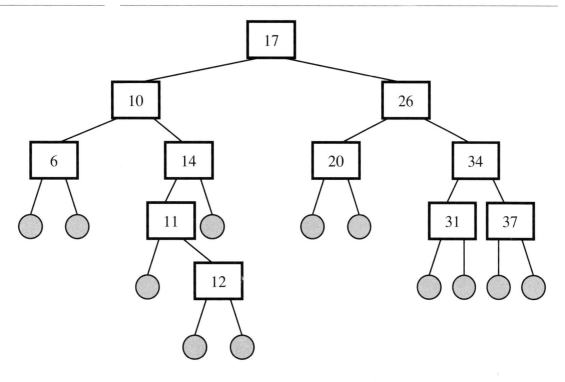

Code Example 11-9   Interface file for Binary Search Tree

```
// cx11-9.h
// Code Example 11-9: Interface File: Binary Search Trees

#ifndef __MB_CX11_9__
#define __MB_CX11_9__

#include "dslib.h"

template < class btElementType >
class BST {
public:
   BST();
   bool isEmpty() const;
   // Precondition: None.
   // Postcondition: None.
   // Returns: true if and only if T is an empty tree
   btElementType getData() const;
   // Precondition: !this->isEmpty()
   // Postcondition: None
```

```
    // Returns: The data associated with the root of the tree
    void insert(const btElementType & d);
    // Precondition: if d is a left child, then d must be < parent->getData();
    //     if d is a right child, then d must be > parent->getData();
    // Postconditions: T->retrieve(k)->getData() == d
    BST * retrieve(const btElementType & d);
    // Precondition: none
    // Postcondition: none
    // Returns: if T contains a node matching d, then
    //     T->retrieve(d)->getData() == d; otherwise, T->isEmpty()
    BST * left();
    // Precondition: !this->isEmpty()
    // Postcondition: None
    // Returns: (a pointer to) the left child of T
    BST * right();
    // Precondition: !this->isEmpty()
    // Postcondition: None
    // Returns: (a pointer to) the right child of T
private:
    bool nullTree;
    btElementType treeData;
    BST * leftTree;
    BST * rightTree;
};

#endif
```

The implementation of the BST, shown in Code Example 11-10, follows the algorithm quite closely. The `insert` function looks at the tree that receives the call, and if it's a null tree, turns it into a non-null tree containing the new data. Otherwise, it's recursively invoked on either the left or right subtree as appropriate.

Code Example 11-10 Implementation file for Binary Search Tree

```
// cx11-10.cpp
// Code Example 11-10: Implementation File: Binary Tree

#include "cx11-9.h"

template < class btElementType >
BST < btElementType > :: BST()
{
    nullTree = true;
    leftTree = 0;
    rightTree = 0;
}
```

```
template < class btElementType >
bool
BST < btElementType > :: isEmpty() const
{
    return nullTree;
}

template < class btElementType >
btElementType
BST < btElementType > :: getData() const
{
    assert(!isEmpty());
    return treeData;
}

template < class btElementType >
void
BST < btElementType >
:: insert(const btElementType & d)
{
    if (nullTree) {
        nullTree = false;
        leftTree = new BST;
        rightTree = new BST;
        treeData = d;
    }
    else if (d == treeData)
        ; // do nothing -- it's already here!
    else if (d < treeData)
        leftTree->insert(d);
    else
        rightTree->insert(d);
}

template < class btElementType >
BST < btElementType > *
BST < btElementType >
:: retrieve(const btElementType & d)
{
    if (nullTree || d == treeData)
        // return a pointer to the tree for which retrieve was called
        return this;
    else if (d < treeData)
        return leftTree->retrieve(d);
    else
        return rightTree->retrieve(d);
}
```

```
template < class btElementType >
BST < btElementType > *
BST < btElementType > :: left()
{
    assert(!isEmpty());
    return leftTree;
}

template < class btElementType >
BST < btElementType > *
BST < btElementType > :: right()
{
    assert(!isEmpty());
    return rightTree;
}
```

BST Client   Code Example 11-11 contains a simple BST client. The client creates the tree shown in Figure 11-21, and then tests to see whether 11 and 13 are contained within the tree. If you run Code Example 11-11, you'll get the following output:

```
11 found.
13 not found.
```

Code Example 11-11 Simple BST client

```
// cx11-11.cpp
// Code Example 11-11: Sample Client of BST

#include "cx11-9.h"

int main()
{
    typedef BST < int > intBST;
    typedef intBST * intBSTPtr;

    intBSTPtr b(new intBST);
    b->insert(17);
    b->insert(10);
    b->insert(26);
    b->insert(6);
    b->insert(14);
    b->insert(20);
    b->insert(34);
    b->insert(11);
    b->insert(31);
    b->insert(37);
    b->insert(12);
    // is 11 in the tree?
    intBSTPtr get11(b->retrieve(11));
    if (get11->isEmpty())
```

```
      cout << "11 not found.\n";
   else
      cout << "11 found.\n";
   // is 13 in the tree?
   intBSTPtr get13(b->retrieve(13));
   if (get13->isEmpty())
      cout << "13 not found.\n";
   else
      cout << "13 found.\n";
   return 0;
}
```

As we mentioned above, the Binary Search Tree shares many characteristics with the Binary Tree. In the next section, we'll see how we can take advantage of this similarity to reuse some of the implementation of the Binary Tree, using an object-oriented programming technique called inheritance.

Exercise 11-15   Trace the process of inserting the following items into the BST on Figure 11-20, and draw the resulting tree:

> 21, 30, 50, 34

Exercise 11-16   Draw the BST that's created when the following items are added to an initially empty tree, *in the order given*:

> 17, 3, 45, 55, 33, 1, 29, 30, 20, 5

Exercise 11-17   Give a possible order that items might have been inserted to create the tree in Figure 11-17.

Exercise 11-18   The BST as shown in the example doesn't meet all our needs, because it contains only a key and no associated data. Explain, in general, how to implement the class `btElementType` so it will contain both a key and data and work correctly with the given implementation.

11.5 Reuse Through Inheritance: A Hierarchy of Trees

An object-oriented programming language generally has the following three features:

- *Encapsulation:* abstractions can be encapsulated as a type, object, or class.

- *Inheritance:* abstractions can be reused through inheritance.

- *Polymorphism:* statements in a program can be written that use more than one abstraction, with the language choosing the right one while the program is running.

Throughout this course we've been using the notion of encapsulating an abstraction as a class. In this section we're going to begin using inheritance.

is-a relations   We observed in the last section that a Binary Search Tree is a kind of binary tree. Thus a Binary Search Tree can be defined using our binary tree abstraction, using an **is-a relationship**. That is, we say that "A Binary Search Tree *is-a* Binary Tree, with additional features." Note that the relationship is *not* symmetric—it would not be correct to say that a Binary Tree is a Binary Search Tree.

Defining one abstraction in terms of another using an is-a relationship can be seen as a kind of inheritance—our definition of Binary Search Tree inherits from the definition of a Binary Tree. In programming, inheritance works the same way. We can define a BST class as inheriting from the BinaryTree class. When we do this, we're telling the compiler that our new BST class should inherit all the features of the BinaryTree class, including its member data and member functions. We refer to the class inherited from as the **base class,** and the class doing the inheriting as the **derived class.** So for our example, BinaryTree will be the base class and BST the derived class. The inheritance relationship can be represented pictorially through an **inheritance diagram;** we've provided one for the BinaryTree and the BST in Figure 11-22.

Figure 11-22   *Inheritance diagram for BinaryTree and BST*

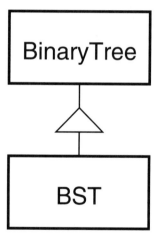

Now let's look at implementing inheritance in C++. First of all, with few exceptions, inheritance only "works" when the base class has been designed to be inherited from. I suggest that you stick to the following rule:

Only inherit from classes that have been designed to be base classes!

The Keyword
"virtual"

How do you know that a class has been designed to be used as a base class? Classes designed to be inherited from will include the keyword "**virtual**" in the declaration of most or all of their member functions. The keyword virtual tells the compiler that derived classes are allowed to provide their own, modified, definitions for the function. Consider, for example, the function insert in a Binary Tree. An insert of a value into a Binary Tree will change the value of the data of the root of the tree; this behavior is shown in Code Example 11-2. However, the insert function in a Binary Search Tree behaves differently—in order to maintain the BST invariant, the data must be inserted at an appropriate leaf. So if we want to use inheritance to define a BST, we have to be able to change the behavior of insert; declaring the insert function to be virtual in the base class allows us to do so. Because, when we define the base class, we don't know which functions a derived class may wish to redefine, we generally make all member functions virtual, with the exception of the constructor. (Since the derived class has a different name, it's going to have its own constructor, rather than inheriting the base's constructor. If necessary, the derived can invoke the base's constructor function to perform appropriate initialization.)

"protected" Members

There's another change that we've made in our definition of BinaryTree that will make things more convenient for the derived class. The member data for BinaryTree has been declared to be **protected** rather than **private.** From the point of view of a client class, there's no difference between protected and private class members. However, for a derived class it makes a big difference—a derived class has access to class members that are protected but no access to private members. Unlike the use of virtual, protected members are optional in a base class, but in many cases they make it much easier to write the derived classes. Code Example 11-12 shows our rewritten declaration of BinaryTree using virtual and protected, as well as the declaration of BST, which we'll look at next.

Code Example 11-12 Interface File for BST implemented with inheritance

```
// cx11-12.h
// Code Example 11-12: Interface File: Binary Search Trees inheriting from
//                     Binary Trees

#ifndef __MB_CX11_12__
#define __MB_CX11_12__

#include "dslib.h"

template < class btElementType >
class BinaryTree {
public:
    BinaryTree();
```

```cpp
        virtual bool isEmpty() const;
        // Precondition: None.
        // Postcondition: None.
        // Returns: true if and only if T is an empty tree
        virtual btElementType getData() const;
        // Precondition: !this->isEmpty()
        // Postcondition: None
        // Returns: The data associated with the root of the tree
        virtual void insert(const btElementType & d);
        // Precondition: none
        // Postconditions: this->getData() == d; !this->isEmpty()
        virtual BinaryTree * retrieve(const btElementType & d);
        // Precondition: none
        // Postcondition: none
        // Returns: this
        // Note: A useless stub, will be redefined by child class
        virtual BinaryTree * left();
        // Precondition: !this->isEmpty()
        // Postcondition: None
        // Returns: (a pointer to) the left child of T
        virtual BinaryTree * right();
        // Precondition: !this->isEmpty()
        // Postcondition: None
        // Returns: (a pointer to) the right child of T
        virtual void makeLeft(BinaryTree * T1);
        // Precondition: !this->isEmpty();
        //     this->left()->isEmpty()
        // Postcondition: this->left() == T1
        virtual void makeRight(BinaryTree * T1);
        // Precondition: !this->isEmpty()
        //     this->right()->isEmpty()
        // Postcondition: this->right() == T1
protected:
        bool nullTree;
        btElementType treeData;
        BinaryTree * leftTree;
        BinaryTree * rightTree;
};
template < class btElementType >
class BST : public BinaryTree < btElementType > {
public:
        virtual void insert(const btElementType & d);
        // Precondition: if d is a left child, then d must be < parent->getData();
        //     if d is a right child, then d must be > parent->getData();
        // Postconditions: T->retrieve(k)->getData() == d
        virtual BinaryTree < btElementType > * retrieve(const btElementType & d);
        // Precondition: none
        // Postcondition: none
        // Returns: if T contains a node matching d, then
        //     T->retrieve(d)->getData() == d; otherwise, T->isEmpty()
};
#endif
```

Now we'll consider the definition of our derived class, BST. We use the following notation to indicate the inheritance relationship:

```
class BST : public BinaryTree
```

The syntax indicates that the class BST is defined in terms of base class BinaryTree. Furthermore, the keyword `public` tells the compiler that we want clients of BST to be able to access the public members of the class BinaryTree. All our examples in this book use **public inheritance.** You can see that our declaration of BST in Code Example 11-12 is a lot shorter than the original one in Code Example 11-9. That's because we only have to declare the functions that we want to redefine; all other member functions are inherited from BinaryTree, and the data fields that appear after the `protected` keyword will also be available to the BST implementation. Hence, when we create a BST object, it will be able to understand the functions `insert` and `retrieve`, as redefined for a BST, as well as functions such as `getData` and `left`, inherited from BinaryTree.

Implementing
Derived Classes   Now let's look at the implementation. There's not really much difference between the implementation of BinaryTree and BST when we use inheritance, with the exception of the constructor. A constructor in a derived class has a special form in order to allow the construction process to proceed in the correct order. For the BST, the constructor implementation includes the following line:

```
BST() : BinaryTree < btElementType > ()
```

This syntax tells the compiler to call the BinaryTree constructor *first* when constructing a BST. In this particular case, there's nothing special that a BST constructor has to do, other than make sure that the BinaryTree constructor is called, so the body of the constructor function is empty. The rest of the implementation details can be found in Code Example 11-13.

Code Example 11-13 Implementation File for BST with inheritance

```
// cx11-13.cpp
// Code Example 11-13: Implementation File: Binary Tree

#include "cx11-12.h"

template < class btElementType >
BinaryTree < btElementType > :: BinaryTree()
{
    nullTree = true;
    leftTree = 0;
    rightTree = 0;
}
```

```
template < class btElementType >
bool
BinaryTree < btElementType > :: isEmpty() const
{
    return nullTree;
}

template < class btElementType >
btElementType
BinaryTree < btElementType > :: getData() const
{
    assert(!isEmpty());
    return treeData;
}

template < class btElementType >
void
BinaryTree < btElementType >
:: insert(const btElementType & d)
{
    treeData = d;
    if (nullTree) {
        nullTree = false;
        leftTree = new BinaryTree;
        rightTree = new BinaryTree;
    }
}

template < class btElementType >
BinaryTree < btElementType > *
BinaryTree < btElementType >
:: retrieve(const btElementType & d)
{
    return this;
}

template < class btElementType >
BinaryTree < btElementType > *
BinaryTree < btElementType > :: left()
{
    assert(!isEmpty());
    return leftTree;
}

template < class btElementType >
BinaryTree < btElementType > *
BinaryTree < btElementType > :: right()
{
    assert(!isEmpty());
    return rightTree;
}
```

```
template < class btElementType >
void
BinaryTree < btElementType >
:: makeLeft(BinaryTree * T1)
{
    assert(!isEmpty());
    assert(left()->isEmpty());
    delete left();
    leftTree = T1;
}

template < class btElementType >
void
BinaryTree < btElementType >
:: makeRight(BinaryTree * T1)
{
    assert(!isEmpty());
    assert(right()->isEmpty());
    delete right();
    rightTree = T1;
}

template < class btElementType >
void
BST < btElementType >
:: insert(const btElementType & d)
{
    if (nullTree) {
        nullTree = false;
        leftTree = new BST;
        rightTree = new BST;
        treeData = d;
    }
    else if (d == treeData)
        treeData = d;
    else if (d < treeData)
        leftTree->insert(d);
    else
        rightTree->insert(d);
}

template < class btElementType >
BinaryTree < btElementType > *
BST < btElementType >
:: retrieve(const btElementType & d)
{
    if (nullTree || d == treeData)
        return this;
    else if (d < treeData)
        return leftTree->retrieve(d);
    else
        return rightTree->retrieve(d);
}
```

Traversing the Inherited BST

You can already see a payoff for the use of inheritance, in the amount of new code we have to write to support the BST. Reducing the amount of code not only means less to write now, but also, more importantly, less to maintain in the future. Now we're going to see an additional advantage you probably didn't expect. If we rewrote the BST implementation from scratch, we'd have to rewrite or modify our traversal code (Code Example 11-8) to work with the BST. However, because of the way we've used inheritance, *our original traversal algorithms will work with our BST!* After all, a BST is a BinaryTree, and if you look at the way the traversal algorithms access the BinaryTree, there's nothing that they do that's inconsistent with a BST. When you call the traversal algorithm and pass it a pointer to a BST, the compiler will recognize that the BST is inherited from BinaryTree and automatically apply the traversal algorithm just as if you'd called it with a BinaryTree. So we can write and maintain a single set of traversal algorithms and use them for all our trees. At this point you can begin to glimpse the power of inheritance.

Exercise 11-19   The inheritance implementation in Code Example 11-12 and Code Example 11-13 has one unattractive feature: the `makeLeft` and `makeRight` functions are inherited by the BST, even though using these functions would allow the client to improperly destroy the structure of the BST. Explain.

Exercise 11-20   Because inheritance allows you to redefine how inherited member functions work, you can get around the problem described in Exercise 11-19, by redefining `makeLeft` and `makeRight` to do nothing. Rewrite the header, and add implementations of `makeLeft` and `makeRight` that simply print a warning to `cerr` and make no changes to the tree.

Exercise 11-21   Write a test driver for the BST that creates the tree in Figure 11-17 and traverses it in each of the three orders.

Exercise 11-22   Experiment with the syntax for inheritance, using Code Example 11-12 and Code Example 11-13. For example, take the `virtual` keyword out of the base class and see what happens when you compile the code.

Exercise 11-23   You can use inheritance to create a class ExpressionTree derived from the base class BinaryTree. The ExpressionTree class should implement one new member function, `evaluate`, which returns the value obtained by evaluating the expression tree at the root. Show the class declaration for ExpressionTree.

11.6 Performance of Binary Trees

11.6.1 The Shapes of Binary Trees

We promised you that Binary Trees would let us implement inserts, retrievals, and traversals, all with excellent running times. Let's now evaluate the performance of a BST for each of these operations. First, let's look at traversals. For convenience, we repeat the Preorder Traversal algorithm, first shown as Algorithm 11-1.

Algorithm 11-4	*Preorder Traversal*

```
if the tree is not empty
    visit the root
    preOrderTraverse(left child)
    preOrderTraverse(right child)
```

If you trace the algorithm carefully, you'll find that the traversal "looks at" each node three times—once for the visit and once for each recursive call. Hence the performance is 3 multiplied by the cost of the operations performed. Because these operations require constant time traversal is an $O(n)$ algorithm. We certainly can't expect to find better asymptotic performance than that.

Inserts and retrievals are a bit more problematic. In order to insert a node, the program has to follow a path from the root of the tree to some leaf, at which point a constant amount of work is required to perform the insertion. Likewise, to retrieve a node, that same path from root to leaf must be travelled. So we see that the key to understanding the performance of the tree lies in the depth of the tree. Unfortunately, in the worst case, the depth of the tree can be quite unfavorable. Consider, for example, adding the item 10 to the tree shown in Figure 11-23. In this case, every single item in the tree has to be processed before the new node can be added as a child of 8. For a tree with this "bad" shape, the insert and retrieve operations will require $O(n)$ —in other words, the performance of the tree will be the same as an ordered list.

On the other hand, the performance of the tree can be much better if the shape of the tree is "short and wide" rather than "long and skinny." Consider the tree in Figure 11-24; this tree, containing 15 nodes, will require traversing just 4 nodes to insert the value 10. How good is this, as a function of n, the size of the tree?

In order to answer this question, we need to come up with a way of expressing the minimum depth of the tree as a function of n, the number of nodes. In Figure 11-25, we show the "shortest" trees we can find for the values of n equal to 1, 3, 7, and 15.

Figure 11-23   *A tree that is expensive to process*

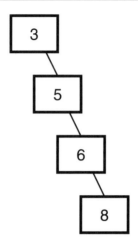

Figure 11-24   *An efficient tree*

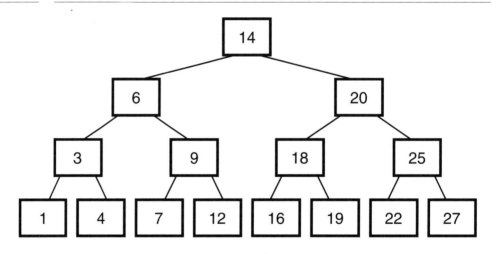

In other words, if *n* is less than or equal to 7, for example, you can make a tree of depth 2. For *n* less than or equal to 15, you can make a tree of depth 3, and so on. Looking at the numbers, can you see the pattern?

Take a look at the tree of depth 2, containing 7 nodes, and then observe that the tree of depth 3 consists of two trees of depth 2, plus 1 more node (the root): $15 = 7 + 7 + 1$. In general, the number of nodes you can fit in a tree of depth *d*, which we'll call $f(d)$, can be expressed by the following equation:

Figure 11-25   *Shallowest trees for n=1, n=3, n=7, and n=15*

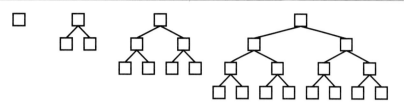

Equation 11-1 $$f(d) = f(d-1) + f(d-1) + 1 = 2f(d-1) + 1$$

Equation 11-1 is an example of a **recurrence relation.** There are various techniques for solving recurrence relations, that is, converting them from the sort of recursive form to one in which the function only appears to the left of the equation. The simplest technique is simply to look at the numbers produced by the equation and infer the value of the function. Look at the values of f for 0 through 4, as shown in Equation 11-2.

$$f(0) = 1$$
$$f(1) = 3$$
Equation 11-2 $$f(2) = 7$$
$$f(3) = 15$$
$$f(4) = 31$$

Can you see the pattern? Each number is 1 less than a power of 2. Using this observation, we can write Equation 11-3:

Equation 11-3 $$f(d) = 2^{d+1} - 1$$

Equations 11-1 and 11-3 are two ways of expressing the same relationship,[2] but the second is easier to manipulate. Equation 11-3 tells us how many nodes can be stored in a tree of depth d, but what we really want to know is, for a tree containing n nodes, how deep is it? Observe that the number of nodes, n, is less than $f(d)$; so

Equation 11-4 $$n \le 2^{d+1} - 1$$

Now we can solve for d, by taking the base 2 log of both sides:

---

2. To prove it, use proof by induction.

Equation 11-5

$$n \le 2^{d+1} - 1 \Rightarrow n < 2^{d+1} \Rightarrow \log_2 n < \log_2 2^{d+1} \Rightarrow \log_2 n < d+1$$
$$\text{hence: } \log_2 n - 1 < d$$

In words, the depth of the tree is greater than the base 2 log of the number of nodes, minus 1. So when there are, say, 26 nodes, the base 2 log of 26 is between 4 and 5 (since $2^4 < 26 < 2^5$) so a tree with 26 nodes has to be at least 4 deep.

Expressing Equation 11-5 in big-O notation, we can see that the depth is $O(\log n)$, and therefore we conclude that the performance of our insert and retrieve operations is logarithmic, *if* we can guarantee that our trees are "as short as possible." We refer to "short" trees as **balanced trees**. In order to guarantee good performance, the tree implementation needs to be modified to guarantee that trees remain balanced. Various balanced tree schemes have been developed, such as AVL trees, 2-3 trees, and red-black trees. The discussion of these schemes is out of the scope of this book; for more information, take a look at an algorithms reference such as Cormen, Leiserson and Rivest (1990). We can observe that in practice, with randomly distributed data, the performance of the BST will be closer to the best case than the worst case, so trees can often work quite well even without a tree balancing method.

Sorting with Trees

We can use BSTs to sort a list; here's how to do it. Take each item from the input list, and insert it into a BST. When you're done, traverse the tree in inorder—the items will be visited in sorted order. Pretty simple, eh? How efficient is it? The cost of insertions depends upon the current size and depth of the tree. *If* we use a balanced tree scheme, then the cost of each insertion is no more than $O(\log n)$; since there are n insertions, the total cost for building the tree is $O(n \log n)$. The traversal requires time $O(n)$; so overall, the **Treesort** method requires $O(n \log n) + O(n) = O(n \log n)$. So asymptotically, Treesort looks about as good as Quicksort and Mergesort, again assuming that our trees remain balanced as we work.

Chapter Summary

- Trees represent data in a hierarchical manner.
- In a Binary Tree, each node has a left and a right child.
- Expression trees are Binary Trees that can represent arithmetic expressions.
- The data in a tree can be visited using inorder, preorder, and postorder traversals.
- Function pointers can be used to pass one function to another as an argument.
- The Binary Search Tree is an ordered tree ADT.
- Binary Search Trees support efficient retrieval by key.

- Inheritance can be used to model is-a relations.
- Inheritance can be implemented in C++ through base and derived classes.
- Inheritance supports code reuse.
- Binary Search Trees can have bad performance if they're unbalanced and very good performance if they're balanced.
- Treesort sorts a list using a Binary Search Tree.

Programming Laboratory Problems

Lab 11-1   An *ancestor tree* lists the names of an individual's ancestors. The root contains the name of a person (whom we'll call the *subject* of the tree), the two nodes at level 1 list the names of the subjects's parents, the four nodes at level 2 list the subject's grandparents, and so forth. Write a program that reads in seven names, representing:

```
subject
subject's mother
subject's father
subject's mother's mother
subject's mother's father
subject's father's mother
subject's father's father
```

These items should be stored in a binary tree, and then the program should answer queries of this form:

```
name1 parent name2
```

or

```
name1 grandparent name2
```

with either "yes" or "no" as appropriate.

Lab 11-2   The Binary Tree ADT 11-1 doesn't provide a way to get from a child to its parent. Define an operation, `T.parent()`, that returns the parent of a node or 0 if that node is the root of the tree. Create a class, BinaryTree2Way, that inherits from BinaryTree, to implement the ADT with the parent operation. Test your derived class thoroughly.

Lab 11-3   Write the following programs that analyze trees:

```
int depth(const BinaryTree * btp)
```

Precondition: None.
Postcondition: None.
Returns: The depth of the BinaryTree rooted at `btp`.

```
int degree(const BinaryTree * btp)
```

Precondition: None.

Postcondition: None.

Returns: The degree of the BinaryTree rooted at `btp`.

I strongly recommend recursive solutions, which will make your programs much simpler. If you write the program correctly it will work with BinaryTrees and BSTs without alteration.

Lab 11-4   Design and implement a program that, given a preorder and an inorder traversal of a tree, constructs the tree (or reports that the input is incorrect). See Exercise 11-10 for further discussion.

Lab 11-5   The examples given for using BSTs all assume that the data is a single `int`. In many cases you want to store more complex data, for example, an employee record. Implement a simple telephone number database in which each entry is an object with the following fields: first name, last name, telephone number. The items should be stored in the tree in alphabetical order by last name/first name. The "key" to making this work lies in overloading the `<` and `==` operations on your object so that the ordering is correct. *(Note: you absolutely need not, and must not, modify the BST implementation to do this assignment.)*

Lab 11-6   Using a BST, implement the Table ADT 10-1. Do *not* modify the BST code.

Lab 11-7   Write a program that reads in a description of a Binary Tree from a file and builds the tree. The file should consist of records in this form:

```
A B C
```

which indicates that A is the parent of B and C.

Lab 11-8   A *forest* is a set of zero or more trees. Design an ADT that will permit you to implement forests of binary trees, then implement it using the List ADT and the Binary Tree ADT. Be sure to test your implementation thoroughly.

Lab 11-9   Implement Treesort. Write a test driver that creates random sequences of `ints`, passes them to Treesort for sorting, and then tests to make sure that the sorting was correct. Use the Timer class[3] to determine average performance of Treesort for lists of size 100 through 10,000 by increments of 100, using 100 random lists at each point. Plot the time function using a spreadsheet or other plotting software. How does the performance of Treesort grow as a function of *n*?

---

3. See the source code distribution for this book.

Chapter Vocabulary

balanced tree

base class

Binary Search Tree (BST)

binary tree

BST invariant

child

degree

depth

derived class

empty tree

encapsulation

expression tree

forest

function pointer

grandchild

grandparent

height

hierarchical

inheritance

inheritance diagram

in-order

internal node

is-a relation

leaf

left child

level

node

parent

polymorphism

postorder

preorder

private (member data)

protected (member data)

public inheritance

recurrence relation

right child

root

sibling

tree

Treesort

tree traversal

virtual

visit

Chapter 12 **Graphs**

Overview   A discussion of the rich and powerful way
                  graphs can model relations.

Chapter Objectives

1. To review basic graph vocabulary and concepts.
2. To develop classes that model various kinds of graphs.
3. To learn some useful algorithms for manipulating graphs.

12.1   Example: Keeping Track of Course Prerequisites

One day at lunch your friend Barry comes by with the university catalog, asking for help. "I'm going nuts trying to figure out these crazy prerequisites," complains Barry. "All I want to know is if I can get in all my courses to graduate next year, but it's so hard to figure out from the catalog which course you have to take when." Being the systematic student of computer science that you are, you offer to help. First, you and Barry list all the courses and prerequisites in his program, producing Table 12-1.

Table 12-1   *Course prerequisites in table form*

Course	Prerequisite(s)	Barry has completed?
Math 101	None	Yes
Math 201	Math 101	Yes
CS 101	None	Yes
CS 102	CS101; Math 201	No
CS 215	CS 102; Math 211	No
Math 211	Math 101; Math 201	No
CS 247	CS 215; Math 211	No
CS 392	CS 215	No
CS 405	CS 247; CS 392	No

"Well, that makes a little more sense now," says Barry, "but I'm still not sure if I can complete all the courses I need to graduate in two semesters." In order to understand the situation better, you decide to lay the information out visually—often a good strategy—and you create Figure 12-1. The courses Barry has completed are shown in grey.

The diagram in Figure 12-1 represents a graph—and Table 12-1 represents the same graph. A *graph* represents relationships among items. In this case, the items (called *vertices*) are the courses, and the relationships (called *edges*) are the prerequisites. This particular example, the edges are *directed* as indicated by the arrows—for example, CS 101 is a prerequisite for CS 102, but not vice versa. When the edges in a graph are directed, we call it a *directed graph,* or *digraph* for short.

Barry takes a look at the graph, and sighs. "I guess I'm headed for summer school. Looks like I need four more semesters to finish." It's easy to tell how long the stu-

Figure 12-1   *Course prerequisites in graphical form*

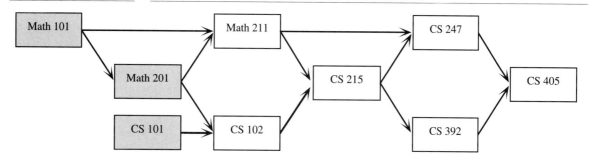

dent's program is in this small graph just by visual inspection, but later on we'll look at algorithms that will automate the processing of graphs.

12.2 Basic Graph Concepts and Terminology

Before we go on, let's review the basic graph terminology we'll need. ***Graph theory,*** a branch of ***discrete mathematics,*** provides us with a rich and comprehensive set of vocabulary and tools we can use to talk about and think about graphs. We'll only scratch the surface of the theory here; instead, we're going to emphasize the use of graphs in software.

Let's start with graphs that are not directed, which we simply refer to as graphs. We define a graph G as a pair of sets: V, the set of vertices in the graph, and E, the set of pairs of edges. For example, consider the graph shown in Figure 12-2.

The graph in Figure 12-2 contains five vertices; so we write $V = \{0, 1, 2, 3, 4\}$. Each edge can be described by a pair of vertices; the complete edge set for this graph is $E = \{\{0, 1\}, \{0, 3\}, \{0, 4\}, \{1, 2\}, \{1, 4\}, \{2, 4\}\}$. By examining E, we can quickly determine that 1 and 2 are connected by an edge, but 1 and 3 are not. We describe the size of a graph in terms of the size of the two sets that define it: for example, in this graph $|V| = 5$ and $|E| = 6$. To summarize, we say that a graph consists of a vertex set and an edge set, or $G = (V, E)$.

Up to now, we've used the variable n to indicate the size of a problem. However, for graphs, we have two separate parameters, namely the size of the vertex set ($|V|$) and the size of the edge set ($|E|$). From now on, we'll let $n = |V|$ and $m = |E|$. We can then express the time required by graph algorithms as a function of n and m.

A digraph can be defined in nearly the same way, except that each edge represents a pair rather than a set. Take a look at Figure 12-3.

Figure 12-2 A graph

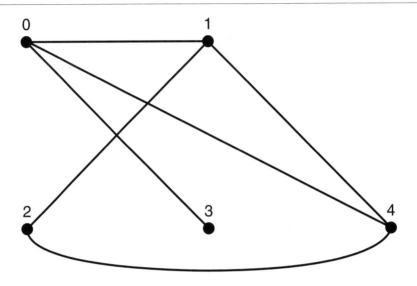

Figure 12-3 A digraph

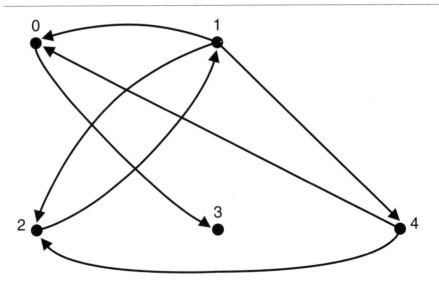

The digraph in Figure 12-3 appears quite similar to the graph in Figure 12-2, except that the lines in the the first graph now have arrows, suggesting the direction of the relationship. We can represent the edge set by

$$E = \{(0, 3), (1, 0), (1, 2), (1, 4), (2, 1), (4, 0),(4, 2)\}\,.$$

Note that because the individual edges are not sets anymore, $(1, 2)$ and $(2, 1)$ each appear as distinct elements.

Exercise 12-1 For an undirected graph of n vertices, what is the largest number of edges it can have? For a directed graph? (Assume that the graph cannot have self-loops; i.e., $\{i, i\} \notin E$.)

Exercise 12-2 For each of the following cases, indicate whether it would best be represented by a directed graph, an undirected graph, or either:

      a.   Vertices: the cast of characters in the soap opera. Edges: "in love with"

      b.   Vertices: countries on a map. Edges: adjacent borders

      c.   Vertices: countries. Edges: major export markets

      d.   Vertices: devices in a computer network. Edges: connectivity

      e.   Vertices: variables in a computer program. Edges: "uses" relations (We say variable x *uses* variable y if y appears on the right-hand side of an expression with x on the left, e.g., $x = y$.)

      f.   Vertices: football teams. Edges: games during a season

Exercise 12-3 Draw a representation of the following graph:

$$G = (V, E); \; V = \{0, 1, 2, 3\};$$
$$E = \{\{0, 3\}, \{1, 2\}, \{2, 3\}, \{0, 1\}\}$$

Exercise 12-4 Draw a representation of the following graph:

$$G = (V, E); \; V = \{0, 1, 2, 3\};$$
$$E = \{(0, 1), (0, 2), (0, 3), (2, 3), (3, 0)\}$$

12.3   Creating Graph ADTs

12.3.1   Data Structures to Model Graphs

How can we represent a graph in the computer? What functionality does a Graph ADT need to provide? The exact set of operations depends on the particular problem that we want to solve, but in addition to the obvious need to be able to add—and, perhaps, remove—edges, there are two general kinds of questions we might want to ask about the graph:

1. Neighbor queries: for a particular vertex, find all the edges connected to that vertex.

2. Edge member queries: determine whether a particular edge is in the graph.

It might seem at first blush that one or the other of these would be enough, but depending on the problem you want to solve one of these may be much more useful than the other. For example, suppose you have a graph with 100 vertices and a few hundred edges. In such a graph, the average number of neighbors is pretty small, say 2 or 3. Now let's suppose I want to find all the neighbors of some vertex, say vertex 17. If all I have is the edge member query, I have to check all the other 99 vertices in the graph to find the neighbors of 17, of which there are only a few. Obviously that's not very efficient. On the other hand, suppose I want to know whether there is an edge connecting 17 and 47. In this case, the edge member query is just what I want. If all I have is the neighbor query, I have to check every one of the neighbors of 17 and see if one of them is 47. So for some problems, the list of neighbors is what I really want, and for others the edge member query fits the bill. Occasionally, you'll find a problem that calls for both.

Adjacency List   Let's look at how we might represent neighbors. Because for each vertex we need a list of neighbors, we can simply keep one list for each vertex, listing the neighbors for that vertex. For rapid retrieval, these lists are generally organized into an array, yielding a structure called an ***adjacency list.*** You can visualize an adjacency list as shown in Figure 12-4, which corresponds with the digraph in Figure 12-3. Of course, we don't necessarily want to implement the linked list directly—instead, we'll use the List class as a component of our Graph class. You can see from the diagram that, given a vertex, the neighbors can be traversed efficiently.

Figure 12-4   *An adjacency list of Figure 12-3*

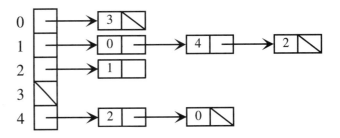

If you imagine writing code to process a structure like the one in Figure 12-4, you can see that it will be easy and efficient to generate a list of all the neighbors of a given vertex. However, to determine whether, say, vertex 1 and vertex 2 are connected will require linear traversal of a list, potentially requiring time $O(n)$.[1]

Adjacency Matrix   If we instead want to make edge queries our most efficient operation, we can represent the edges in the graph using a matrix, an ***adjacency matrix.*** In its most basic form, an adjacency matrix is a two-dimensional array A of 0's and 1's, where

$$A[i][j] \ = \ 1 \ \textit{if and only if} \text{ there is an edge from } i \text{ to } j \text{ or } i \ = \ j.$$

In Figure 12-5, we show an adjacency matrix for the graph in Figure 12-3. The diagonal of the matrix represents a special case; generally, by convention, we want to set $A[i][i]$ to 1, to indicate that every vertex is connected to itself.

By examining the adjacency matrix, it's easy to see that checking for an edge between two vertices is trivial—you simply look at the appropriate entry in the matrix. On the other hand, finding all the neighbors of a vertex requires looking at a whole row of the matrix. Hence, generating the neighbors will always take $O(n)$, even when most vertices have few neighbors.

Figure 12-5   *An adjacency matrix representation of Figure 12-3*

	0	1	2	3	4
0	1	0	0	1	0
1	1	1	1	0	1
2	0	1	1	0	0
3	0	0	0	1	0
4	1	0	1	0	1

1. Recall that n is the number of vertices, not the size of the entire graph, which is the sum of the vertices and the edges, or $n + m$.

12.3.2   Defining Graph ADTs

You may have noticed that we've looked at graphs a bit differently than we looked at most of the data structures we've considered in that we examined representational issues before defining an ADT. That's because efficiency considerations make it quite difficult to divorce representation issues from the external definition of the ADT. Let's look at one possible set of ADT definitions, and then we'll examine alternative designs we might consider.

First, note that we need definitions addressing both directed and undirected graphs. Furthermore, we'll present for each type of graph a definition inspired by the adjacency list and adjacency matrix representations for a graph, yielding a total of four ADTs.

ADT 12-1

Undirected Adjacency List Graph

Characteristics:

An Undirected Adjacency List Graph $G = (V, E)$ stores an undirected graph so that vertex neighbors can be found efficiently.

The number of vertices in the graph, $n = |V|$, is fixed when the graph is created.

The vertices are labelled $0...n-1$.

Operations:

int vertexSize()

Precondition: None.
Postcondition: None.
Returns: The number of vertices in the graph, $|V|$.

int edgeSize()

Precondition: None.
Postcondition: None.
Returns: The number of edges in the graph, $|E|$.

void addEdge(i,j)

Preconditions: $0 \le i < n$; $0 \le j < n$; $\{i, j\} \notin E$.
Postcondition: $\{i, j\} \in E$

int nextNeighbor(i)

Precondition: $0 \le i < n$

Postcondition: If the current iterator position is within the neighbor list, it's advanced to the next neighbor; if it's at the end of the neighbor list, it's reset to the beginning.

Returns: The next neighbor of i, or n if at the end of the list.

A couple of comments: it aids the simplicity and the efficiency of both graph representations to fix the number of vertices in advance. In the exercises you can explore the consequences of relaxing this requirement. The `nextNeighbor` function describes an iterator, which as we shall see will give us an efficient and flexible way to generate the neighbors of a vertex. The `nextNeighbor` iterator is designed so that there's no need for a "`firstNeighbor`" operation — each time you get to the last neighbor in the list, the `nextNeighbor` function returns the value n, to let the client know that the end of the list has been reached, and resets the internal iterator so that the neighbor list can be traversed from the beginning in future calls.

Next we consider a directed graph implemented with an adjacency list. As you'll see, this ADT is nearly identical to ADT 12-1, a similarity we'll exploit using inheritance once we get to the implementation.

ADT 12-2 Directed Adjacency List Graph ∨

Characteristics:

A Directed Adjacency List Graph $G = (V, E)$ stores a directed graph so that vertex neighbors can be found efficiently.

The number of vertices in the graph, $n = |V|$, is fixed when the graph is created.

The vertices are labelled $0 \ldots n - 1$.

Operations:

int vertexSize()

Precondition: None.
Postcondition: None.
Returns: The number of vertices in the graph, $|V|$.

int edgeSize()

Precondition: None.
Postcondition: None.
Returns: The number of edges in the graph, $|E|$.

void addEdge(i,j)

Preconditions: $0 \le i < n$; $0 \le j < n$; $(i,j) \notin E$.
Postcondition: $(i,j) \in E$

int nextNeighbor(i)

Precondition: $0 \le i < n$.

Postcondition: If the current iterator position is within the neighbor list, it's advanced to the next neighbor; if it's at the end of the neighbor list, it's reset to the beginning.

Returns: The next neighbor of i, or n if at the end of the list.

Next we define graph ADTs based upon the performance characteristics of the adjacency matrix representation. Again, the undirected and directed definitions are quite similar.

ADT 12-3

Undirected Adjacency Matrix Graph

Characteristics:

An Undirected Adjacency Matrix Graph $G = (V, E)$ stores an undirected graph so that vertex connectivity can be queried efficiently.

The number of vertices in the graph, $n = |V|$, is fixed when the graph is created.

The vertices are labelled $)...n - 1$.

Operations:

int vertexSize()

Precondition: None.

Postcondition: None.

Returns: The number of vertices in the graph, $|V|$.

int edgeSize()

Precondition: None.

Postcondition: None.

Returns: The number of edges in the graph, $|E|$.

void addEdge(i,j)

Preconditions: $0 \le i < n$; $0 \le j < n$; $\{i, j\} \notin E$.

Postcondition: $\{i, j\} \in E$

bool edgeConnected(i,j)

Preconditions: $0 \le i < n$; $0 \le j < n$.

Postcondition: None.

Returns: True if and only if $\{i, j\} \in E$. Note that by convention $\{i, i\} \in E$.

ADT 12-4 Directed Adjacency Matrix Graph

Characteristics:

A Directed Adjacency Matrix Graph $G = (V, E)$ stores a directed graph so that vertex connectivity can be queried efficiently.

The number of vertices in the graph, $n = |V|$, is fixed when the graph is created.

The vertices are labelled $)...n-1$.

Operations:

int vertexSize()

Precondition:	None.
Postcondition:	None.
Returns:	The number of vertices in the graph, $|V|$.

int edgeSize()

Precondition:	None.
Postcondition:	None.
Returns:	The number of edges in the graph, $|E|$.

void addEdge(i,j)

Preconditions:	$0 \le i < n$; $0 \le j < n$; $(i,j) \notin E$.
Postcondition:	$\{i,j\} \in E$

bool edgeConnected(i,j)

Precondition:	$0 \le i < n$; $0 \le j < n$.
Postcondition:	None.
Returns:	True if and only if $(i,j) \in E$. Note that by convention $(i, i) \in E$.

Design Choices In a sense, we've compromised our usual notions of encapsulation by suggesting the implementation of each graph ADT in the name. Note, though, that it's just a suggestion: there's nothing in the definitions that require a adjacency lists or adjacency matrices—rather, the adjacency list ADTs require that the client list the neighbors of a vertex efficiently, and the adjacency matrix ADTs require that edge queries are efficient. My feeling is that among computer scientists, the adjacency list and adjacency matrix representations are so well known and widely accepted that to try to use a different name, such as "Undirected graph with fast edge queries," would add unnecessary confusion. Furthermore, we'll see that even with the broad designations "adjacency list" and "adjacency matrix" there are significant design choices that affect the exact representation of the graph, choices that certainly can be encapsulated from the client.

Another choice we've made is to only include the relatively efficient operations within each definition. For example, there's nothing that prevents us from including an `edgeConnected` operator in the adjacency list ADTs. However, I think it makes more sense to leave them out, for two reasons. To include an `edgeConnected` operator in the adjacency list operation seems to me to be a sort of false advertising—an operation is provided that can't be implemented efficiently. The client can write an `edgeConnected` operator, using the `nextNeighbor` iterator, thus making the inefficiency apparent. The same argument can be made about including a `nextNeighbor` iterator in the adjacency matrix ADT. By providing only the operation that the representation supports directly, we have emphasized the difference between the two approaches and forced the client to make a clear and conscious decision when selecting an ADT to represent the graph.

Exercise 12-5   Show the adjacency list and adjacency matrix representations for the graph shown in Figure 12-6.

Figure 12-6   *Undirected graph for Exercise 12-5*

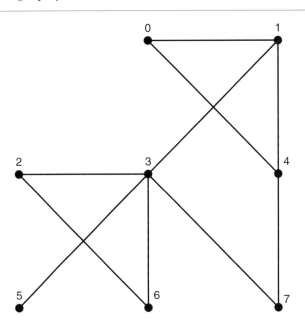

Exercise 12-6   Show the adjacency list and adjacency matrix representations for the graph shown in Figure 12-7.

Exercise 12-7   Draw a representation of the graph defined by the adjacency list shown in Figure 12-8.

Exercise 12-8   Draw a representation of the (undirected) graph defined by the adjacency matrix shown in Figure 12-9.

Figure 12-7   *Directed graph for Exercise 12-6*

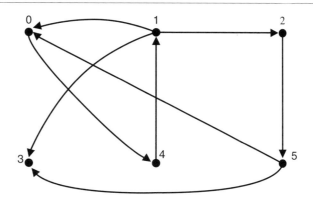

Figure 12-8   *Adjacency list for Exercise 12-7*

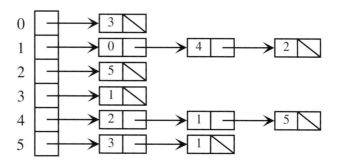

Exercise 12-9   Write pseudo-code for the procedure a client can use to write an `edgeConnected` function for an adjacency list graph.

Exercise 12-10 Write pseudo-code for the procedure a client can use to write a `nextNeighbor` function for an adjacency matrix graph.

Exercise 12-11 How much space does an adjacency list graph require? State your answer in big-O notation, as a function of n and m.

Exercise 12-12 How much space does an adjacency matrix require? State your answer in big-O notation, as a function of n and m.

Exercise 12-13 In an adjacency matrix for an undirected graph as presented in Figure 12-9, approximately half the storage space required by the graph is unnecessary. Explain, and suggest a modification that uses less space.

Figure 12-9   *Adjacency matrix for Exercise 12-8*

	0	1	2	3	4	5	6
0	1	0	1	1	0	1	0
1	0	1	1	0	1	0	1
2	1	1	1	0	0	1	1
3	1	0	0	1	0	0	0
4	0	1	0	0	1	1	0
5	1	0	1	0	1	1	1
6	0	1	1	0	0	1	1

12.3.3   A Hierarchy of Graphs

We can observe that all four of our graph definitions are versions of the same abstraction: the graph. We can implement this abstraction hierarchy directly in C++ using inheritance. Figure 12-10 illustrates our initial hierarchy for graphs.

Figure 12-10   *Inheritance hierarchy for graphs*

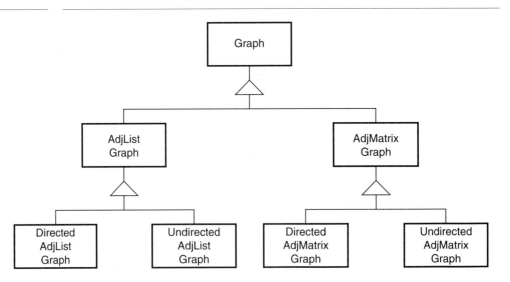

Abstract Classes   Note that the only classes we're actually going to use are the leaves of the hierarchy. In other words, we will want to use, say, an Undirected AdjList Graph, but we'll never use a "Graph" or an "AdjList Graph." The inner nodes in the hierarchy are called ***abstract base classes*** or just ***abstract classes.*** The word *base* suggests the use of these classes as the base for inheriting new classes. For example, the Directed AdjList Graph uses AdjList Graph as its base class and, implicitly, uses the Graph class as well. Abstract classes serve as placeholders, representing the common features of their children. You can start to see how this works as C++ code in Code Example 12-1, which represents the top of the hierarchy.

Code Example 12-1   *Header file for Graph abstract class*

```
// cx12-1.h
// Code Example 12-1: Header for graph hierarchy

#ifndef __MB_CX12_1__
#define __MB_CX12_1__

class graph {
public:
    graph(int size) : n(size), m(0) { }
    virtual int vertexSize() { return n; }
    virtual int edgeSize() { return m; }
    virtual void addEdge(int fromV, int toV) = 0; // specify abstract class
protected:
    int n; // number of vertices
    int m; // number of edges
};

#endif
```

Some new syntax appears here. First of all, the declaration for the Graph constructor specifies the way in which the member variables, *n* and *m*, are initialized. The expression

```
    Graph(int size) : n(size), m(0) { }
```

tells the compiler to use the argument size to initialize *n* and initialize *m* to 0. Furthermore, the empty brackets "{   }" tell the compiler that there's nothing else the constructor has to do, so we don't need to include code for it in another file.

Inline Declarations   The declarations for the functions `vertexSize` and `edgeSize` also include definitions of the action of these functions—in each case, they simply return the relevant value. Declarations of this kind, called ***inline,*** provide a convenience to the programmer, but I suggest you don't overuse them. Restrict your use of inline declarations to functions that have very simple and transparent implementations, such as `vertexSize`, and avoid them for more complicated functions that should be implemented in a separate file.

Declaring Abstract
Classes As we described above, we wish to use the Graph class as an abstract class; we will inherit from the Graph class, but we will not create objects of type Graph. We specify this explicitly by the special "= 0" syntax for `addEdge`. This declaration for `addEdge` does something else: it specifies a particular interface for graphs, with a specific method for adding new edges.

Now that we've developed the base class to represent the root of the hierarchy, we'll look at the adjacency list and adjacency matrix classes.

12.4   Implementing and Using Adjacency List Graphs

Again, we're going to create an abstract base class to represent adjacency lists, and then we'll inherit from it to create directed and undirected graph classes. We want to put as much functionality as we can into the Adjacency List class, leaving to the child classes only those functions that they have to implement. Our design will put the iterator in the Adjacency List class, and then leave the directed and undirected graph classes to implement `addEdge`. In a directed graph, we'll keep edges only on the neighbor list of the vertex they come from, while in an undirected graph adding an edge will put it on the neighbor list of both vertices it connects.

12.4.1   Implementing Lists with Iterators

The main issues for implementing the Adjacency List class (which we'll call ALGraph) revolve around the neighbor list iterator. We might try to use the Lists we implemented in Chapter 7. The original ADT definition, shown as ADT 7-1, is repeated here as ADT 12-5.

ADT 12-5 List ADT (Same as ADT 7-1)

Characteristics:

A List L stores items of some type, called ListElementType.

The items in the List are *ordered*; the Lists (1,2) and (2,1) are distinct.

Operations:

void L.insert(ListElementType elem)

Precondition: None.
Postcondition: L = L with an instance of elem added to the end of L.

bool L.first(ListElementType &elem)

Precondition: None.

Postcondition: If the list is empty, none. Otherwise, the variable elem contains the first item in L; the "next" item to be returned is the second in L.

Returns: True if and only if there is at least one element in L.

bool L.next(ListElementType &elem)

Precondition: The "first" operation has been called at least once.

Postcondition: Variable elem contains the next item in L if there is one, and the next counter advances by one; if there is no next element, none.

Returns: True if and only if there is a next item.

Our method of providing iterators through two internal functions, `first` and `next`, while adequate for some purposes, has some real limitations when we try to use the lists within the ALGraph class. Note that we now have an array of lists, and in order to make sure we don't violate the invariant for the `next` function, we have to make sure that when we go to find the next neighbor, we've called `first` previously. Furthermore, the simple internal iterators don't allow for more than one iterator to be used at one time. If, for example, we want to create a function that searches the neighbor list, it's going to have to start at the beginning of the list and iterate to the end, which means that if the client is also trying to iterate through the same list, the position within the list may be lost.

Fortunately, there's a more flexible, if somewhat more complicated, way to implement iterators by creating an *iterator class.* The Iterator class will, in effect, encapsulate a pointer that keeps track of a position in the list. Because the iterator is now a class, we can declare multiple iterator objects if we need them, each one of which can be at a different position in the list.

Friend Classes   Because the Iterator class has to know about the internal representation of the class it iterates on, it has to have a way to "get inside" the encapsulation boundary for the class. In C++, we can allow a class to use the private implementation of a class by using a ***friend class.*** In Code Example 12-2, you'll find the declaration of the List class and of its iterator, which we call ListIter. Look first at List, and note that within the declaration we've included the line

```
friend class ListIter < ListElementType >;
```

This tells the compiler that the ListIter class can use the internal, protected part of the List implementation. Note that because we've moved the responsibility for iteration to ListIter, there's not much for the List class to do, other than construct a list and insert new members.

Code Example 12-2   Header for List implementation with Iterator class

```
// cx12-2.h
// Code Example 12-2: Header, List class with List Iterator class

#ifndef __MB_CX12_2__
#define __MB_CX12_2__

#include "dslib.h"

template < class ListElementType >
class List {
public:
    List() : head(0) { }
    virtual void insert(const ListElementType & elem);
    friend class ListIter < ListElementType >;
protected:
    struct Node;
    typedef Node * Link;
    struct Node {
        ListElementType elem;
        Link next;
    };
    Link head;
};

template < class ListElementType >
class ListIter {
public:
    ListIter(const List < ListElementType > & l, ListElementType endFlag)
        : myList(l), myEndFlag(endFlag), iterPtr(0) { }
    virtual ListElementType operator++();
protected:
    const List < ListElementType > & myList;
    List < ListElementType >::Link iterPtr;
    ListElementType myEndFlag;
};

#endif
```

Constant Reference Variables

The member variable `myList` is an example of a ***constant reference variable.*** A reference variable is like a pointer that you can't manipulate directly. Because `myList` is declared to be `const` it can't be changed, and it has to be initialized by the constructor. The parts of the constructor declaration after the colon:

```
: myList(l), myEndFlag(endFlag), iterPtr(0)
```

will initialize the data members when the constructor is called, including `myList`.

Constructing a List
Iterator

For the ListIter class, note first of all that we have to use the same template as we do for this list, because the iterator is going to return items of type `ListElementType`. Next, take a look at the constructor. The first argument, l, specifies which list the particular ListIter object will iterate through. Remember, now, we're declaring classes—there may be many lists, and, possibly, many iterators. In fact, this implementation will allow more than one iterator for a given list. So we have to have a way to bind iterators to lists, and that's what the first argument to the constructor does.

The second argument handles the following issue: How do we know when we've reached the end of the list? Our implementation back in Chapter 7 used a boolean flag, but that's a bit clumsy. Instead, we'd like to return a sentinel marking the end of the list. However, what can we return? Because the list is templated by class `ListElementType`, we don't even know much about the object the iterator returns, let alone a good value to use as a sentinel. However, the *client* knows about the data stored in the list, so we'll let the client tell us what to use. That's the purpose of the argument `endFlag` and the protected member `myEndFlag`. The user of the list iterator tells us what to return as a sentinel; we remember it and return it when we get to the end of the list. Given these two arguments, the constructor can initialize `myList` as a reference to the list we're going to iterate, `myEndFlag` as the sentinel, and `iterPtr` to the value 0, which we'll recognize as meaning that we're ready to start at the beginning of the list.

The iteration operator itself overloads the familiar ++ operator. Each use of ++ will return an element from the list, and update the iterator, except that when we get to the end of a list we return the `endFlag` sentinel. Reaching the end of a list also resets the `iterPtr` to 0, so we can reuse the iterator to make another pass through the list. The details can be found in Code Example 12-3, along with the implementation of the `insert` function for the List class.

Code Example 12-3 *Implementation for List class with iterator*

```
// cx12-3.cpp
// Code Example 12-3: Implementation, List class with List Iterator class

#include "cx12-2.h"

template < class ListElementType >
ListElementType
ListIter < ListElementType > :: operator++()
{
    if (iterPtr == 0)
        iterPtr = myList.head;
    else
```

```
        iterPtr = iterPtr->next;
    if (iterPtr)
        return iterPtr->elem;
    else
        return myEndFlag;
}

template < class ListElementType >
void
List < ListElementType > :: insert(const ListElementType & elem)
{
    Link addedNode = new Node;
    assert(addedNode);
    addedNode->elem = elem;
    addedNode->next = head;
    head = addedNode;
}
```

Dangers of Using Iterators

One problem that can arise from iterators results from changing the list during the iteration process. For example, suppose we had a List class that supported deletions from the list. Then it's possible that the `iterPtr` could point to a List element that no longer exists. The implementation here doesn't have this danger because it doesn't support deletions, but this is a subtle and tricky issue you ought to be aware of. Generally, if an operation can potentially "mess up" an iterator we say that the operation *invalidates* the iterator, and that the results of calling the iterator afterward are undefined.

Now that we have a List class with the flexibility we need, we can start to implement our ALGraph class.

12.4.2 The Adjacency List Abstract Base Class

The ALGraph class will create an array of lists. For convenience, we use `typedef` to create symbols of integer lists and integer list iterators. The protected member variable, `vertexList`, will be used to declare the array dynamically in the constructor. The NeighborIter class will allow clients to iterate through the neighbor lists. It inherits from ListIter—a NeighborIter is a special kind of ListIter. When the NeighborIter constructor runs, it calls the parent constructor to create a list iterator for the specified vertex. Because the vertices are labelled from 0 to $n-1$ the value n serves as the end flag. Interestingly enough, we don't need an implementation file here—the only thing that either class requires is a constructor, and we've included both of them inline, as shown in Code Example 12-4.

Code Example 12-4   *Adjacency list abstract base class header*

```
// cx12-4.h
// Code Example 12-4: Header for adjacency list base class

#ifndef __MB_CX12_4__
#define __MB_CX12_4__

#include "cx12-1.h" // graph base class
#include "cx12-2.h" // list class

typedef List < int > IntList;
typedef ListIter < int > IntListIter;

class ALGraph : public graph {
public:
    ALGraph(int size) : graph(size)
        { vertexList = new IntList[n]; assert(vertexList); }
    friend class NeighborIter;
protected:
    IntList * vertexList;
};

class NeighborIter : public IntListIter {
public:
    NeighborIter(const ALGraph & G, int startVertex) :
    IntListIter (G.vertexList[startVertex], G.n)
        { assert(startVertex < G.n); }
};

#endif
```

12.4.3   The Undirected and Directed Adjacency List Graphs

We've finally worked our way down to the leaves of the inheritance tree, and we can define the undirected and directed adjacency list graphs, which we'll call UALGraph and DALGraph. We'll actually create objects of these classes. The implementation of the addEdge member function marks the only difference between the undirected and directed graphs. For a UALGraph, adding an edge from, say, vertex 1 to vertex 2 requires two steps—adding vertex 2 to the neighbor list for vertex 1, *and* adding vertex 1 to vertex 2's list. On the other hand, adding an edge to a DALGraph results in just a single list entry being added. The details appear in Code Examples 12-5 through 12-8.

Code Example 12-5   Header file for undirected adjacency list graph

```cpp
// cx12-5.h
// Code Example 12-5: Header for Undirected Adjacency List Graphs

#ifndef __MB_CX12_5__
#define __MB_CX12_5__

#include "cx12-4.h"

class UALGraph : public ALGraph {
public:
    UALGraph(int size) : ALGraph(size) { }
    virtual void addEdge(int fromV, int toV);
};

#endif
```

Code Example 12-6   Implementation file for undirected adjacency list graph

```cpp
// cx12-6.cpp
// Code Example 12-6: Implementation file for Undirected Adjacency List Graph

#include "cx12-5.h"

void
UALGraph::addEdge(int fromV, int toV)
{
    assert(fromV < n && fromV >= 0 && toV < n && toV >= 0);
    vertexList[fromV].insert(toV);
    vertexList[toV].insert(fromV);
    m++;
}
```

Code Example 12-7   Header file for directed adjacency list graph

```cpp
// cx12-7.h
// Code Example 12-7: Header for Directed Adjacency List Graph

#ifndef __MB_CX12_7__
#define __MB_CX12_7__

#include "cx12-4.h"  // ALGraph -- Adjacency List Base Class

class DALGraph : public ALGraph {
public:
```

```
    DALGraph(int size) : ALGraph(size) { }
    virtual void addEdge(int fromV, int toV);
};

#endif
```

Code Example 12-8 Implementation file for directed adjacency list graph

```
// cx12-8.cpp
// Code Example 12-8: Implementation file for Directed Adjacency List Graph

#include "cx12-7.h"

void
DALGraph::addEdge(int fromV, int toV)
{
    assert(fromV < n && fromV >= 0 && toV < n && toV >= 0);
    vertexList[fromV].insert(toV);
    m++;
}
```

Preconditions: A Trade-off If you refer back to the ADT for the Undirected Adjacency List Graph, ADT 12-1, you'll find the following preconditions for the addEdge operation, which we re-write here using the variable names from our implementation:

$$0 \le \text{fromV} < n \, ; \; 0 \le \text{toV} < n \, ; \; \{\text{fromV}, \text{toV}\} \notin E$$

The first two preconditions, requiring that the vertex labels lie in the proper range, can be checked easily, and in Code Examples 12-6 and 12-8 you can find appropriate calls to assert to do just that. However, the third precondition, which states that the new edge must not already be in the graph, poses a tougher problem. In an adjacency list, checking to see whether a particular edge is in the graph requires traversing a neighbor list. To check every edge as it's added would greatly boost the cost of adding edges to the graph—exactly how much we leave for Exercise 12-14.

Exercise 12-14 What is the big-O cost of checking the precondition $\{\text{fromV}, \text{toV}\} \notin E$ in a single call to addEdge? If we check the precondition, what is the cost of creating the entire graph using a sequence of calls to addEdge?

Exercise 12-15 For the function UALgraph::addEdge, does checking the precondition $\{\text{fromV}, \text{toV}\} \notin E$ require traversing one neighbor list or two? Explain.

Exercise 12-16 Modify the addEdge functions to check the precondition $\{\text{fromV}, \text{toV}\} \notin E$. (*Hint:* Use an iterator.)

Exercise 12-17   Assuming that `addEdge` does not check the precondition {fromV, toV} $\notin E$, what are the effects of a call to `addEdge` that violates the precondition?

12.4.4   Topological Sort

The problem that started the chapter—finding a sequence of courses that fit a set of prerequisites—is a particular example of a more general problem known as ***topological sort,*** or ***Topsort*** for short. In Topsort, we're given a set of relationships among items that can be modelled by a directed graph. These relationships form what we call a ***partial order.*** The course prerequisites in Figure 12-1 are an example of such a partial order. The topsort problem is, given a partial order, find a ***total order*** that's ***consistent*** with the partial order. In other words, we want to take all the items and put them into a sequence, called the total order, in which the order of the items doesn't violate any of the relationships in the partial order.

Let's take a specific example. Suppose we have 5 items labelled 0 through 4, and the following relations: 0:2, 0:3, 2:4, 1:4. This partial order requires that, for example, 0 must come before 2 and 2 must come before 4. Because these relationships are transitive—like the < relationship, for example—we can see that 0 has to come before 4, even though this relationship is not explicitly stated. One possible order for the example is 0, 1, 2, 3, 4. Another is 0, 2, 3, 1, 4. As we see from this example, generally there's more than one total order that's consistent with the partial order.

Figure 12-11   *Partial order example*

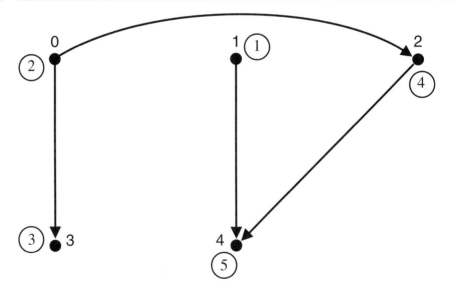

In Figure 12-11, we illustrate our partial order as a directed graph. Let *a* and *b* be any two vertices in a digraph. The goal of Topsort is to label the vertices of the graph so that if there's an edge from vertex *a* to vertex *b*, the label on vertex *a* is less than the label on vertex *b*. The numbers in the circles represent one possible answer to Topsort. For example, there's an edge from 0 to 2, and the label for vertex 0, 2, is less than the label for vertex 2, 4. So we can state the Topsort problem as the problem of coming up with such a labelling.

A Topsort Algorithm   One Topsort algorithm works like this. Observe that if a particular vertex doesn't have any in-edges, its label doesn't have to be larger than any other label. So we pick any vertex with no in-edge. In the example graph, we could pick 0 or 1; let's suppose we pick 1. Give vertex 1 the first label (1) and then remove all its out-edges, resulting in the graph shown in Figure 12-12. Now we pick another vertex with no in-edg-

Figure 12-12   *Topsort algorithm after first step*

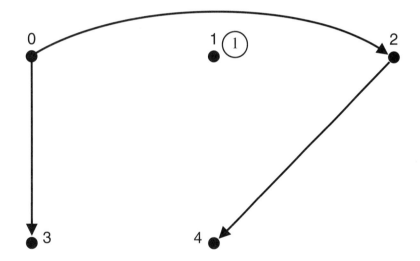

es, give it the next label (2), and repeat the process; we show this in Figure 12-13. You should continue the process until you get a completed Topsort.

Now, for some partial orders there is no total order that is consistent with them. If there is a *cycle* in the set of relations, it's not possible to label the nodes in Topsort order. To see why, take a look at the graph in Figure 12-14. You could set label(0) to 1 and label(2) to 2, but then what label could you assign to vertex 1? The label for 1 has to be greater than label(2), because there's an edge from 2 to 1, but it has to be less than label(0), because there's an edge from 1 to 0. Obviously, no such label exists, and there's no correct Topsort labelling for this graph.

Figure 12-13   *Topsort after the second step*

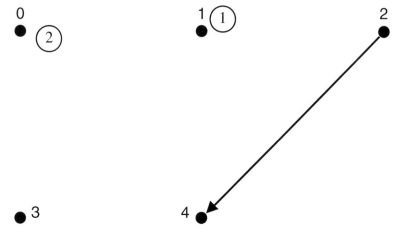

Figure 12-14   *Graph with a cycle*

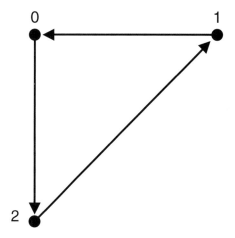

In terms of the algorithm, you can see that when you have a cycle, there's no vertex without an in-edge. We'll write the algorithm so that it halts when it no longer can apply a new label, and at the end we'll check to see that every vertex was labelled. If not, the algorithm will report that we've detected a cycle and no Topsort exists.

Improving the Algorithm   There's one more observation we can make to improve the efficiency of the algorithm. Searching the entire graph each time through to find nodes with no in-edges is clearly inefficient. Instead, we can note that the only vertices whose number of in-edges is decreasing are the neighbors of the vertex being labelled. So each time we label a vertex, we check all its neighbors and, if the number of in-edges has gone to zero, we push it onto a stack that will keep track of all the vertices ready to label. You can see the final algorithm in Algorithm 12-1.

Algorithm 12-1   *Topsort*

```
nextLabel = 1
find all vertices with no in-edges and push them onto a stack
while the stack is not empty do
        pop a vertex v from the stack
        label(v) = nextLabel
        add 1 to nextLabel
        remove all out-edges from v
        if any neighbor of v now has no in-edges, push it onto the stack
if all vertices are labelled,
        report the labels
else
        report that the digraph has a cycle
```

The Topsort
Program   To turn the algorithm into a program that uses our Graph class, we make a few small changes. First of all, our Graph class doesn't support removing edges. While this could be added to the class, we don't really need it. Instead, we start by counting the number of in-edges for each vertex, then each time we label a vertex we reduce the in-edge count by one. To see how this works, take a look at Figure 12-15. The first step in computing the Topsort will be to preprocess the graph and count the in-edges for each vertex; these values are shown in the boxes next to each vertex. When the first vertex receives the label 1, the in-edge counts of vertices 3 and 4 will be reduced by one. Because the count of vertex 3 is reduced to 0, it's now ready to take a label, so it will be pushed onto the stack. The count of vertex 4 will be reduced from 2 to 1.

The code for the Topsort is shown in Code Example 12-9. The program begins by reading in a description of the graph. Then it builds the array `vertices`, containing the number of in-edges for each vertex. The program adds vertices with no in-edges to a stack and then begins the process of adding the vertices to a queue one at a time. The first vertex on the queue implicitly carries the label 1, the second 2, and so forth. Finally, after checking to make sure all vertices have been labelled, the program reports the results.

Code Example 12-9   *Topsort*

```
// cx12-9.cpp
// Code Example 12-9: Topological Sort
```

Figure 12-15   *One step in a Topsort*

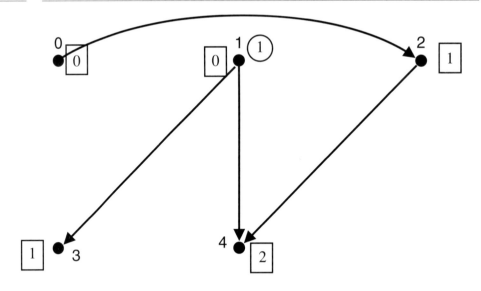

```cpp
#include "dslib.h"
#include "cx12-7.h"   // directed adjacency list graphs
#include "sx8-1.h"    // stacks (supplemental version)
#include "cx9-4.h"    // queues
#include <fstream.h>

int main()
{
    // read graph from a file
    // first entry is size of graph
    const char * inFileName = "graph.dat";
    ifstream ifs(inFileName);
    assert(ifs); // make sure graph exists
    int n;
    ifs >> n;
    DALGraph G(n);
    cout << "Created graph; n = " << G.vertexSize() << endl;
    // now read in the edges and add to the graph
    int u, v;
    while ( ifs >> u ) {
        ifs >> v;
        G.addEdge(u,v);
    }
    cout << "Edges in graph: m = " << G.edgeSize() << endl;

    // count the number of in-edges for each vertex
    int * vertices(new int[n]);
    assert(vertices);
    for (u = 0; u < n; u++)
```

```
      vertices[u] = 0;
for (u = 0; u < n; u++) {
    NeighborIter ni(G,u);
    while ((v = ++ni) != n)
        vertices[v]++;
}

// put vertices with no in-edge onto a stack
Stack < int > s;
for (u = 0; u < n; u++)
    if (vertices[u] == 0)
        s.push(u);
if (s.isEmpty()) {
    cout << "graph has a cycle!\n";
    return 0;
}

// begin topological sort
// As each vertex is identified, put it into a queue and
// decrement the number of in-edges for its neighbors
int count = 0; // number of vertices found so far
Queue < int > sortedEdges;
while (!s.isEmpty()) {
    count++;
    u = s.pop();
    sortedEdges.enqueue(u);
    // reduce in count for u's neighbors;
    // for each that goes to zero, put on stack
    NeighborIter ni(G,u);
    while ((v = ++ni) != n) {
        --vertices[v];
        if (vertices[v] == 0)
            s.push(v);
    }
}

// check results
if (count < n)
    cout << "Couldn't complete top sort -- cycle present.\n";
cout << "Ordering for top sort: \n";
while (!sortedEdges.isEmpty())
    cout << sortedEdges.dequeue() << '\t';
cout << endl;
return n;
}
```

Exercise 12-18   Explain the relationship between the Topsort algorithm and the example in Section 12.1. Test the Topsort program using the graph in Figure 12-1.

Exercise 12-19   Analyze the runtime of Topsort, as a function of *n* and *m*.

Exercise 12-20   Prove that if a directed graph does not have a cycle, then it must include a vertex with no in-edges. (*Hint:* Assume the contrary and show a contradiction.)

Exercise 12-21   In general, a graph has more than one possible Topsort ordering. Propose an algorithm that will list *all* legal Topsorts. (*Hint:* Use recursion.)

12.5   Implementing and Using Adjacency Matrix Graphs

12.5.1   Implementation of the Adjacency Matrix Classes

Next we consider the implementation of graphs based upon adjacency matrices. The header file for the abstract base class for adjacency matrices is shown in Code Example 12-10. You may be confused by the declaration of the adjacency matrix am. Declaring a pointer to a pointer will allow us to dynamically declare the memory for a two-dimensional graph. As you can see from the header file, we will implement a constructor for the amGraph class, as well as the member function edgeMember.

Code Example 12-10   Header file for adjacency matrix base class

```
// cx12-10.h
// Code Example 12-10: Header for adjacency matrix base class

#ifndef __MB_CX12_10__
#define __MB_CX12_10__

#include "dslib.h"
#include "cx12-1.h" // graph base class

class amGraph : public graph {
public:
    amGraph(int size);
    virtual bool edgeMember(int fromV, int toV);
protected:
    int * * am; // am points to pointers to int
};

#endif
```

In the implementation file, Code Example 12-11, the constructor has the responsibility to create the adjacency matrix. In order to allocate the memory for the two-dimensional array, an array of pointers is declared to point to each of the rows of the matrix. Then each row is declared, and the entries are initialized to zero. The edgeMember function simply examines the appropriate entry in the matrix.

Code Example 12-11 *Implementation of adjacency matrix base class*

```cpp
// cx12-11.cpp
// Code Example 12-11: Implementation for adjacency matrix base class

#include "cx12-10.h"

amGraph::amGraph(int size) : graph(size)
{
    int i;
    am = new int * [n]; // make an array of pointers to int
    assert(am);
    for (i = 0; i < n; i++) {
        am[i] = new int[n];  // make an array of ints
        assert(am[i]);
        int j;
        for (j = 0; j < n; j++) // initialize the array to 0
            am[i][j] = 0;
    }
}

bool amGraph::edgeMember(int fromV, int toV)
{
    assert (fromV < n && toV < n && fromV >= 0 && toV >= 0);
    return bool(am[fromV][toV] != 0);
}
```

Now we declare the Undirected and Directed Adjacency Matrix classes. Their only responsibility is to properly insert new edges. Thus the two header files, Code Example 12-12 and Code Example 12-14 are nearly identical. The difference can be seen in the implementation files—in Code Example 12-13, the `addEdge` member function adds new edges in a single direction, while the implementation for the undirected graph, Code Example 12-15, adds a 1 for both pairs of vertices.

Code Example 12-12 *Header file for the Directed Adjacency Matrix class*

```cpp
// cx12-12.h
// Code Example 12-12: Header for directed adjacency matrix class

#ifndef __MB_CX12_12__
#define __MB_CX12_12__

#include "cx12-10.h" // adjacency matrix base class

class dAMGraph : public amGraph {
public:
    dAMGraph(int size, int initialValue = 0) :
            amGraph(size) { }
```

```
    virtual void addEdge(int fromV, int toV);
};

#endif
```

Code Example 12-13 Implementation file for Directed Adjacency Matrix class

```
// cx12-13.cpp
// Code Example 12-13: Implementation for directed adjacency matrix class

#include "cx12-12.h"

void dAMGraph::addEdge(int fromV, int toV)
{
    assert(fromV < n && toV < n && fromV >= 0 && toV >= 0);
    if (!edgeMember(fromV, toV)) {
        m++;
        am[fromV][toV] = 1;
    }
}
```

Code Example 12-14 Header file for Undirected Adjacency Matrix class

```
// cx12-14.h
// Code Example 12-14: Header for undirected adjacency matrix class

#ifndef __MB_CX12_14__
#define __MB_CX12_14__

#include "cx12-10.h"

class uAMGraph : public amGraph {
public:
    uAMGraph(int size, int initialValue = 0) :
            amGraph(size) { }
    virtual void addEdge (int fromV, int toV);
};

#endif
```

Code Example 12-15 Implementation file for Undirected Adjacency Matrix class

```
// cx12-15.cpp
// Code Example 12-15: Implementation for undirected adjacency matrix class

#include "cx12-14.h"

void uAMGraph::addEdge(int fromV, int toV)
```

```
{
    assert(fromV < n && toV < n && fromV >= 0 && toV >= 0);
    if (!edgeMember(fromV, toV)) {
        m++;
        am[fromV][toV] = 1;
        am[toV][fromV] = 1;
    }
}
```

12.5.2   Finding the Transitive Closure

Let's suppose that we're using an undirected graph to model a communications net-work. In our model, each vertex represents a node in the network, and each edge represents a direct connection between two nodes. If there's an edge between vertex *x* and vertex *y*, it means that information can pass directly between *x* and *y*. However, even if there's no direct connection between two nodes, the nodes can communicate if there's a path through the graph that connects them. For example, take a look at Figure 12-16. Nodes 2 and 6 can communicate, by passing a message via nodes 1 and 3, but there is no way for nodes 2 and 5 to talk to each other.

Figure 12-16   *A communications network*

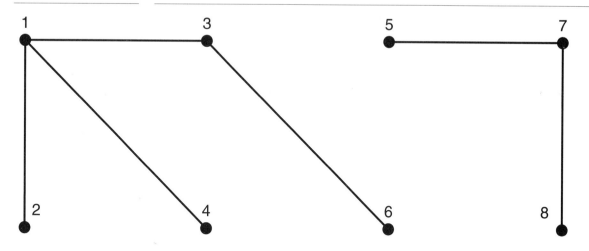

Paths in a Graph   We refer to the sequence of vertices such as [2, 1, 3, 6] as a ***path.*** We define a path more precisely in Definition 12-1.

Definition 12-1   A sequence $v_0, v_1, \ldots, v_k$ is a *path* from v_0 to v_k in an undirected graph $G = (V, E)$ if and only if $\{v_i, v_{i+1}\} \in E$ for all $1 \leq i < k$. The *length of the path* is k.

In other words, a sequence of vertices is a path if each pair of vertices is an edge. Note that if there's an edge between two vertices there's also a path (of length 1).

The Transitive
Closure Graph   Now we can state the problem. We want to know, for each pair of nodes, whether that pair can communicate. In terms of our graph, we want to know for each pair of vertices whether there's a path that connects them. We'll start with our input graph, and compute a new graph called the ***transitive closure*** graph, as defined in Definition 12-2.

Definition 12-2   For a graph $G = (V, E)$, the transitive closure graph $G^* = (V, E^*)$ has edge $\{v_1, v_2\} \in E^*$ if and only if there's a path $v_1, \ldots, v_2$ in graph G.

In Figure 12-17 you'll find the transitive closure graph for the communications network shown in Figure 12-16.

Figure 12-17   *Transitive Closure of Graph from Figure 12-16*

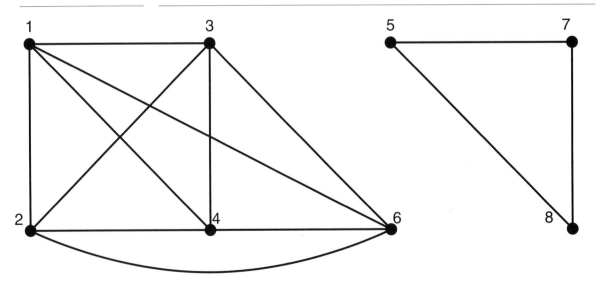

An Algorithm for
Transitive Closure   One algorithm to compute the transitive closure graph looks a lot like matrix multi-plication and lends itself well to the adjacency matrix representation. If we start out with the initial graph, we see that we get all the length = 1 paths "for free"—these are just the edges in the graph. The first phase of the algorithm looks at each vertex to see whether it can link two vertices together. For example, take vertices 2, 1, and 3 in the graph shown in Figure 12-16. The algorithm will find the path [2, 1, 3] and add a transitive closure edge between 2 and 3. In the next phase, the algorithm finds an edge between 2 and 3, and between 3 and 6, and adds a transitive closure edge be-tween 2 and 6. The algorithm consists of nested loops that add these edges until all possible paths have been found and the new transitive closure graph is complete. The code for a transitive closure program, using the adjacency matrix classes, is shown in Code Example 12-16. A data file corresponding to Figure 12-16 can be found in Supplementary Example 12-1, included with the source code distribution.

Code Example 12-16 A transitive closure program

```
// cx12-16.cpp
// Code Example 12-16: Transitive Closure

#include "dslib.h"
#include "cx12-14.h"
#include <fstream.h>

int main()
{
    const char * inFileName = "graph2.dat";
    // read graph from a file
    // first entry is size of graph
    ifstream ifs(inFileName);
    assert(ifs);
    int n;
    ifs >> n;
    uAMGraph G(n);
    cout << "Created graph; n = " << G.vertexSize() << endl;
    int u, v;
    while ( ifs >> u ) {
        ifs >> v;
        G.addEdge(u,v);
    }
    cout << "Edges in graph: m = " << G.edgeSize() << endl;

    int step;
    for (step=0; step < n; step++)
        for (u = 0; u < n; u++)
            for (v = 0; v < n; v++)
                if (G.edgeMember(u,step) && G.edgeMember(step,v))
                    G.addEdge(u,v);
```

```
// print results
for (u=0; u < n; u++) {
    cout << u << "\t: ";
    for (v = 0; v < n; v++)
        cout << (G.edgeMember(u,v)? "T " : "F ");
    cout << endl;
}
return 0;
}
```

Exercise 12-22   Analyze the worst-case complexity of the transitive closure algorithm.

Exercise 12-23   Look up the definitions of the mathematical terms *transitive* and *closure*, and explain the name "transitive closure graph."

Exercise 12-24   Prove that the *n* steps in the outer loop of the transitive closure algorithm are both necessary and sufficient to compute the transitive closure graph.

Modify Code Example 12-16 so that it computes the transitive closure graph without modifying the original input graph.

Chapter Summary

- A graph represents relationships among items. Vertices represent the items, and edges represent the relationships.

- In an undirected graph, an edge is a set; in a directed graph, it's a directed pair.

- An adjacency list is a data structure for representing a graph by keeping a list of the neighbor vertices of each vertex.

- An adjacency matrix is a data structure for representing a graph by keeping a matrix of 0's and 1's in which each 1 corresponds with an edge.

- An inheritance hierarchy can be used to represent the variations on a graph.

- Abstract base classes allow the programmer to specify an interface for inherited objects.

- Iterator classes, implemented via friend classes, provide the most flexible way to create iterators.

- A Topsort finds an ordering of vertices consistent with the partial order represented by the edges.

- The transitive closure of a graph contains an edge for every path in the original graph.

Programming Laboratory Problems

Lab 12-1 In a *weighted graph,* a numeric value is associated with every edge. Weighted graphs have many useful applications—for example, vertices can represent airports that a particular airline services, and the weighted edges can represent the cost of a ticket between airports that the airline flies between.

  a. Create an ADT for an undirected, weighted graph, represented by an adjacency matrix. Use floating point numbers for the weights.

  b. Write the code for your ADT, inheriting from the `uAMGraph` class.

  c. Write a simple application that simulates an airline's graph of ticket prices. The program should read in vertices and prices and keep an array that maps vertices to the names of the airports. Store a very high cost, representing "infinity" for each route that the airline does not fly. Once the graph is set up, the program should accept queries consisting of the names of two airports and either report a cost or report that no flight is available.

Lab 12-2 The Depth-First Search (DFS) algorithm can be used to traverse all the vertices of a graph. DFS works as shown in Algorithm 12-2.

Algorithm 12-2 *Depth-First Search*

```
put the initial vertex into a stack;
while the stack is not empty do {
        pop a vertex v from the stack;
        visit vertex v;
        push all unvisited neighbors of v onto the stack;
}
```

  a. Under what conditions does the DFS algorithm visit every vertex in the graph?

  b. Write a program that reads in a directed graph, stores it in an adjacency list, and performs a DFS, printing each vertex as it's visited.

Lab 12-3 An *Eulerian tour* is a sequence of vertices that crosses every edge exactly once. For example, take a look at Figure 12-18. The sequence [3, 0, 4, 2, 0, 1, 4] is an Eulerian tour for this graph.

  a. (*Optional*) Prove that an Eulerian tour exists if and only if the number of neighbors of every vertex is even, except for the beginning and end vertices, which can have an odd number of neighbors.

b.   Write an algorithm that finds an Eulerian tour in a graph, if such a
      tour exists.

c.   Write a program that reads in an undirected graph, stores it in an ad-
      jacency list, and finds an Eulerian tour or else reports that no such
      sequence exists.

Figure 12-18   *Sample graph for Eulerian Tour*

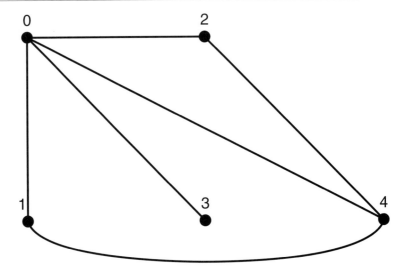

Lab 12-4   Write a program that reads in a directed graph, stores it in an adjacency list, and uses
              Depth-First Search (see Lab 12-2) to answer a series of connectivity queries. Each
              query will consist of a pair of vertices, and the program should answer "connected"
              if there is a path from the first vertex to the second and "not connected" if there is no
              such path.

Lab 12-5   Write a program based on the example in Section 12.1. The program should first
              read a directed graph that represents a set of course prerequisites. A table should be
              used to map vertices to strings representing the names of the courses. Then, a series
              of courses should be read in, representing all the courses a particular student has
              completed. Finally, the program should print out all courses the student is ready to
              take next.

Chapter Vocabulary

abstract base class

abstract class

adjacency list

adjacency matrix

consistent order

constant reference variable

digraph

directed (edges)

directed graph

discrete mathematics

edges

friend class

graph

graph theory

inline declaration

invalidated iterator

iterator class

path

partial order

topological sort

total order

transitive closure

vertices

Appendix A A Brief Review of C++

Overview   A primer to get the student started using C++.

Appendix Objectives

1. To learn to read and write simple, procedural C++ programs.

2. To understand how C++ programs are built from separately compiled source files.

A.1   Things You Won't Learn From This Appendix

Reading this appendix won't turn you into an expert C++ programmer, or even into a good one. Instead, it is intended to teach you enough about the basics of C++ so that you can get started. If you already know another language such as Pascal, C, or Ada, you can apply what you've learned about programming to the study of data structures, using the C++ language. As you probably know, C++ was designed to support what is known as object-oriented programming (OOP), as introduced in Chapter 4. However, C++ also supports procedural programming[1]—the style of programming exemplified by Pascal. Thus, you can take most of what you already know about writing programs in Pascal or some other language, learn some new—but not totally dissimilar—syntax, and be able to write and read simple C++ programs.

I also intend for this appendix to provide a reasonable review of the language for those who have learned it before. If you learned some C++ at some point in the past, but it's a bit rusty, a pass or two through this appendix may be useful. You will probably also wish to have a comprehensive C++ reference handy. My favorite is Lippman's *C++ Primer* (1991).

You might think that the procedural parts of C++ are the same as its ancestor, the C language, but that's not quite right. They are similar, but there were a number of innovations in C++ to make it a "better C"—changes that, most would agree, make C++ a better language even when OOP is not considered. If you do know C, however, you'll find that the subset of C++ introduced here will be quite familiar. The C programmer should pay particular attention to Sections A.4.3 and A.5.1, which describe features that are somewhat different in C++.

We'll offer some hints as we go along to make your indoctrination into C++ as quick and easy as possible, but be aware that without additional care on your part there's a potential for real frustration in debugging C++ programs. You'll find that the same techniques you learned, or were supposed to learn, in your first programming class will help just as much or more with C++; good planning and design, using formal or informal techniques to reason about loops, and thorough testing will all help you avoid those late nights in the lab. You should also be sure to learn to use any tools that are available to help you, such as a debugger. The time you spend becoming proficient with such tools will be paid back many-fold.

---

1. Acronym intentionally omitted.

A.2 Naming Things

A.2.1 Variables

The names of things, or *identifiers*, in C++ are built from the characters A-Z, a-z, the underscore "_", and the digits 0-9. Note that, unlike some languages, upper- and lower-case characters are distinct, so that the names "bullseye" and "BullsEye" are different. Names begin with a character or an underscore; names beginning with an underscore, and those containing double underscores "__", are used by libraries and system facilities, so it's generally not a good idea to use indentifiers starting with underscores in your own programs.

Most C++ programmers use lower-case letters for variable and function names. If a variable name is made from more than one word, it's customary to use a single underscore to separate the words, or to use an upper-case letter to highlight the start of each word; for example: long_identifier, longIdentifier. You can't use keywords for identifiers; for example, "if" can't be an identifier, because it's a keyword. A complete list of keywords appears in Table A-1. In addition, certain operators and punctuators have an alternative representation, listed in Table A-2; these are also reserved and must be avoided when you pick your identifiers.

Table A-1   *C++ keywords*

asm	do	inline	short	typeid
auto	double	int	signed	typename
bool	dynamic_cast	long	sizeof	union
break	else	mutable	static	unsigned
case	enum	namespace	static_cast	using
catch	explicit	new	struct	virtual
char	extern	operator	switch	void
class	false	private	template	volatile
const	float	protected	this	wchar_t
const_cast	for	public	throw	while
continue	friend	register	true	
default	goto	reinterpret_cast	try	
delete	if	return	typedef	

Table A-2   *Alternative representations*

bitand	and	bitor	or	xor	compl
and_eq	or_eq	xor_eq	not	not_eq	

Tips   • *Choose names that are descriptive but concise.*
        • *Don't start names with underscores.*
        • *Generally, use lowercase letters.*
        • *Don't forget that upper- and lower-case letters are distinct!*

A.2.2 Types

Every variable and function in C++ has a *type*; these types must be *declared*. A type specifies the set of legal values a variable can hold. For example, an int can hold integer values. A simple variable is declared by an expression consisting of the name of a type, followed by the name of the variable and a semicolon. Some examples:

```
int i;
float x_coord, y_coord;
```

The expressions above declare three identifiers; i is an integer, x_coord and y_coord are floating point numbers.

The programmer can specify that a larger or smaller space be reserved for the variable. In particular, integers can be specified by all of the following:

```
char   short int   int   long int
```

The range that each can store varies from compiler to compiler. The only thing that's guaranteed is that in the list above, each type can store items as big as or bigger than the type to its left. Note that while a char is the right size to store a single character, the value stored can be interpreted as a character or an integer depending on the context. (After all, a character is represented in the computer by a number, its ASCII code.) Floating point numbers are declared as one of the following:

```
float   double   long double
```

Just as with the integer types, a double is as big as or bigger than a float, and a long double is as big as or bigger than a double.

The integer types can also be modified by the keyword unsigned to indicate that all the bits in the variable should be treated as positive, rather than reserving a bit to indicate whether the value is positive or negative.

In many languages, variable declarations must appear in a special section or at the beginning of a block, but in C++ a declaration can appear almost anywhere. The main restriction is that the declaration must precede all uses of the variable. You can see an example of this in Code Example A-1, when `operand1` and `operand2` are declared in the middle of the `perform_calculations()` function.

Code Example A-1   *Example of declaration within a function*

```cpp
// cxa-1.cpp
// Code Example A-1: perform_calculations function

void perform_calculations()
{
    int Done(0);
    char op;
    const char sp = ' ';
    const char eq = '=';
    while (!Done) {
        cout << "Select operations: +, -, *, /, or q for quit: ";
        cin >> op;
        if (op == 'q' || op == 'Q')
            Done = 1;
        else if (op == '+' || op == '-' || op == '*' || op == '/') {
            double operand1(get_operand());
            double operand2(get_operand());
            double result;
            switch (op) {
                case '+':
                    result = add(operand1, operand2);
                    break;
                case '-':
                    result = subtract(operand1, operand2);
                    break;
                case '*':
                    result = multiply(operand1, operand2);
                    break;
                case '/':
                    result = divide(operand1, operand2);
                    break;
            }
            cout << operand1 << sp << op << sp << operand2
                << sp << eq << sp << result << '\n';
        }
        else
            print_error(op);
    }
}
```

The declarations of `operand1` and `operand2` are also interesting because they are combined with a call to a function that sets the initial values. You can also use an equal sign "=" to give a variable an initial value, for example,

```
double operand1 = get_operand();
```

There's no difference in the effect, but I prefer to use the parentheses form because that's consistent with giving initial values to user-defined objects, as you'll see later.

Any declaration of a simple variable may specify an initial value, but the declaration of a constant must do so. An example of a constant declaration is repeated from the `perform_calculations()` function:

```
const char sp = ' ';
const char eq = '=';
```

As you can see, the keyword `const` specifies that the name declared refers to a constant; that is, the value in the declaration cannot change during the execution of the program.

Tips
- *Keep declarations close to initial use.*
- *Use initial values where appropriate.*
- *Keep things simple by picking just a couple of types (I recommend* int *and* double*), and use those unless you specifically need another size.*

A.2.3   Arrays

An array is specified in C++ by including an integer value in square brackets after the name of the array. For example, here's a declaration of an array of 100 integers:

```
int a[100];
```

In general, for an array of size n, the elements are indexed from 0 to $n-1$. The individual elements are referenced in a manner similar to other languages; for example, `a[50]` refers to the 51st integer in the array `a`.

When you write an array reference in C++, the compiler doesn't check to make sure that you are referencing an item that's actually in the array. To continue with the example of the array above, executing the following expression will have unpredict-able results:

```
a[100] = 17;
```

By "unpredictable" I mean that just about anything can happen, including nothing —what you *won't* get is a message like "Array reference out of range."

To understand what happens, we need to consider briefly how arrays are implement-ed by a compiler. When an array is declared, the compiler allocates the amount of storage needed to store the array. For example, if a particular compiler uses 4 bytes for each `int`, then the array declaration for a will result in 400 bytes set aside for the array. The space for the array will be located in memory, mixed in with other da-ta.

Let's look at an example. A C++ program contains the following declarations:

```
float x;
int a[3], b[2];
```

Figure A-1 illustrates one possible configuration for memory when the program ex-ecutes. Note that this is only one possibility—the compiler isn't obliged to store the items in the same order in which they are declared.

Figure A-1   *Memory configuration at execution*

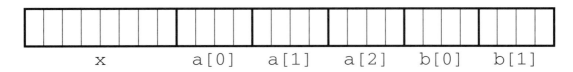

            x   a[0]   a[1]   a[2]   b[0]   b[1]

Now, let's suppose that the expression

```
a[3] = -1;
```

is executed. Remember, C++ doesn't check to see that the reference is in the proper range. Instead, it knows where array a starts and computes the location for a[3]. But as we see in the diagram, there *is* no a[3]. The spot where C++ puts –1 is actu-ally b[0]. By "magic," b[0]'s value has changed without an explicit reference to it.

Sometimes, even worse things happen. The computed location may refer to memory that is allocated to some other purpose by the operating system. The results of refer-encing such a location depend upon the system you're using. In a Unix system, memory references outside the area allocated for data will typically cause your program to halt with a cryptic message along the lines of "Segmentation Fault." In the less-sophisticated MS-DOS system, any memory reference will be treated as valid, which means you can do nasty things like change the operating system itself! Typically, this locks up the computer, but more cryptic outcomes are possible.

Fortunately, if you are aware of and understand the problem, you are well on your way to avoiding it most of the time, and fixing it if it occurs. First, careful design of your loops, using loop invariants, will prevent most out-of-range references. Second, in any case where the value of the index cannot be known reliably in advance, such as when it depends on user input, a *guard* in the form of an if statement can be used to assure that the index is in range. For example:

```
if (i >= 0 && i < n)
    a[i] = 0;
else
    // take error action
```

The syntax "&&" specifies a logical "and" operation. This if statement assures that the reference a[i] is in the proper range (assuming that n is the size of a). We'll look at the if statement in Section A.5.2. You can find more strategies for avoiding range errors in Chapter 3.

Tips • *Don't forget: An array of size* n *ranges from 0 to n–1.*

  • *Use loop invariants and guards to avoid referencing invalid indexes.*

A.2.4 Strings

A standard string in C++ is simply an array of char, with a special value used to mark the end. The null character, typed "\0" in a C++ program, is used by string manipulation functions to determine the end of a string. Note that even though "\0" is typed using two keys, the backslash and the zero (not the letter *O*), it represents a single character. For example, the string "Tighten up" could be stored in an array, as shown in Figure A-2.

Figure A-2   *Storage of a standard string*

Note that this array has space for 12 characters, but only 11 are in use. C++ strings, as provided by the base language, are also of fixed length. Of course, since C++ is an object-oriented language it is possible to create or obtain more sophisticated and flexible string implementations. But most programmers will need to know how to use this standard string format. Functions for manipulating strings are provided in a library; see Section A.6.2 for examples.

A string is declared in exactly the same way as any other array. For example:

```
char song_title[14];
```

You can also initialize a string when you declare it. C++ automatically puts the null character at the end of the string:[2]

```
char song_title[14]("Tighten up");
```

When you give a string an initial value, you need not specify the length; for example:

```
char song_title[]("Like a Sturgeon");
```

The string has 15 characters, so `song_title` will be 16 characters long, since space has to be reserved for the null character at the end.

While the double quote character specifies a string, single quotes are used to write a single literal character. The following illustrates correct and incorrect syntax for strings and characters:

```
char c, s[10];   // c is a character, s is a string
c = '$';         // OK: c assigned the dollar sign character
c = "$";         // ERROR: c is char, but "$" is a string
s = "dollar";    // ERROR: can't assign one array to another
s = 'dollar';    // ERROR: the syntax 'dollar' will be
                 // rejected since '' used only for chars
s = c;           // ERROR: the types are incompatible
s[0] = c;        // OK: first character in s set to '$'
```

Tips
- *If you manipulate a string, be sure you put a null character at the end.*
- *Remember when allocating space for strings that you need one extra array element to hold the null character.*
- *Be sure you know when to use single quotes and when to use double quotes.*

---

2. But only for initialization—when you manipulate a string directly, *you* have to make sure to put the null character on the end.

A.2.5   Structures

C++ provides a mechanism that's useful for grouping heterogeneous information. For example, suppose you want to create variables that can store names, telephone numbers, and zip codes:

```
struct person {
    char first_name[20];
    char middle_initial;
    char last_name[25];
    int area_code;
    long int phone_number;
    int zip_code;
};
```

This assumes that you can fit a seven-digit phone number into a `long int`, and a five-digit zip code into an `int`. The `struct` statement in effect creates a model for a particular type of structure, but it doesn't actually define any variables. In the example above, a new type `person` has been defined by the `struct`, and subsequently variables of type `person` can be declared; for example:

```
person p;
person person_list[100];
```

The first statement declares a variable `p` that can store a single person's data; the second declares an array of 100 structures.

The items in the structure are referenced using the following syntax:

```
p.phone_number = 5551212;
```

`Phone_number` above is called a *field specifier*. To reference one field in an array of structures, you first indicate the index element and then follow it with the field specifier:

```
person_list[i].zip_code = 10012;
```

A.2.6   Multidimensional Arrays

To create a multidimensional array in C++, you declare the size of each dimension within its own pair of square brackets. For example, here's the declaration of a 10-by-20 array of `int`s:

```
int a2d[10][20];
```

Note that combining the two dimensions within a single pair of brackets will not work:

```
int a2d[10,20]; // ERROR
```

You access elements using the same style:

```
a2d[i][j] = 7;
```

All the same caveats that apply to one-dimensional arrays apply to multidimensional arrays as well; in particular, most C++ implementations do not verify that your indices are in the proper range. Beware!

A.3 Expressing Things

A.3.1 Express Yourself

A simple C++ expression looks like this:

```
answer = 3*a + 2*b;
```

An expression combines literals and variables, called *operands*, with *operators*, and yields a value. The sequence "3*a + 2*b" is an expression. Expressions can appear in assignment statements, function calls, and as the control values for statements such as if and while.

In C++, some surprising things are treated as expressions. For example, in the assignment statement x = b + 1, the entire statement is an expression and has a value. The value of the statement in this case is the same as the value of x after the assignment is performed. This can be used to create compound expressions that many C++ beginners find daunting; for example,

```
if (x = b + 1 > 3)
```

This if statement changes the value of x as a *side effect*. We'll return to this type of expression, and its pitfalls, in Section A.3.3 below.

A.3.2 Arithmetic Expressions

C++ provides arithmetic operators that you are familiar with, plus a few that may be new. Addition, subtraction, multiplication, and division are indicated by the symbols "+", "−", "*", and "/". The operator "%", which requires the operands to be integral, yields the remainder after division; it's often called the modulus or mod operator. Trying to divide by 0 results in a runtime error.

As in most (but not all) languages, the C++ expression "2+3*2" yields 8, not 10; that is, the multiplication is performed first, yielding "2+6", and then the numbers are added. The rules that determine the order of evaluation are called *precedence rules*. C++ evaluates the subexpression with the highest precedence first. For operators of equal precedence, evaluation is from left to right. As in other languages, C++ lets you use parentheses to change the default order of evaluation: for example, (2+3)*2 evaluates to 10. We'll get to a table of operator precedence in Table A-7, after we've seen most of the available operators.

In addition to the *binary* operators—that is, operators that take two operands—C++ provides several *unary* operators—operators that work with a single operand. One familiar unary operand is the unary minus "–", which negates the value of its operand. A unary plus "+" is also defined, but has no effect.

A more interesting class of unary operators are the *increment* "++" and *decrement* "--". These operators are applied to a variable, and have the side effect of adding 1 to (incrementing) or subtracting 1 from (decrementing) the operand. For example:

```
int a(0), b;
++a;        // a is now equal to 1
b = --a;    // a is now equal to 0
```

Since "--a" is an expression, it has to have a value—for the decrement in the expression b = --a, it's equal to the value of the operand *after* it's decremented, which in this case is zero. In many cases, we don't care about the value of the expression, but just want to perform the effect of incrementing the variable. In this case the effect of a++ is the same as the assignment statement a = a + 1.

For situations in which the value of the expression is significant, there is another form that is often handy. If the increment or decrement operator appears *after* its operand, the value of the expression is equal to the value of the operand *before* it is changed. When the operator appears before the operand, it's called a *prefix* operator; when it follows, it's a *postfix* operator. Here are some examples:

```
int a(1), b(2);
a = b++;      // a equals 2, b equals 3
b = --a;      // a equals 1, b equals 1
a++ = b++;    // ERROR: can't assign value to a++
```

An easy way to remember the difference between prefix and postfix forms is this: when the increment (or decrement) operator is in the prefix position, it's as if the operator is applied first, and then the value returned; when the operator is in the postfix position, the value is returned first and then the operator applied.

While the experienced C++ programmer needs to know and understand the increment and decrement operators in postfix and prefix form, in order to read code produced by others, you can always avoid them in your own code, by making it just a bit longer. For example, the following three code examples have the same effect:

```
// first example: most terse
b = --a;

// second version: uses decrement op, but less terse
--a;
b = a;

// third version: most verbose
a = a - 1;
b = a;
```

Some people find the second or third easier to digest. If you don't fully understand these expressions, I suggest you simply do not use them, especially when you are first getting used to C++.

Tips • *If you're uncertain about the effect of an increment or decrement expression, rewrite it without "++" or "--".*

A.3.3   Other Types of Expressions

Relational and Equality Operators   Relational and equality operators are used to compare arithmetic operands. The relational operators are shown in Table A-3. Relational expressions return 0 to indicate false, and 1 to indicate true. The returned value is an int.

Table A-3   *Relational operators*

>	greater than
>=	greater than or equal to
<	less than
<=	less than or equal to

The equality operators work in just the same way, to determine whether the two operands are equal or not equal, as shown in Table A-4. Let's jump ahead for a moment and use an if statement, to show one of the nastiest problems that tends to plague the

Table A-4   *Equality operators*

==	equal to
!=	not equal to

C++ neophyte. Suppose that the programmer intends to compare variables x and y and take action in an `if` statement based upon the result. But by mistake, he or she uses "=", the assignment operator, instead of "==", the equality operator:

```
if (x = y) ...
```

What happens? The assignment statement copies the value of y into x, and then returns the resulting value of x. Recall that there is no boolean type in C++, so `if` statements interpret 0 as false and non-zero as true. Suppose that before the `if` statement was reached, x was 1 and y contained 2. Since the value of the expression $x = y$ is 2, the `if` statement will be treated as true, which is not what the programmer expects. Furthermore, the value of x has changed, which was not intended.

You can often avoid the unexpected in an `if` statement by putting the constant part, if any, on the left. For example, suppose you want to compare x to 0. You can write it either way:

```
if (x == 0)
if (0 == x)
```

but there's an advantage to the second form, if you make the mistake of using a single equals sign. Compare the following:

```
if (x = 0)
if (0 = x)
```

The compiler will accept the first line, and running the program will cause an unexpected side effect; the compiler will reject the second line, because you can't have a constant on the left side of an assignment. So if you can get in the habit of putting the constant on the left, you can often detect this error while compiling, when it's easy to fix, rather than having to debug the program when it's running but you're getting the wrong answer.

Many compilers will give you a warning for an expression that modifies a variable within an `if` statement. For example, Borland compilers warn you of a "possibly incorrect assignment." The compiler designer puts in warnings for a reason, and it behooves you to treat them seriously and make sure that you either remove them or be sure that the line that triggers the warning really does what you want. Ignoring warnings you don't understand often leads to logic errors later on.

Expressions can be categorized by the type of the value returned. We'll next look at the different types of expressions available in C++.

Tips • *Watch out for the difference between "=" and "==".*

• *Put constants on the left side when using "==" in a statement.*

• *Heed and understand compiler warnings.*

Logical Operators C++ provides the logical operators "and", "or", and "not". These operators are defined by how they operate on zero and non-zero numbers.

Take for example the "not" operator, which is expressed by the notation "!". The exclamation point is sometimes referred to as the "bang" by C++ programmers. If x is 0, then !x is 1; if x is non-zero, then !x is 0. For example:

```
int a = 0, b = 1, c;
c = !(a < b);// c is 0, i.e., "false"
```

The *logical and* operator is expressed by "&&". If both operands to && are non-zero, then the result is 1; otherwise, the result is zero. In logical terms, "a && b" is true (non-zero) if both a and b are true (non-zero) and false (zero) otherwise.

The *logical or* operator is "||". If both operands to || are zero, then the result is zero; otherwise, the result is 1. Thus "a || b" is true (non-zero) if either or both of a and b are true (non-zero) and false (zero) otherwise. Note that this is the form of logical or sometimes known as *inclusive or* since it's true not only when one of the operands is true, but also when they're both true. Another type of *or*, called *exclusive or*, is true only when exactly one of the operands is true; there is no logical exclusive or operator in C++.

Conditional Expression C++ has an unusual but handy operator called the *conditional expression*. The conditional expression consists of three subexpressions, separated by the characters "?" and ":"; for example:

```
x > y ? x - y : y - x
```

In this case, the first expression is "$x > y$". The first expression is evaluated; if it is non-zero (true) the second expression will be the result, otherwise the third expression will be the result. In the example, suppose $x == 5$ and $y == 10$. Then, since $x > y$ is false, the value of the first expression is 0, so the value of the conditional expression is $y - x$, or 5.

A useful example of a conditional expression is to avoid division by zero:

```
z = y? x/y : 0;
```

In this case, if y is non-zero, then z will be set to the quotient x/y; otherwise, z is set to 0. Note that this also demonstrates that the first expression need not contain a relational or equality operator if all you need to know is whether the operand is zero or non-zero.

As with increment and decrement operators, you really don't need to use conditional expressions unless you like and understand them. There's always another way to express the same thing.

Bitwise operators   C++ provides operators that treat the operand as a string of bits. For example, `&` is the operator for *bitwise and*. Suppose that `int i` is 127 and `int j` is 64. To determine the value of `i&j`, look at the binary representations of `i` and `j`: `i == 01111111`$_2$, and `j==01000000`$_2$. Wherever both bits in the operands are 1, there will be a 1 in the result, and everywhere else there will be a 0. In this case, `01111111`$_2$ `& 01000000`$_2$ `== 01000000`$_2$ `== 64`. So `i & j == 64`.

A detailed discussion of the bitwise operators is outside the scope of this appendix. For your reference, they are listed in Table A-5.

Table A-5   *Bitwise operators*

~	unary complement (change each 0 to 1, each 1 to 0)
<<	shift left
>>	shift right
&	bitwise "and"
^	bitwise exclusive "or"
|	bitwise inclusive "or"

Assignment
Operators   In addition to the standard assignment operator "`=`", C++ features a set of special assignment operators that allow the programmer to express an arithmetic or bitwise operation and an assignment at the same time. For example,

```
a *= 2
```

means, multiply `a` by 2 and put the result back in `a`. The arithmetic assignment operators are

```
*=    /=    %=    +=    -=
```

and the bitwise assignment operators are

```
>>=   <<=   &=    ^=    |=
```

These complex assignment operators take some getting used to, but experienced programmers tend to like their conciseness.

Sequencing
Operator The comma—", "—is called the sequencing operator. Because it is most often used in conjunction with the `for` statement, we will return to it in Section A.5.3.

A.3.4 Conversion

Conversion occurs when expressions combine operands of different types. For example, consider the following expressions:

```
int i(1), j(2);
double x(1.0), y(2.0);

i = x * j;
y = y + i / j;
```

In the first expression, a `double` is multiplied by an `int`, with the result assigned to an `int`. In C++, the language uses conversion rules. The compiler evaluates this expression via the following steps:

1. It converts `j` to an equivalent double precision number and multiplies `1.0` by `2.0`.

2. It converts `2.0` back to an `int`, and sets `i` to `2`.

The compiler evaluates the second expression as follows:

1. It treats `i/j` as integer division, yielding the `int` `0`.

2. It converts the result to the `double` `0.0`, so it can be added to `double` `y`, yielding `2.0`.

3. It assigns `2.0` to `y`.

A conversion from an integer type to a floating point type is usually simple, just a matter of, in effect, adding ".0" to the integer. Converting a floating point type to an integer type can be problematic, since the fractional part is lost. Furthermore, any conversion from a larger type to a smaller type can lose information; such a conversion is said to be *narrowing*.

You can also trigger a conversion when you use pass values via *reference parameters*. We discuss parameter passing in Section A.4.3.

The rules for conversion are rather complicated but can be summarized by the following three rules:

1. If either operand is a floating point type, convert both to the largest floating point type.

2. Otherwise, if both operands will fit in `int`, convert both to `int`.

3. Otherwise, convert both to the larger of the two integral types.

Table A-6 shows some examples.

Table A-6   *Examples of type conversion*

Operand 1	Operand 2	Result
int	double	double
char	short int	int
float	long double	long double
long int	double	double
long int	int	long int

You can also explicitly convert an operand to a specific type by an operation called *explicit conversion* or *casting*. C++ has two syntaxes for casting: the traditional, or cast notation, and functional notation. In cast notation, the type is enclosed within parentheses. For example:

```
y = (double) x;
```

Functional notation has the same effect, but a different form:

```
y = double(x);
```

Many people prefer the functional notation, but unfortunately there are situations (involving pointers) where the cast notation is needed.

Tips   • *If you're not sure how a conversion will work, use explicit conversion.*

• *Avoid narrowing conversions, which have system-dependent consequences.*

A.3.5   Precedence Rules

The precedence rules for the operators we've seen so far are shown in Table A-7. We only show the operators that we have discussed here; for a complete list, consult a C++ reference. All the operators within a single box have the same precedence. You probably didn't think of array subscripting and function calls as operators, but that's how C++ treats them.

Table A-7   *Operator precedence*

[ ]	subscripting
( )	function call
( )	functional conversion
++	post increment
++	pre increment
- -	post decrement
- -	pre decrement
~	complement
!	not
-	unary minus
+	unary plus
( )	cast
*	multiply
/	divide
%	modulo (remainder)
+	add (plus)
-	subtract (minus)
<<	shift left
>>	shift right
<	less than
<=	less than or equal
>	greater than
>=	greater than or equal
==	equal
!=	not equal
&	bitwise "and"
^	bitwise exclusive "or"

Table A-7   *Operator precedence*

|		bitwise inclusive "or"
&&		logical "and"
||		logical inclusive "or"
?:		conditional expression
=		simple assignment
*=		multiply and assign
/=		divide and assign
%=		modulo and assign
+=		add and assign
-=		subtract and assign
<<+		shift left and assign
>>=		shift right and assign
&=		"and" and assign
|=		inclusive "or" and assign
^=		exclusive "or" and assign
,		comma (sequencing)

Tips • *If you can't remember the precedence rule for a particular set of operators, use parentheses.*

A.4 Calling Things

A.4.1 Functions

You can build a C++ program from functions—procedural programming—or from composing objects—object-oriented programming. You can read about object-oriented programming in Chapter 4; here we focus on the procedural approach. A function can be fully described by a function header followed by a function body, although as we will see these are often written separately. Let's start with a small example:

```
// is_lower returns true if the argument is a lower case
// character, otherwise false
int is_lower(char c)
{
   return c >= 'a' && c <= 'z';
}
```

The function header specifies three things:

1. The name of the function is "is_lower".

2. The function returns a value of type int.

3. The function has a single parameter of type char.

The body of the function is surrounded by curly brackets "{" and "}".

The special keyword "return" serves two purposes: it specifies the value that the function should return, and it terminates the execution of the function and returns control to the calling function. Here's another example that illustrates the dual nature of "return":

```
// sign returns -1 if its argument is less than zero,
// zero if the argument is zero, and +1 if the argument
// is greater than zero.
int sign(float x)
{
   if (x < 0) return -1;
   if (x == 0) return 0;// (*)
   return 1;
}
```

Suppose that x==0. When the line marked (*) is executed, the flow of control returns to the calling function, with a value of 0. The last line of the program will never be executed in this case. Sometimes we wish to create a function that is called only for its side effects; that is, we don't care for it to return a value. The keyword "void" is used to specify a function of this kind. For example:

```
void line_feeds(int n)
{
   int i;

   for (i = 0; i < n; i++)
      cout << '\n';
}
```

We'll see soon how the `for` loop works; for now, take my word for it that this loop executes its body n times. The body of the loop, "`cout << '\n'`", sends a line feed to the output device. Note the use of the keyword "`void`" to indicate that there is no return value. Note also that there's no need for a `return` statement in this function because no value is returned. You can use `return` statements in a `void` function if you want to specify a return of control within a function.

Here are calls to the functions above:

```
if (is_lower(ch)) . . .// ch is a char variable
if (sign(z) != 1) . . .// z is an int variable
line_feeds(5);
```

If you have a function with no arguments, you need to include an empty pair of parentheses when you call the function. For example:

```
r = random();
```

calls a function `random` with no parameters. Trying to write

```
r = random;
```

will, if you're lucky, trigger a compiler error, or, if you're unlucky, will lead to a logic error, since the expression treats `random` as the name of a *variable* rather than the name of a function. So if your function doesn't have a variable `random`, the compiler will flag the error; if it does have a variable `random`, `r` will get the value of the variable rather than the result of a function call.

A.4.2 Programs

Every program must have a function called "`main`". When the program is executed, control begins with the first executable line of the `main` function. Traditionally, the `main` function has no parameters and is written without a return type:

```
main()
{ ...
```

Actually a function is assumed to return `int` by default, so writing `int main()` has the same effect; I prefer to make the return type explicit by using

```
int main()
{ . . .
```

If a `main` function returns a value, the effect is operating-system dependent. The arguments to the `main` function can be used to pass information to the program when it's called; the use of these arguments is outside the scope of this appendix.

Note that because the `main` function as written above has type `int`, some compilers will warn you that your `main` function doesn't have a `return` statement. You can eliminate this warning by adding `return 0;` at the end of the `main` function.

A.4.3 Parameters

C++ uses parameters to pass information to and from functions. Let's review some terminology. Parameters in a function header are called *formal parameters*. The parameters in a function call are *actual parameters*.[3] By default, C++ uses the parameter passing method referred to as *call by value*. The ideas are easier than the terminology makes them sound; let's look at an example:

```
float square(float x)
{
   return x*x;
}

int main()
{
   cout << square(4.0) << '\n'; // prints result of square
   return 0;
}
```

In the `square` function header, the formal parameter is x. In the call to the function `square`, within the `main` function, `4.0` is the value of the actual parameter. In a call by value, the *value* of the actual parameter is *bound* to the formal parameter. In effect, the formal parameter x within the body of `square` works just like a local variable that is initialized to the value of the actual parameter. At the beginning of the execution of the `square` function, the value of x is set to 4.0. The function is free to change the value of a formal parameter later on, with no effect on the calling program.

By its nature, a call by value parameter is useful only for passing information from the calling program *to* the called function. But in many cases it's desirable to use parameters to pass information back from a called function to the function doing the calling. C++ accomplishes this by using what are called *reference parameters* and a mechanism referred to as *call by reference*.

The motivation for call by reference is clear—to pass information back from a called function—but the mechanism is a bit more difficult to understand than call by value. Instead of binding a value when the function is called, the compiler binds a memory

---

3. Actual parameters are sometimes referred to as *arguments*.

location. That is, the formal parameter and the actual parameter become synonyms or *aliases* for the one memory location. Here's a concrete example:

```
void square(float &x)
{
  x = x * x;
}

int main()
{
  float y(4.0);
  square(y);
  cout << y << '\n'; // prints result of square
  return 0;
}
```

The ampersand "&" preceding formal parameter x indicates that it should be passed by reference rather than by value. You may mix value and reference parameters in a single call—the "&" refers only to the parameter that immediately follows it, so if you want to use more than one reference parameter, you need to put the ampersand in front of each one. In this example, the call to square within main binds the formal parameter x to point to the same memory location as the variable y. Thus any change to x during the execution of function square will be reflected in the value of y afterward. Note that it's permissible for the formal parameter and the actual parameter to have the same name—I could have given the formal parameter in square the name y, and everything would have worked in the same way.

When you have a reference parameter, it doesn't make any sense to use a constant for the actual parameter. For example, suppose I replace the call to square with square(4.0). What memory location should I bind x to within the square function? When I change x, what do I want to change? Because there's really no reasonable answer to these questions, using a constant or any expression other than the name of a variable is not allowed for a reference parameter.

A.4.4 Scope

In a large program, it's often the case that the same name will be used in different places for different variables. The *scope rules* for a language specify how the program determines which variable is associated with a particular reference. In C++, functions cannot be nested. Except for classes, which we introduced in Chapter 4, there are only two kinds of scope: *global* and *local*. Local identifiers are declared within the header or body of a function, while global identifiers are declared outside any function. The scope of a local identifier, that is, where it can be referenced, begins at the point following its declaration and extends to the end of the body. Global identifier scope also begins following the declaration and extends to the end of the file in which it is declared. (Note that a single program can, and generally is, built from more than one file; see Section A.6.) With these rules in mind, examine the following example:

```
int x, y;
int f1(int a)
{
    return x = y;
}
int f2(int y)
{
    return x = y;
}
int main()
{
    y = 1;
    y = f1(1) + f2(2);
    ...
}
```

Note that the second reference to y refers to the formal parameter, rather than the global variable y.

A.5   Doing Things

A.5.1   Input and Output

Most programs are useless without input and output (I/O). One of the advances of C++ over C is the simplified method for I/O, based on a standard library of functions called *iostream*. A *library* is a set of functions (and variable declarations) that provide useful services to a program; a *standard library* is one that is provided by every C++ compiler. We'll discuss libraries in more detail in Section A.6.2. Technically, I/O is not part of the C++ language itself, since these services are provided by the library rather than the compiler. This is not an important practical distinction for the beginner, since every modern C++ compiler provides these services through the standard library iostream.[4] Note however that compilers often expand upon the core definition of iostream, so that the exact features provided vary from one compiler to another. After all, many aspects of I/O depend upon the specific operating environment in which a program is run.

---

4. Older versions of C++ use the *stream* library. The stream library works somewhat differently from iostream, so if you are using an older compiler consult your reference materials.

Iostream defines input and output streams for your programs. Input and output normally consists of a stream, or sequence, of characters, while the information within the program consists of characters, integers, floats, and other types. The iostream routines perform this conversion for you automatically.

Please note that in order to use the iostream library, you need to include the following line at or near the top of your program:

```
#include <iostream.h>
```

The purpose of this line is discussed in Section A.6.2

Output   Let's look at output first. The primary output stream is called cout, sometimes referred to as *standard output*. In most cases, standard output appears on the screen, but it's possible that standard output might be a printer, a file, or a dialog box in a windowed system. We'll assume here that the characters sent to standard output simply appear on the computer screen. The operator <<, called the *insertion operator*, is used to specify that characters are to be inserted onto the output stream. For example:

```
char str[]("a string");
cout << str;
char c('x');
cout << c;
int i(17);
cout << i;
double x(6.5);
cout << x;
```

The output from this sequence of statements would be

```
a stringx176.5
```

All the output has run together on a single line. With stream I/O, no extra spaces or line feeds are provided—the programmer must explicitly request them.

Here's an alternative version of the code above, in which the output is separated by tabs and appears on two lines. The special character code '\t' indicates that a tab character should be sent to the output stream. The code '\n' stands for a *newline*, which specifies that the next character in the stream should appear at the beginning of a new output line. The exact interpretation of these characters is system-dependent; for example, Unix files use a single character to represent a new line, while DOS files have two.

```
char str[]("a string");
cout << str << '\t';
char c('x');
cout << c << '\n';
int i(17);
cout << i << '\t';
double x(6.5);
cout << x << '\n';
```

On my system, the output from these statements looks like this:

```
a string        x
17       6.5
```

In the last example, we've sent more than one thing to output in a single line, by separating each item with the insertion operator. In fact, we could combine all the output into a single statement, as in the following example:

```
char str[]("a string");
char c('x');
int i(17);
double x(6.5);
cout << "str[] = " << str << '\t' << "c = " << c << '\n' <<
        "i = " << i << '\t' << "x = " << x << '\n';
```

The final statement of the code above contains a char variable, an array of char, an int, a double, literal strings, and literal characters. The iostream library takes care of converting everything to appropriate characters and sending the result to standard output. When I executed the statements, I got the following output:

```
str[] = a string        c = x
i = 17   x = 6.5
```

In addition to the cout output stream, another stream called cerr is also provided. The cerr stream is associated with *standard error*. This is useful when the user wants to instruct the program to send standard output to a file. In such a situation, there may be output that needs to go directly to the primary output device (typically, the screen) so that the user can act upon it. In this category are important error messages, hence the name standard error. Other than the possibility of splitting standard output and standard error, cout and cerr work essentially the same way. Here's an example using cerr:

```
cerr << "Warning: could not open file " << filename << '\n';
```

On most systems, cout and cerr go to the same place by default.

Input   You can think of the symbol "<<" as an arrow that says "put this stuff onto `cout`."
For input, you turn the arrow around to get ">>", the *extraction operator*, and use
the `cin` input stream. Here's a familiar code fragment, rendered in C++:

```
char answer;
cout << "Do you want to continue? Enter y or n: ";
cin >> answer;
```

Iostream performs any conversion, if necessary, to put the input into the argument to
the right of the extraction operator. As with output, you can include more than one
argument on a single line:

```
cout << "Enter last name and zip code: ";
cin >> last_name >> zip_code;
```

Iostream puts a null character at the end of the array. As usual, a statement such as
`cin >> answer` is an expression. The value of the expression is nonzero when
characters are read in; when the end of the input file is reached, the value will be zero. This can happen when reading from a disk file, or if the user enters the "end of
file" character for the system, for example, control-Z for MS-DOS, control-D for
Unix. This lets you write loops that continue until all input has been read, for example:

```
while (cin >> x)
{
   . . .
}
```

The loop terminates once you get to the end of the file.

Note that when reading a string—a char array—characters are extracted until
whitespace is encountered. So if you want to read in a string with embedded spaces
you need more than one `cin`. For example, if you try to use the following code to
read a name, it won't do what you want:

```
cout << "Enter your full name: ";
cin >> name;
```

If the user types "`George Washington`", only "`George`" will be inserted into
name, while "`Washington`" remains in the input buffer and will be read by the
next input statement.

One handy thing to know about the way input works is that you can check the return
value from an input expression to determine whether or not the expected type of data

has been entered. This is useful when you input numbers. For example, suppose you have the following code:

```
int i;
cout << "Enter a number: ";
cin >> i;
```

Now suppose the user hits the wrong key by mistake and enters a letter on the keyboard rather than a number. After the input takes place the contents of i will be unpredictable and system dependant, and in any case certainly not what you want. The following code is much more robust:

```
int i; char b[80]
cout << "enter a number: ";
while ((cin >> i) == 0) {
    cout << "invalid input -- try again: ";
    cin.clear (0); cin.getline(b,80); // clear input
}
```

The expression cin >> i will return non-zero if an integer was entered by the user; so as long as the expression cin >> i has a non-zero value you can continue with the assurance that i has been set to some reasonable value. (You still may need to check the value of i to make sure it makes sense in the context of your program, but at least you know the user did enter a number.) On the other hand, an invalid input will cause cin >> i to return zero. As shown above, you can use this information to take appropriate action.

You can read a line with spaces by using the getline function, as shown in Code Example A-2.

Code Example A-2   *Use of the iostream getline function*

```
// cxa-2.cpp
// Code Example A-2: Example of using the getline function

#include <iostream.h>

int main()
{
    const int maxNameLength = 40;
    char name[maxNameLength+1];
    cout << "Enter your first and last names: ";
    cin.getline(name, maxNameLength);
    cout << "Your name is " << name << endl;
}
```

The first argument to `getline` specifies the name of the array that will hold the characters; the second argument indicates the maximum number of characters that will be read. The call to `getline` will read to the end of the input line, or until `maxNameLength` chars are read, whichever comes first. In addition to reading through spaces, the ability to specify the maximum length of the input offers greater safety, because the simple "`cin >>`" expression can cause the program to go beyond the intended end of the input array, with consequences like those discussed in Section A.2.3.

Iostream provides additional input facilities, but you know enough now to get started. Consult a C++ book or manual for additional details.

A.5.2 Selection

Selection is the process of choosing which action a program will pursue based on the state of some variable. Selection can be two-way—the `if` statement—or multi-way, which is called a `switch` in C++.

if Statements   In C++ the argument to the `if` is treated as true if it is non-zero, and false if it is zero. The argument must appear in parentheses. Here's an example:

```
if (x != 0)
    cout << "x is not zero.\n";
```

Because the argument will be true whenever it's non-zero, the above `if` statement can be more concisely written as

```
if (x)
    cout << "x is not zero.\n";
```

The consequent of the `if` can be a single statement or a block of statements. The block in C++ is expressed by enclosing it within curly brackets:

```
if (x) {
    cout << "x is not zero.\n";
    cout << "Really, I'm not kidding!\n";
}
```

The style of indentation of brackets shown here is the most popular; you should pick a style you like and stick to it consistently to make your programs as readable as possible.

You can also express an `else` condition in C++:

```
if (x > 0)
   cout << "x is positive\n";
else
   cout << "x is less than or equal to zero.\n";
```

Note that you need a semicolon at the end of the statement before the `else`. Omitting it will confuse the compiler and result in a syntax error. However, if the clause after the `if` is a block, that is, is surrounded by curly brackets, it *doesn't* end with a semicolon.

You can nest or cascade `else` statements, and with the same semantics: an `else` is always paired with the closest unmatched `if`.

```
if (x > 0)
   cout << "x is positive\n";
else if (x < 0)
   cout << "x is negative\n";
else
   cout << "x is zero";
```

Note that using an `if` statement to set the value of a variable can often be done more conveniently with a conditional expression. For example, here is an `if` statement and its conditional expression equivalent:

```
if (x >= 0)
   y = x;
else
   y = -x;

y = x >= 0? x : -x;
```

Depending on your taste (and perhaps your instructor's or boss's taste) one form is as good as the other.

Switch Statement   The `switch` statement provides a multi-way selection statement, but it is a bit tricky to use. Here's an example:

```
switch(age) {
  case 1:cout << "Just begun\n";
         break;
  case 2:cout << "Almost new\n";
         break;
  case 3:cout << "Hardly me\n";
         break;
  case 4:cout << "Not much more\n";
         break;
```

```
      case 5:cout << "Barely alive\n";
            break;
      case 6:cout << "Clever, so clever!\n";
            break;
    }
```

Note the presence of the `break` keyword. When `break` is encountered, control passes to the end of the block. Without the `break`, C++ will continue execution at the next line. For example, suppose you wrote this:

```
switch(age) {
   case 1:cout << "Just begun\n";
   case 2:cout << "Almost new\n";
   case 3:cout << "Hardly me\n";
   case 4:cout << "Not much more\n";
   case 5:cout << "Barely alive\n";
   case 6:cout << "Clever, so clever!\n";
}
```

When this `switch` is executed with `age == 3`, the output will be

```
Hardly me
Not much more
Barely alive
Clever, so clever!
```

Usually, this is not what you want, and the `switch` statement can be the source of many tricky bugs. But sometimes this behavior is exploited, typically when there are several cases that you want to handle in the same way:

```
switch(sensor) {
   case 'h':
   case 'm': temp = 75;
         break;
   case 'l':temp = 65;
         break;
}
```

Note that the last `break` never has an effect and hence can always be eliminated. However, most programmers include it so that if a new case is added to the end of the switch, they won't have to remember to add a `break` to the previous case.

The argument after the keyword "case" has to be *integral*, that is, a `char`, `int`, or `long int`. Furthermore, there is no way to express a range of values. Generally, you use a cascade of `if/else if/ ... / else` to express complicated multi-way selection in C++.

There is one additional keyword that is available for use with the `switch`: `default`. The default case is taken if no matches occur between the `switch` argument and the listed cases. For example:

```
switch(sensor) {
  case 'h':
  case 'm': temp = 75;
            break;
  case 'l': temp = 65;
            break;
  default:  temp = 70;
            break;
}
```

If there is no match, and no `default` present, then execution simply continues after the `switch`. Note that this is *not* a runtime error.

Tips
- *Remember the syntax for `if`s includes parentheses around the condition.*
- *Because non-zero is "true" you needn't use "!= 0" in a condition.*
- *Use conditional expressions rather than `if`s when it makes the code clearer.*
- *Always include a break after each case in a switch (unless you want execution to "fall through").*

A.5.3 Loops

`while` *Loops* The most generally useful looping structure in C++ is the `while` loop. Here's an example, written in a style similar to most other procedural languages:

```
// compute n factorial in C++
fact = n;
while (n > 1) {
  n = n - 1;
  fact = fact * n;
}
```

An experienced C++ programmer wouldn't write it quite like that, however. The more concise version below is more typical.

```
fact = n;
while (--n)
  fact *= n;
```

do/while *Loops*
The do/while loop in C++ is always executed at least once—conceptually, the condition is checked at the end of the iteration rather than the beginning. For example:

```
do {
  cout << "Do you want to continue? (y/n)";
  cin >> ans;
  if (ans != 'y' && ans != 'n')
    cout << "Please answer y or n.";
} while (ans != 'y' && ans != 'n');
```

Note that for both varieties of while loop, C++ syntax requires that the condition be enclosed in parentheses.

for *Loops*
In most programming languages, the for loop is a counting loop. The C++ for loop can be used in this manner, but it also has many other uses. Here's an example of a for loop for summing up an array a of size n.

```
long int sum(0);
for (i = 0; i < n; i++)
  sum += a[i];
```

(Remember, to iterate through an array of size *n,* you start at 0 and go up to *n* – 1.) There are three parts inside the parentheses in the for statement. The first part contains initialization; the expression here is executed once before the body of the loop. The second part is an iteration test; when this condition is true, the loop continues execution. The third part is used for updating; the expression here is evaluated at the end of every iteration. Thus, the for loop above could be rewritten using a while loop as follows:

```
long int sum(0);
i = 0; // initialization
while (i < n) { // iteration test
  sum += a[i];
  i++; // updating
}
```

Of course, the two statements within the body of the loop could be combined into

```
sum += a[i++];
```

but this makes the relationship between the while and for loops less obvious.

Since any for loop can be expressed with an equivalent while loop, you might wonder why it's included in the language. While it certainly is not necessary, it does improve program readability, because it clearly sets off the initialization and updating steps and includes them as part of the loop. For the `while` loop above, the relationship between the assignment `i = 0` and the loop is not immediately obvious, especially if the comment is omitted; but in the `for` loop it's clear that the programmer intended the assignment to initialize a loop counter.

To illustrate the flexibility of the `for` loop, here's the first `while` loop example rewritten as a `for` loop:

```
for (fact = n; n > 1; fact *= --n)
   ;
```

Here we've put everything the loop has to do within the three `for` clauses, so we don't even need a body for the loop! When you write a loop with no body, it's customary to put the semicolon—which represents a null statement—on a line by itself, just to make it clear that you did indeed intend an empty loop body.

Any of the three parts can be empty if unneeded. You always include the two semicolons to make it clear what's there and what's missing. Here's another version of the last loop, omitting the third part—it has been moved to the loop body.

```
for (fact = n; n > 1;)
    fact *= --n;
```

If you omit the second clause, it is treated as always true; hence one way to write an endless loop in C++ is

```
for (;;) {
  // endless loop
...
}
```

You might think that you would never want to write such a loop, but as we'll see next there are various ways to jump out of a loop even if the iteration test remains true. (In fact, you've already seen one way—the `return` statement.) So you may well encounter intentionally "endless" loops in C++.

Jumping out and about

C++ provides a couple of ways to jump out of the middle of a loop, plus the powerful and dangerous unconditional branch—the `goto`.

We've already seen the `break` statement in the context of a `switch`. Within a `for`, `while`, or `do/while` loop, encountering a `break` causes the flow of control to pass to the first statement after the end of the loop; that is, it breaks out of the loop. This is quite a convenience in many situations, such as handling interactive I/O:

```
int sum(0);
cout << "Enter numbers to average, terminated by a zero:";
int count;
for (count = 0;;count++) {
  cin >> num;
  if (!num) break; // jumps out of loop if num is 0
  sum += num;
}
cout << "Average is " << (count? sum/count : 0) << '\n';
```

Because the execution of the break terminates the loop, count will not be incremented when num is zero. Note the use of a conditional expression on the last line to avoid the possibility of division by zero. This conditional expression must appear within parentheses because the precedence of the "<<" is higher than that of the "?:".

Sometimes rather than breaking out of a loop, the programmer wants to skip the remainder of the loop body and iterate again. This facility is provided by the continue statement:

```
int sum(0);
cout << "Enter numbers to average, terminated by a zero:"
int count;
for (count = 0;;) {
  cin >> num;
  if (num < 0) {
    cout << "Negative numbers not allowed! Try again.\n";
    continue;
  }
  if (!num) break; // jumps out of loop if num is 0
  sum += num;
  count++;
}
cout << "Average is " << (count? sum/count : 0) << '\n';
```

I had to move count++ out of the for statement, because I don't want count to be incremented when a negative number is entered.

C++ also provides the dangerous, brute force unconditional branch, the goto. It's danger lies in the ability to transfer the flow of control willy-nilly through a program. But there are a very few situations where it does come in handy. In particular, a break statement only takes you out of the loop that immediately encloses it, so if you need to jump all the way out of nested loops you need to use a `goto`. Here's an outline of the use of a `goto` with nested loops:

```
while ( . . . ) {
  while ( . . . ) {
    . . .
    if (some condition) goto leave_loops;
    . . .
  }
}
leave_loops: ...
```

As shown in the example, you label a point to branch to with an identifier followed by a colon.

Because of the potentially tricky nature of using `goto`, most programmers-in-training are probably better off avoiding them altogether.

A Loose End   As we promised back in Section A.3, there's one more operator that is usually used in conjunction with `for` loops. This is the comma operator ", ". The comma operator allows you to combine a sequence of expressions into a single expression. C++ executes the sequence from left to right, with the value of the last expression in the sequence returned as the value for the sequence. For example, you could write something like this:

```
a = b + c, x = y, t = 0;
```

The value of the expression is 0. The question is, why would you want to do this? The answer is that within the `for` loop, there is a place for exactly three expressions — the first typically used for initialization and the third for updating. What if you want to initialize two (or more) variables for the loop? This is a job for the comma operator:

```
cout << "Enter numbers to average, terminated by a zero:"
int count, sum
for (count = 0, sum = 0;;count++) {
  cin >> num;
  if (!num) break; // jumps out of loop if num is 0
  sum += num;
}
cout << "Average is " << (count? sum/count : 0) << '\n';
```

Outside of `for` loops, the comma operator is rarely used. Note that a comma operator has the lowest precedence around, so you don't need to enclose the constituent expressions within parentheses.

A.6   Putting Things Together

A.6.1   Building Systems from Multiple Files

The design of C, and later C++, assumed that a program is built from multiple files, compiled separately, which are put together by a program called a *linker* to form the final product. Figure A-3 illustrates a simple version of this process for two C++ files.

Figure A-3   *Linking C++ files—a simple example*

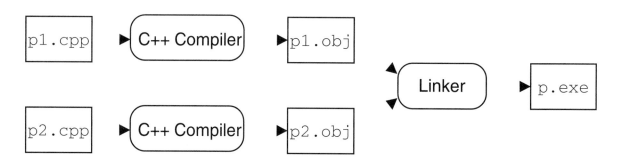

The files containing C++ code are called *source files*. In many operating systems, the second part of the name of a file, called the *extension*, is used to indicate the type of file. Unfortunately, there is no universal naming convention for C++. Borland C++ users use .cpp for source files. Unix users generally use .C. Some compilers prefer .c++. Be sure you know the standard conventions for your environment and stick with them to avoid confusion; some compilers won't even compile your source code unless you use the correct extension.

The output files from the compiler are called *object files*. Like the naming of source files, naming conventions for object files differ from system to system. MS-DOS systems typically use .obj, while Unix uses .o. The object files are combined by the linker to form an *executable file*. This is a program "ready to run." In MS-DOS, most executable files have the extension .exe; executables in Unix generally have no extension.

What are the advantages of separate compilation using multiple files? There are several:

1. The time it takes to compile a source file is largely determined by its size. If a program consists of a million lines of code in a single file, a compilation might take an annoying amount of time. If, instead, it consists of several hundred files, each one might compile in a few minutes or less.

2. Large systems are built by teams of programmers, not by individuals. Having many programmers attempt to work with a single source file is much too difficult to manage. (It's hard enough to manage with multiple source files, but software is available that assists in the process.) Each programmer can generate her or his own files and perform preliminary testing — *unit testing.* Once unit testing is complete, a *system build* is performed to link the files together. For more information about testing, see Section 3.2.

3. Separate compilation makes it possible to distribute *libraries* without delivering source code. This means that a software company can sell a library of functions while maintaining a proprietary interest in the source code. One of the important goals of OOP is to support libraries of objects that can be sold without "giving away" the source code.

In the remainder of this section we'll look at the nuts and bolts of the process of separate compilation and linking. First, we examine a related issue: the C++ preprocessor.

A.6.2   The Preprocessor and Libraries

The C++ *preprocessor* is part of the C++ compiler. Before most of the compilation process takes place, the preprocessor examines the source code for preprocessor directives, which begin with a pound sign "#". The two most important preprocessor directives are #define and #include.

#define provides *macro expansion.* If you've studied an assembler language before, you've probably seen this. In its simplest form, #define specifies that whenever a particular preprocessor variable appears, it should be replaced by a specified string of characters. For example, if the input to the preprocessor is

```
#define x 25
y = x;
```

the output from the preprocessor—the *expansion* of the code—is

```
y = 25;5
```

___

5. If you look at the actual output from the preprocessor, you will generally see extra newlines and spaces added in the expansion process; in this example and below, we've simplified the output without making any semantic changes.

In older C code it was common to use #define in just this way—to declare a constant value. However, in newer C and in C++ the preferred way to handle constants is by declaring them using const. Using a const forces you to declare a type for the value, and it puts the name of the constant into the *symbol table*, which means that it can be accessed later for debugging purposes. You will see other uses of #define in the main part of this text.

#include is used to specify *source file inclusion*. For example, suppose you have the following two files, f1.cpp and f2.cpp:

```
//f1.cpp
int x;
```

```
//f2.cpp
#include "f1.cpp"
int y = x;
```

After passing f2.cpp through the preprocessor, the following output will be sent on to the main compilation process:

```
int x;
int y = x;
```

The line "#include "f1.cpp"" has been replaced by the contents of the file f1.cpp. (The preprocessor discards comments.) When including a file that you've created, the file name is contained within double quotes.

The most important use for file inclusion is to support separate compilation, by including *header files*. To understand this process, let's look more closely at the line

```
#include <iostream.h>
```

First, a syntactic issue: the name iostream.h is enclosed within "<" and ">" rather than within quotation marks. This indicates that the preprocessor should expect to find iostream.h in whatever location is reserved for system include files, rather than those belonging to individual programmers. Include files enclosed in quotation marks, for example, "myfile.h", are assumed to be stored with the user's source files. The exact process by which the preprocessor searches for include files is system dependent, but the basic idea is that system include files are installed in a standard, accessible location, while user include files reside wherever the programmer keeps source files.

What is contained within iostream.h? If you're curious, you might want to go ahead and take a look on your system. What you *won't* find, however, is the complete source code for the implementation of iostream.[6] A header file contains the declarations needed to use some set of functions. The definitions of the functions is contained within source code files that, typically, don't come with your compiler. The compiled functions are stored in *libraries* that will be linked with your program to form the executable. A library is similar to an object file, except that it's usually bigger and the linker can pick and choose from the code in the library rather than including the whole thing in the executable. Figure A-4 illustrates this process.

Figure A-4   *Linking iostream.h*

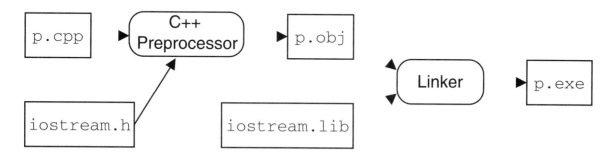

In the main body of the textbook, nearly all the code was designed with separate compilation in mind.

A.6.3   The "Assert" Macros

One useful service provided by C++, and used throughout the book, is the `assert` macro. You use the `assert` macro to check for conditions that could cause a catastrophic failure or unpredictable results in your program, for example, exceeding array bounds. The argument to `assert` contains an expression; if the expression evaluates non-zero (true), the `assert` macro has no effect. However, if the condition evaluates to zero (false), the program will terminate. Most implementations of `assert` will print a message indicating the line in the program where the assertion was violated. Obviously, this is a drastic response, so you should only use the `assert` macro in places where continuing to operate would lead to unpredictable results.

---

6. It's possible that some header files will contain the actual code, but this is the exception not the rule.

Here's a brief example. Note that files that access the `assert` macro should include the header `<assert.h>`. The ellipses represent parts of the code that have been omitted because they're not relevant to demonstrating `assert`.

```
#include <assert.h>
...
int a[100], i;
...
assert(i >= 0 && i < 100); // check array bounds
a[i] = j;
```

Programming Laboratory Problems

Lab A-1   Write a program that has variables of all the following types:

char	short int	int	long int
float	double	long double	

Determine, by experimentation, the largest and smallest value each type will hold. Try all possible conversions between these types, and determine which are legal.

Lab A-2   Take any integer, and apply the following function:

$$f(x) = \begin{cases} x \text{ divisible by } 2 \Rightarrow \dfrac{x}{2} \\ \text{otherwise} \Rightarrow 3x + 1 \end{cases}$$

$f(x)$ is called the *Hailstone function*. It is believed, although not proven, that if you start with any positive integer and apply the Hailstone function repeatedly, you will eventually get to 1. Write a program that prompts the user for an integer and applies $f(x)$ until the value is equal to 1. Print out each value of the function as you go, and keep track of the number of iterations and report it at the end.

Lab A-3   Write a program that reads in a money amount between $0.01 and $100.00 and prints out the smallest set of bills and coins that add up to that amount. For example, if the entry is $25.74, a correct answer would be

```
1 Twenty-Dollar Bill
1 Five-Dollar Bill
1 Fifty-Cent Coin
2 Dimes
4 Pennies
```

Lab A-4   Using the following table:

Freshman:	0–24 credits
Sophomore:	25–58 credits
Junior:	59–89 credits
Senior:	90 or more credits

write a program that prompts the user for the number of credits completed and prints out his or her status.

Lab A-5   A number is said to be *perfect* if the sum of its divisors (except for itself) is equal to itself. For example, 6 is a perfect number because the sum of its divisors (1 + 2 + 3) is 6. The number 8 is said to be deficient because the sum of its divisors (1 + 2 + 4) is only 7. The number 12 is said to be abundant because the sum of its divisors (1 + 2 + 3 + 4 + 6) is 16. Write a program that prompts the user for an integer, prints out its factors, and classifies the number as perfect, deficient, or abundant.

Lab A-6   Write a program that will read in a set of data from standard input and draw a histogram representing the frequency distribution of the data. The input is a sequence of floating point numbers greater than 0.0 and less than or equal to 100.0. The sequence is terminated by 0.0. The output will be a histogram (bar graph) representing the percentage of inputs that fall in each of ten ranges between 0 and 100. The range labeled "10" on the histogram represents the items between 0.0 and 10.0; the range labeled "20" goes from > 10.0 to <= 20.0, and so forth. Each bar in the histogram should display the *percentage* found in each range (*not* the number of inputs). The size of the bar should be rounded to the nearest 10%. In addition, summary data about the input will be presented. The mean of the inputs is the sum of the inputs divided by the number of inputs.

Here's a sample run:

```
Input:   50.1 50.5 75.1 0.0
Output:
# of inputs: 3
largest input: 75.1
smallest input: 50.1
mean input: 58.567
```

```
HISTOGRAM
100%
 90%
 80%
 70%                    **
 60%                    **
 50%                    **
 40%                    **
 30%                    **      **
 20%                    **      **
 10%                    **      **
      10  20  30  40  50  60  70  80  90  100
```

Lab A-7   The monthly payment for a loan can be computed with the following formula:

$$\text{payment} = \frac{\text{monthlyRate} \times \text{expRate}^{\text{months}} \times \text{loanAmount}}{\text{expRate}^{\text{months}} - 1.0}$$

where
    monthlyRate = rate as an annual percentage / 1200
    expRate = 1 + monthlyRate
    months = the duration of the loan in months
    loanAmount = the amount borrowed

Write a program that prompts the user to enter the annual rate, the amount borrowed, and the duration of the loan and computes the monthly payment.

Lab A-8   Write a function that meets the following specification:

```
int search(int a[], int n, int target)
```

Precondition: a is an array of integers indexed from 0 to n-1.

Postcondition: None.

Returns: If target is in array a, then the value x is returned, such that a[x] == target; otherwise, n is returned.

Write a main function that can be used to test the search function.

Lab A-9   Write a pair of functions with the following specifications:

```
int romanToInt(char * romanNumeral)
```

Precondition: romanNumeral is a properly terminated string representing a Roman Numeral.

Postcondition: None.

Returns: An integer having the same value as `romanNumeral`.

```
void intToRoman(int i, char * romanNumeral)
```

Precondition: `i` is an integer; `romanNumeral` points to memory large enough to store the `romanNumeral` presentation of `i`.

Postcondition: `romanNumeral` contains the Roman Numeral representation of `i`.

Recall that M=1000, D=500, C=100, L=50, X=10, V=5, I=1, and that you represent 4 by IV, 9 by IX, etc.

Write a program to test these functions.

Lab A-10 Write a function that meets the following specification:

```
void reverse(int a[], int n)
```

Precondition: `a` is an array of integers indexed from 0 to `n-1`.

Postcondition: the items in the array `a` are in the reverse order from when the function was called.

Write a `main` function that can be used to test the `reverse` function.

Lab A-11 Write a program that reads characters from standard input and counts the number of times each letter between `A` and `Z` occurs. Group upper- and lower-case letters together, and ignore any characters that are not letters. Compute the percentage for each letter and print out a table with the results.

Lab A-12 Every computer connected to the Internet has a unique number called its IP Address. IP stands for "Internet Protocol." The number is 32 bits long and is often written as a sequence of four numbers in the range from 0 to 255. For example, one of the machines on my campus has the following IP address: 150.250.10.217

A number in the range 0 to 255 requires 8 bits to store, and hence this address can be stored in a single 32-bit variable. It's easiest to understand the conversion if you treat each of the four chunks as a hexidecimal (base 16) number, since two hexidecimal digits can store numbers from 0 to 255. For example, the IP Address 150.250.10.217 can be written as 96FA0AD9, which requires 32 bits to store (each hex digit is 4 bits long).

Host IP Addresses consist of three parts: a Class Identifier (classid), a Network Identifier (netid), and a Host Identifier (hostid) and are broken into three classes as follows (note that the bits are numbered from 0 on the left to 31 on the right):

Class A: classid is bit 0; netid is bits 1–7; hostid is bits 8–31.

Class B: classid is bits 0 and 1; netid is bits 2–15; hostid is bits 16–31.

Class C: classid is bits 0, 1, and 2; netid is bits 3–23; hostid is bits 24–31.

Furthermore, you can identify which class an IP Address belongs to by looking at the classid bits -- Class A starts with 0, Class B with 10, and Class C with 110 (all in binary).

For example, the address 150.250.10.27, written in hex as 96FA0AD9, is written in binary as: 10010110111110101011001. So we see that it's a Class B address (because it starts with 10); hence the netid is 01011011111010 binary = 16FA hex, and the hostid is 0AD9 (bits 16 through 31).

The lab problem consists of the following parts:

1. Write a function `readIP` that will read an IP address in the dotted notation form (e.g. 150.250.10.217) and return it as a single unsigned `long int` (this is a 32-bit integer in C++). This function should take an istream reference and use that to get the input.

2. Write a function with the following prototype:
   ```
   enum ipClass {classA, classB, classC, badClass};
   ipClass interpretIP(unsigned long int ipAddress,
       unsigned long int & netid,
       unsigned long int & hostid);
   ```
   `interpretIP` should return the class of the address (note that you could get an address with an invalid IP Address, e.g., starting with 1111, in which case return `badClass`), and it should set netid and hostid to contain the correct network id and host id.

3. Write a program to thoroughly test your functions.

Appendix B C++ for the Pascal Programmer

Overview

An outline of C++ from the point of view of the Pascal programmer.

Appendix Objectives

1. To help the Pascal programmer get started using C++.

B.1　Introducing C++ for the Pascal Programmer

Students often wonder why, if C and C++ are so pervasive in industry, Pascal has been so popular as a first language of instruction in colleges and high schools. Habit plays some part in this, but there are certainly advantages to Pascal for the beginner. In order to provide greater flexibility and power, and to support systems programming, C (and now C++) permit the programmer much more latitude in manipulating system memory directly. This power is like a sharp knife, and the apprentice programming wizard often gets cut.

In many ways, you'll find C++ quite familiar. The basic structures—loops, `if/then/else`, procedures and functions, are all here, although they tend to look a little different and sometimes they go by different names. Once you get used to these differences, you'll find that you can quickly apply what you already know from your Pascal experience.

In order to illustrate the similarities and highlight the differences, we'll start with a sample Pascal program and "translate" it into C++. Once you've carefully examined the example, you'll be ready to go on to study Appendix A.

B.2　Simple Sample

We start with a sample Pascal program of the type that you might write in an introductory programming course. This program is a (very) simple, and fairly useless, interactive calculator. The user is offered a choice of four calculator operations (+, −, *, /) then prompted to enter two operands; the program performs the operation and displays the result. Code Example B-1 is a sample Pascal solution.

Code Example B-1　　*Interactive calculator in Pascal*

```
{ cxb-1.pas }
{ Code Example B-1: Simple calculator written in Pascal }

program I_Calc(input, output);
{ I_Calc is a (very) simple Interactive Calculator }

procedure welcome_user;
begin
    writeln('Welcome to the Interactive Calculator.')
end;

procedure perform_calculations;
const
```

```
    eq = '=';
    sp = ' ';
var
    Done: Boolean;
    op: char;
    operand1, operand2, result: real;

    function get_operand: real;
    var
    n: real;
    begin
        write('Enter number: ');
        read(n);
        get_operand := n
    end;

    function add(a, b: real): real;
    begin
        add := a + b
    end;

    function subtract(a, b: real): real;
    begin
        subtract := a - b
    end;

    function multiply(a, b: real): real;
    begin
        multiply := a * b
    end;

    function divide(a, b: real): real;
    begin
        if b <> 0 then
            divide := a / b
        else begin
            writeln('Oops! Attempting to divide by zero.');
            divide := 0
        end
    end;

    procedure print_error;
    begin
        writeln('Sorry, operation "', op, '" unknown; try again.')
    end;

begin
    Done := false;
    while (not Done) do
    begin
        write('Select operation: +, -, *, /, or q for quit: ');
        readln(op);
```

```
        if op in ['q','Q'] then
            Done := true
        else if op in ['+','','*','/'] then
        begin
            operand1 := get_operand;
            operand2 := get_operand;
            readln;
            case op of
                '+': result := add(operand1, operand2);
                '-': result := subtract(operand1, operand2);
                '*': result := multiply(operand1, operand2);
                '/': result := divide(operand1, operand2)
            end; {case}
            writeln ( operand1:1:3, op:2, sp, operand2:1:3,eq:2, sp, result:1:3 )
        end
        else
            print_error
    end
end;

begin
    welcome_user;
    perform_calculations
end.
```

The next program, Code Example B-2, is a "translation" of this program into C++. By a translation, I mean that I first wrote the program in Pascal and then wrote the C++ version referring directly to the Pascal implementation. It's quite possible that had the direction been reversed, the programs would look quite different. It's also important to point out that a programmer experienced in object-oriented techniques might write a rather different solution. But the (limited) purpose here is to help the reader get started with simple C++ programs. You should compare the two programs carefully to get a feel for some of the differences between the two languages.

Code Example B-2   *Interactive calculator in C++*

```
// cxb-2.cpp
// Code Example B-2: A (very) simple Interactive Calculator

#include <iostream.h>

void welcome_user()
{
    cout << "Welcome to the Interactive Calculator.\n\n";
}

double get_operand()
{
```

```
        double n;
        cout << "Enter number: ";
        cin >> n;
        return n;
}

double add(double a, double b)
{
        return a + b;
}

double subtract(double a, double b)
{
        return a - b;
}

double multiply(double a, double b)
{
        return a * b;
}

double divide(double a, double b)
{
        if (b)
            return a / b;
        else {
            cout << "Oops! Attempting to divide by zero.\n";
            return 0;
        }
}

void print_error(char op)
{
        cout << "Sorry, operation \"" << op
             << "\" not known; try again.\n";
}

void perform_calculations()
{
        int Done(0);
        char op;
        const char sp = ' ';
        const char eq = '=';
        while (!Done) {
            cout << "Select operations: +, -, *, /, or q for quit: ";
            cin >> op;
            if (op == 'q' || op == 'Q')
                Done = 1;
            else if (op == '+' || op == '-' || op == '*' || op == '/') {
                double operand1(get_operand());
                double operand2(get_operand());
                double result;
```

```
        switch (op) {
            case '+':
                result = add(operand1, operand2);
                break;
            case '-':
                result = subtract(operand1, operand2);
                break;
            case '*':
                result = multiply(operand1, operand2);
                break;
            case '/':
                result = divide(operand1, operand2);
                break;
        }
        cout << operand1 << sp << op << sp << operand2
             << sp << eq << sp << result << '\n';
    }
    else
        print_error(op);
    }
}

int main()
{
    welcome_user();
    perform_calculations();
    return 0;
}
```

B.3   Random Notes for the Pascal Programmer

Here are a few things that you will want to keep in mind as you learn about C++. Each note is followed by reference to the appropriate section(s) in Appendix A.

- C++ is a case-sensitive language; unlike Pascal, "IF", "If" and "if" are all distinct identifiers. (Section A.2.1)

- C++ has a type called "char" but unlike Pascal, the "char" type holds positive integers, which are interpreted as characters in certain contexts. (Section A.2.2)

- All arrays start with the first item at position 0. So if you declare an array of size 100, the members of the array range from 0 to 99. (Section A.2.3)

- Most implementations of C++ do not check array indices to make sure they are in the proper range. (Section A.2.3)

- C++ uses the double-quote character—"—to indicate a literal string, as opposed to the single quote in Pascal. (Section A.2.4)

- When referencing items in a multi dimensional array, each index gets its own set of brackets, like this: `a[i][j]`. (Section A.2.6)

- The assignment operator in C++ is "`=`" instead of "`:=`". (Section A.3.1)

- Instead of relational operators returning a "boolean" type for expressing the results of the comparisons, they return a `0` or `1`. (Section A.3.3)

- The equality operator in C++ is a double equals sign, "`==`". The similarity between the assignment operator and the equality operator in C++ is a major pitfall. (Section A.3.3)

- C++ converts between types in expressions much more freely than Pascal. (Section A.3.4)

- Curly braces, "`{`" and "`}`", serve essentially the same purpose as "`begin`" and "`end`" in Pascal. Note, however, that unlike Pascal, every statement in C++ ends with a semicolon ("`;`"), so omitting the semicolon after the last statement in the function will result in a syntax error. (Sections A.4.1 and A.5.2)

- Instead of the "procedures" and "functions" in Pascal, all subprograms in C++ are called "functions." However, you can have a C++ function that doesn't return a value—similar to a procedure in Pascal—by indicating a return type of "`void`". (Sections A.4.1 and A.4.2)

- If you call a C++ function with no arguments, you need to include an empty pair of parentheses when you call the function. (Section A.4.1)

- To return a value from a function, the keyword "`return`" is used, rather than assigning a value to the name of the function. (Section A.4.1)

- Just as in Pascal, C++ parameters can be passed by value (the default) or by reference. To pass a variable by reference (a "Var parameter" in Pascal) precede the variable's name with the symbol "`&`". (Section A.4.3)

- In C++, there are no nested functions. (Section A.4.4)

- The C++ `if` statement requires parentheses around the argument, and there is no "`then`" keyword. (Section A.5.2)

- In Pascal, you can't put a semicolon after the "then" clause of an `if`; in C++, you *must* put a semicolon in that position. (Section A.5.2)

- The C++ `switch` statement provides a multi-way selection, similar to `case`, but it's not quite as flexible as `case`, and it's harder to use. (Section A.5.2)

Programming Laboratory Problems

Lab B-1   Take one of your programs you've written in Pascal, convert it into C++, compile and test it.

Lab B-2   Create a Pascal program that contains an array of 100 elements. Include a line that attempts to reference an item outside the range of the array. What happens?[1] Now convert the program to C++, and run it.[2] Contrast the results.

---

1. In most Pascal systems, array bounds checking, or range checking, is always on. However, if you are using Borland's Turbo Pascal, make sure to turn range checking on — consult the Help system for the language to determine how to do this.

2. Be sure you save your program before you run it, especially on a microcomputer, because on some systems referencing an array item out of bounds can cause the system to lock up, requiring rebooting.

Appendix C C++ for the C Programmer

Overview

An introduction to C++ from the point of view of the C programmer.

Appendix Objectives

1. To help the C programmer get started using C++.

C.1 Introducing C++ for the C Programmer

C.1.1 A "Better C"

As a C programmer, you'll find much of C++ quite familiar to you. Unfortunately, the close relationship between C and C++ also presents some pitfalls. In many cases, you'll have a choice between writing a piece of code "the C way" or "the C++ way." Because C++ has some big advantages over C, you should avoid the tendency to stick to the familiar. Your goal should be to "speak C++ like a native." Paying attention to the points raised in this appendix should help you get started.

Of course, support for object-oriented programming distinguishes C++ from C more than anything else. However, in this appendix we focus on the "procedural" parts of C++, the features that make C++ "a better C." The main body of the textbook covers the use of C++ for object-oriented programming. The next few pages focus on leveraging your C knowledge to help you get started quickly with C++.

C.1.2 A Sample Program in C and C++

To illustrate the most important "better C" features of C++, let's compare a simple program written in C, and see how we might rewrite it in C++. In fact, the C program shown in Code Example C-1 will also compile and run in C++, but it fails to take full advantage of C++. The example program simply reads some numbers into an array, uses a very simple implementation of Bubble Sort to sort the numbers, and prints the result.

Code Example C-1 *A Bubble Sort written in C*

```
/* cxc-1.c
   Code Example C-1: sample C program
   This program reads integers into an array, sorts them with
   Bubble Sort, and prints the result. */

#include <stdio.h>

/* swap the values of two integers */
void swap(int *a, int *b)
{
    int temp = *a;
    *a = *b;
    *b = temp;
}

#define SENTINEL -1
```

```
#define MAX_ARRAY 10

main()
{
    int a[MAX_ARRAY];
    int n = 0;
    int input;
    int i, j;

    /* read ints from stdin, until sentinel encountered */
    printf("Enter integers, terminating with %d.\n", SENTINEL);
    while (n < MAX_ARRAY) {
        scanf("%d", &input);
        if (input == SENTINEL) break;
        a[n++] = input;
    }

    /* sort the list, using Bubble Sort */
    for (i = 0; i < n; i++)
        for (j = n - 1; j > i; j--)
            if (a[j] < a[j-1])
                swap(&(a[j]), &(a[j-1]));

    /* report the results */
    printf("Sorted list is:\n");
    for (i = 0; i < n; i++)
        printf("%d\t", a[i]);
    printf("\n");
    return 0;
}
```

Now compare the C++ version, in Code Example C-2. You'll certainly see more similarities than differences, but there are significant changes.

Code Example C-2   *Bubble Sort rewritten in C++*

```
// cxc-2.cpp
// Code Example C-2: sample C++ program
// This program reads integers into an array, sorts them with
// Bubble Sort, and prints the result.

#include <iostream.h>

// swap the values of two integers
void swap(int & a, int & b)
{
    int temp(a);
    a = b;
    b = temp;
}
```

```
const int SENTINEL = -1;
const int MAX_ARRAY = 10;

int main()
{
    int a[MAX_ARRAY];
    int n(0);
    int input;

    // read ints from stdin, until sentinel encountered
    cout << "Enter integers, terminating with " << SENTINEL << ".\n";
    while (n < MAX_ARRAY) {
        cin >> input;
        if (input == SENTINEL) break;
        a[n++] = input;
    }

    // sort the list, using Bubble Sort
    int i, j;
    for (i = 0; i < n; i++)
        for (j = n - 1; j > i; j--)
            if (a[j] < a[j-1])
                swap(a[j], a[j-1]);

    // report the results
    cout << "Sorted list is:\n";
    for (i = 0; i < n; i++)
        cout << a[i] << "\t";
    cout << endl;
    return 0;
}
```

C.1.3   C and C++: Some Important Differences

**stdio *vs.*
iostream**   Just like C, C++ depends upon a library to perform input and output (I/O). In C, the most commonly used I/O features can be found in the stdio library; to use the functions in stdio, the programmer writes

```
#include <stdio.h>
```

C++ provides a much nicer set of functions, called the iostream library, that does everything stdio does, but in a manner that most programmers will find easier to use. To use iostream, write

```
#include <iostream.h>
```

The most common use of the iostream functions is for simple input from standard input and output to standard output. As shown in Code Example C-2, you can read from standard input into a variable using the *extraction operator* "`>>`":

```
cin >> input;
```

Since using the scanf function incorrectly leads to some of the most common C runtime errors, this change alone is worth the price of admission.

For output, use the *insertion operator* "`<<`":

```
cout << a[i] << "\t";
```

As shown, you can string together several items and each will be sent to the output stream in turn. The value endl, defined by iostream, sends an endline character to the output stream, and then flushes the output buffer. You don't use the specification string as you do with printf and scanf—instead, the library functions automatically figure out an appropriate format. For those situations when you need more control, iostream provides it, but the insertion and extraction operators make I/O easy most of the time. More details on iostream can be found in Section A.5.1.

references vs. pointers

C++ includes a built-in type specifier called "reference to." The addition of the reference overcomes one of the significant drawbacks of C, by allowing scalar variables to be passed by reference.[1] To understand why this is useful, consider the following incorrect implementation of a function to swap two integers in C:

```
void swap(int a, int b)
{
    int temp = a;
    a = b;
    b = temp;
}
```

Why doesn't this work? Recall that when the compiler executes a function call in C, it copies the values of the actual parameters (the ones in the call) into the formal pa-

---

1. *Scalar variables* hold a single value, as opposed to arrays and structures, which can hold more than one value.

rameters (the ones in the declaration of the function). For example, if the following code calls the swap function:

```
i = 1;
j = 2;
swap(i, j);
```

then the swap function will execute with a set to 1, and b set to 2. After executing the last line of the swap function, a=2 and b=1. *However, when returning to the point of function call, the new values of* a *and* b *will not be copied back to* i *and* j. So the swap function has no effect on the variables in the function that called it.

To get the effect we want, we have to pass pointers instead, as shown in the swap function in Code Example C-1, repeated here:

```
void swap(int *a, int *b)
{
    int temp = *a;
    *a = *b;
    *b = temp;
}
```

Now, a and b are pointers to int, and we have to dereference them, using the "*" operator. The call to the swap function looks like this:

```
swap(&(a[j]), &(a[j-1]));
```

The compiler binds a to the location of a[j] in memory, and b to the location of a[j-1]. So when the swap function executes, it can change the actual values of a[j] and a[j-1], as desired. This gets the job done, but it's easy to mess up—for example, if you forget to dereference the pointers within the swap function, the program may still compile, but the values don't get updated in the way you expect.

In C++, we can pass a variable by reference—which really means that we do the same thing we did with pointers in C, but we can do it more cleanly and we are less prone to error. Since the declaration of swap looks like this:

```
void swap(int & a, int & b)
```

the compiler knows from the "&" symbol that we want to pass the parameters by reference. That's all you have to do! The compiler takes care of binding the location rather than the value of the parameter, and we can dispense with the use of pointers. For another discussion of passing by reference, see Section A.4.3.

#define *vs.* const

New features of C++ eliminate many uses of the C preprocessor. In particular, the use of `#define` to declare constants becomes obsolete in C++. As you can see in Code Example C-2, the `const` keyword lets you specify that a variable's value cannot change, for example:

```
const int SENTINEL = -1;
```

By using a variable rather than `#define`, you give the compiler the ability to check for the proper type when it uses your constant. Plus, most preprocessors won't let you view the value of a `#define` macro, while a `const` variable will be available.

C.2   Random Notes for the C Programmer

Here are a few things that you will want to keep in mind as you learn about C++. Each note is followed by reference to the appropriate page(s) in Appendix A.

- Use pass-by-reference rather than passing pointers. (Section A.4.3)
- Use `iostream` instead of `stdio`. (Section A.5.1)
- Use `const` instead of `#define`. (Section A.2.2)

Programming Laboratory Problems

Lab A-1   Take one of your programs you've written in C, convert it into C++, compile and test it.

Bibliography

Bentley, Jon. *Programming Pearls*. Addison-Wesley, 1986.

Berman, A. Michael, "When words collide: Network simulation as an exercise in a CS2 course," *Journal of Computing in Small Colleges* 11(4), March 1996, 264–274.

Berman, A. Michael and Robert C. Duvall, "Thinking about binary trees in an object-oriented world," *Proceedings of the Twenty-Seventh SIGCSE Technical Symposium on Computer Science Education*, 1996, 185–189.

Comer, Douglas E. *Internetworking with TCP/IP, Volume I. Principles, Protocols, and Architecture*. Second Edition. Prentice Hall, 1991.

Cormen, Thomas H., Charles E. Leiserson, and Ronald L. Rivest. *Introduction to Algorithms*. MIT Press/McGraw-Hill, 1990.

Gamma, Erich, Richard Helm, Ralph Johnson, and John Vlissides. *Design Patterns: Elements of Reusable Object-Oriented Software*. Addison-Wesley, 1995.

Leveson, Nancy G. and Clark S. Turner, "An investigation of the Therac-25 accidents," *Computer*, July 1993, 18–41.

Lippman, Stanley B. *C++ Primer*. Second Edition. Addison-Wesley, 1991.

Meyers, Scott. *Effective C++: 50 Specific Ways to Improve Your Programs and Designs*. Addison-Wesley, 1992.

Neumann, Peter G. *Computer Related Risks*. Addison-Wesley, 1995.

Perl, Y., A. Itai, and H. Avni, "Interpolation search—a log log n search," *Communications of the ACM* 21, 1978.

Plauger, P.J. *The Draft Standard C++ Library*. Prentice Hall PTR, 1995.

Stroustrup, Bjarne. *The C++ Programming Language.* Second Edition. Addison-Wesley, 1991.

Stroustrup, Bjarne. *The Design and Evolution of C++.* Addison-Wesley, 1994.

Tanenbaum, Andrew S. *Computer Networks.* Third Edition. Prentice Hall PTR, 1996.

van Vliet, Hans. *Software Engineering: Principles and Practice.* John Wiley & Sons, 1993.

Weiner, Lauren Ruth. *Digital Woes: Why We Should Not Depend on Software.* Addison-Wesley, 1993.

Wirfs-Brock, Rebecca, Brian Wilkerson, and Lauren Wiener. *Designing Object-Oriented Software.* Prentice Hall PTR, 1990.

Wirth, N. *Algorithms + Data Structures = Programs.* Prentice Hall, 1976.

Index

Abstract base class, 375–76
Abstract class. *See* Abstract base class
Abstract Data Types. *See also* specific
    abstract data types
  characteristics, 5
  definition of, 5
  examples of, 68
  operations, 5
  and reuse, 74–75
  why use, 69–70
Abstraction
  definition, 2
  of processes, 100
  use of experiments in, 3
  use of models in, 2
Accessor function, 205
ACM, 2
Activation record. *See* Stack frame
Adjacency list
  base class, 381
  illustrated, 366
Adjacency matrix
  base class, 390–91
  illustrated, 367
ADT. *See* Abstract Data Type
Aggregate data, 70
Algorithm, 2, 100
Algorithm analysis. *See also* specific
    algorithms
  history of, 101
  types of, 100

Algorithmic decomposition, 20–25
Alias, 424
Analysis of algorithms. See Algorithm
    analysis
Anthropomorphization, 26
Array
  dangers of, 406–8
  dynamically allocated, 200–201
  implementation of, 407
  live portion of, 108
  multidimensional, 410–11
  relationship with pointers, 200–201
  of string objects, 91
Ascending order, 108
`assert` (macros) 180
Assertions, 50
Association for Computing Machin-
    ery, 2
Asymptotic efficiency, 102
Average case, 105

Back-tracking, 213–16, 237
Bandwidth ratio, 266
Bentley, Jon, 108
Best case, 105
Big-O notation, 106
Binary Search
  algorithm for, 108
  analysis of, 109–10
  defective code for, 110
  implementation, 110–14

  invariants in, 111–12
  recursive, 137–39
Binary Search Tree ADT
  client of, 344–45
  definition, 338
  header file, 341–42
  implementation, 342–44
  implemented with inheritance,
    349–51
  implemented with inheritance,
    header file, 347–48
  traversal, 352
Binary search tree. *See also* Binary
    Search Tree ADT
  algorithms for, 339–40
  BST invariant, 336, 339
  definition, 336
Binary Tree. *See also* Binary Tree ADT
  application of, 311–14
  definition, 309
  distinguishing, 310–11
  empty tree, 309
  left child, 309
  right child, 309
  shape of, 353–54
  traversal. *See* Tree traversal
Binary Tree ADT. *See also* Binary
    Tree
  client for, 318–20
  definition, 314–15
  header file, 316

Binary Tree ADT (*cont.*)
  implementation, 317–18
  performance, 353–55
Bitstring (C++ library), 86
  bool, 166
  boolean type, 166
BST. *See* Binary search tree
Bubble Sort
  algorithm, 119
  analysis of, 121
  compared with Quicksort, 145–47
  implementation, 120–21
  phase, 119–20

C
  popularity of, 15
  relationship with C++, 14, 456
C string, 89
C++
  arrays, 406–8
  arrays, multidimensional, 410–11
  as a better C, 456
  assert macros, 441–42
  casting, 418
  conversion, 417–18
  declarations, 404–6
  explicit conversion, 418
  expression, 411
  expression, arithmetic, 411–13
  expression, conditional, 415
  expression, relational, 413–15
  function, 420–22
  function header, 421
  function with no parameters, 422
  getline, 429
  header file, 440
  identifiers, 403
  initialization, 406
  input, checking return type, 429
  iostream library, 425–30
  libraries, 440–441
  linker, 438
  loops, 433–437
  loops, breaking out of, 435–37
  loops, endless, 435
  macro expansion, 439
  main program, 422
  narrowing, 417
  newline, 426
  null statement, 435
  parameters, 423
  pitfalls of = vs. ==, 414
  precedence rules, 412, 418–20

preprocessor, 219, 439–40
reference parameter, 417
references vs. pointers, 459–60
relationship with C, 14, 456
relationship with Pascal, 448
scope rules, 424
selection, 430–31
separate compilation, 438–41
source file inclusion, 440
standard error (cerr), 427
standard for, 14
standard input (cin), 428
standard output (cout), 426
stdio vs. iostream, 458
string, 408–9
structure, 410
symbol table, 440
template, 211–24
type, 404–6
C++ keywords
#define, 219, 439–40
#ifndef, 219
#include, 439–40
break, 432, 435
case, 431–33
char, 404
class, 79
complete list of, 403–4
const, 165, 204
default, 433
delete, 196
do, 434
double, 404
else, 431
float, 404
for, 434–35
goto, 436–37
if, 430–31
int, 404
long, 404
main, 422
new, 179
operator, 205
private, 79
protected, 347
public, 79
return, 421
short, 404
struct, 410
switch, 431–33
this, 81
virtual, 346
void, 421

while, 433–34
C++ operators
!, 415
!=, 414
%, 411
%=, 416
&&, 415
&, 165, 416, 424
&=, 416
*, 411
--, 412
-, 411
, , 417, 437
/, 411
/=, 416
::, 85
?:, 415
^, 416
^=, 416
|, 416
||, 415
|=, 416
~, 416
+, 91, 411
++, 412
+=, 416
+=, 416
<, 413
<<, 87, 416, 426–28
<<=, 416
<=, 413
-=, 416
=, 414
==, 414
>, 413
>=, 413
>>, 87, 416, 428–29
>>=, 416
assignment, 416–17
bitwise, 416
extraction operator, 428–20
insertion operator, 426–28
logical, 415
precedence, 418–20
prefix vs. postfix, 412
sequencing, 417, 437
C++ standard class libraries, 85–92.
    See also individual libraries
Call stack
  defined, 232
  example of, 233–37
Call-by-reference, 423
Call-by-value, 165, 423

Carrier Sense Multiple Access with Collision Detection, 252
Choose
  definition, 132
  implementation, 134
cin, 86. *See also* C++
Circular linked list, 196
Class. *See also* Abstract base class; Iterator class; Friend class
  data member, 79
  declaration, 79
  formal parameters for, 165
  header file, 80
  in C++, 78–79
  instance of, 26, 81
  member function, 79, 204–5
  protected member, 347
  providing encapsulation, 78
  use in design, 26
Client
  definition, 77
  role of, 52
Code reuse. *See* reuse
Coding specification, 11
Cohesion, 24
Collision (in Ethernet), 265–66
Combinatorics, 132
Complex (C++ library), 86
Computer network performance
  controller class, 271–72
  controller state machine, 269–70
  controller, 265, 268–69
  device class, 272–73
  device, 266
  main function, 267–68
  problem described, 252–54
  simulation results, 273–74
Computer science, 2
Computer Society, 2
Const member function, 204–5
Constant function, 102
Constant reference variable, 378
Constant reference, 165
Constructor function
  copy constructor, 165
  default, 90
  described, 87–88
Constructor. *See* Constructor function
Container, 215
Contiguous list, 166
Contract, 52
Copy constructor. *See* Contructor function, copy constructor

Cost-benefit analysis, 10
Coupling, 24
cout, 86
Critical operations, 101
CSMA/CD, 252
Cursor, 168

Data abstraction, 14
Data structures, definition of, 4
Declaration without definition, 176
Decomposition, 20
Decoupling, 6
Deliverables, 9
Depth-First Search, 397
Dequeue. *See* Queue ADT
Descending order, 108
Design
  anthropomorphization in, 26
  collaborators, 27
  definition, 3
  goals of, 20
  methodologies for, 20
  methodologies, evaluation of, 31–32
  object-oriented, 20, 25–31
  phase of software life cycle, 11
  responsibility-driven, 26–27
  scenarios, 26
  top-down, 20–25
Design pattern, 13
Destination network, 280
Dice ADT
  definition of, 5–6
  implementation of, 6–7
Digraph. *See* Directed graph
Directed Adjacency List Graph ADT
  defined, 369–70
  header file, 382–83
  implementation file, 383
Directed Adjacency Matrix Graph ADT
  defined, 371
  header file, 391–92
  implementation, 392
Directed graph. *See also* Graph; Adjacency list; Adjacency matrix
  cycle in, 385
  example, 362
Discrete mathematics, 363
Documentation, 13–14, 88–89
Domain experts, 10
Doubly linked list
  header file for, 198
  insert function, 199

previous function, 197, 199
  when to use, 199
dslib.h, 165
Dummy head node
  compared with standard linked list, 192
  header file, 191
  implementation, 193–94
  remove function, 195–96
Dynamic linear list, 200–202
Dynamic memory allocation. *See* Memory allocation, dynamic
Dynarray (C++ library), 86

Edge. *See also* Graph; Directed graph
  directed, 362
  example, 362
  set, 363
Encapsulation, 78
Enqueue. *See* Queue ADT
Errors. *See* Software errors
Ethernet, 252–53
Eulerian tour, 397–98
Examination of alternatives, 10
Expression tree
  code to create, 324–25
  described, 311
  evaluation of, 312
  header file, 321
  implementation, 322–23
  tree rewriting, 312, 322

Factorial function, 132
Failure to build the right system. *See* Software errors, verification
Failure to build the system right. *See* Software errors, validity
Feasibility study, 10
FIFO, 253
File
  executable, 438
  object, 438
  source, 438
First In First Out, 253
First. *See* Iterator function
Forwarding network, 280
4GL, 13
Fourth-generation language, 13
Free store, 180. *See also* Memory allocation, dynamic
Friend class, 377
Function calls, implementation of, 151–52, 232–37

Function curve, shape of, 150
Function pointer, 333–34
Functional decomposition. See Design, top-down
Functional specification, 10

Gauss's formula, 118, 145
Generic class. See Template
Graph ADT. *See also* Undirected Adjacency List Graph ADT; Directed Adjacency List Graph ADT; Undirected Adjacency Matrix Graph ADT; Directed Adjacency Matrix
  design choices, 371
  efficiency in, 372
  inheritance hierarchy, 374
Graph theory. See Graph
Graph. *See also* Directed graph; Adjacency list; Adjacency matrix; Transitive closure
  defined, 363
  depth-first search of, 397
  Eulerian tour, 397–98
  example, 362
  path, 393–94
  queries in, 366
  size of, 363
  weighted, 397
Gray Code, 157
Guard, 408

Hash table
  chained hashing, 297
  clustering, 292
  collision, 286
  collision, handling, 288
  deletion, 289–91
  division hashing, 287
  hash function, 285
  hash function, selection of, 287
  home address, 288
  implementation, 292–93
  linear probing, 288
  performance, 291
  quadratic probling, 303
  slot, 288
Header file, 219
Hierarchical, 308
High-order term (of a polynomial), 106
Hoare, C.A.R., 139
Homogenous data structure, 216
Host, 280

IEEE, 2
IEEE 802.3, 252
Inductive hypothesis, 139
Infix expression, 227, 311
Infix notation. *See* Infix expression
Information hiding
  definition, 77
  example of, 73
Inheritance. *See also* Abstract base class
  base class, 346
  derived class, 346
  implementing derived classes, 349
  inheritance diagram, 346
  virtual, 346–47
Initializer. *See* Constructor function
Inline declaration, 375
Inorder List ADT
  definition, 183–84
  insert, code for, 189
  inserting into, 185–90
  invariant for, 184
  rationale, 183
Insertion Sort
  idea of, 57
  implementation, 59
  insert next item, 59–60
  invariant for, 57–58
Instance variable. *See* Class, data member
Institute for Electrical and Electronic Engineering, 2
Interface between functions, 52–53
Internet Protocol, 280
Internet worm, 89
Invariant. See Loop invariant
iostream, 86
IP address, 280
IP, 280
Is-a relation, 345–46
Iterator class
  defined, 376
  invalidated iterator, 380
Iterator function, 168, 182

Key comparison, 104–5
Key, 103

LAN, 280
Last In First Out, 215
Laude, Mary, 43n
Lexical analysis, 228
LIFO, 215

Linear function, 106
Linear list, 166
Linear Search
  algorithm, 104
  analysis of, 105–7
  recursive, 135–37
Linear Selection, 100
Link, 171. *See also* Linked list
Linked list. *See also* Dummy head node; Circular linked list; Doubly linked list
  abstract representation, 171
  adding node to, 172–73
  external link, 171
  head link, 171
  node, 171
  null link, 174
  rationale, 170
  tail, 173
  traversing, 174
List ADT
  array implementation, 167–68
  array implementation, header for, 166–67
  client for, 169
  constructor, 166
  definition, 163
  linked list implementation, header for, 175–76
  rationale for, 162
  with iterator, 378–79
List traversal, 163, 182
Local Area Network, 280
Logarithm, base-2, 149
Logarithmic algorithm, 109
Loop, steps for analyzing, 55
Loop invariant
  description, 51, 53
  establishing, 54
  in Binary Search, 112
  useful, 53
  using examples to understand, 60–61

Maintenance
  errors, 42
  programmer, 43
  types of, 12
Make-or-buy study, 10
Maximum in an array, finding, 115
MaxSelect function, 116
Maze class. *See* Robot navigation
Median, 49n, 100n

Member function. *See* Class, member function
Membership management program, 162, 202–6
Memory allocation, dynamic
deallocating memory, 196
memory leak, 196
process of, 180
Memory allocation, static, 180
Memory leak. *See* Memory allocation, dynamic, memory leak
Merge Sort, 156
Method. *See* Class, member function
Modula 2, 15
Modular programming, 15
Module, 15
Multiprocessing system, 42
n choose *k, see* Choose

Neighbor, 366, 368–69
Next. *See* Iterator function
NULL, 177n
Null character, 409
Null pointer, 176. *See also* Pointer

Object, 15, 21, 81
Object-Oriented Design. *See* Design, object-oriented.
Object-oriented programming
and encapsulation, 345
and inheritance, 15, 93, 345
and polymorphism, 15, 94, 345
and reuse, 13, 93
relationship to Abstract Data Types, 68
Operand, 227, 411
Operator (in expression), 227
Operator overloading, 72, 87, 205, 379
Operator, 411
Order (of a function), 102, 106
Order of magnitude. See Order (of a function)
Ordered list. See Inorder List ADT
ostream, 86

Parameters
actual, 423
binding of, 151
formal, 423
Partial order, 384
Pascal, 14, 448
Pointer. *See also* Memory allocation, dynamic; Link

dereferencing, 177
function pointer. *See* Function pointer
null, 176
using null pointer to dereference, 178
Polynomial, 106
Pool monitor, 38
Pop. *See* Stack ADT, pop
Postcondition, 51
Postfix expression, 228
Postfix notation. *See* Reverse Polish Notation
Precedence rules (in expression), 227
Precondition
checking, 51, 220
definition of, 51
Preprocessor. *See* C++, preprocessor
Program correctness, proving, 50
Proof by induction, 54, 139
Protocol, 252
Prototype, 12, 71
Proving loop termination, 55
Push. *See* Stack ADT, push

Quadratic algorithm, 118
Queue ADT
array and list implementations compared, 265
array implementation, code for, 261–62
array implementation, complications of, 256–58
array implementation, header file, 260
circular queue, 258–60
comparison with buffer, 253
defined, 254–55
dequeue, 254
dynamic list implementation, code for, 264–65
dynamic list implementation, header file, 263
enqueue, 254
example of use, 255–56
use in simulation, 265
Quicksort
analysis of, 144
compared with Bubble Sort, 145–47
idea of, 139
implementation, 140
partition implementation, 143
partition invariant, 141–42
pivot, 139
worst case, 144–45

Rank, 115
Rate of growth, 101
Real-time environment, 42
Record, 103
Recurrence relation, 130, 355. *See also* Recursion
Recursion
back substitution in, 131
base case, 130
closed form, 131, 133
correctness of, 139
efficiency of, 153
evaluation by substitution, 131
implementation of, 151–55, 232–37
partial definition, 133
recursive definition of, 130
recursive function call, 152–53
recursive function, 129
recursive routine, 135
recursive search algorithm, 135
use of memory, 153
when to use, 155
Recursion tree
balanced, 147
depth of, 155
use of, 144
Recursive. *See* Recursion
Reference parameter, 165
Refinement, 22
Reinventing the wheel, 74
Reliability. See Software reliability
Responsibility-driven design. See Design, responsibility-driven
Reuse
and ADTs, 70
by copying code, 92
by inheritance, 93, 352
code reuse, 74
design reuse, 13
example of, 92
goals of, 13
object-oriented programming and, 13
Reverse Polish notation, 228, 330
Robot navigation
coordinates for, 237
directionQuery, 243–44
introduced, 212–15
main function, 240–41
Maze class, 238
MazeCoordinate class, 239
moveAttempt, 241–43
tryMove, 244–45
Router, 280

Routing, 280
RPN. 228, 330

Scope operator, 84
Search algorithm, 103. *See also* Linear
    Search, Binary Search
Search. *See* Linear Search; Binary
    Search
Selection algorithm, 115
Selection Sort
    algorithm, 114–15
    implementation, 116–17
Side effect, 411
Signature, 71, 205
Smalltalk, 15
Software crisis, 9
Software engineering, 2
Software errors
    cost to repair, 43
    logic, 41
    maintenance, 42
    run-time, 42
    syntax, 40–41
    validity, 41
    verification, 41–42
Software life cycle, 10–14
Software reliability. *See also* Testing
    costs of software errors, 39–40
    ethics of, 39
    risks of faulty software, 38–40
Sorted order, 108
Sorting. *See also* Insertion Sort, Selec-
    tion Sort, Bubble Sort, Quicksort,
    Treesort
    description, 57
    in-place, 57
Specification language, 5
Stack ADT
    applications of, 227–31
    array implementation, 216–18
    array implementation, header for,
        218–19
    defined, 215–16
    dynamic list implementation, advan-
        tage of, 225
    dynamic list implementation, header
        for, 225
    dynamic list implementation, opera-
        tions, 226
    full, 220–21
    generic, 222–24
    pop, 215–17
    push, 215–17

Stack frame, 232
Standard C libraries, 86
Standard Template Library (STL), 86
String (C++ library), 86, 89–91
String class. *See* String (C++ library)
String concatenation, 91
Stroustrup, Bjarne, 14
Structure chart, 22
Symbol Table ADT, 303–4
Symbol table, 302
System architect, 11
System build, 45
System documentation, 14
System integration, 45

Table ADT
    definition, 281
    hash table implementation, 294
    hash table implementation, header
        file, 292
    hash table with chaining implementa-
        tion, 299–301
    hash table with chaining implementa-
        tion, header file, 298–99
    simple implementation, 282–84
    using, 302
Target key, 104
Technical specification, 11
Technical writer, 13
Template
    instantiation, 224
    linking, 224
    purpose, 221
    syntax of, 222–24
Term (of a polynomial), 106
Testing
    acceptance, 45
    approaches to, 44
    beta, 45
    black-box, 44
    code coverage, 44
    driver, 47–48
    functional, 45
    glass-box, 44
    goal of, 40
    inputs to test, 46
    plan, 11, 45–47
    stub, 48–49
    system build, 45, 439
    system integration, 45
    system, 44
    unit, 44, 47, 439
    who does it, 45

Theory, 2
Therac-25, 38–39
This (pointer), 81
Time ADT
    client of, 83
    definition, 71
    header file, 80–81
    implementation, 75
    revised using class syntax, 82
Token class, 229–30
Token, 228
Tokenization, 228
Top-down decomposition. *See* Design,
    top-down
Top-Down Design. *See* Design, top-
    down.
Topological Sort
    algorithm, 385–87
    defined, 384
    implemented, 387–89
Topsort, see Topological Sort
Total order, 183, 384
Towers of Hanoi, 158
Transitive closure
    algorithm, 395
    described, 393
    defined, 394
    graph, 394
    implementation, 395
Tree. *See also* Binary tree; Binary
    search tree; Tree traversal
    ancestor, 357
    balanced, 356
    children in, 309
    degree, 309
    depth, 309
    forest, 358
    grandchild, 309
    grandparent, 309
    height, 309
    leaf, 309
    level, 309
    node, 309
    parent in, 309
    root, 309
    sibling, 309
    sorting with, 356
Tree traversal
    of Binary Search Tree ADT, 352–53
    described, 325–26
    implementation with function
        pointer, 332–33
    inorder, 326, 328–29

Tree traversal (*cont.*)
performance, 353–55
postorder, 326, 329
preorder, 325–28
simple implementation, 330–32
using, 329–30
visit, 325
why it works, 326

Treesort, 356
Turbo Pascal, 15
Type, 26

Undirected Adjacency List Graph ADT
defined, 368–69
header file, 382

implementation, 382
preconditions in, 383
Undirected Adjacency Matrix Graph
ADT
defined, 370
header file, 392
implementation, 392–93
Uniform likelihood, 149

Vacuous statement, 56, 117
Vertex. *See also* Graph; Directed graph
example, 362
set, 363
Vertices. *See* Vertex
Video rental system
console class, 29

object-oriented design for, 30–31
patron class, 29
printer class, 30
scanner class, 29
specification of, 21
tape class, 28
top-down design for, 25
used to illustrate reuse, 92

Waterfall
critiques of, 12
phases of, 11–12
Wirth, Niklaus, 15
Worst case, 105

Xerox, 252